To our wives, Robin and Lin, for their continuous support and encouragement over 3 years of work on this book.

Published by Global Sports Insights, LLC, 716 Kimwood Place, Eugene, Oregon 97401 (541) 484-5209

MUST-HAVE RESOURCE

The sports industry is a $2.3 trillion global economic engine and among the top 10 worldwide business sectors. The Best-Howard Model described in The Sports Industry works from the bottom up with well-defined sports segment revenue measures aggregated into three core areas. Prior reports of sports industry revenues varied from $450 billion to $1.3 trillion and rarely detailed how their estimates were determined.

The Best-Howard Model's well-defined structure relies on more than 250,000 sports industry data points. The model is global in scope but local in detail, as it includes country- and city-level revenues. The Sports Industry is available as a digital book featuring direct links to the model's underlying data.

The Sports Industry reports revenues by country alongside population and economic data. The strategy allows readers to understand how and why revenues vary around the globe. The digital book offers interactive tables and graphs describing sportswear sales per household versus disposable income for the top 25 countries based on revenues. Click on country GDP, consumer spending or population age to gain insights into how revenues vary. For example, annual sportswear spending per U.S. household is almost $1,100, while it is $696 in Norway, $108 in Brazil, $29 in India and $166 on average worldwide.

The Sports Industry digital book is updated annually. The book also offers strategic insights into the numbers and deep understanding of every aspect of the industry. Beyond revenues, the book examines the sports and outdoor activities inspiring industry trends. The United States accounts for about 37% of the global sports industry spending. This book provides detail on how the revenues are produced and examines the remaining 63% worldwide.

The Sports Industry is a must have resource for students studying sports and professionals working in the industry, as well as journalists, advertisers, government agencies and investors. And the book's trove of sports industry revenue data and analysis is available at all times on any digital device.

AUTHORS

ROGER BEST: Dr. Best is an Emeritus Professor in Marketing at the University of Oregon and co-founder of the UO Sports Product Management Program. He is the author of **Market-Based Management**, over 40 marketing publications and **The Academy of Marketing Science** article of the year. Recent publications include "To Cut Cost, Know Your Customers, **Sloan Management Review** and "Customer Satisfaction: An Organizing Framework for Strategy," **Journal of Marketing Research**.

Roger started his career at GE in engineering and product management where he earned a patent. As a professor he has taught at the University of Arizona, INSEAD in Fontainebleau, France, and University of Oregon. He has been awarded numerous teaching awards and honored as **AMA Distinguished Teacher of the Year**. He currently serves on the advisory board for the UO Lundquist College of Business.

Roger has worked extensively in consulting and executive education with companies including 3M, Dow, DuPont, ESCO, GE, HP, James Hardie, Lucas Industries, Media One, Tektronix, Sprint and US West. He also developed several commercial products, which include the Marketing Excellence Survey, BIDSTRAT, Mark-Plan, and Marketing Metrics Handbook.

DENNIS HOWARD: As an educator, author, and consultant, Dennis' focus has been on the financial and economic aspects of sport over the past 30 years. He has been on the faculty at Texas A&M, Penn State, Ohio State and over the last 20 years at the Lundquist College of Business at the University of Oregon. He has received outstanding teaching awards at every institution he served. In 2008, Dennis was endowed a **Philip H. Knight Professor of Business**.

He has published nearly 100 academic and professional articles and authored several books, including the most recent, **Financing Sport (4th edition)** with his long-time colleague and friend, John Crompton. Dennis is co-editor (with Brad Humphreys) of the 3-volume series, **The Business of Sport**. He is also the **founder** and **former editor** of the **International Journal of Sport Finance**. For his scholarly contributions, Dennis was the recipient of the North American Sport Management Association's prestigious **Earle F. Ziegler Award**.

At the University of Oregon, Dennis served for many years as the Academic Director of the **James H. Warsaw Sports Marketing Center**, which developed the first MBA program dedicated to the business of sport. The program's success has inspired many universities to establish sport-specialty programs in business schools around the globe. Dennis also served as the Head of the Marketing Department and Dean of the Lundquist College of Business. He is now an Emeritus Professor of Marketing and Sports Business.

ACKNOWLEDGEMENTS

KRISTY NEVES: Kristy is a partner with Global Sports Insights, LLC and manages the overall database, and business operations. She has over 25 years in database, systems management, & accounting. Most recently, (2008-2019), she managed a large marketing manager database and information system for Gartner.

OLIVER BEST, MILLIE VELASQUEZ & IRENKA ANGELOVA: Oliver and Millie provide the graphics, production and website, as well as a website video and payment system. Irenka leads GSI market research, and all three participate in social media marketing. Their contribution to the creation and production of this book was invaluable.

GLOBAL SPORTS INSIGHTS INTERNS: We have had many outstanding interns who have done incredible research on the sports industry. They attended weekly team meetings and contributed student perspectives we would have not considered without their user insights. To each we are extremely grateful for the work they have provided.

GRADUATE INTERNS
University of Oregon, Sports Product Management Masters Program
 - Ben Hogan, (Summer 2018)
 - Nathan Trautman, (Summer 2019)
 - Sherry Dai, (Summer 2019)
 - Narkie Nartey, (Summer 2020)
 - Krystal Yeh, (Summer 2021)
 - Josh Daniel, (Summer 2021 to Spring 2021)
 - Kyle Crawford, (Fall 2021 to Spring 2022)
 - Maren Troitsky, (Fall 2021 to Spring 2022)

University of Oregon, Warsaw Sports Business MBA Program
 - Ofuma Eze-Echesi, (Summer 2019 and Fall 2020)
 - David Borlack, (Fall 2020)
 - Landon Wright, (Fall 2021 to Spring 2022)
 - Andy Fain (Fall 2021 to Spring 2022)

UNDERGRADUATE INTERNS
University of Oregon, Sports Business Program
 - Maggie Bidasolo, (Fall 2020)
 - Abby Dolioso, (Fall 2020)
 - Braden Buerk (Fall 2021 to Spring 2022)
 - Issa Malik (Fall 2021 to Spring 2022)
 - Meagan Kiefer (Fall 2021 to Spring 2022)

University of Oregon, Journalism School
 - Chloe Colligen, (Fall 2020)

American University - Nicaragua
 - Irenka Angelova (Summer 2020, Summer & Fall 2021)

We would also like to make a special thank you to Dean Sarah Nutter, Lundquist College of Business who provided two summer internships when starting this project, Professor Bettina Cornwell who helped start the research of this book, and John Elkins for his generous support of eight year-long internships and Dr. Ellen Schmidt-Devlin for her spirited encouragement.

We would also like to thank Elizabeth Brock-Jones, Nike Senior Developer for her detailed comments and edits that set the direction of our book. Paul Swangard and Merryn Huntley Roberts for providing valuable feedback and encouragement. We would like to recognize Katy Lenn, UO Reference Librarian who was of great assistance throughout this project. We also want to thank copy editor Shea Gibbs. His detailed copy editing and writing of our chapters were a humbling experience but a much needed level of professional writing.

CONTENTS

PART I:
Structure of the Sports Industry

The sports industry includes a wide range of events, products and activities that engage people around the world. More than any other industry, sports are truly global and serve our planet with a unifying spirit of competition, enjoyment and health. Our goal in this book is to account for all these factors and explore how they shape the scope of the sports industry.

To understand the complexities of today's global sports industry, let us consider where it came from and how it evolved.

Sports and competition have been around as long as individuals could run faster, throw farther or jump higher than their peers. Sports and competition are an innate part of our human structure and cultural condition.

FIGURE I

Sports competition was first formalized in training soldiers to run, jump, fight and ride horses, as well as use poles, spears and rocks in combat. The intense training inevitably led to competition among soldiers. We can assume some observers even placed wagers on the contests. Hence, one of competitive sports' first derivatives may have been betting. The early period also produced the first signs of sports-as-entertainment and the importance of fan engagement.

Military competitions eventually led to the inaugural Olympic games in 776 BCE (*Figure I*). The games were the first documented organized sports competition with athletes, events, spectators and a venue. The events included boxing, discus, equestrian, long jump, javelin, running and wrestling.

Beyond entertainment, what motivated the first Olympic competition? Many would be surprised to learn the answer is war. The Olympic Truce is a tradition originating in ancient Greece the year of the first games. The laying down of arms was announced before and enforced during the competition to ensure the host city-state was not attacked and athletes and spectators could travel safely to and from the games.

From the beginning, sports and competition played a positive role in society, bringing together people traditionally at war.

SPORT CREATION: While the origins of sports are generally traced to 776 BCE, sports emerged in the years between the first Olympics and 1850. The new sports and their rules evolved primarily in Europe, with some coming to be in Asia. Their development also led to the first cataloguing of world records.

FIGURE II
Sports Developed by 1850

SPORTS	YEAR	COUNTRY	SPORTS	YEAR	COUNTRY	SPORTS	YEAR	COUNTRY
Polo	550 BC	Persia	Ice Skating	1500	Holland	Rugby	1749	England
Soccer	300 BC	China	Bowling	1511	China	Squash	1830	England
Rowing	1454	England	Cricket	1600	England	Swimming	1836	England
Tennis	1500	England	La Crosse	1600	Canada	Skiing	1840	Sweden
Golf	1500	Scotland	Horse Racing	1670	England	Baseball	1847	USA

The era between 776 BCE and 1850 saw the creation of the sports shown in *Figure II*. For the most part, sports venues at the time consisted of fields, courts and pools. Unlike the giant arenas where the ancient Greeks and Romans showcased their skills, the new venues had limited room for spectators. The sparse seating offered the only form of sports fan engagement, aside from informal wagers among spectators.

FIGURE III
Sports Developed From 1850 to Today

SPORTS	YEAR	COUNTRY	SPORTS	YEAR	COUNTRY	SPORTS	YEAR	COUNTRY
Water Polo	1850	England	Ice Hockey	1875	France	Surfing	1900	USA
Australian Football	1858	Australia	Table Tennis	1880	England	Skeet Shooting	1920	USA
Motocross	1861	England	Rodeo	1880	USA	Water Skiing	1922	USA
Canadian Football	1861	Canada	Softball	1887	USA	Snowboarding	1965	USA
College Football	1862	USA	Basketball	1891	USA	Windsurfing	1967	USA
Auto Racing	1867	France	Pro Football	1892	USA	Ultimate Frisbee	1975	USA
Bicycle Racing	1868	England	Volleyball	1895	USA	Esports	1974	USA

The modern sports era began around 1850 and continues today. Shown in *Figure III* are many of the sports evolving during the period. In the early years, a dramatic shift occurred, with new leagues, teams and stadiums added for a variety of sports like baseball, football, basketball, ice hockey, water sports, bicycle racing and auto racing. By 1880, the United States became a driving influence in sports creation. As the new sports drew greater interest with the support of emerging media, fan engagement and venues showcasing the events also grew.

THE SPORTS INDUSTRY: As sports venues grew in size and complexity, sponsors rushed to put their brands alongside events. Merchandise and broadcast media began to contribute a large part of the revenues produced by sporting events.

Emerging technology drove the growing sports media and allowed events to reach audiences outside the venues in which they were played. The telegraph allowed scores to be shared, and radio broadcasts allowed fans to listen to entire events. Television, cable TV and later live internet streaming allowed more fans to watch and listen to events than could attend them. The new broadcast audiences quickly attracted new advertisers and sponsorships. The wide array of sports that could be viewed from almost any location also opened the market for sports betting and the evolution of sports entertainment products, including fantasy sports, video games and sports bars.

Athletes participating in sports need footwear, apparel and equipment. All sports require at least some specialized equipment and sportswear. Companies emerged to make balls, bats, sticks, rackets, golf clubs and poles, as well as mitts, gloves and skis. Over time, style and fashion became critical among sports products, as did health products like hydration beverages, energy bars and nutritional aids. Today, athletes rely on their health and wellness to compete, and innovations in medicine and physical therapy have become a large and growing part of the massive sports industry.

Sports have also come to include outdoor recreation, including camping, rafting, fishing and hunting. The evolution of gymnasiums for boxers and weightlifters—and later health and fitness clubs—expanded sports participation into the exercise arena. Boating and recreational vehicles drew even more individuals to outdoor recreation.

Each new area of the sports industry has come to generate revenue around the world. While the U.S. market is the largest for most sports, the rest of the world still contributes more than 60% of worldwide revenue.

In Chapter 1 of this book, we review past definitions of the sports industry and provide a comprehensive scope and structure to measure its size accurately. While we attempt to present an accurate picture of today's global sports industry, one thing is certain: The industry will continue to change as it evolves with new sports, ways to view and enjoy sports, products and ways to participate in sports and outdoor recreation. And as worldwide prosperity grows, more of the world's population will become part of the sports industry. We can also expect the industry will continue to play a growing role in worldwide health and wellness.

DEFINING THE SPORTS INDUSTRY
CHAPTER 1

Scope, Structure & Size

Sports are universal. Around the globe, sports teams perform before enthusiastic fans at modern venues, and even larger audiences watch on TV or stream online. An increasing number of interested viewers now wager considerable sums on sports outcomes.

Millions of people of every race, ethnicity and nationality spend countless hours participating in their favorite sports and recreation activities and considerable money purchasing the equipment they need, from golf clubs to cricket bats. How much do the revenues generated by sporting events, participation costs (e.g., fees, lessons, travel), and sportswear and equipment purchases total?

It would seem to be a straightforward question. But the answer is complicated.

The Best-Howard Sports Industry Model systematically estimates the sports industry's size using a unique, well-defined structure and scope (*Figure 1.1*). The model also offers a framework for understanding the 2020 COVID-19 pandemic's impact on the sports industry and forecasting recovery prospects for many sectors in the near future.

FIGURE 1.1
What is the Sports Industry?

SCOPE *(Boundaries)* What is included?	**STRUCTURE** *(Composition)* How is it organized?	**SIZE** *(Measurement)* How big is it?

Most would expect a vast global industry, which inspires millions of people to spend countless hours and considerable money, to have up-to-date, accurate revenue figures and forecasts. Yet, revenue data for sports and recreation activities—including purchasing necessary equipment, paying fees to participate and buying sportswear—has never before been available in one readily-accessible place.

Existing revenue estimates for the global sports industry range from $471 billion to $1.4

trillion. What leads to the nearly trillion-dollar discrepancy? Sports industry revenue estimates have traditionally lacked a well-defined structure and failed to measure all, or even the same, essential dimensions.

A closer look at the many available sports industry estimates raises several questions. How comprehensive are they? Do they encompass sports engagement from what consumers pay to attend or watch events to their spending on team merchandise and memorabilia? Do they capture the enormous corporate investments made in sports teams and events sponsorships and media rights partnerships? Do they incorporate the full range of available sportswear, including athleisure, and specialized gear and equipment? What about costs associated with direct participation in sports, fitness and outdoor recreation, as well as their expensive consequences like physical therapy? Finally, do the estimates fully attend to the world's fastest-growing sports fan engagement segments, such as video games, fantasy sports, wagering and even sports movies?

Building A Comprehensive Model

The Best-Howard Model fully captures the sports industry's scope and structure. As shown in *Figure 1.2*, the model includes three core domains: Fan Engagement, Sport Products and Sports Participation. The domains capture the complete breadth and detail of the industry and provide a comprehensive structure for estimating the economic magnitude of sports and recreation activity worldwide. The domains and their core area breakdowns serve as a framework for collecting participation and spending data for every industry segment. The aggregated totals across the domains provide a composite measure of the sports industry's overall size.

FIGURE 1.2
The Best-Howard Sports Industry Model

Existing efforts to model and measure the sports industry all suffer from one major challenge: The U.S. government does not recognize sports as a separate or standalone industry. As a result, it is impossible to find a single definition of what constitutes the industry or consolidated figure representing its economic magnitude. Sports-related activity segments are scattered, without apparent rationale, across several categories of the North American Industry Classification System (NAICS). Sports and Athletic Goods Manufacturing is classified under NAICS code 339920, while Spectator Sports is under 711219, and yet another category, Sports Teams and Clubs, is under 711211.

It is possible to combine figures across categories to estimate the size of the U.S. sports industry. Using Department of Commerce guidelines, researchers Milano and Chelladurai create a Gross Domestic Sports Product (GDSP) metric by aggregating "the market value of the nation's output of sports-related goods and services"(1). Their analysis produces three GDSP estimates for the year 2005, ranging from a conservative $168.5 billion to $207.5 billion ($281 billion on the high-end accounting for 2020 inflation). The researchers' use of the U.S. government classification system captures more relevant sports content than any other industry estimate. It is the only estimate to include entertainment and recreation activities, such as parimutuel betting and fantasy sports, and sports medicine.

While their estimate is broadly inclusive, Milano and Chelladurai recognize concerns related to its "ambiguous classification of certain expenditures related to the sport industry," narrow sports gambling definition and reliance on data collected from nongovernment sources (e.g., the National Sporting Goods Association) for product-related expenditure estimates. While credible, the National Sporting Goods Association omits several prominent equipment and apparel categories, including for all equestrian sports and emerging outdoor activities like bouldering/mountaineering. The researchers' estimate also ignores digital technology rapidly ascending in many sports dimensions, from wearable devices to online gambling and media streaming services. Finally, the estimate does not include global sports activity.

Plunkett Research (2) provides the most complete descriptive overview of the global sports market. It is one of many commercial firms offering sports industry market forecasts, trend analyses and financial performance data. The ReportLinker.com site Sports Industry 2021 contains thousands of market intelligence reports focused on the sports industry.

Plunkett's Sports & Recreation Industry Almanac offers currency and a global perspective. The almanac provides an extensive description of the sports industry's many products and services and the trends—particularly related to technology—influencing its growth. The industry overview recognizes the emerging prominence of esports, fantasy sports and sports betting and estimates the size of the U.S. and global sports and recreation markets. The 2020 Almanac estimates that 2018 U.S. sports market revenues reached $539.7 billion. The rest of the world's spending amounted to $763 billion in 2018, bringing the global sports market's estimated aggregate value to $1.33 trillion. Plunkett Research's estimate (*Figure 1.3*) is far greater than those of most other commercial research outlets.

Figure 1.3 provides Plunkett's breakdown of the revenue sources used to estimate the global sports market's size in 2017 and 2018. The categories represent the breadth of the industry and include: 1) a range of spectator sporting events, 2) retail sportswear and equipment purchases, 3) the costs of participating in fitness, indoor and outdoor recreation and sports activities, and 4) diverse sports engagement opportunities bundled under the broad "Other" heading.

Plunkett's "Other" category accounts for more than half of the firm's estimated total $1.33 trillion spent globally on sports and recreation in 2018.

FIGURE 1.3
Plunkett's Sports & Recreation Industry Almanac 2020 Global Sports Revenues (U.S. billions)

CORE AREAS	2017	2018	GROWTH
Professional Leagues & Teams	$ 37.4	$ 37.7	0.8 %
College Sports	$ 1.7	$ 1.7	0.0 %
Other Spectator Sports	$ 16.1	$ 15.4	–4.3 %
Sporting Goods at Retail	$ 158.4	$ 164.8	4.0 %
Sporting Apparel at Retail	$ 132.3	$ 142.9	8.0 %
Amusement and Recreation	$ 218.4	$ 229.7	5.2 %
Sports Goods Manufacturing	$ 57.5	$ 59.8	4.0 %
Other Sports Related Revenues	$ 655.9	$ 682.1	4.0 %
TOTAL	$ 1,277.7	$ 1,334.1	4.4 %

Source: Plunkett Research Estimate, Plunkett Research, Ltd. Note: Professional Leagues & Teams revenues figures pertain to North America leagues only and two corrections were made to 2017 figures reported by Plunkett, in which Professional Leagues & Teams revenues were listed as $93.6 billion and total revenues at $1.333.8 bn

Optimizing the Model

The data sourcing for the Plunkett Research estimate lacks specificity. The reference provided for *Figure 1.3* does not include the underlying data used to arrive at each category's revenue estimate. The Almanac's limitations, therefore, are as follows:

• While Plunkett Research lists multiple credible data sources—including the U.S. Census Bureau, U.S. Bureau of Labor Statistics and Forbes—elsewhere in the Almanac, sources are not included for the tables showing revenue data, as in the *Figure 1.3* example.

• All the Almanac's references are U.S. sources and provide data exclusively attributable to American sports leagues, events and companies. The narrative portion of the Almanac includes participation and spending statistics from global organizations like the International Health, Racquet & Sportsclub Association, but the numbers are not referenced in data tables.

What sources does Plunkett Research use to reach its $1.34 trillion global estimate? The U.S. contribution, $539.7 billion, accounts for 41.5% of the total but leaves almost $800 billion of economic activity to the rest of the world.

The Best-Howard Model estimates the global sports industry is worth $2.3 trillion. The estimate is almost $1 trillion dollars greater than the next highest number. More extensive and credible sourcing is therefore required to understand the global sports industry.

Two other frequently referenced publications also offer sports industry market size forecasts, trend analyses and financial performance statistics. ResearchAndMarkets.com released a report in 2019 (3) estimating the value of the 2018 global sports market at $488.5 billion and projected growth to $614 billion in 2022. The growth figure has been widely referenced in news and journal reports around the globe.

In The Sporting Goods Industry, Richard Lipsey offers a detailed analysis of the major segments comprising the market (4). While Lipsey focuses primarily on consumer products and sports participants' equipment, he provides a thoughtful overview of the cultural and technological dynamics influencing the industry's shape and structure. His chapter on the U.S. industry's size provides a template for capturing participation and spending data for a range of sports activities and product categories. While the data cited in Lipsey's 2006 publication is no longer current, his approach to identifying and assembling data is a useful resource.

The Best-Howard Model uses nine core areas under its three primary domains to capture the size of the sports industry: Sports Events, Sports Media, Sports Entertainment, Sportswear, Sports Equipment, Sports Health, Sports Recreation, Fitness & Exercise and Outdoor Recreation. Each major sports industry model addresses the core areas to different extents. In *Figure 1.4*, the core areas are organized under the Best-Howard Model's three domains. Comparing the models' coverage breadth and depth, the number of stars in each column shows the extent to which the category is addressed, with three to zero stars representing complete, adequate, deficient and no coverage.

FIGURE 1.4
The Sports Industry Structure – Models

SPORTS INDUSTRY — MODEL STRUCTURE & CORE AREAS	FAN ENGAGEMENT			SPORTS PRODUCTS			SPORTS PARTICIPATION		
	Sports Events	Sports Media	Sports Enter.	Sports Wear	Sports Equipment	Health & Wellness	Sports Recreation	Fitness & Exercise	Outdoor Recreation
Best-Howard	★★★	★★★	★★★	★★★	★★★	★★★	★★★	★★★	★★★
Milano & Chelladurai	★★	★★	★★	★★	★★★	★★	★		★
Plunkett Research Group	★★★	★★	★★	★★★	★★		★★★	★★	★
Research & Markets	★★	★★					★★★	★★	
Lipsey		★		★★	★★★	★	★★★	★★	★★

The Best-Howard Model to some degree represents a consolidation of the available market studies' common elements. ResearchAndMarkets.com provides sufficient transparency to include a representation of the firm's model, the Milano and Chelladurai paper serves as a foundation for the Best-Howard Model's development and the Plunkett Research Group offers the most comprehensive inventory of sports categories and activities and includes global estimates.

The video below (*Figure 1.5*) provides an overview of the Best-Howard sports industry domains and core areas highlighted in *Figure 1.4*. We belief the scope of this sports industry more is more comprehensive, and the structure offers and better organization.

FIGURE 1.5
Overview of the Sports Industry

Source: https://www.youtube.com/watch?v=F98Td4pl_Cw

The Best-Howard Model's comparative analysis reveals many sports products and service areas are either missing from the other prominent models or only partially covered. The missing or incomplete elements are shown in *Figure 1.6*.

FIGURE 1.6
Missing Elements of a Sports Industry Model

Sport Venue Construction	Sports Betting (casino & online)	Digital Sports Media Advertising	Sports Media Subscription Fees
Sports Wearable Devices	Sports Streaming Services	Sports Video Games	Esports
Fantasy Sports	RVs, Campers, ATVs	Recreation Boats	Sports Nutrition & Drinks
Sports Medicine & Theraphy	Sports, Outdoor & Recreation Fees	Equestrian Sports	Youth Sports

Understanding the Best-Howard Model

The Best-Howard Model, shown in *Figure 1.7*, includes each of the features missing from other prominent sports industry models. The model includes an inventory of 36 categories, known as segments, with participation and revenue data collected for each. The model assigns each segment to one of the three major domains—Fan Engagement, Sports Products and Sports Participation—and each domain is further divided into three core areas.

FIGURE 1.7
BEST-HOWARD MODEL: Domains, Core Areas & Segments

FAN ENGAGEMENT
3 CORE AREAS
15 Segments

SPORTS PRODUCTS
3 Core Areas
10 Segments

SPORTS PARTICIPATION
3 Core Areas
11 Segments

FAN ENGAGEMENT		
Sports Events	Sports Media	Sports Enter.
Gate Revenues	Media Adv.	Sports Betting
Media Rights	Media Subs.	Fantasy Sports
Sponsorships	Digital Adv.	Esports
Sports Merch	Digital Subs.	Video Games
Venue Construction		Collectibles
		Sports Bars

SPORTS PRODUCTS		
Sports Wear	Sports Equipment	Sports Health & Wellness
Footwear	Sports & Fitness	Sports Medicine
Apparel	Outdoor Recreation	Wellness Products
Wearables Devices	Recreation Vehicles	Sports Therapy
		Sports Nutrition

SPORTS PARTICIPATION		
Sports Recreation	Fitness & Exercise	Outdoor Recreation
Outdoor Sports	Sports & Fitness	Camping Hiking
Indoor Sports	Coaches Trainers	Hunting Fishing
Youth Sports	Specialty Gyms	Water Sports
		Snow Sports
		Equestrian

DOMAIN I: Fan Engagement – Experiencing. Fan Engagement includes all sports fan-related experiences, including attending sporting events, watching them on a preferred media platform and participating in sports entertainment like fantasy sports, video games and wagering. All are ways in which fans engage with their preferred sports.

Fan Engagement includes the core areas Sports Events, Sports Media and Sports Entertainment. Each core area is subdivided into four to six segments representing distinctive revenue-producing categories.

The Sports Entertainment core area includes several of the world's fastest growing activity segments—sports betting, esports and fantasy sports. Increased worldwide internet access and smartphone use, coupled with many new and attractive mobile applications, allow hundreds of millions of people around the globe to engage in sports in ways not possible a decade ago.

Today, fans can wager, manage their own fantasy sports teams and watch the world's best video gamers compete directly on their mobile devices. The 2020 global COVID-19 pandemic accentuated the activities' entertainment appeal. With live attendance limited, fans found easily accessible online platforms an attractive way to engage with their favorite sports.

Wagering on sports has also become a popular form of engagement. Legal betting on games and matches around the world topped $250 billion in 2020, making it the single highest revenue-producing segment in the Best-Howard Model.

The Sports Events core area includes five segments, which analysts PricewaterhouseCoopers and Deloitte use in their financial reviews of the global sports market and European soccer leagues:

1. Gate revenues (ticket sales, food and beverage sales, etc.).

2. Media rights.

3. Sponsorships.

4. Merchandise sales.

5. Sports venue construction costs.

Sports Events are the wellspring of engagement. Without league games, matches, tournaments and road races, fans would have nothing to watch, stream and bet on. Much of the Best-Howard Model depends on fan-engaging events. And the event producers—from professional sports leagues to the Boston Marathon—depend on revenues produced from ticket sales, registration fees, television broadcast rights, and corporate sponsorships and licensed merchandise.

The growing worldwide, interdependent fan engagement ecosystem includes both media companies televising and streaming sporting events and corporate partners aligning their brands with highly visible sports properties. The Sports Media core area and its prominent role in engaging sports fans represents a significant opportunity as media outlets increasingly target digital devices and streaming platforms. All the segments included in the core area of Sports Entertainment, such as wagering and fantasy sports, are also integral to the Fan Engagement ecosystem and highly dependent on a robust sports events calendar.

DOMAIN II: Sports Products – Using. The Sports Products domain includes the core areas Sportswear, Sports Equipment, and Sports Health, which covers sports medicine, nutrition and sports drinks. The domain includes all products athletes and consumers use in sports, exercise, recreation and everyday living.

Sports Equipment includes the specialized gear used across three major areas of sports and recreation—mainstream recreational sports like golf and tennis, gym and fitness activities from yoga to CrossFit, and outdoor pursuits like hunting, fishing and backpacking. The closely related recreational vehicles segment recognizes the growing popularity of campervans, caravans, camper trailers, truck campers and all-terrain vehicles.

The Sportswear core area focuses on specialized footwear and clothing designed for engaging in sports and recreation activities, as well as wearable health monitors and smart watches. The Best-Howard Model also highlights the growing trend of sportswear being used in everyday, non-sports contexts—from the workplace to leisure activities—leading to a new fashion category, Athleisure.

The third core area in the Sports Equipment domain, Sports Health, is often overlooked but rapidly growing. Consumer spending related to sports medicine and nutrition products collectively surpassed $50 billion worldwide in 2020.

DOMAIN III: Sports Participation – Doing. Sports Participation includes all the sports activities in which people engage as direct participants. In addition to traditional sports, the domain includes fitness and exercise-based events and recreational sports.

Sports Participation includes three core areas: Sports Recreation, Fitness & Exercise and Outdoor Recreation. An abundance of credible data shows the number of people in the United States participating in sports and recreation activities in each of the core areas.

Credible annual spending data are provided for a number of sport and recreation activities by U.S. government organizations. The U.S. Fish and Wildlife Service, U.S. Forest Service and National Park Service collect annual data on user, licensing and permit fees related to hunting, fishing, camping and boating. In addition, sports industry trade associations (e.g., for fitness and health clubs, golf, boating and downhill skiing) report annual revenues from membership fees, greens fees, ski passes, moorage fees, etc. The Best-Howard Model draws on the data wherever available to complement its participation trends analysis in 12 Sports Participation segments. Of special consideration are the challenges facing youth sports organizations, such as declining participation, rising costs and their role in combating the growing obesity crisis.

The Best-Howard Model: Scope & Size

The Best-Howard Model provides a broad and inclusive sports industry outlook, both from a geographic and content perspective. *Figure 1.8* highlights the most popular sports around the world (5). By some measures, soccer is the one true global sport. It has a passionate following in most world regions, highly developed sports leagues and prolific participation at the recreational and amateur levels. The same devotion is shown for cricket in India and Pakistan and American football in the United States, but both are geographically limited.

FIGURE 1.8
The Best-Howard Model's Global Perspective

WORLDWIDE SPORTS FANS

Soccer	Cricket	Basketball	Hockey	Tennis	Volleyball	Table Tennis	Baseball	Football	Rugby
3.5 Billion	2.5 Billion	2.4 Billion	2.2 Billion	1 Billion	900 Million	850 Million	500 Million	410 Million	400 Million

Basketball, tennis and volleyball are also played in every world region. More people watch NBA basketball in China than any other nation outside the United States. Baseball, once considered the U.S. "National Pastime," is now well established across most of Asia, the Caribbean, Australia and South America. Many countries have developed their own culturally unique sports, like sumo wrestling in Japan, bandy in Russia and korfball in the Netherlands.

The Best-Howard Model takes a global perspective, drawing from every credible data source on sports participation and spending from all regions and countries of the world. Oxford Economics, a leader in global forecasting and quantitative analysis, provides the model data on personal and household spending patterns for 10 countries and 25 major cities worldwide. The Best-Howard Model uses the robust economic data to correlate the impact of variables like household disposable income on average annual sports spending. The analysis allows comparisons of average household spending on categories like sportswear from one city to another.

The Best-Howard Model includes several previously overlooked sports industry segments. The model places heavy emphasis on the Fan Engagement domain, recognizing fan attachment to sports leagues and teams is critical for behaviors like attending, viewing, traveling and wagering.

The model also incorporates the many ways and settings in which people can engage in sports, from video gaming, to fantasy sports, to sharing experiences with friends in sports bars.

In addition to equipment used directly in sports, the Sports Products domain captures all the products and services sustaining the health and wellbeing of those who actively participate, from sports nutrition products to the rapidly growing core area of Sports Medicine.

The Best-Howard Model also recognizes a range of recreational sports, including enormously popular activities like RV camping and the new and rapidly growing luxury camping, or "glamping," segment, as well as emerging outdoor pursuits like bouldering. Also included is the nearly $200 billion global equestrian industry, which has been largely ignored in previous sports industry estimates.

FIGURE 1.9
Size of Sports Industry 2019 (U.S. billions)

DOMAINS	U.S.	GLOBAL	%U.S.
FAN ENGAGEMENT	$ 173.2	$ 586.3	29.5 %
SPORTS PRODUCTS	$ 352.9	$ 968.1	36.5 %
SPORTS PARTICIPATION	$ 307.7	$ 762.4	40.3 %
TOTAL	$ 833.8	$ 2,316.8	35.9 %

The Best-Howard Model, as described in *Figure 1.9*, measures each segment of its three major domains separately. The model uses a bottom-up approach to collecting and aggregating participation and revenue data starting with the 36 segments shown in *Figure 1.7*. For each segment, the model uses data specific to the United States and, where possible, from other world countries and regions. The Best-Howard Model synthesizes segment-level spending to provide an expansive size estimate of the nine core areas. The model then uses the core area revenues to produce size estimates for each domain.

The Best-Howard Model finds the sports industry's total value came to $2.3 trillion in 2019, the largest estimate of the industry's economic magnitude and exceeding the nearest estimate by Plunkett Research by almost $1 trillion dollars.

COVID-19 dramatically impacted sports industry revenues worldwide beginning in 2020. Highlighted throughout this book are assessments of the virus's impacts on each sports industry segment. In future editions, 2019 participation and spending data will serve as benchmarks against which the Best-Howard Model will measure recovery rates across each core area.

Still, $2.3 trillion is likely a conservative estimate for the value of the global sports industry. Credible global data does not exist in several areas. For example, estimated annual sports wagering spending ranges from $200 billion to $500 billion. While IBISWorld (6) offers credible annual global sports betting estimates, its revenue figure represents net income, or what is left after prize money is removed. As much as 7% to 10% of the actual amount wagered (i.e., the "handle") is not included. The Best-Howard Model adjusts the IBISWorld figure by reintroducing the 7% and providing a more accurate wagering estimate. However, the model's estimate of $234 billion includes only legal activity in 2019, ignoring the significant amount of illegal betting taking place in every corner of the world. It is possible the Best-Howard Model's estimate captures only half the money spent on sports gambling.

Data Warehousing

The Best-Howard Model serves as a framework for aggregating sports industry data. As shown in *Figure 1.10*, the data is allocated and stored in a warehouse containing more than 250,000 data points. The data are assigned to one of the model's three major domains: Fan Engagement, Sports Products or Sports Participation. They are then further sorted by best fit to a core area (e.g., Sports Events, Sports Entertainment) and assigned to the most relevant segment (e.g., media rights, sponsorships). The tiered arrangement allows users to move quickly from a broad to focused perspective.

The data warehouse also stores socioeconomic data, drawn mainly from population statistics and Oxford Economics metrics like retail sales and household consumer spending. The data, which extends back to 1980 and projects to 2050, is updated monthly. The data features prominently in Chapters 11 and 12 of this book, revealing key socioeconomic variables' impact on sports spending across segments, including apparel and event revenues, in 10 countries and 50 major cities worldwide.

Some challenges arise when collecting sports, recreation products and activity data in several Best-Howard Model core areas. U.S. data is typically more trustworthy than that from other world regions. Reputable publishers like IBISWorld and Statista provide reliable figures on U.S. participation rates and spending across a broad spectrum of sports, fitness and recreation activities. While both organizations aggregate data on a global perspective, their worldwide coverage is not comprehensive. IBISWorld focuses mostly on U.S. sectors, with the exception of sports betting, which the firm analyzes around the world.

Several U.S. government agencies provide information on sports and recreation activities. The U.S. Census Bureau tracks product and activity expenditures across almost all 36 Best-

FIGURE 1.10
Sports Industry - Data Warehouse

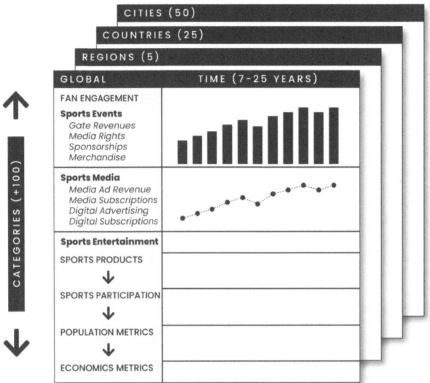

Howard Model segments. The U.S. Forest Service, U.S. Fish & Wildlife Service and National Park Service collect and publish detailed annual participation and fee data across a range of outdoor activities. And many U.S. nonprofit organizations, such as the Aspen Institute (youth sports), Outdoor Industry Association (outdoor recreation) and American Horse Council Foundation (equestrian), publish sector-specific data. Sports and fitness trade associations and private organizations produce well-constructed, detailed annual reports. Examples include the National Sporting Goods Association's annual Market Report, the Sports and Fitness Industry Association's Topline Participation Report and Kampgrounds of America's North American Camping Report. Finally, several business publications offer dedicated sports content, most prominently Forbes magazine's annual financial North American sports league valuations and, more recently, Sportico.com's in-depth insights into the business of sports.

On a global scale, reputable research aggregating firms like Statista and Euromonitor International provide market research on several Best-Howard Model segments. Euromonitor's Passport site is the gold standard for understanding consumer spending across all Sportswear segments in 210 countries. High-quality industry-specific international reports include the International Health, Racquet & Sportsclub Association's Global Report: State of the Health Club Industry, Laurent Vanant's International Report on Snow & Mountain Tourism and Future Market's Camping and Caravanning Markets.

Multinational firms like Deloitte and PricewaterhouseCoopers contribute significantly to the Best-Howard Model's Sports Events core area. Both organizations provide valuable data and insights into the financial operations of major professional sports leagues and teams in North America and Europe. While the firms provide credible annual data for most of the Best-Howard Model's components, global participation and revenue figures in areas like hunting and fishing, equestrian sports and youth sports are elusive. The model therefore uses either a conservative estimate or does not report data (NA) for those activities.

The extensive Best-Howard Model data warehouse also chronicles the impact of COVID-19 on every sports industry segment, allowing analysts to draw meaningful comparisons between recovery rates by sports type across countries and cities. The data is updated regularly, making the warehouse a vital resource for assessing how the sports industry rebounds from the virus.

Finally, the data warehouse is easily accessible. By clicking on the citation reference numbers throughout this digital book, readers can quickly see full underlying datasets. Many of the book's interactive figures allow readers to navigate through several data layers, with each providing additional detail.

Breaking Down the Sports Industry

The Best-Howard Model shows the full economic value of the global sports industry is $2.3 trillion. The value is derived from a bottom-up approach, in which revenue estimates for 36 segments are compiled, then combined and summed for nine core areas, which are in turn aggregated for three domains (*Figure 1.11*).

FIGURE 1.11
Sports Industry – Bottom-Up Revenue Method

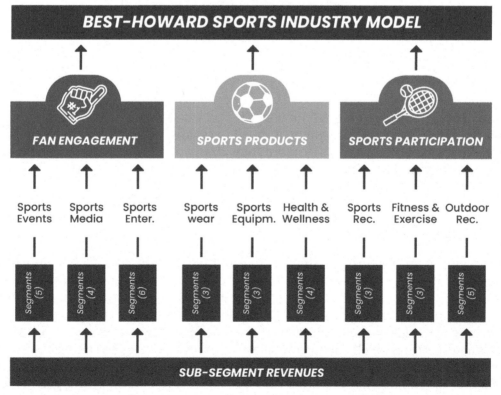

Figure 1.12 shows total revenues for the Best-Howard Model's three domains. Sports Products, with its core areas of Sportswear, Sports Equipment and Sports Health & Wellness, is the largest contributor at $968.1 billion. One segment, recreational vehicles, accounts for $152.5 billion of the total. Unlike many market reports, which provide one summary estimate for the RV category, the model's estimate includes revenues from six sub-segments: RVs, Recreational Boats, All-Terrain Vehicles, Jet Skis, Golf Carts, & Snowmobiles. Revenues for all six categories are used to estimate total annual RV spending. The Best-Howard Model replicates the bottom-up approach in all its model segments.

FIGURE 1.12
BEST-HOWARD Sports Industry Domains

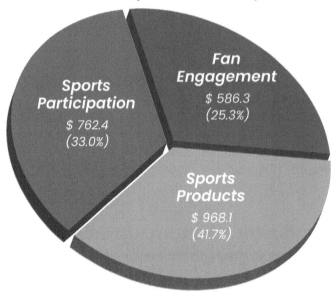

Sports Participation is the next largest domain, with total revenues of $762.4 billion. Annual sports and recreation participant spending is growing rapidly, primarily due to the expanding popularity of outdoor activities. In 2019, more than 70% of all Sports Participation domain revenues came from outdoor sports.

Outdoor pursuits continued to flourish during the COVID-19 pandemic, as individuals seeking refuge from the virus flocked to open-air, natural spaces. Leading the way was the surge in RV sales and the emergence of glamping.

Fan Engagement, while currently the smallest of the three domains at $586.3 billion, has a high revenue ceiling. The explosive sports betting growth around the globe drives the domain's potential. Widespread legal sports wagering is a recent development in the United States. With as many as 30 states soon to offer legalized gambling, from lotteries to online sportsbooks, America's share of worldwide betting is expected to soar over the next decade. Recently developed micro-betting, which allows enthusiasts to wager on every pitch of a baseball game or shot in an NBA telecast, stands to grow sports gambling further. For example, bettors might predict whether the NFL's Dallas Cowboys will make a first down on their next play. The discrete occurrences offer hundreds of betting opportunities within every sporting event, and analysts believe micro-betting will soon account for a substantial share of all sports wagering.

The total global sports betting handle is forecast to exceed $300 billion by the mid-2020s. While more money is spent on global sports gambling than any other Best-Howard Model segment, other Sports Entertainment activities are also growing at spectacular rates. Fantasy sports, esports and sports video games all grew in popularity as restrictions imposed by the COVID-19 pandemic eliminated or diminished alternatives.

The Sports Industry: One of the World's 10 Largest Industries

As shown in *Figure 1.13*, the Best-Howard Model has estimated the worldwide sports industry in 2019 to $2.3 trillion. This estimate is based on revenues from three major domains of the sports industry. Each domain is strategically unique, and its revenue derived from three core areas.

FIGURE 1.13
BEST-HOWARD MODEL – Sports Industry Revenues (U.S. billions)

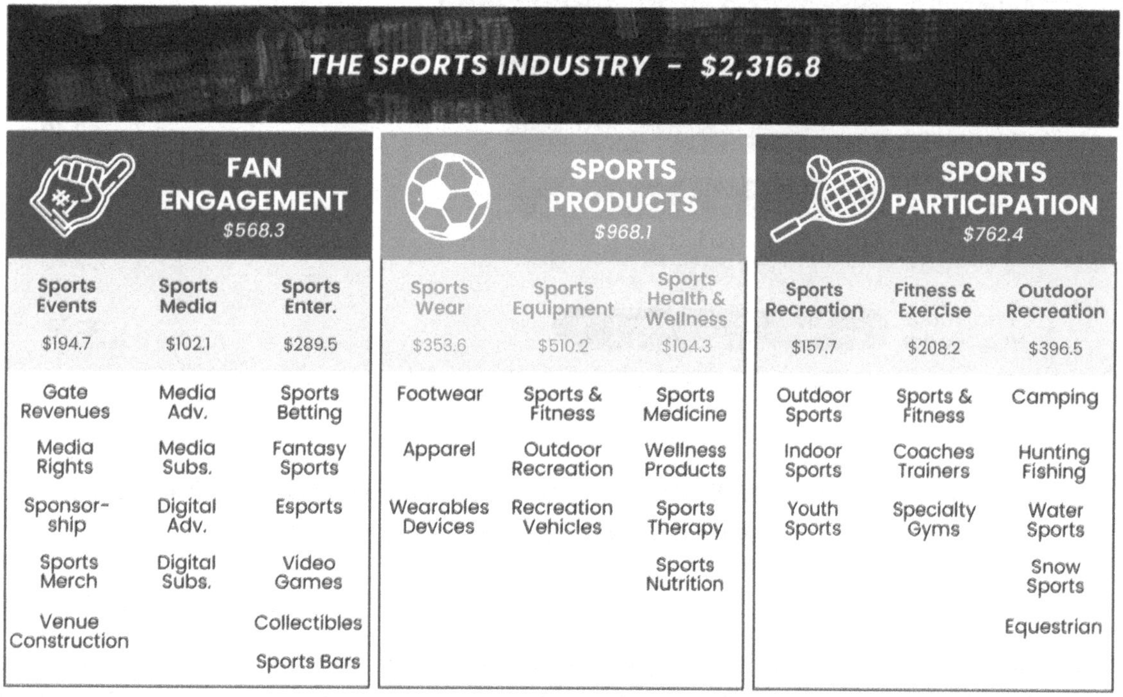

THE SPORTS INDUSTRY – $2,316.8

FAN ENGAGEMENT $568.3			SPORTS PRODUCTS $968.1			SPORTS PARTICIPATION $762.4		
Sports Events	Sports Media	Sports Enter.	Sports Wear	Sports Equipment	Sports Health & Wellness	Sports Recreation	Fitness & Exercise	Outdoor Recreation
$194.7	$102.1	$289.5	$353.6	$510.2	$104.3	$157.7	$208.2	$396.5
Gate Revenues	Media Adv.	Sports Betting	Footwear	Sports & Fitness	Sports Medicine	Outdoor Sports	Sports & Fitness	Camping
Media Rights	Media Subs.	Fantasy Sports	Apparel	Outdoor Recreation	Wellness Products	Indoor Sports	Coaches Trainers	Hunting Fishing
Sponsor-ship	Digital Adv.	Esports	Wearables Devices	Recreation Vehicles	Sports Therapy	Youth Sports	Specialty Gyms	Water Sports
Sports Merch	Digital Subs.	Video Games			Sports Nutrition			Snow Sports
Venue Construction		Collectibles						Equestrian
		Sports Bars						

The segments under each core area create the core area revenue in this bottoms-up estimate of the worldwide sports industry. Part II of this book examines the fan engagement core areas and segment revenues in Chapters 2, 3 and 4. Part IV reports the core area and segment revenues for sports products in Chapters 5, 6 and 7. Part V focuses on the core areas and segments that make up sports participation domain in Chapters 8, 9, and 10. With regard to sports industry revenue, Chapter 11 presents the Top 10 sports cities and Chapter the Top 50 sports cities.

Aggregating all revenues from each Best-Howard Model domain, the total exceeds $2.3 trillion. The value places the global sports industry among the 10 largest industries in the world. In 2020, Forbes magazine reported the sales revenues for the top 10 industry sectors around the globe

(*Figure 1.14*) (7). At the top of the list is oil and gas at $4.8 trillion, followed by technology and communication ($4.73 trillion) and banking ($4.42 trillion). The global sports industry, valued at $2.3 trillion, ranks as the ninth largest industry, falling between consumer-packaged goods at $2.37 trillion and pharmaceuticals and healthcare at $2.10 trillion.

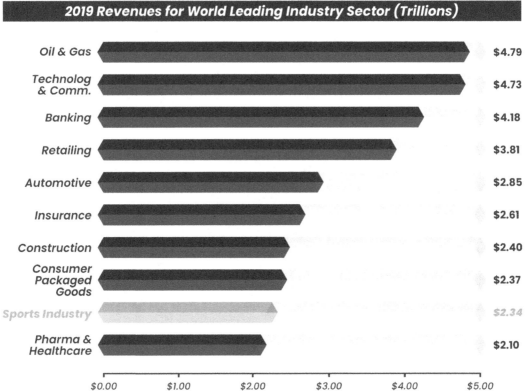

FIGURE 1.14
The Sports Industry Among Top 10 Industries in the World

2019 Revenues for World Leading Industry Sector (Trillions)

Industry	Revenue
Oil & Gas	$4.79
Technolog & Comm.	$4.73
Banking	$4.18
Retailing	$3.81
Automotive	$2.85
Insurance	$2.61
Construction	$2.40
Consumer Packaged Goods	$2.37
Sports Industry	$2.34
Pharma & Healthcare	$2.10

The Impact of the COVID-19 Pandemic on the Global Sports Industry

The COVID-19 pandemic altered the sports industry in ways no one could have predicted.

While its financial impacts have been substantial and enduring, they are also highly differential. Some sports and recreation activity areas flourished over the second half of 2020, while others suffered deep losses. Easily accessible online Fan Engagement options like sports betting and fantasy sports thrived. Providers of outdoor sports and recreation experiences, led by RV camping and pleasure boating, also did well. Hardest hit were professional and collegiate sports leagues deprived of live audiences and health and fitness clubs plagued by lockdowns and restrictions.

The final section of each of the next 9 chapters assesses the financial impact of the COVID-19 pandemic on each of the segments comprising the Best-Howard Model domains. The analysis will use 2019 pre-COVID revenues as the baseline for comparing 2020 gains and losses for each segment of the sports industry both globally and in the U.S.

To provide a more vivid and detailed understanding of the differential impacts of the virus across the sports industry, *Figure 1.15* uses a heat map to show changes in revenue for each of the three domains of the Best-Howard Model (7). The heat map highlights the changes in magnitude along a continuum from -50% to +50%. Each interval represents a change of 10%. Declines on the left side of the spectrum range from intense red, representing losses up to 50%, to orange-yellow for losses less than 10%. On the right side of the scale, revenue increases move from pale green (+1.0% to 9.9%) to vivid green, representing a jump from 40% to 50%.

Figure 1.15 illustrates the severe impact of the novel coronavirus on two of the three Best-Howard Model domains in 2020. Both Fan Engagement and Sports Participation revenues fell dramatically in the United States and worldwide. Only the Sports Product domain continued to expand during the pandemic. Its growth resulted largely from the robust increase of the Recreation Vehicle segment, which set a new record for sales in 2020.

FIGURE 1.15
COVID-19 Impact Heat Map (U.S. billions)

Global Sports Industry	2019	Growth	2020	-50% 0% 50%	2020	2020
Domains	(billions)	Rate	Forecast		(billions)	% Change
Fan Engagement	$586.3	3.0%	$603.8	-14.6%	$500.9	-14.6%
Sports Products	$968.1	4.7%	$1,013.2	-15.6%	$817.0	-15.6%
Sports Participation	$762.4	5.7%	$805.8	-26.7%	$576.4	-26.7%
TOTAL	$2,316.8	4.6%	$2,422.8	-19.1%	$1,894.3	-19.1%

U.S. Sports Industry	2019	Growth	2020	-50% 0% 50%	2020	2020
Domains	(billions)	Rate	Forecast		(billions)	% Change
Fan Engagement	$173.2	6.8%	$184.9	-12.9%	$150.8	-12.9%
Sports Products	$352.9	7.7%	$380.0	-7.4%	$327.0	-7.4%
Sports Participation	$307.7	-1.5%	$303.0	-23.5%	$235.4	-23.5%
TOTAL	$833.8	4.1%	$867.9	-14.5%	$713.2	-14.5%

The heat maps show the variable effects of the pandemic across the three domains. The substantial revenue declines suffered by the Sports Participation and Fan Engagement domains resulted in a massive loss of $500 billion (US$) for the global sports industry in 2020.

Healthy pre-COVID-19 annual growth rates of 4.6% globally and 4.1% for the United States over the past decade plunged by 20% during the pandemic. Total global sports industry revenues fell from $2.32 trillion in 2019 to $1.89 trillion in 2020.

To better understand how the industry experienced a loss of such magnitude, we provide heat map analyses at the end of each chapter to illustrate the pandemic's impact on each of the 36 Best-Howard model segments.

The segment heat maps provided in each chapter are shown in *Figure 1.16*. The colors indicate the magnitude of loss or gain for each segment, the brighter the red, the greater the loss; the deeper the green, the greater the gain. The deep losses suffered in the Sports Participation domain can be explained by the fact that 9 of the 12 segments experienced revenue losses, some very severe including all four Fitness & Exercise segments, as well as youth sports and snow sports.

In contrast, the Sport Products domain shows the spectacular gains in green (40%+) for all four segments of the sports gear and equipment core area. Each of these segments benefited from the pandemic's adverse impacts, from closed gyms and health clubs to a new-found urgency to find safe space outdoors.

FIGURE 1.16
Best-Howard Model Segment Heat Maps

SPORTS INDUSTRY MODEL

FAN ENGAGEMENT			SPORTS PRODUCTS			SPORTS PARTICIPATION		
Sports Events	Sports Media	Sports Enter.	Sportswear	Sports Equipment	Sports Health & Wellness	Sports Recreation	Fitness & Exercise	Outdoor Recreation
Gate Revenues	Ad Revenue	Sports Betting	Footwear	Sports & Fitness	Sports Medicine	Outdoor Sports	Fitness Clubs	Camping
Media Rights	Subscriptions	Fantasy Sports	Apparel	Outdoor Recreation	Wellness Products	Indoor Sports	Exercise Studios	Hunting/ Fishing
Sponsorships	Digital Ad Revenue	Esports	Wearables	Recreation Vehicles	Sports Therapy	Youth Sports	Coaches/ Trainers	Water Sports
Merchandise	Digital Subs	Video Games			Sports Nutrition		Specialty Gyms	Snow Sports
Construction		Collectibles						Equestrian
		Sports Bars						
Chapter 2	Chapter 3	Chapter 4	Chapter 5	Chapter 6	Chapter 7	Chapter 8	Chapter 9	Chapter 10

Near-Term Prospects for the End of the COVID-19 Pandemic

The record-breaking pace at which new highly effective COVID-19 vaccines were developed in early 2021 brought hope that life would return to a post-pandemic "normal" by the end of the year.

Instead the slow rollout of vaccine supply and distribution and the emergence of new coronavirus variants early in the spring of 2021 led to a new spike in infection rates throughout most of the world. As summer approached, new cases were still rising across most of Europe, India, Russia, Brazil, as well as in the United States.

The widespread belief among health experts is that the spread of the COVID-19 virus won't stop until enough people become vaccinated. The prevailing view is that "herd immunity" occurs when about 70% of the population becomes fully vaccinated. Achieving this threshold by the end of 2021 appears to be highly unlikely. As of April 15, 2021, only 11% of the world's population had been vaccinated. In many wealthy western European nations, including Germany, France and Spain, less than 10% of the population had received all required doses by mid-April. Unless, the supply of vaccines can be dramatically increased and more evenly and efficiently distributed, it's quite probable that the global pandemic will extend well into 2022.

Relative to many countries, the United States has a much higher probability of reaching the immunity threshold by year's end. By May 15, 2021, nearly 25% of Americans were fully vaccinated. With approximately, 4 million shots being administered each day, the U.S. is on pace to achieve control of the virus' spread as early as the fall of 2021. Of course, this all depends on the current vaccines providing protection against the constant threat of the emergence of new virus variants.

Given all the uncertainty, The Sports Industry will closely monitor the continuing impacts of the pandemic. Subsequent editions will track the recovery rates of every Best-Howard Model segment as the United States and other countries around the globe emerge from the pandemic.

References

We have added links to many references for direct and easy access. While we have tested each link, there are a few instances where the websites are no longer accessible. We will continue to monitor the accessibility of citation references and remove any links no longer active. In many instances the referenced data was purchased, this is noted.

1. *Michael Milano and Packianathan Chelladurai, "Gross Domestic Sport Product: The Size of the Sport Industry in the United States," Journal of Sport Management, 2011, 25 24-35.*

2. *Plunkett's Sports & Recreation Industry Almanac 2020, Plunkett Research., Ltd, Houston Texas.*

3. *"Sports - $614 Billion Global Market Opportunities & Strategies to 2022," May 14, 2019. Research and Markets. Businesswire (www.businesswire.com).*

4. *Richard Lipsey, "The Sporting Goods Industry," McFarland Publishers, 2006.*

5. *Top 10 List of the World's Most Popular Sports. BallerStatus (ballerstatus.com).*

6. *Shawn McGrath, "Global Sports Betting & Lotteries," November 2020. IBISWorld (my.ibisworld.com). (GSI Purchased Report)*

7. *"Oil and gas sector tops Forbes 2019 list of world's largest public firms in revenue generation, finds Global Data," August 20, 2019. Global Data (www.globaldata.com).*

PART II:
Fan Engagement

Where would the sports industry be without fans? It wouldn't exist.

Fan engagement is the driving force of the sports industry. Pre-pandemic revenues—just more than $600 billion in 2019, including media rights and advertising—resulted entirely from fans who paid to go to sports events, watched media broadcasts, bought team and player merchandise, bet on events, played fantasy sports, and purchased sports video games.

Fans' enthusiasm and loyalty to the teams and players they support is at the heart of the sports industry. Indeed, the term "fan" is derived from the word "fanatic," a person displaying excessive enthusiasm and intense devotion. Fans often identify with the teams they support (*Figure 1*), and after "big wins," avid fans often wear their team's apparel, buy more team merchandise and use phrases like "we won" when describing the victory. Following disappointing losses, fans tend to distance themselves from their team by not wearing apparel and using language like "they lost," omitting reference to the team by name.

SPORTS EVENTS

SPORTS MEDIA

SPORTS ENTERTAINMENT

Fans often place the blame for their favorite team's losses on external factors like poor officiating, injuries and weather. Some observers have labeled fans' two modes of behavior BIRGing and CORFing: "Basking In Reflected Glory" and "Casting Off Reflected Failure." As evidenced by their BIRGing and CORFing, fans so strongly identify with their sports teams, their own self-esteem is often closely tied to team performance.

FIGURE I
Fan Passion Provides Pride, Belonging & Self-Esteem

FAN ENGAGEMENT: Fan Engagement is the first domain in the Best-Howard Sports Industry Model. The model divides fan engagement revenues into three core areas:

- Sports Events. Gate revenues, media rights, sponsorships and advertising, merchandise sales and facility construction.

- Sports Media. Television sports broadcast subscriptions and advertising, digital subscriptions and advertising.

- Sports Entertainment. Sports betting, fantasy sports, sports video games and sports bars.

Part II of this book takes a detailed look at the three Fan Engagement core areas. And as shown in *Figure II*, each played a significant role in yielding the sports industry's pre-pandemic revenues of $2.3 trillion.

While Sports Events are at the heart of the sports industry, they create only 30% of Fan Engagement revenues. In 2019, Sports Events totaled $204.8 billion of the $648.3 billion attributed to the domain. The core area also included monies derived from gate revenues, media rights, sponsorships and advertising, merchandise sales and venue construction. Chapter 2 examines the Sports Events core area, exploring every revenue segment in the United States and worldwide over the past 10 years.

Sports Media, the Best-Howard Model's second Fan Engagement core area (*Figure II*), represents only 17% of the domain's total revenues in 2019. But digital sports subscriptions and advertising are expected to grow significantly and drive the revenues up over the next decade. Today, fans can follow their teams in real time on a day-to-day basis with team app subscriptions on smartphones. Chapter 3: Sports Media covers all aspects of the rapidly growing core area around the world.

The Sports Entertainment core area (also shown in *Figure II*) accounts for more than half of Fan Engagement's $648.3 billion in revenues. Chapter 4 takes a deep dive into the core area's revenue generating segments, which are expected to grow rapidly alongside worldwide online sports gambling. Add to this a growing interest in fantasy sports and sports video games, and Fan Engagement's importance in the sports industry is clear.

FIGURE II
Fan Engagement Core Area Revenues, 2019 (U.S. billions)

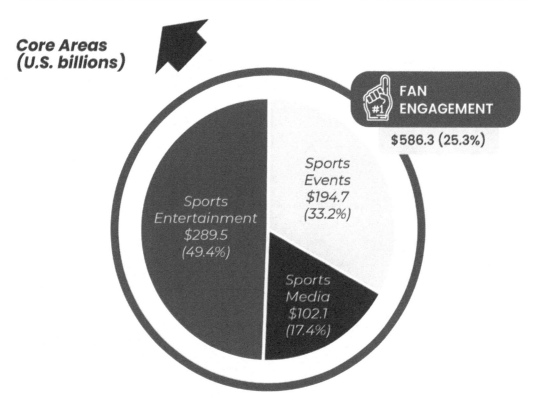

Copyright Best-Howard Model 2022. All Right Reserved.

SPORTS EVENTS
CHAPTER 2

The Heart of the Sports Industry

The heart of the sports industry is the hundreds of thousands of organized games, matches and races that occur around the globe each year. Fueled by competition, drama and pageantry, passionate fans numbering in the hundreds of millions attend and watch sport events played in ever more lavish and expensive stadiums and arenas.

Gate receipts are just one component of the revenues derived sports events. Money spent by fans to park and to purchase food and beverages adds to event revenue, as does the sale of media rights. Teams and leagues are paid by media companies to broadcast their events on TV, radio or the Internet. (*Figure 2.1*)

FIGURE 2.1
Sports Events Segments

GATE REVENUES	MEDIA RIGHTS	SPONSORSHIPS	MERCHANDISE	CONSTRUCTION
Ticket sales, parking and food sales	Revenues from brodcasting events	Venue and sports events sponsors	Licensed merchandise sold	New and renovation construction

Sponsorships - money paid by a corporation to a team to advertise and promote its brand at events – are another important source of sport event revenue. Sponsorships can range from the placement of brand names or logos on player jerseys to investing millions to place a corporation's name on a stadium or arena.

Sale of team or league merchandise at events, in retail stores or online are also provides revenues for team, leagues and sometimes athletes.

Finally, the billions invested in the construction of a new generation of "state of the art" stadiums and arenas full of expensive luxury seating options and amenities has produced abundant income streams for team owners and event operators.

An in-depth discussion (examination) of each of the major event revenue sources presented in *Figure 2.1* will be the focus of this chapter.

FIGURE 2.2
Sports Industry

$2.3 Trillion (Worldwide)

Domains (U.S. billions)

FAN ENGAGEMENT	SPORTS PRODUCTS	SPORTS PARTICIPATION
$586.3 (25.3%)	*$968.1 (41.8%)*	*$762.4 (32.9%)*

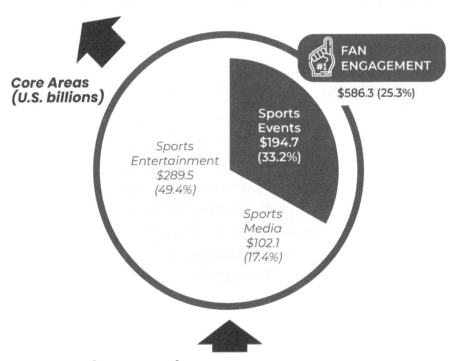

Core Areas (U.S. billions)

FAN ENGAGEMENT
$586.3 (25.3%)

Sports Events $194.7 (33.2%)

Sports Entertainment $289.5 (49.4%)

Sports Media $102.1 (17.4%)

Segments (U.S. billions)

Sports Events Segments	Revenues	Percent
Gate Revenues	$ 49.4	25.4 %
Media Rights	$ 37.8	19.4 %
Sponsorship	$ 68.5	35.2 %
Merchandise	$ 22.2	11.4 %
Construction	$ 16.8	8.6 %
TOTAL	**$ 194.7**	**100.0 %**

Copyright Best-Howard Model 2022. All Right Reserved.

Before we get started, it is important to understand where sports events fit into the Best-Howard Sports industry Model. As shown in *Figure 2.2*, sports events are one of three core areas of Fan Engagement in the Best-Howard Sports Model. The $194.7 billion generated from all five event segments accounted for 31.5% of the $586.3 billion total global revenues produced by all three Fan Engagement core areas, including sports media ($102.1 billion) and sports entertainment ($339.7 billion) in 2019.

Sports have steadily grown in popularity over the past decade (*Figure 2.3*). Worldwide sporting event revenues increased almost $50 billion over the period, reaching $177.5 billion in 2019 (1, 2), and yielding a 3.2% compound annual growth rate (CAGR). The dominant revenue share was produced in North America, with the United States and Canada accounting for nearly half the global total at 43% to 45% over the decade. The North American share grew from $55.4 billion in 2010 to $80.3 billion in 2019, outpacing the rest of the world with a compound annual growth rate of almost 4 percent. North America's preeminent revenue-producing position is due largely to the prosperity of its top four professional sports leagues (the Big 4), led by the world's most prosperous entity, the National Football League. Each of North America's pro leagues have flourished over the last five years.

FIGURE 2.3
Global & North American Sports Events Revenues (U.S. billions)

	2010	2011	2012	2013	2014	2015	2016	2017	2018	2019	CAGR
GLOBAL	$ 130.1	$ 131.0	$ 140.1	$ 143.2	$ 155.2	$ 157.7	$ 162.4	$ 167.3	$ 172.9	$ 177.5	3.2 %
NORTH AMERICAN	$ 55.4	$ 57.5	$ 59.1	$ 62.6	$ 63.9	$ 69.4	$ 73.2	$ 75.7	$ 79.1	$ 80.3	3.8%
% NORTH AMERICAN	42.6 %	43.9 %	42.2 %	43.7 %	41.2 %	44.0 %	45.1 %	45.2 %	44.8 %	45.2 %	

The annual event revenues pertaining to "North America" provided by PwC apply only to the U.S. and Canada

The first portion of this chapter examines the primary revenue generated from sports events, including ticket sales, media rights, sponsorships and merchandise. The model draws on the latest financial data for each revenue source from the four major leagues in North America and the five biggest soccer leagues in Europe over the past decade. The annual figures provide pre-COVID-19 performance profiles over an extended period. However, the pandemic severely impacted 2020 event revenues. Later in the chapter we will examine the severe impact of the pandemic on 2020 event revenues on a number of major sports leagues. We also provide post-COVID-19 recovery forecasts for each of the primary event revenue sources.

Following our examination of revenues generated from live sporting events, we devote a section of the chapter to the critical and increasingly prominent role of new sports facility construction around the globe. Over the past decade, nearly $140 billion has been invested worldwide in building a new generation of sports facilities. Many of these new multi-billion dollar "sport palaces" serve as entertainment destinations, complete with night clubs, amusement centers, and even casinos. While these new amenities greatly enhance the fan experience, they also generate abundant new income streams for stadium operators and their corporate partners. We account for the impact of capital investment in new sports venue construction as a separate but increasingly important component of sports event revenues. Much of the revenue spent by fans attending live events and companies sponsoring their brands is directly attributable to the new generation of modern "fully-loaded" sports venues.

SPORTS EVENT REVENUE SOURCES. The four primary sources of event-generated income, gate revenues, media rights, sponsorships and merchandise sales, are universal to live sporting events, from games and matches to golf tournaments:

- **Gate Revenues:** Ticket sales for live events, parking fees and concession sales.

- **Media Rights:** Revenues obtained from sports media rights to broadcast events.

- **Sponsorships:** Venue, event and athlete sponsorships, as well as event and venue advertising.

- **Merchandise:** Licensed product sales by teams, leagues and athletes.

FIGURE 2.4
Global & North American Sports Events Segments Revenues (U.S. billions)

SPORTS EVENTS - SEGMENTS				
$ 194.7 Billion Global Total				
Gate Revenues	**Media Rights**	**Sponsorships**	**Merchandise**	**Construction**
$ 49.4 Billion	$ 37.8 Billion	$ 68.5 Billion	$ 22.2 Billion	$ 16.8 Billion
25 %	**19 %**	**35 %**	**11 %**	**9 %**

Figure 2.4 shows each revenue source in the Sports Events core area and its relative contribution to overall industry spending in 2019. Corporate and brand sponsorships contributed the largest share at $68.5 billon, accounting for one third of all income generated by global events. Gate revenues from fans' spending on tickets, parking, food and beverages accounted for $49.4 billion, about one quarter of the core area's value. The sale of television network, sports cable platform and streaming service broadcast rights totaled nearly $40 billion, and licensed merchandise sales, from team jerseys to player bobble-head dolls, were $22.2 billion. Included in *Figure 2.4* is $16.8 billion spent building new sports venues, bringing total global sports events revenues to $194.7 billion in 2019.

Direct attendance accounts for a diminished share of event revenues: When we examine the relative contribution of each source over the decade, it is evident that the portion of total event revenues contributed by those fans actually attending events has declined. This trend is most apparent in North America, where gate revenues have fallen steadily from close to a third of all event revenues in 2010 to 26.8% in 2019. The factors contributing to live attendance declines, such as rising costs and enhanced live viewing options, are discussed below. As fans increasingly choose to watch events at home or at sports bars, spectators' direct contributions to event revenues have been surpassed by corporations investing billions in reaching fans through sponsor partnerships with sports teams and leagues and media companies buying the rights to live broadcast games and events.

Figures 2.5 and *2.6* provide a breakdown of the four revenue sources over the past decade, both worldwide and for North America. From a global perspective, sponsorships are the fastest growing category, while media rights have more than doubled in the United States.

FIGURE 2.5
Global Sports Event Revenue Sources 2010-2019 (U.S. billions)

	2010	2011	2012	2013	2014	2015	2016	2017	2018	2019	
Gate Revenues	$ 39.6	$ 39.0	$ 40.6	$ 41.3	$ 43.5	$ 44.8	$ 45.9	$ 47.0	$ 48.2	$ 49.4	2.2 %
Media Rights	$ 29.2	$ 26.9	$ 32.1	$ 30.1	$ 37.8	$ 35.3	$ 35.8	$ 36.5	$ 37.2	$ 37.8	2.5%
Sponsorships	$ 44.7	$ 47.3	$ 49.4	$ 53.2	$ 55.3	$ 57.5	$ 60.1	$ 62.7	$ 65.8	$ 68.5	4.4%
Merchandising	$ 16.6	$ 17.8	$ 18.0	$ 18.6	$ 18.6	$ 20.1	$ 20.6	$ 21.1	$ 21.7	$ 22.2	2.9%

On the other hand, the United States has seen stagnating gate receipts. Game attendance revenues from tickets, parking, food and beverages increased less than 1% from 2017 through 2019, as prominent sports leagues from Major League Baseball to NASCAR struggled to attract new fans.

FIGURE 2.6
North American Sports Event Revenue Sources 2010-2019 (U.S. billions)

	2010	2011	2012	2013	2014	2015	2016	2017	2018	2019	
Gate Revenues	$ 16.2	$ 16.1	$ 15.8	$ 17.4	$ 17.5	$ 17.9	$ 18.5	$ 19.1	$ 19.2	$ 19.6	2.6 %
Media Rights	$ 9.4	$ 10.8	$ 11.6	$ 12.3	$ 12.3	$ 16.3	$ 18.4	$ 19.1	$ 21.1	$ 20.9	7.2 %
Sponsorships	$ 17.2	$ 18.1	$ 18.9	$ 19.8	$ 20.6	$ 21.4	$ 22.3	$ 23.1	$ 24.2	$ 25.1	3.9 %
Merchandising	$ 12.6	$ 12.5	$ 12.8	$ 13.1	$ 13.5	$ 13.8	$ 14.0	$ 14.4	$ 14.6	$ 14.7	1.4 %

GATE REVENUES ($49.4 billion). Admission ticket sales have long been a prominent source of worldwide sports event revenues as shown in *Figure 2.7*. Other live game revenue streams are pay-to-park fees for fans driving to venues—the average pre-COVID-19 NFL parking cost was $31 in 2019 (3)—and food and beverage services.

FIGURE 2.7
Gate Revenues: North America, Rest of World and Global Total (U.S. billions)

	2010	2011	2012	2013	2014	2015	2016	2017	2018	2019
North America	$ 16.2	$ 16.1	$ 15.8	$ 17.4	$ 17.5	$ 17.9	$ 18.5	$ 19.1	$ 19.2	$ 19.6
Rest of World	$ 23.4	$ 22.9	$ 24.8	$ 23.9	$ 36.0	$ 26.9	$ 27.4	$ 27.9	$ 29.0	$ 29.8
Global Total	$ 39.6	$ 39.0	$ 40.6	$ 41.3	$ 43.5	$ 44.8	$ 45.9	$ 47.0	$ 48.2	$ 49.4
% North America	40.1 %	41.3 %	38.9 %	42.0 %	40.2 %	40.0 %	40.3 %	40.6 %	39.8 %	39.7 %

While beer and hot dogs remain popular, new venues offer fans diverse concessions, from steak to sushi and imported Italian wine to craft beer and premium mixed drinks. Hungry to highlight their city's culinary culture, Chicago's ballparks offer fans Italian beef sandwiches, Philadelphia's Citizens Bank Park serves Philly cheesesteaks and Boston's Fenway Park allows Red Sox fans to enjoy crème brulee french toast (4).

No single development in decades has had a more transformational effect on major sports teams than premium seating. Luxury suites, loge boxes and club seating now account for as much as 20% of new sports venue seating (5). In North America, the Big 4 major league venues contain more than 12,000 luxury suites and close to 500,000 club seats (5). The inventory sells at a premium, with suites going for as much as $300,000 and club seats for up to $15,000. Premium seating produces average "per cap" or person yields of three to four times that of regular game tickets, and new venues are taking advantage. See chapter 10 of Financing Sport (Howard and Crompton, fourth edition) for more information, and take a four-minute tour of the premium seating at the NFL's Nashville Titans' Nissan Stadium by clicking on the video in *Figure 2.8.*

FIGURE 2.8
Nissan Stadium Premium Seating Offerings

Tour the Premium Seating Offerings at Nissan Stadium

Scan to Watch Video

Source: https://www.youtube.com/watch?v=dWL9HNHBmT0

Worldwide gate revenues grew at an annual rate of 2.2% from $39.6 billion in 2010 to $49.4 in 2019 (*Figure 2.5*). North American gate receipts grew at a slightly higher annual rate of 2.6%, but live attendance plateaued at the end of the decade. From 2017 to 2019, the region's gate receipts grew at a rate less than 1 percent.

The United States and Canada's gate income was consistently around 40% of the world's total throughout the past decade, but the countries' gate revenue annual growth rate has stagnated. More and better media viewing options allow fans to substitute high quality broadcasts for live experiences. In 2019, television and digital platforms offered Americans 127,000 hours of sports programming, much of it live. To a growing number of fans, watching at home eliminates the inconvenience and cost of going to stadiums. Major sports events' rising costs are also a significant barrier to attendance in many world regions. For example, the cost of attending a major league game in the United States or Canada has almost tripled over the past two decades.

As shown in Figure 2.9, the average price of an NFL game ticket was $102 in 2019. When adding parking, food and beverages, souvenirs, etc., the cost grows substantially. According to Team Marketing Report's NFL Fan Cost Index (3), a single NFL game cost a family of four $540 on average in 2019. The same family of four would pay $234 to attend a Major League Baseball game. The median income for a full-time or salaried U.S. worker prior to COVID-19 was around $900 a week, making even the lower MLB price a financial challenge for many American households.

FIGURE 2.9
Average North American Big 4 Cost of Attendance

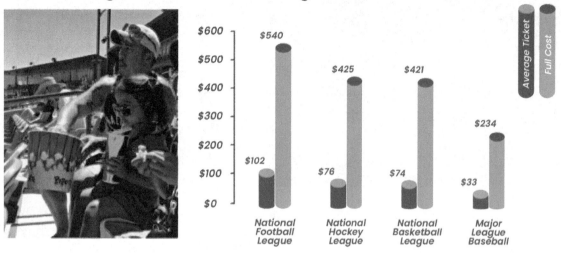

	Average Ticket	Full Cost
National Football League	$102	$540
National Hockey League	$76	$425
National Basketball League	$74	$421
Major League Baseball	$33	$234

For many, nothing replaces the pageantry and excitement of attending live sports events. But fans are increasingly experiencing major sporting events through the many electronic and wireless platforms now available. Both traditional and emerging digital media viewing options provide sports consumers with attractive, affordable and convenient alternatives to live sporting events. And sporting event producers are exploiting media's enormous potential to engage more fans.

MEDIA RIGHTS ($37.8 billion). With growing audiences, media companies are now spending more for the rights to broadcast and stream sporting events, often committing billions of dollars for extended and exclusive coverage. In 2019, worldwide sports media rights spending amounted to $37.8 billion (6). North America accounted for more than half of the total (55.3%). Over the past decade, media rights were the fastest growing sports industry income source, increasing at a compound annual rate of nearly 9% and totaling $20.9 billion in North America alone in 2019 (*Figure 2.10*).

FIGURE 2.10
Worldwide Sports Media Rights Spending, 2010–2019 (U.S. billions)

	2010	2011	2012	2013	2014	2015	2016	2017	2018	2019
North America	$ 9.4	$ 10.8	$ 11.6	$ 12.3	$ 12.3	$ 16.3	$ 18.4	$ 19.1	$ 21.1	$ 20.9
Rest of World	$ 19.8	$ 16.1	$ 20.5	$ 17.8	$ 25.5	$ 19.0	$ 17.4	$ 17.4	$ 16.1	$ 16.9
Global Total	$ 29.2	$ 26.9	$ 32.1	$ 30.1	$ 37.8	$ 35.3	$ 35.8	$ 36.5	$ 37.2	$ 37.8
% North America	32.2 %	40.1 %	36.1 %	40.9 %	32.5 %	46.2 %	51.3 %	52.3 %	56.7 %	55.3 %

In no place in the world are media rights sales, via broadcast, cable or satellite television, more dominant than North America. *Figure 2.11* summarizes the latest television broadcast deals for major North American sports properties (7,8,9,10,11,12).

Sports Events Broadcast

Three of the Big 4 professional leagues, NFL, MLB and NHL, recently signed long-term extensions with their media partners. In April 2021, WarnerMedia's Turner Sports and the NHL struck a 7-year multimedia deal worth $1.58 billion. While ESPN will retain first-tier rights, the partnership with Warner Media will allow the NHL to stream games on HBO Max "that attracts young, diverse digital first audiences (13).

Major broadcast and cable networks and streaming platforms like WarnerMedia and Amazon Prime have collectively committed more than $140 billion to the Big 4 leagues through the end of the decade—and beyond that for the NFL.

FIGURE 2.11
Selected Major North American Sports TV Deals

National Football League	CBS	Sunday Afternoon (AFC)	$2.1 billion per year, 2022-2033
	Fox	Sunday Afternoon (NFC)	$2.25 billion per year, 2022-2033
	ESPN, ABC	Monday Night Football	$2.7 billion per year, 2021-2033
	NBC	Sunday Night Football	$2 billion per year, 2022-2033
	Amazon	Thrusday Night Football	$1.32 billion per year, 2022-2033
	DirecTV	Sunday Ticket	$1.5 billion per year, 2014-2022
Major League Baseball	Fox	Regular Season, All-Star, World Series	$729 million per year, 2022-2028
	ESPN	Regular Season, Sunday Night Baseball	$550 million per year, 2022-2028
	TBS	Regular Season, Post-Season Series	$470 million per year, 2022-2028
National Basketball Association	ESPN, ABC	Regular Season, Playoffs, Finals	$1.45 billion per year, 2017-2025
	Turner	Regular Season, Playoffs	$1.25 billion per year, 2017-2025
National Hockey League	ABC, ESPN	Regular Season, Playoffs, All-Star, 4 Stanley Cups	$400 million per year, 2022-2028
	NBC	Regular Season, Winter Classic, 3 Stanley Cups	$200 million per year, 2022-2028
NASCAR	Fox, NBC	Regular Season Series	$820 million per year, 2015-2024
NCAA Basketball Tournament	CBS	NCAA Championship "March Madness"	$700 million per year, 2010-2024
	TSN		$1.1 billion per year, 2025-2032

The NFL claims the lion's share of the enormous broadcast rights sum. Broadcasters will pay nearly 75%, as much as $113 billion, over 11 years to the world's most prosperous professional sports league (14). In the first year of its extensions with CBS, Fox, Disney (ABC and ESPN), NBC and Amazon, the NFL will receive nearly $12 billion in media rights payments, doubling the $6 billion the league received in 2021.

Remarkably, the NFL negotiated many of the terms during the catastrophic pandemic, a period in which the league lost $4 billion. Even more compounding was that all four major networks were willing to pay twice as much as they had previously to renew their NFL partnerships—without any competitive bidders. As Sports Business Journal analyst Ben Fischer asserted at the time, "what an incredible business situation when you don't have to get into a traditional auction and can still double your rights fees" (15). Fischer's colleague, Abe Madkour, suggested the networks had all the leverage and could have played "hardball." He said the fact that they didn't "shows how powerful the NFL is in the media ecosystem" (15). Is the league worth it? Some would argue yes. In 2020, the league accounted for 32 of the 50 most-watched TV broadcasts in the United States (8).

The huge rights fee payouts are expected to accelerate the NFL's post-pandemic recovery. Under the league's revenue sharing arrangement, each team receives an equal share of the annual income. Every team will receive more than $300 million in 2022. Before the season starts, NFL television revenue alone will cover close to 75% of each team's annual operating expenses.

SKY TV logo

Media rights revenues in the United Kingdom, Germany, France, Spain and Italy have doubled in the last seven years, reaching $11.9 billion in 2019. Two traditional broadcast networks, Sky in the United Kingdom and Telefonica in Spain, are the biggest spenders, together paying $7 billion for sporting event rights (16,17). While the five premier European soccer leagues account for more than half of the nearly $12 billion spent in 2019, the rapid growth in rights values has benefitted many less prominent leagues and smaller competitions. In 2018, secondary level European sports properties received 44% of total broadcast rights fees.

Online streaming services—Apple TV+, Disney+, Hulu, Peacock and others—are growing rapidly and expected to continue creating opportunities for sports leagues and event producers. Even with online, direct-to-consumer viewing options fracturing television content, media analysts anticipate the next round of media rights fees for the Big 4 North American major leagues will be historically high.

The robust sports television market has also benefitted the Professional Golf Association, which recently signed an agreement with CBS, NBC and the Golf Channel totaling $1.1 billion a year, a 74% increase over its previous broadcast rights deal (18). Even with the uncertainty the COVID-19 virus creates, analysts project massive increases in sports media rights revenues over the next five to seven years.

SPONSORSHIPS ($68.5 billion). Sports sponsorships' unique and versatile benefits attract a growing number of companies around the globe. Over the past decade, corporate sponsorships have provided the fastest growing and single largest sports event revenue stream worldwide. As shown in *Figure 2.12*, companies worldwide spent $68.5 billion sponsoring teams, leagues and major events in 2019 (19). The North American share, $25.1 billion, accounted for 36.6% of the total (20). Companies eager to connect their brands to passionate fans have found sports teams and athletes serve as powerful marketing platforms and brand ambassadors.

FIGURE 2.12
Worldwide Sports Sponsorship Annual Revenues, 2010–2019 (U.S. billions)

	2010	2011	2012	2013	2014	2015	2016	2017	2018	2019
North America	$ 17.2	$ 18.1	$ 18.9	$ 19.8	$ 20.6	$ 21.4	$ 22.3	$ 23.1	$ 24.3	$ 25.1
Rest of World	$ 27.5	$ 29.2	$ 30.5	$ 33.4	$ 34.7	$ 36.1	$ 37.8	$ 39.6	$ 41.5	$ 43.4
Global Total	$ 44.7	$ 47.3	$ 49.4	$ 53.2	$ 55.3	$ 57.5	$ 60.1	$ 62.7	$ 65.8	$ 68.5
% North America	38.5 %	38.3 %	38.3 %	37.2 %	37.3 %	37.2 %	37.1 %	36.8 %	36.9 %	36.6 %

Benefits companies seek from sponsoring sports teams and events include the following:

• Differentiating established brands in cluttered markets and introducing new products.

• Providing on-site sampling for product trials or demonstrations to highlight superior technology and to engage consumers directly on-site.

• Using sports to facilitate hospitality opportunities: Relationship marketing is a central facet of many companies' goal to attract, develop and retain customers. Hospitality at sport events facilitates this bonding and client cultivation in exclusive hospitality suites.

Over the past decade, European association soccer leagues have achieved steady sponsorship revenue growth. During the 2018–2019 season, the top leagues in the United Kingdom, Germany, France, Spain and Italy all reported sponsorship income as their second largest operational revenue source. The English Premier League led the way, with sponsorship sales reaching $1.62 billion, followed by Spain's La Liga at $1.02 billion (17).

FIGURE 2.13
Toyota Sponsorship Signage at Chicago's Wrigley Field

The most lucrative sponsorship deals in European soccer are on team jerseys, where global companies pay for the rights to display their brand name and logo. In 2012, the American automobile company Chevrolet signed a seven-year, $600 million deal with the Premier League's Manchester United. It was the largest shirt sponsorship deal ever recorded for a European soccer club (*Figure 2.14*). The agreement guaranteed the team an annual payout of $88 million and expired at the end of the 2020-21 season.

FIGURE 2.14
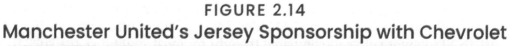
Manchester United's Jersey Sponsorship with Chevrolet

After a long search for a new sponsor, Manchester United announced a five-year deal with global technology company TeamViewer in March 2021. The deal's terms were considerably less than those of the Chevrolet contract. TeamViewer agreed to pay about $325 million over five years, equating to annual payments of $65 million. The result is an annual loss of $23 million for Manchester United (21). Pundits attributed the loss to the Man U's failure to win championships in either the Premier League or Champions League after 2013. But the COVID-19 pandemic also likely restricted the team's prospects, and analysts disagree about whether the smaller sponsorship deal was an aberration, short-term casualty of the economic downturn or an indication of a more cautious, conservative approach to the market in uncertain times.

Other sizeable pre-pandemic jersey or "kit" deals include two La Liga clubs, with Middle Eastern airline Emirates paying Real Madrid $77 million a year and Japanese electronics company Rakuten paying FC Barcelona $60.5 million annually.

Sports have come to dominate all sponsorship types in North America. By 2019, sports accounted for 70% of total sponsorship spending in the region. The sponsorships' growth has accelerated over the past four years, increasing at a compound annual rate of 5.6% to $25.1 billion in 2019. And while the increased investment is dramatic, it underestimates the full costs associated with activating a sponsorship. For every dollar they spend on rights fees, companies spend an additional $1.80 on staffing, promoting, developing and executing the sponsorship. The expenses can include signage, logoed merchandise, security, infrastructure development (e.g., on-site hospitality suites) and appearance fees for celebrity athletes.

The most prominent form of sports sponsorships in North America is stadium and arena naming. Almost 90% of teams in the region's Big 4 professional leagues play in venues with corporate or brand names (5). The entitlement deals, with teams or community stadium authorities, have exploded in recent years. Companies commit hundreds of millions of dollars to attach their names to high profile, iconic venues like the New Orleans Mercedes-Benz Superdome (*Figure 2.15*), which has hosted seven NFL Super Bowls and five college football championships and is the home of the NFL's Saints. Software technology company SoFi signed the richest naming rights agreement in the world in 2018, agreeing to pay $600 million over 20 years to sponsor the new home of the NFL's Los Angeles Rams and Chargers. The venue will host at least 16 NFL games per year (compared to eight for most stadiums), the 2022 NFL Super Bowl, the 2023 College Football Championship game, one to three 2026 FIFA World Cup games, and the opening and closing ceremonies of the 2028 Summer Olympics.

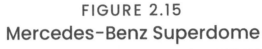

FIGURE 2.15
Mercedes-Benz Superdome

Why are companies willing to pay so much for naming rights? Analysts suggest the sponsorships offer unique 24/7 exposure, particularly appealing for companies with little or no existing brand recognition. Swedish telecom giant Ericsson, Inc. was virtually unknown in the U.S. before it paid $20 million in 1995 to name the NFL's Carolina Panthers' new stadium in Charlotte, North Carolina. In just three years, 50% of Carolinian adults and 44% of Americans recognized the Ericsson brand. Brand building and incremental sales opportunities are also attractive. When PepsiCo purchased the naming rights to the Pepsi Center in Denver, Colorado, home of the NBA's Nuggets and NHL's Avalanche, the transaction also conveyed exclusive soda pouring rights for all arena events.

Companies also receive hospitality opportunities through naming rights partnerships. Almost universally, the agreements grant the corporate partner access to at least one luxury suite, and other premium seating opportunities are often made available. The seating allows sponsors to create direct, casual selling opportunities with key clients, and the goodwill engendered by the hospitality efforts can strengthen business relationships and lead to increased or renewed sales opportunities.

MERCHANDISE SALES ($22.2 billion). Licensed sports merchandise sales, while the smallest of the Best-Howard Model's four event revenue categories, contributes considerably to worldwide sports spending. In 2019, fans spent more than $22 billion on authentic, logoed league and team sports merchandise, from jerseys to player-replica bobblehead dolls (See *Figure 2.17*). As shown in *Figure 2.16*, North Americans accounted for a dominant share, spending $14.7 billion on all sports merchandise in 2019. Consumers can buy licensed goods and products online, in department stores, in sports specialty stores or in a growing number of league- and team-themed merchandise outlets.

FIGURE 2.16
Worldwide Annual Merchandise Sales (U.S. billions)

	2010	2011	2012	2013	2014	2015	2016	2017	2018	2019
North America	$ 12.6	$ 12.5	$ 12.8	$ 13.1	$ 13.5	$ 13.8	$ 14.0	$ 14.4	$ 14.5	$ 14.7
Rest of World	$ 4.0	$ 5.3	$ 5.2	$ 5.5	$ 5.1	$ 6.3	$ 6.6	$ 6.7	$ 7.2	$ 7.5
Global Total	$ 16.6	$ 17.8	$ 18.0	$ 18.6	$ 18.6	$ 20.1	$ 20.6	$ 21.1	$ 21.7	$ 22.2
% North America	75.9 %	70.2 %	71.1 %	70.4 %	72.6 %	68.7 %	68.0 %	68.2 %	66.8 %	66.2 %

FIGURE 2.17
NFL Bobblehead Dolls: Popular Fan Promotional Giveaways

Sports entities maintain ownership of their intellectual property (IP), such as their team logo, name, mascot, nickname and symbol, through the licensing process. A sports team, league or event first registers the symbols, designs, colors, phrases and combinations of words distinctively identified with their organization. In the United States, organizations must submit trademark applications to the U.S. Patent and Trademark Office, which grants exclusive use protection for each approved trademark. Once the sports organization has legal ownership of its IP, it can enter agreements with licensees to manufacture, distribute and promote logoed goods and products. The four major professional sports leagues in North America all operate their own centralized properties office (e.g., NFL Properties) to manage licensing concerns for their league and teams. The offices negotiate with manufacturers to create official league merchandise; Nike and Adidas might produce themed sportswear, EA Sports might make video games featuring teams and players, and Marvel Comics might print comic books featuring player "superheroes."

Mass distribution retail outlets like Walmart and Target, as well as national sporting goods chains like Dick's Sporting Goods and global brand stores like Nike, Adidas and Puma, sell the majority of licensed sports merchandise available today. In turn, leagues and their members receive licensing revenue in the form of royalty payments, usually based on a total sales revenue percentage for each good or product. On average, sports organizations charge 11% to 14% of net sales for the use of their trademarks.

While revenues realized from licensing royalties provide substantial income for major sports properties, they are likely to remain the smallest contributor among the Best-Howard Model's four Sports Events revenue sources. Over the last three years, the segment's annual growth rate has diminished to less than 1% in North America and 2.5% in Europe.

SPORTS VENUE CONSTRUCTION SPENDING ($16.8 Billion). North America, led largely by the United States, invested over $100 billion in new sports facility construction from 2010 to 2019, nearly three times more than the rest of the world (*Figure 2.18*). Drawing from various credible sources, the Best-Howard Model estimates global spending on new and renovated sports facilities over the past decade totaled $136.1 billion (5,22,23).

FIGURE 2.18
Worldwide Sports Venue Construction Spending 2010-2019 (U.S. billions)

	2010	2011	2012	2013	2014	2015	2016	2017	2018	2019
North America	$ 10.12	$ 9.43	$ 9.12	$ 8.55	$ 8.80	$ 9.92	$ 10.19	$ 11.66	$ 11.85	$ 12.00
Rest of World	$ 1.65	$ 1.99	$ 3.18	$ 6.25	$ 4.54	$ 1.29	$ 2.82	$ 3.41	$ 4.66	$ 4.80
Global Total	$ 11.77	$ 11.42	$ 12.30	$ 14.80	$ 13.34	$ 11.21	$ 13.01	$ 15.07	$ 16.51	$ 16.80
% North America	86.7 %	85.3 %	74.1 %	57.8 %	66.0 %	88.5 %	78.3 %	77.3 %	71.8 %	75.0 %

Rest of World annual figures are estimates compiled from a search of 553 venues listed on Wikipedia's "List of Stadiums by Capacity." Construction cost figures were retrieved from credible sources for all venues opening between 2010 and 2019. Currencies were converted to U.S. dollars, and all construction costs were inflation adjusted to March 2021. Construction cost figures were not retrievable from approximately 5% of facilities listed.

Three new major league stadiums opened in the United States—two new NFL stadiums in Las Vegas and Los Angeles and one MLB ballpark in Arlington, Texas—even as the COVID-19 pandemic took hold in early 2020. The total construction cost exceeded $8 billion. Since MLB's New York Yankees and the NFL's Dallas Cowboys both eclipsed the billion-dollar barrier in 2009, nine of the 14 major U.S. sports facilities constructed have also crossed the threshold.

The most expensive of the new facilities is SoFi Stadium, home of both the NFL's Los Angeles Rams and Chargers (*Figure 2.19*). The stadium's full development cost is estimated to have reached $4.97 billion (24). It offers 260 luxury suites, a 120-yard double-circular video board and a translucent roof also serving as a movie screen. The stadium is surrounded by entertainment options, including a 6,000-seat performance center, the 2.5-acre American Airlines Plaza, more than 1.5 million square feet of retail and office space, a 250-room hotel and 20 acres of parks.

FIGURE 2.19
SoFi Stadium, the World's Most Expensive Sports Facility

SPORTS VENUES AS ENTERTAINMENT DESTINATIONS. California's SoFi Stadium exemplifies a new wave of event facilities commonly called sports and entertainment districts (SEDs). North American sports venue developers and team owners have created SEDs in St. Louis, Missouri (Ballpark Village), Philadelphia, Pennsylvania (Xfinity Live!), Edmonton, Ontario (Ice District), San Diego, California (Ballpark District), Houston, Texas (Avenida District), Atlanta, Georgia (The Battery), and Arlington, Texas (Texas Live!). In the new development model, arenas and stadiums are the primary attraction for mixed-use developments integrating entertainment elements like casinos, sportsbooks, amusement parks and amphitheaters, as well as dining and retail shopping options.

The Battery hospitality district in Atlanta, the new home of MLB's Braves, includes a Professional Bull Riders–branded restaurant. The PBR Atlanta provides a unique "cowboy" experience, including a ride on "the world's meanest" mechanical bull and a large dance floor, stage, lounge area with fire pits and bars. (*Figure 2.20*)

Scan to Watch Video

Source: https://www.youtube.com/watch?v=Fy28ZtAZN-k

FIGURE 2.20
Battery District Attractions

Both Allegiant Stadium in Las Vegas, Nevada, and Capital One Arena in Washington, D.C., include sportsbooks, areas in which ticket holders can wager on competitions. Gamblers can place bets on Major League Baseball, UFC bouts, NASCAR auto racing and golf tournaments. The Staples Arena in Los Angeles includes a night club, the Hyde Lounge, where membership is modeled after an iconic club of the same name on Hollywood's Sunset Strip. The 4,000-square-foot space features two salons, three bars, a dance hall and a private great room with floating LCD television screens. The lounge includes ledge seating overlooking the floor from the arena's stage end, offering members intimate views of concerts and sporting events featuring the NBA's Lakers and Clippers and NHL's Kings. In all cases, the developers intend to attract fans to the venues earlier and make them stay longer and spend more.

Europe has experienced a stadium building boom, as well. The English Premier League's Tottenham Spurs joined the billion-dollar club with its $1.3 billion, 62,026-seat stadium in 2019. The stadium is England's first cashless sports venue and features the two largest video boards in western Europe and the world's first retractable soccer pitch. (*Figure 2.21*)

FIGURE 2.21

Source: https://www.youtube.com/watch?v=ZA6cbCe3vnA

Spain's Real Madrid is investing $680 million to renovate its iconic Santiago Bernabeu stadium, intending to create "the digital stadium of the future." The arena will be the world's first with a 5G network; the network's heightened speed and capacity is intended to provide fans greater team access by streaming 360-degree images of players and coaches arriving on buses or in locker rooms before and after matches. The remodeled venue will also incorporate shops, restaurants and a hotel with some rooms overlooking the pitch. The renovation is due for completion in summer 2022. Insiders reported in March 2021 that Real Madrid was considering building a casino in the new stadium. The dramatic new feature was considered a strategy for recouping the heavy losses Real Madrid suffered during the COVID-19 pandemic (25). While the casino's addition has not been confirmed, the club's consideration of it is further evidence of gambling's increased prominence in sports culture.

FIGURE 2.22

For a look inside the club's new 80,000-seat domed stadium

Scan to Watch Video

Source: https://twitter.com/realmadriden/status/1249766803800276992

The new Emirates Stadium, home of the English Premier League's elite Arsenal Football Club, has had a significant impact on the team's financial fortunes. For nearly 100 years, the London soccer team played in Highbury Stadium, affectionately known as the Home of Football. Despite resistance from Arsenal fans, team owners believed building a larger stadium capable of generating increased revenues was the only way to keep pace with the world's best soccer teams. Highbury Stadium's limited 38,400-fan capacity and lack of revenue-enhancing assets had handicapped Arsenal's ability to stay competitive, and the move to the new 60,361-seat, state-of-the-art stadium in 2006 proved to be a financial success. Arsenal's matchday revenues more than doubled from $45.5 million to $109.5 million. The team's conversion of the Highbury site to residential housing resulted in an even larger revenue stream of about $200 million annually. Arsenal now arguably has the strongest financial footing of any soccer team in Europe.

Find a comprehensive list of future sports facilities either currently under construction or on the drawing boards in countries around the globe.

Scan for List of Future Stadiums

Source: https://en.wikipedia.org/wiki/List_of_future_stadiums

COVID-19 Impacts on Sports Events

Sports leagues' stable growth across the globe came to an abrupt halt in 2020. The COVID-19 pandemic led to more than 20,000 cancelled events and attendance losses of 198.2 million fans in the United States alone (26).

As shown in *Figure 2.23*, the pandemic forced many leagues to suspend play for several months (27). Several leagues shut down by the pandemic, such as the French Ligue 1 and Russian Kontinental (hockey) League, never resumed play for the season. Those resuming regular-season games, like Europe's five largest soccer leagues and the NHL, played in empty stadiums. The NBA created a "bubble," or isolation zone, in Orlando, Florida, to continue playing safely.

To learn more from Commissioner Adam Silver about the NBA's innovative approach.

Scan to Visit Site

Source: https://edition.cnn.com/2020/12/09/business/nba-chris-paul-michele-roberts-adam-silver-risk-takers/index.html

FIGURE 2.23
COVID-19 Pandemic's Impact on Global Sports Events

SUSPENDED / RESUMED COMPETITION

League/Event	Length Suspended (mos.)	Resume NO Live Attendance
German Bundesliga	2	X
English Premier	3	X
Italian Serie A	3	X
Spanish La Liga	3	X
Turkish Super Lig	3	X
S. Korean Football	1	X
S. Korean Baseball	1	X
World Rugby Sevens	5	X
National Hockey League (NHL)	5	X
National Basketball Association (NBA)	4.5	X
UEFA Europe League	4	X

POSTPONED / ALTERED

League/Event

2020 Summer Olympic Games (Tokyo, Japan) until summer 2021
2020 World Track & Field Championships until summer 2021
Major League Baseball - delayed season opening 3 months, shortened season from 162 to 60 games
Tour de France - from June 2020 to August 2020
Chinese Grand Prix - indefinitely
Dubai World Cup (horse race) - until 2021
Kentucky Derby (horse race) - from May 2020 to September 2020

TERMINATED (Ended Season Prematurely)

League/Event

Dutch Football League
EuroLeague (basketball)
Russian Kontinental Hockey League
Pakistani Super League (cricket)
Indian Premier League (cricket) - tournament shifted to the United Arab Emirates.

CANCELLED

League/Event

French Ligue 1
NFL Pro Bowl
British Open Golf-Tournament
Euro Cup Basketball Tournament

REGULAR SCHEDULE WITH NO OR LIMITED LIVE ATTENDANCE

League/Event

PGA (Professional Golf Association) Tour
LPGA (Ladies Professional Golf Association) Tour

The world's biggest event, the 2020 Summer Olympics, was postponed along with several other prominent sporting events. The Tokyo Olympics were rescheduled to start July 23, 2021, but in a reorganized fashion. Because of continuing COVID-19 concerns, the Tokyo Organizing Committee in March announced that no overseas spectators would be allowed at the Games, even if they were vaccinated (28). Many other global events rescheduled for 2021 face uncertainty. In spring 2021, a new coronavirus strain spread rapidly across Europe. While millions had received coronavirus vaccines, the number was not sufficient to stop the pandemic.

Figure 2.24 details the financial impact of COVID-19 on each of the top professional sports leagues around the world (29). Every one of the leagues suffered substantial losses over the past year. The five major North American leagues were the hardest hit, losing a collective $12.8 billion (*Figure 2.26*). All of Europe's association soccer experienced significant revenue declines, with combined losses totaling $3.85 billion. Seven of the 10 leagues examined suffered one-year losses greater than 25% of their 2019 revenues. No previous global crisis has had such a deleterious effect on sports leagues and teams.

FIGURE 2.24
COVID-19 Impact on 2020 Top Global Sports League Revenues (U.S. billions)

LEAGUES	2019 REVENUES	2020 # OF GAMES, MODIFICATIONS	2020 EST. REVENUES	LOSS (%/$)
NFL	$ 15.3	Full 16 reg. seaspn games; No or limited live attend.	$ 12.2	−20% $3.1 bn
NBA	$ 8.8	90% of reg. season games played before season suspended; post-season played in 'bubble', no fans.	$ 7.5	−10% $1.3 bn
MLB	$ 10.4	Reduced reg. season to 60 games, No fans; post-season limited attend.	$ 3.7	−54% $6.7 bn
NHL	$ 5.1	85% of reg. season games played before season suspended; post-season games confined to 2 sites. No fans.	$ 4.4	−14% $0.7 bn
MLS	$ 2.0 (est.)	65% of reg. season games played before suspended play for 5 months, resumed to complete season. No or limited fans.	$ 1.0	−50% $1 bn
English Premier	$ 7.1	Regular season suspended for 3 months, resumed June 19 to complete schedule and FA cup. No fans.	$ 5.75	−19.0% $1.35 bn
German Bundesliga	$ 4.7	Regular season suspended for 2 months, resumed May 16 to complete schedule. No fans.	$ 4.5	−4.2% $0.20 bn
Spanish La Liga	$ 4.0	Regular season suspended for 3 months, resumed June 12 to complete schedule. No fans.	$ 3.25	−18.8% $0.75 bn
Italian Serie A	$ 3.0	Regular season suspended for 3 months, resumed June 14 to complete schedule. No fans.	$ 2.15	−28.3% $0.85 bn
French Ligue 1	$ 2.3	Cancelled 2019/20 season with 25% of games left to play; Brodcast partner Mediapro failed to pay $400M.	$ 1.6	−30.4% $0.70 bn

As shown in *Figure 2.24*, the combined impact of disruptive shutdowns, cancelled games and months of empty stadiums deprived teams of game- and match-day revenues from ticket, concession and souvenir sales and parking fees. For leagues without significant media rights deals, the loss of live gate income was devastating.

North America's Major League Soccer suffered the greatest decline of any organization, losing more than half of the revenues generated in its banner 2019 season. After shutting down two weeks into its season, the league faced daunting challenges as the first in America to welcome fans back to games. Some states and cities imposed bans on spectators; others, like Texas, imposed 50% capacity restrictions. Some MLS teams placed their own limitations on fans (*Figure 2.25*). FC Dallas restricted games to 25% capacity. Other jurisdictions created attendance-squelching barriers like requiring cashless in-stadium transactions and spectators to sign liability waivers saying they would not bring lawsuits should they contract COVID-19.

FIGURE 2.25
MLS Fans Dispersed and in Face Masks

The combination of empty stadiums and cancellations made it impossible for leagues and teams to satisfy their contractual obligations to corporate sponsors during the 2019-2020 season. International Events Group (30) reports that the pandemic adversely impacted more than 120,000 active sponsorship agreements and left more than 5,000 brands "needing to recoup the lost value" (31) in the United States alone. In 2019, brands invested $25 billion in sports league and event sponsorships in North America. The International Events Group study found that as much as $14 billion went unfulfilled. Will the lost sponsorship value be refunded or deferred and honored in the future? The study found brand sponsors and event producers/properties (leagues, teams, events) disagreed. Almost two-thirds of properties believed they could deliver full value, while only 45% of the sponsors agreed. How the issue will be resolved through 2021 and beyond remains uncertain, but the unfulfilled obligations will impact new and incremental sponsorship spending, most likely causing it to decline until existing inventory is expended.

BOUNCING BACK. While the mass sporting event cancellations and postponements due to COVID-19 hit the industry hard, most analysts believe it will rebound and thrive. Leading sports business publication Sportico asserts, "the big four leagues [in North America] all seemingly managed to survive the financial challenges COVID-19 brought on in 2020" (32).

As of early summer 2021, the pandemic was still far from under control. With an outbreak of virus variants around the globe, 2021 looks to be another difficult year. Will the teams and leagues incurring losses in 2020 withstand a second straight year of declines? The chairman of the European Club Association recently expressed concern. Andrea Angelli believes that 2020-2021 will be "much worse" than 2019-20, as the coming year will be a "full season without fans in the stadiums" (33). Angelli said Europe's soccer clubs are facing "bottom line losses of around $7.7 billion and $10.1 billion for the combined two years…and about 360 clubs are in need of cash injections" (33). Don Garber, MLS commissioner, echoed the concern. Garber said his league's almost $1 billion 2020 losses "were probably deeper than what we expected" (34). Recognizing the grim consequences facing the league if the pandemic disrupts the 2021 season, Garber remarked, "I don't think any business can sustain the kind of impact that we sustained in 2020 for two years in a row" (34). Shown in *Figure 2.26* are the estimated losses in 2020 for top professional global sports (35).

Established leagues, particularly those with significant television broadcast deals, will likely endure extended adverse impacts of the COVID-19 pandemic. Europe's Premier League and Bundesliga and North America's Big 4 all have the financial resources to withstand multiple difficult years. Below the elite level, many leagues are dependent on game day revenues and corporate sponsors and face a different reality. They will rely on COVID-19 vaccines to be rapidly administered around the world to return fans to their stadiums and arenas. As of mid-April 2021, more than 800 million vaccine doses had been administered to about 10% of the world's population. Even in highly developed, wealthy nations, the percentage of people fully vaccinated was small: 22% in the United States, 11% in the United Kingdom and less than 7% in Germany (6.1%), Spain (6.6%) and France (5.5%).

While worldwide communities are now in better position to combat the COVID-19 pandemic than they were one year ago, they have a long ways to go before infection rates are low enough to allow sports events to return to normalcy. Indeed, the coronavirus likely will never be totally eradicated. The key to controlling the pandemic is vaccinating enough people so the virus has nowhere to spread. Current estimates place the COVID-19 herd immunity threshold between 65% and 80%. Reaching even the low end of that threshold will take several months at current vaccination rates in the U.S. and likely a year or more in most of Europe or Asia. It appears that the most optimistic forecast for returning to a post-pandemic sports world will be sometime in 2022, when fans in most places around the globe will likely feel safe once again returning to crowded stadiums, arenas or race tracks to watch their favorite sports with family and friends.

Fan response to the resumption of three major sports leagues in the fall of 2021 offers optimism for the recovery of North American sport leagues heading into 2022. Despite COVID-19 infection rates still at a high level in many parts of the U.S., American fans filled NFL stadiums and NBA and NHL arenas to near capacity. Only four NFL teams required vaccine mandates, with all 32 stadiums open to full capacity. Home attendance reached 4.3 million over the first four weeks – 22 times greater than compared to the 197,000 attending during the COVID-19 restricted 2020 season (35). Opening night for the NBA's 75th season achieved nearly 95% capacity in 16 arenas across the United States. NBA Commissioner, Adam Silver, optimistically projects attendance revenue for the 2021-22 season reaching $10 billion, an almost 50% increase over the previous shortened season (36). NHL attendance averaged over 90% of capacity over the first week of leagues' 2021-22 season (37).

References

We have added links to many references for direct and easy access. While we have tested each link, there are a few instances where the websites are no longer accessible. We will continue to monitor the accessibility of citation references and remove any links no longer active. In many instances the referenced data was purchased, this is noted.

1. At the Gate and Beyond: Outlook for the Sports Market through 2023 (2019). *PwC* (www.pwc.com). (GSI Purchased Report)

2. Changing the Game – Outlook for the Global Sports Market to 2015 (December 2015). *PwC* (www.pwc.com). (GSI Purchased Report)

3. Team Marketing Report (September 2019). *NFL* Fan Cost Index (www.nfl.com).

4. Daniel Smith (May 2018). How sports stadiums are stepping up their foodservice game. *QSR* (www.qrsmagazine.com).

5. Dennis Howard & John Crompton (2018). Financing Sport (4th edition). FIT Publishers

6. Scott Roxborough (October 16, 2019). Sports rights now make up 26% of global content spend, Advanced Television

7. NFL Communications, "NFL completes long-term media distribution agreements providing fans greater access to NFL games than ever before," March 18, 2021. *National Football League* (www.nflcommunications.com).

8. Anthony Crupi, "NFL inks 11-year, $105 billion media rights renewals with partners," March 18, 2021. *Sportico* (www.sportico.com).

9. Craig Edwards, "Should MLB worry about its new deal with ESPN," January 11, 2021.

10. Jabari Young, "Major League Baseball's new media rights deal with Turner Sports worth over $3 billion," *CNBC* (www.cnbc.com); Evan Altman, "Latest report of MLB's reduced ESPN deal may not tell the whole story," January 8, 2021. *Cubs Insider* (www.cubsinsider.com).

11. Jabari Young, "NBA is next up for a big rights increase, and $75 billion is the price," March 22, 2021. CNBC

12. Paulsen, "NBA announces 9-year extension with ESPN, Turner through 2025," *Sports Media Watch* (www.sportsmediawatch.com).

13. Jabari Young, "NHL moving to Turner Sports is $1 billion risk-reward for hockey," April 27, 2021. CNBC

14. Justin Birnbaum, "NFL's new TV deal hands teams $300 million a year, and still won't drive franchise values," March 19, 2021. *Forbes* (www.forbes.com).

15. SBJ Unpacks Podcast, "The Road Ahead: NFL Media Rights Deal with Abe Madkour, Ben Fischer and John Ourand," March18, 2021. Sports Business Journal

16. "Annual Review of Football Finance 2019," May 2019. *Deloitte* (www2.deloitte.com).

17. Home Truths: Annual Review of Football Finance, June 2020. *Deloitte* (www2.deloitte.com).

18. Brian Steinberg, "PGA Tour strikes massive golf-rights deal with CBS, NBC and ESPN," March 9, 2020. Variety

19. A Guttman, "Global sponsorship spending by region from 2009 to 2018 (in billion U.S. dollars)," November 16, 2019. *Statista* (www.statista.com). (GSI Purchased Report)

20. Christina Gough, "Sports sponsorship spending in the United States from 2014 to 2024," March 17, 2021. *Statista* (www.statista.com). (GSI Purchased Report)

21. Mark Ogden, "Man U to lose $23m a year with TeamViewer shirt sponsor deal," *ESPN* (www.espn.com).

22. Gordon Zheng, "Sports Stadium Construction in the U.S.," December 2019. IBISWorld (my.ibisworld.com). (GSI Purchased Report)

23. David Broughton, "Sports venue construction spending to take off again in 2019," January 12, 2018. Sports Business Journal (www.bizjournals.com).

24. Jay Paris, "Costly SoFi Stadium gets a financial handout from NFL," May 20, 2020. Forbes (www.forbes.com).

25. Arnold Dzouza, "Real Madrid's revamped 575M Santiago Bernabeu Stadium to have a casino?" March 31, 2021. Republicworld.com

26. David Broughton, " SBJ Unpacks: Highlights from a most unusual year," December 27, 2020. Sports Business Journal (www.sportsbusinessjournal.com).

27. Sources for Figure 2.15 - Al Jazeera, Deloitte, PwC. and others (www.aljazeera.com).

28. Andrew Dawson, "Everything you need to know about the 2021 Tokyo Olympics and Paralympics," March 25, 2021. Runner's World (www.runnersworld.com).

29. Sources for Figure 2.24 -- David Lange, "Potential revenue loss of Serie A due to the coronavirus 2019-2020, by source," February 9, 2021 Statista (www.statista.com); Frank Pingue, "MLS concerned after COVID-19 take bite out of 2020 revenue," December 8, 2020. Reuters (www.reuters.com); "Home Truths: Annual Review of Football Finance," June 2020. Deloitte (www2.deloitte.com); PwC 2021 Sports Outlook, (www.pwc.com); "Coronavirus: What sporting events are affected by the pandemic?" September 20, 2020. Al Jazeera (www.aljazeera.com); Chris Smith, "Major League Soccer's most valuable teams 2019: Expansion Fees, Sale Prices Surge May 4, 2019 Forbes (www.forbes.com); Bobby McMahon, "How Ligue 1's dream TV deal has turned into a financial nightmare," January 18, 2021. Forbes (www.forbes.com) ESPN (www.espn.com). (GSI Purchased Report)

30. IEG, "$10 billion in sports and entertainment sponsorship value gap will need to be made up." 2021 IEG (www.sponsorship.com).

31. Ed Dixon, "Study: US$ 10bn in sponsorship value need to be made up in the US," April 17, 2020. SportPro Media (www.sportspromedia.com).

32. John Wall Street, Covid-19 spawns sports advertising 'Buyer's Market,'" September 20, 2020. Sportico

33. "ECA chief spells out COVID-19 impact, backs Champions League reform," January, 21, 2021. Sports Business (www.sportbusiness.com).

34. Sam Carp, "MLS confirms US$1bn revenue hit due to COVID-19," December 10, 2020. SportsPro Media (www.sportspromedia.com).

35. Kurt Badenhausen, "NFL Stadiums, Back to Capacity, to Bag $1 billion through Week 4," September 4, 2021 Yahoo (www.yahoo.com).

36. Jabari Young, "NBA projects $10 billion in revenue as audiences return after COVID, but TV viewership is the big question," October 18, 2021 CNBC (www.cnbc.com).

37. NHL Attendance Report – 2021-22, ESPN (www.espn.com).

SPORTS MEDIA

CHAPTER 3

Extending Fan Engagement

Many sports fans around the globe will never attend a live event to watch their favorite teams or players in person. For them, the only way to experience a sports event is by watching it on a television, computer or mobile device screen or listening to it on the radio.

While sports venues catered to fans who attended a sports event, the advent of sports media brought a new dimension to the world of sports. Now fans could experience a sports event from their own living room.

By the late 1800s newspapers had begun to include a sports section (*Figure 3.1*). The 1921 baseball World Series was broadcast on radio. The first sports magazine appeared in 1946, and small-screen black-and-white TV broadcasts brought sports to homes by 1950. The advent of color television in the 1960s, cable TV in the 1970s, and satellite television broadcasts in the late 1980s transformed the reach of sports media and access to sports events. In the early 2000s Internet streams beamed sports through our computers. Today sports streaming channels and apps allow for 24/7 access to almost every sport.

FIGURE 3.1
Evolution of Sports Media and Fan Engagement

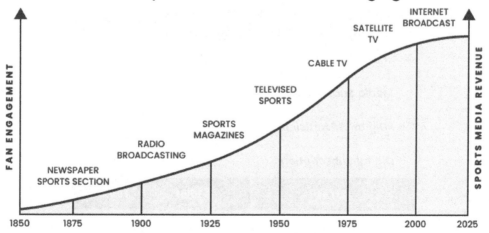

FIGURE 3.2
Sports Media Revenues in the Best-Howard Model (U.S. billions)

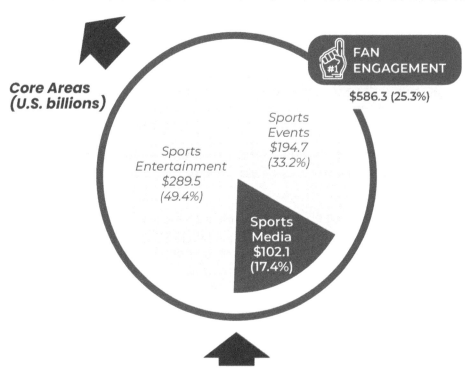

Domains (U.S. billions)

FAN ENGAGEMENT	SPORTS PRODUCTS	SPORTS PARTICIPATION
$586.3 (25.3%)	$968.1 (41.8%)	$762.4 (32.9%)

$2.3 Trillion (Worldwide)

Core Areas (U.S. billions)

FAN ENGAGEMENT $586.3 (25.3%)

Sports Events $194.7 (33.2%)

Sports Entertainment $289.5 (49.4%)

Sports Media $102.1 (17.4%)

Segments (U.S. billions)

Sports Media Segments	Revenues	Percent
Media Advertising	$ 71.9	70.4 %
Media Subscriptions	$ 25.3	24.8 %
Digital Advertising	$ 4.9	4.8 %
Digital Subscriptions	NA	NA
TOTAL	**$ 102.1**	**100.0 %**

More people watch sports now than ever before, but the way consumers view sports is transforming rapidly. For most of the world, traditional television has been the dominant sports viewing platform for more than half a century. Many sporting events are available to fans via zero-cost, over-the-air broadcasts from several major networks. In the United States, three networks dominated for many years: ABC, CBS and NBC. Another major broadcaster, Fox, first aired in 1986. Companies paying networks to promote their brands to TV audiences, typically in the form of 30- or 60-second commercials, bore the broadcasting costs. And advertising sales remain the predominant revenue source for traditional broadcast and cable television networks.

Sports Media, a Fan Engagement core area in the Best-Howard Sports Industry Model, examines how broadcasters provide audience reach and allow sports events to be watched live or replayed around the world at any time. In the Best-Howard Model, Sports Media accounted for 16% of 2019 worldwide Fan Engagement revenues. The model derives its 2019 Sports Media revenues from the four segments shown in *Figure 3.2*. Media advertising and subscriptions represented close to 75% of 2019 Sports Media revenues. Revenue data for digital advertising and subscriptions, a relatively new phenomenon, are more difficult to obtain, but the Best-Howard Model estimates that their volume is rapidly increasing.

The sports media landscape began to change rapidly in the 1990s with the growth of cable television networks, inspired by the enormous success of America's Entertainment and Sports Network (ESPN, shown in *Figure 3.3*). Cable's broadcasters began offering specialized sports programming to fans on a subscription fee basis. Today, the United States has nearly 70 national and regional cable networks dedicated to sports (1).

FIGURE 3.3
ESPN's Baseball Tonight on a Cable Television Broadcast

The emergence of digital television, or streaming technology, in the 2010s has dramatically impacted sports viewing behavior. YouTube TV, Hulu and Fubo TV have become increasingly popular sports content sources. In the three to four years prior to 2020, sports-only streaming services gave fans another digital viewing platform. The specialized networks offer 24/7 live and on-demand programming for a range of mainstream and niche sports, including mixed martial arts, sailing, wrestling and boxing.

Users' ability to access streaming content on any device, including tablets, laptops and mobile phones, has accelerated digital sports media's growth. In 2019, U.S. adults for the first time spent more hours on their mobile phones than watching TV. For many fans, particularly the young, smartphones are now the default device for consuming sports through online blogs, team apps and live game action.

Traditional TV Still Dominates

Increased competition has steadily eroded traditional television's once overwhelming sports viewing audience share, but over-the-air and cable television networks still dominate emerging alternative media platforms.

Global revenues from commercial advertising sales on traditional broadcast and cable networks reached $71.9 billion in 2019 (*Figure 3.4*) (2). Corporations spent $23.2 billion promoting their brands on U.S. sports programs aired on the four major national networks and cable stations like ESPN and Fox Sports. Sports media monitoring firm Nielsen Sports has collected ad spending data on digital platforms since 2016. The company's data reflect modest growth to $1.32 billion by 2019.

FIGURE 3.4
Global and U.S. Spending on Sports Media, 2012 & 2019 (U.S. billions)

REVENUES ($ Billions)	U.S.	Global	U.S.	Global	U.S.	Global	U.S.	Global
Media Sources	*2010*	*2010*	*2015*	*2015*	*2019*	*2019*	*CAGR*	*CAGR*
Sports Media Ad Revenue	$ 14.8	$ 55.6	$ 18.7	$ 63.1	$23.2	$71.9	2.6 %	2.5 %
Sports Media Subscriptions	$ 10.0	$ 20.7	$ 12.3	$ 23.1	$ 15.3	$ 25.3	4.3 %	2.0 %
Digital Sports Advertising	NA	NA	NA	NA	$ 1.3	$ 4.9	NA	NA
Digital Sports Subscriptions	NA		NA	NA				
TOTAL	**$ 24.8**	**$ 76.3**	**$ 31.0**	**$ 86.3**	**$ 39.8**	**$ 102.1**		

The Nielsen data used in *Figure 3.4* are the only data of its kind available from a reputable source. Until 2016, Nielsen reported only revenues paid by companies to advertise their brands on traditional network sports broadcasts. In 2016, the media tracking company began collecting data on advertising sales paid to sports streaming services. The $1.32 billion adverting revenues reported for 2019 do not reflect the full financial impact of digital sports networks like ESPN+, DAZN and Vegas Stats and Information Network (VSiN).

Unreported in *Figure 3.4* are revenues digital sports platforms receive annually from subscription fees. While no credible summary data exist, reported information on the number of subscribers and monthly and annual subscription fee rates for some prominent streaming services offers evidence of the magnitude of subscription revenues. As detailed later in this chapter, ESPN+ and DAZN generate an estimated $630 million and $800 million a year, respectively in subscriber fees. That combined amount of $1.43 billion exceeds the total digital sports ad sales revenues reported by Nielsen for 2019. The inability to include digital subscription fee revenue represents an omission of billions of dollars in our reported estimate of U.S. sports media spending.

The major television networks still deliver large audiences, and traditional television continues to offer the deepest household penetration of any media type. TV reaches 96% of U.S. homes, while smartphones reach 89% and laptops reach 72%. Ad Age reports that the United States' National Football League accounted for 45 of the 50 most watched television programs in 2019 (3), and the league's Super Bowl championship game (*Figure 3.5*) has been the single most watched television event in America for decades, with 184.5 million people viewing at least part of the game in 2020. Still, the figure is small compared to the global audience viewing the 2018 World Cup final; 885 million tuned in to the TV coverage and 232 million streamed the game on digital devices.

FIGURE 3.5
Super Bowl TV and Streaming Audience Tops 100 Million

Recent technological advances have helped sustain TV's sports broadcasting preeminence. High-definition television's introduction in 1998 enhanced the viewing experience. By 2017, 89% of U.S. households had at least one HD TV, and 52% had more than one. Televised sports program ratings are 21% higher on HD TVs than traditional televisions (1).

Internet-ready smart TVs have also expanded conventional television's versatility. Connected televisions, or CTVs, directly deliver digital content and provide integrated access to streaming providers like Netflix, Hulu and Slingbox. By 2020, Nielsen reported that 76% of U.S. homes had at least one connected device. The market research firm expects the percentage of CTV households to grow to 82% by 2023 (4). Americans have collectively spent almost 8 billion hours using CTV devices, including Xboxes, PlayStations, Rokus and Apple TVs. The platforms now offer a range of sports programming, from live events to broad national and local channel coverage. Analysts suggest that relatively inexpensive access to streaming packages has solidified sports fans' commitment to traditional TV programming options.

Many countries have established their own national sports television channels offering coverage of domestic and international competitions. Prominent examples include Brazil's SporTV, Iran's IRIB Varzesh and Spain's Movistar Deportes. Other countries offer sport-specific channels. The United Kingdom's Sky Sports offers 11 separate channels.

Satellite company Sky, a division of America's Comcast Corporation, operates the network's subscription-based channels. Sky's menu of niche sports pay channels offer programming dedicated to cricket, golf, Formula 1 racing, soccer and mixed martial arts. Global sports broadcasting giants like ESPN, Fox Sports and Eurosport enhance many nations' domestic public and cable sports broadcasting networks. Paraguay's sports TV lineup includes four ESPN, three Fox Sports and two Movistar channels.

While TV viewing options are plentiful around the world, paid television's cost is out of reach for many in countries like India and Brazil. As a result, viewers most commonly access sports through mobile networks. Telecommunications firms play an active role in streaming sports video, whether of cricket in India or soccer in Brazil, to viewers' connected devices.

FIGURE 3.6
A Family in India Watches Cricket

U.S. broadcasters now offer more than 127,000 hours of televised sports programming per year, an increase of 232% over the past decade (1). Much of the programming is live. Live sporting events appeal both to fans and advertisers, as emotionally engaged viewers are likely to stay tuned to full broadcasts and pay close attention to commercials.

> *Live sports content is one of the strongest and drivers and last remaining drivers of value for traditional pay TV – for both viewers and advertisers alike.*
>
> *Business Insider (April, 2020)*

Twenty-seven national cable sports networks (e.g., the Golf Channel, Tennis Channel and Outdoor Channel) provide year-round, 24/7 sports content coverage in the United States (1). Each of the four major leagues in North America—the National Football League, the National Basketball Association, Major League Baseball and the National Hockey Association—has established its own cable network. The NBA led the way in 1999 with NBA TV, which broadcasts games, highlights and commentary.

THE UNCERTAIN FUTURE OF RSNS. Regional sports networks (RSNs) provide another layer of targeted sports programming in the United States. A typical RSN covers one or two sports teams in a single market and partners with a major cable distributor, such as Comcast, broadcasting live games and specialized programming. The New England Sports Network (NESN) covers the MLB's Boston Red Sox and NHL's Boston Bruins on a cable network (Comcast), satellite provider (DirecTV) and streaming service (YouTube TV). For decades RSNs have served as the "go-to" source for fans to watch their favorite local college and professional sports teams.

In 1976, Ed Snider, visionary owner of the NHL Philadelphia Flyers, was the first sports executive to establish a channel featuring local market sports teams. Originally called PRISM, the "extra-charge" cable channel aired live broadcasts of Snider's Flyers and the NBA 76ers in the Philadelphia market. According to Andy Dolich, former President of the Golden State Warriors, Snider was the first owner to see "the crazy DNA fans have for their sports teams" (5). PRISM was sold to Comcast and eventually became NBC Sports Philadelphia, providing live telecasts and programming for three of the City's major sports teams, the Flyers, Sixers and (MLB) Phillies.

The new revenue streams produced by Snider's successful innovation inspired the rapid growth of RSNs in markets across the United States. By 2010, 40 premium regional sports networks were operating, many achieving margins of 30% to 40% from cable subscription fees ranging from $2 to $6 per month (1).

In 2002, in an effort to gain greater control over their own broadcast rights, the New York Yankees baseball team and the, then, NBA New Jersey Nets, launched the YES Network with support from major investors, including Goldman Sachs. The YES Network quickly became the largest and most profitable RSN. In 2014, Rupert Murdoch's News Corp, owner of the Fox Sports Network, became majority owner of the network. In March of 2019, the New York Yankees repurchased the YES Network for $3.47 billion (6).

While the impact of the global pandemic could not have been foreseen at the time this record-breaking transaction occurred, less than a year later the RSN market began a rapid decline. The COVID-19 outbreak had a devastating effect. Revenues plummeted as sports leagues shortened or cancelled their seasons in 2020. The loss of 1,000s of games and the pressure to refund pay TV customers for undelivered games pushed many RSNs to the brink of bankruptcy. RSN distributors like Comcast and AT&T continued collecting subscriber fees for RSN-affiliates' sports programming even as games were cancelled due to COVID-19. Total repayment compensation from RSN's for cancelled games is estimated to exceed $1 billion (7).

No media company took a greater hit during the pandemic than Sinclair Broadcast Group, the second largest TV station operator in the United States. In May 2019, Sinclair purchased 21 former Fox Sports RSNs for $9.6 billion. The deal provided transmission rights to 42 major league franchises across the MLB (14), NBA (16 and NHL (12). In 2018, the 74 million subscribers to these RSNs produced $3.8 billion (8). The timing of the deal could not have been worse. Within 12 months, the promising investment turned into a financial disaster. The 14 MLB teams alone each lost 100 cancelled games during the 2020 season. In the 3rd quarter of 2020, Sinclair reported a $3.2 billion loss, raising concerns about the future of Sinclair's RSN subsidiary, the Diamond Sports Group (8). Facing an uncertain future, Sinclair is not the only RSN owner/distributor exploring exiting or selling its stake in RSNs. In fall of 2021, several media outlets reported that NBCUniversal (Comcast) and AT&T are seeking buyers for at least some of their RSNs (9,10).

Despite the upheaval and uncertainty, many analysts believe RSNs will continue to remain as a prominent feature of the media landscape in the United States. NBCUniversal is considering putting its regional sports networks on the company's streaming service, Peacock (10). Sinclair recently rebranded its RSNs as Bally Sports under a partnership agreement with Bally's

Corporation. The new arrangement is expected to position the networks to take full advantage of the explosive growth of sports wagering.

ESPN (*Figure 3.7*) launched in 1979 and has inspired cable networks around the world.

FIGURE 3.7
The Sports-Dedicated Network ESPN Broadcasts Around the World

It was the first national cable channel to devote its programming to a single subject. ESPN has grown into the leading viewing destination for American sports fans, reaching more than 100 million homes at its peak in 2011. And the network has launched even more targeted channels, including ESPNU for college sports, ESPN Deportes for the U.S.-based Hispanic population and ESPNews offering 24/7 sports updates.

ESPN also pioneered a new business model based on subscription revenues. The network demanded substantial premiums from pay-TV providers like Comcast to deliver its content to customers. ESPN currently charges an average subscription fee of $7.64 per month per customer (11). In most cases, cable networks carrying ESPN channels include the charges in a bundled package. ESPN's fee often represents the largest portion of a consumer's cable TV bill. By comparison, the Fox Sports channel fee is $1.12 per month.

U.S. consumers' average monthly cable bill in March 2020 was $217.42, more than the average spent on all major utilities combined (12). The significant cost burden for consumers, along with attractive and less expensive streaming media alternatives, has led to fewer cable network subscribers. By the end of 2022, analysts expect 55.2 million Americans will have cancelled their paid cable service (13). ESPN has particularly suffered as consumers have left cable. During the eight years prior to 2021, ESPN subscriptions fell nearly 20% to 84 million. And while the United States has seen the most dramatic pay-TV declines, a recent report showed revenues have fallen in 61 countries as viewers move to less-expensive streaming services offering substantial sports content (14).

Digital Sports Streaming Emerges

While prominent global sports pay-TV networks like ESPN and Sky Sports remain popular and profitable, viewers migrating to attractive and inexpensive streaming services has eroded their dominant market presence. (See the 2020 Business Insider Intelligence report, click on the *The Sports Streaming Ecosystem*, to examine a detailed summary of sports viewers' changing media consumption patterns produced by Business Insider.) As noted by Business Insider (15), the migration has been driven by:

- **Media-Branded Over-the-Top Services.** ESPN+, Paramount+ (formerly CBS All Access) and NBC's Peacock feature live sports furnished by their parent networks.

- **Skinny Bundles.** Fubo TV, Sling TV, YouTube TV and other streaming platforms offer live sports programming via traditional broadcast networks.

- **League-Branded Services.** NBA League Pass, NFL Game Pass and MLB TV offer league-specific game broadcasts.

- **Sports-Exclusive Streaming Services.** Digital startups DAZN, Fite TV and VSiN offer sports-specific content highlighting niches like boxing and sports betting.

- **Social Media Platforms.** YouTube, Facebook, Twitter and other popular social media platforms have partnered with sports leagues and broadcasters worldwide to offer highlight packages and/or live short-form sports event programming.

ESPN's ratings remain strong, with annual earnings topping $10 billion per year. However, its parent company Disney expected 12 million people to discontinue their cable subscriptions between 2018 and 2020, making its ratings unsustainable. Disney joined the wave of new sports streaming services by establishing ESPN+ in 2018, and the service has grown from 1.4 million to 12.1 million subscribers (16). Like many sports streaming services, ESPN+ is priced modestly, at $4.99 per month, and offers subscribers a blend of live sports, analysis and other programming. Despite the COVID-19 pandemic limiting live sports in 2020, ESPN+ continued to grow, adding 600,000 new subscribers during the year's fourth quarter. ESPN+ issued its first price increase in January 2021, raising its monthly rate to $5.99 and annual subscriptions to $59.99 (17).

Disney is just one of many global entertainment and internet companies to have established digital streaming services featuring sports content (*Figure 3.8*). AT&T TV Now, YouTube TV and Apple TV have done the same. Several live streaming networks, such as Hulu TV, Sling TV and Fubo TV, feature sports in their promotional messaging. For $65 per month, YouTube TV offers all four major U.S. networks, RSNs (e.g., the New England Sports Network in Boston), all major cable sports networks (e.g., ESPN, Fox Sports and NBC Sports) and several league networks (e.g., NBA TV and MLB Network). For about $50 per month, Fubo TV offers international sports programming, including soccer games from the English Premier League and Spain's La Liga. It also offers NBA TV, the NFL Network (including Thursday Night Football), the Golf Channel and the Tennis Channel. Each of the streaming options is priced at about 25% of the average cable bill.

FIGURE 3.8
Streaming Networks on a Connected Television

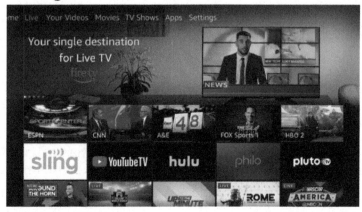

Sports superfans can also subscribe to a growing number of standalone, sports-exclusive streaming services, such as DAZN. For subscription fees from $4.99 to $30 a month, fans receive sports programming bundled to meet their unique viewing interests. The sports-centric services operate direct-to-customer sales models over the internet. Most of the platforms, such as Fite TV (*Figure 3.9*), FloSports and VSiN, aggregate rights to two or three sports not owned by established cable networks. Forbes magazine describes Fite TV as the "leading independent digital streaming platform for combat sports" (18). The four-year-old platform has acquired the rights to stream 1,000s of live and on-demand matches from mixed martial arts, boxing and wrestling leagues and promotional companies, including Top Rank Boxing, Rizin MMA, Bare Knuckle FC, ROH Wrestling and Combate Americas, a franchise targeting Hispanic audiences. Fite TV offers access to major pay-per-view championship bouts, meaning fans can stream premier events using the digital device of their choice, rather than through the traditional pay-per-view arrangement. The niche service is available for $5 per month or $50 per year and has more than 1.5 million registered subscribers.

FIGURE 3.9
Standalone Niche Sports Streaming Services Include FiteTV

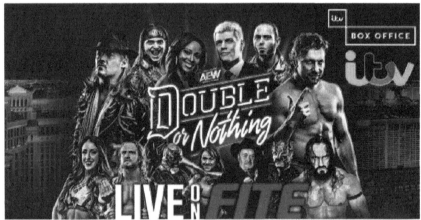

VSiN is "dedicated to delivering news and analysis and proprietary data on sports betting." The Las Vegas-based network was launched in 2017 and is run by the family of longtime sportscaster Brent Musburger, who hosts a weekday program. VSiN's 24/7 video stream provides more than 80 hours of live programming weekly from a studio in the South Point Casino & Spa sportsbook. Authoritative gaming industry analysts and oddsmakers host shows on the basics of sports betting, handicapping and advanced betting strategies. For $39.99 a month or $240 per year, subscribers receive an all-access package, including VSiN's betting guide the Point Spread Weekly. In January 2021, VSiN transitioned its audio content from the SiriusXM satellite radio platform to iHeartRadio, making it available subscription-free to larger audiences (19).

DAZN launched in 2016 in Germany, Austria, Switzerland and Japan and has grown rapidly to become the largest standalone sports streaming company in the world with 8 million subscribers worldwide by 2020 (20).

The network offers extended services to fans in Canada, Brazil, Spain, Italy and the United States. Subscription rates are $19.99 per month or $99.99 per year. In June 2020, DAZN became the "new home of football" in Germany (*Figure 3.10*) after acquiring the Bundesliga broadcast rights for four seasons (21). The watershed deal represented the largest package of European domestic soccer rights ever awarded to a streaming service (22). The agreement grants DAZN exclusive live match coverage of half the annual Bundesliga matches from 2021 to 2025. The other half will be broadcast by longtime partner Sky TV. While agreement details were not released, analysts believe DAZN and Sky will split a $5.1 billion rights fee over four years.

FIGURE 3.10
Sports-Exclusive Streaming Service DAZN Wins Soccer Contract

In 2021, DAZN expanded its commitment to European soccer by becoming the senior broadcast partner for Italy's Serie A league. The streaming service outbid Sky Sports, paying $3 billion for exclusive rights to broadcast seven out of 10 games per match day through 2024. Forbes magazine called the deal a "tipping point" in the history of sports broadcasting (22)—it was the first time a major sports league had sold a majority share of its broadcast rights to a streaming service.

DAZN's diverse programming also includes combat sports, and the network recently contracted with Matchroom Boxing and Golden Boy Promotions to broadcast a series of on-demand bouts between prominent opponents. DAZN has acquired rights to the European Rugby Champions Cup, PDC Darts and the World Rally Championships, and the group owns Goal.com and U.S.-based Sporting News and uses the media platforms' content to augment its live and on-demand event programming.

FloSports started as a website featuring wrestling and running events, such as the USA Wrestling Freestyle World Team Trials, but the streaming service has expanded to incorporate live Major League Soccer and college basketball game streaming. A 2019 Inc. magazine article reported FloSports averaged more than 30,000 new subscribers per month and investors included Discovery Communications and World Wrestling Entertainment (23).

Sports Streaming Revenues

Credible revenue figures are not widely collected for sport-specific or standalone streaming services, but media outlets have begun examining the platforms' growing popularity and success. The Best-Howard Model therefore uses reported subscription numbers and fees to estimate annual streaming revenues.

DAZN, one of the first entrants into the space, is reported to have 8 million subscribers globally. When the service was first introduced in the United States, its subscription service price was $9.99 per month. DAZN raised the fee to $19.99 per month in 2019 but added an annual pass option at $99.99. Multiplying the service's subscribers by its annual cost yields a yearly revenue figure of about $800 million.

Disney's ESPN+ has 12 million subscribers and began by offering an introductory price of $4.99 per month or $49.99 per year. Disney raised the price to $5.99 in January 2021. The average monthly revenues per ESPN+ subscriber for most of 2020 were $5.33 (24). Applying the monthly rate to 12.1 million subscribers yields annual subscription revenues of about $775 million.

The estimated figures for DAZN and ESPN+ do not account for non-subscription revenues. App analytics firm Sensor Tower Inc. recognized DAZN as the top grossing sports app worldwide in 2019 (25). Over the last two months of the year, consumers spent $30.1 million downloading the DAZN app, bringing its total 2019 app sales revenues to more than $150 million. Add the nearly $800 million DAZN generates from its 8 million subscribers, and the sports streaming service's annual revenues approach $1 billion.

Ad sales are another important revenue source for streaming services. Many advertisers have found dedicated streaming services an effective way to reach consumers passionate about specific sports. Streaming services typically sell video ads from five to 15 seconds, some of which viewers can skip and others they cannot. However, the services do not publicize their ad sales revenues, and the Best-Howard Model therefore does not include them. The model speculates, however, that leading digital sports streaming services like DAZN, ESPN+ and Fite TV generate hundreds of millions of dollars in ad sales. DAZN likely generates more than $1 billion in annual ad revenues.

Recognizing the potential of direct-to-consumer (DTC) content delivery models, a growing number of professional European sports leagues and teams have established their own premium streaming services. The English Premier League was the first elite-level professional league to explore a DTC service. In 2019, the EPL partnered with tech giant Amazon to stream 20 league matches exclusively over a three-year period. The agreement marked the first time the EPL sold broadcast rights to a non-TV platform. Analysts suggested the move signals a shift in in the league's direction as it seeks to boost media rights fees. By creating its own streaming service, the EPL could become the "Netflix of football," according to the Crystal Palace Football Club's former chairman Simon Jordan (26). Jordan believes the EPL could more than triple its broadcast rights' value by eliminating TV broadcasters as middlemen. Imagen, a global video management company, suggests that the emergence of DTC streaming is a revolutionary step in sports media: "While it's not sounding the death knell for traditional TV coverage just yet, it does signal a huge shift in power" (27).

More than one-third of the top 25 EPL soccer teams and six of the world's 10 largest soccer leagues and federations now offer paid DTC online content to their fans. Clubs charge modest subscription fees to encourage fan engagement and enhance sponsor visibility and value. Two EPL clubs, Chelsea and Liverpool, charge $63 for a year's subscription. Italy's Juventus Football Club's annual streaming pass costs only $25.

Sports broadcasters, leagues and teams have also found social media outlets highly effective platforms for engaging fans and generating revenues. Sky Sports, the dominant pay-TV sports network in the United Kingdom and Ireland, began placing its coveted EPL highlights on

THE GLOBAL MARKET FOR PREMIUM SPORTS OTT SERVICES

For an overview of the changing global sports media landscape and challenges and opportunities facing pay-TV service providers, download the 2019 Pay-TV Innovation Forum's "The Global Market for Premium Sports OTT Services"

Scan to *View Report*

Source: https://www.mesaonline.org/2019/07/17/nagra-report-sports-ott-ramps-up/

YouTube free of charge immediately following matches in 2019 (28). The network made the decision in an effort to reach new audiences as its subscriptions slumped. YouTube reaches more than 1.9 billion monthly users, and Sky Sports established the Sky Sports Football channel to allow fans to subscribe to the free EPL highlight packages.

As shown in *Figure 3.11*, Sky Sports' collaboration with YouTube has been a success, garnering about 1.5 million subscribers (29). Matchday highlights have generated as many as 3.6 million views in around 24 hours. YouTube has also created an algorithm funneling viewers to Sky Sports' post-match analyses, which include coach and player interviews. Sky Sports has added 200,000 subscribers since creating the channel and generates more than $1 million per month from advertising and merchandise sales (30).

FIGURE 3.11
European YouTube Soccer Channel Subscribers and Monthly Earnings

YOUTUBE CHANNEL	SUBSCRIBERS	MONTHLY EARNINGS (U.S. $)
Sky Sports Football	1,500,000	1,060,192
Liverpool FC	3,100,000	663,940
FIFATV	8,200,000	503,870
FC Barcelona	8,150,000	415,552
Manchester City	2,070,000	222,689
Chelsea FC	1,370,000	186,146
Arsenal FC	1,520,000	169,317
UEFA	2,180,000	128,033
Paris Saint Germain	2,000,000	123,316
Real Madrid	5,130,000	85,880
Juventus	2,300,000	79,652

In addition to Sky Sports, several other European soccer broadcasters, administrative bodies and clubs have more than 1 million subscribers. FIFATV and Real Madrid top 8 million subscribers. Nine of the properties generate more than $100,000 per month. The potential for growth in both fan subscribers and revenues are considerable, as YouTube sports content views have grown by 60% per year and highlight-consumption is up by 80%.

As illustrated in *Figure 3.12*, most U.S. ad spending is aligned with the country's largest sports audiences. In 2019, companies spent $23.2 billion to promote their brands on U.S. broadcast and cable television sports programs. As the most popular league in North America, the NFL attracts the largest audiences of any U.S. television offering. Brands are therefore willing to pay a premium to advertise during NFL telecasts, and the league's 2019 championship playoffs generated $1.12 billion in ad revenues.

FIGURE 3.12
U.S. Sports Advertising Spending (U.S. billions)

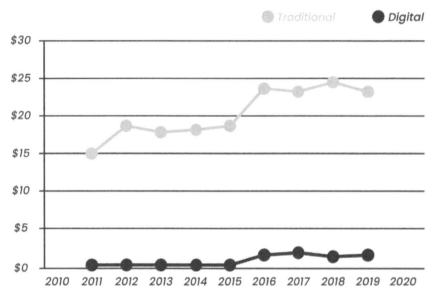

As shown in *Figure 3.13*, total ad spending at the 2019 NFL Super Bowl reached $412 million. That single event generated nearly as much the $479 million in total ad revenue produced across the combined total of 12 games played in the World Series and NBA Finals (31). The Super Bowl draws more than 100 million viewers every year, and adverting rates are the most expensive in the world for a single sporting event. In 2019, companies paid an average of $5.3 million to highlight their brands for 30 seconds during the Super Bowl telecast (32).

FIGURE 3.13
National TV Ad Spending at Major Sporting Events, 2015–2019 (U.S. millions)

EVENT	SUPER BOWL	WORLD SERIES	OLYMPIC GAMES	NBA FINALS
2015	$ 268	$ 102	NA	$ 304
2016	$ 287	$ 173	$ 1,706	$ 366
2017	$ 325	$ 170	NA	$ 252
2018	$ 341	$ 130	$ 837	$ 198
2019	$ 412	$ 191	NA	$ 288

Brands also dedicate a significant share of their advertising budgets to other major U.S. sports properties. Both Major League Baseball and the National Basketball Association complete their regular seasons with a playoff series among the best teams, culminating in a best-of-seven championship series. MLB's 2019 World Series, in which the Houston Astros beat the Washington Nationals in six games, resulted in nearly $200 million in ad spending. In the 2019 NBA Finals, the Toronto Raptors defeated the Golden State Warriors in six games generating $288 million in ad revenues (32).

With 228.5 million listeners, radio's reach exceeds that of TV (216.5 million viewers), smartphone apps/web (203.8 million users) and smartphone video (127.6 million viewers). In the United States, sports talk radio stations have grown dramatically between 2005 and 2020. By 2019, 205 commercial radio stations were dedicated to sports discussion and event broadcasting. Sirius XM offers 21 satellite channels featuring sports talk programming (33).

What began primarily as a local market phenomenon in the early 1980s has become dominated by syndicated national radio networks, with ESPN, CBS Sports and Fox Sports cornering the 24-hour sports talk market. The major networks broadcast to numerous affiliate stations and subscribers on Sirius XM radio across the United States and Canada. NBC and Yahoo Sports recently have joined the market. According to the market manager for an ESPN radio affiliate in Minneapolis, "It's a pretty simple calculation. With sports come passion. There's a new storyline every day. Sometimes it changes hourly. From a programming standpoint, it's the gift that keeps on giving" (34).

FIGURE 3.14
Sports Radio Reach

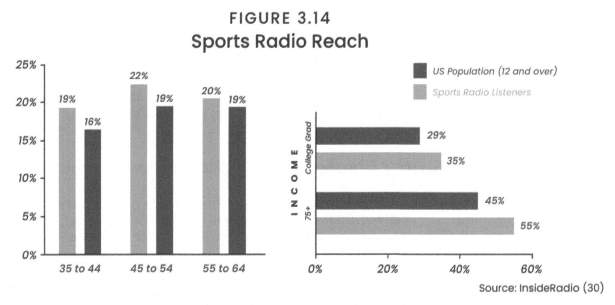

Source: InsideRadio (30)

Many brands are attracted to sports radio by its high number of qualified consumers. As shown in *Figure 3.14*, Nielsen reported that 23 million Americans tuned into sports radio weekly in 2018, and the audience outperformed average consumers on personal income ($75k+), college education and employment status (35). Sports radio attracted listeners with a median age of 44, while cable and broadcast television drew 48- and 49-year-old listeners on average.

SPORTS BETTING TO THE RESCUE: Little credible data is available on the amount spent by brands advertising on sports radio shows and broadcasts. Sports Business Journal provided one benchmark figure in 2010, reporting sports talk shows drew nearly $690 million in advertising revenues. According to the editor, Michael Harrison, of Talkers Magazine, "radio is going through a tough time right now, financially" (36). Ad revenues are down and many of the large radio station networks are "smothered in debt." But, the huge amount of advertising dollars spent by online sports betting companies, nearly $200 million in the 1st quarter of 2021, appears to be a financial life line for radio, especially for sports radio.

Mr. Harrison declared it a "godsend for sport talk radio." Sports betting is a spending category that is growing exponentially. From Q1 2020 to Q1 2021, sportsbook advertising revenue increased 4,000% (36).

Currently, radio claims only a modest share of total sports advertising in the United States. Of the $200 million spent during Q1 of 2021, local radio stations received only $4 million. But, the Vice President of the nation's third largest radio network expressed confidence that as the sports betting revenue pool grows rapidly larger, so will sports talk radios' share. He believes that sports radio is the "audience they (sportsbooks) are looking for (36)."

With the radio industry placing so much hope on sports betting, "a market that came out of nowhere," it will be interesting to see whether sportsbooks will allocate a larger share of ad dollars to local radio stations. The article in Sports Handle, sees more than just financial benefits from sports gambling's investment in sports radio. Sports betting appeals to a younger listening audience. According to Harrison, "The infusion of betting and gambling into the conversation on sports talk radio is attracting younger demos. It's changed the culture and nature of sports talk, as the conversation is now leaning toward the betting action. And that's a big game changer" (36).

Esports, or video game-based sports competitions, has emerged as a small but growing digital advertising platform. eMarketer.com reported 2019 esports digital ad revenues in the United States reached $175 million, a 23% increase over 2018 (37), and projected a 12% increase to $196 million in 2020. While only U.S. data is available, given esports' growing popularity in southeast Asia, particularly China, the Best-Howard Model projects comparable or greater global growth.

Smart Phones and Digital Growth

In a world where 57% of consumers use more than one device at a time, namely the smartphone, it only makes sense for brands to break the shackles and reach out to their audience on a channel that users will always have in their hand.

Inmobi Blog

Mobile cell phone advertising spending reached $93 billion in 2019, 38% of the U.S. total (38). And it was around 2015 when advertisers began to realize the opportunity mobile devices presented to engage and connect with sports fans.

The trend toward smartphone use first became evident at major sporting events like the NFL Super Bowl and 2016 Copa America Centenario soccer tournament, where users downloaded sports apps at unprecedented levels. Fans' use of apps to check scores, match results and game commentary increased 200% during the soccer championship (39).

According to Accenture, 87% of consumers engage with a second screen, primarily their smartphone, while watching television (40). Smartphones allow advertisers to reach target audiences at the most opportune micro-moments during sporting events. As one analyst asserts, "the biggest opportunity for brand advertisers today is to find ways to grab shorter consumer attention spans on the 'one thing' they can't live without—their mobile device—and to show game specific content." Mobile platforms are now considered a central fan engagement strategy, offering unique on-demand accessibility and ways to enhance the live event viewing experience through mobile ticketing, in-seat concession services and video streaming.

While most sports advertising still goes toward television, many advertisers recognize the advantages of digital media and are adopting multi-channel tactics, combining traditional TV buys with investments in mobile apps, email and social networks.

Despite the growth of digital devices, traditional broadcast and cable television remains the dominant viewing platform for sports fans around the globe. Consequently, brands continue to invest billions of dollars to reach large TV-based audiences. In the United States, brands spent $23 billion on commercial airtime during sporting events on broadcast television in 2019. Radio also remains a relevant platform for advertisers. The almost 250 sports talk shows on syndicated radio and satellite stations in the United States connect with 23 million listeners weekly. Nevertheless, brands have not yet optimized mobile devices to meaningfully engage sports fans, and digital platforms will become an increasingly prominent advertising opportunity in the near future.

"Young audience flees TV, creating an uncertain future for sports"

Anthony Crupi, Sportico, April 16, 2021

Viewers began shifting away from cable TV in the early 2010s, and the latest Nielsen audience report indicated TV viewing among young audience members was down 77% from 2016 to 2021, prompting a dire headline from Sportico: "Young audience flees TV, creating an uncertain future for sports" (41). In the third quarter of 2020, average weekly live viewing time among 18- to 34-year-olds plunged 23% compared to the same period the previous year.

Millennials' rapid move away from has had a significant impact on sports viewing, as Sportico reporter Anthony Crupi noted: "Even the most watched show in prime time is having a hard time reaching younger fans. NBC's Sunday Night Football [in 2020] averaged 2.43 million adults 18-34 per game...it was 21% smaller than the year-ago audience (41)."

FIGURE 3.15
WAVE.tv Targets Young Sports Fans

**We entertain modern day sports fans
with the programming they love,
produced for the digital platforms where they
spend the most time.**

Are young people turning away from sports viewing? CEO Brian Verve of new digital platform WAVE.tv (*Figure 3.15*), which targets "next generation" sports fans with programming "when they want it and how they want it," says no. "There's a massive misconception that fandom is decreasing amongst young people or that the next generation isn't watching or talking about sports," Verve says (42). In fact, young viewers have just shifted their viewing behavior from linear television to a "second screen world," according to Verve, and traditional TV ratings have slipped as a result.

FIGURE 3.16
The Chinese Super League to Stream on Tencent

China's technology giant Tencent acquired domestic live streaming rights to the Chinese Super League (*Figure 3.16*) in April 2021. The three-year deal grants Tencent the right to broadcast the league's matches on several streaming platforms. The deal is the latest sign that digital programming and streaming are the future of sports programming. Some suggest DAZN becoming the primary rightsholder of Italy's Serie A was the tipping point, but well before the agreement, Disney had begun transitioning ESPN from a cable to streaming network. Over the several years leading up to 2020, Disney moved growing amounts of content to ESPN+ as the service's subscriptions grew. The NFL granting Amazon exclusive streaming rights to Thursday Night Football further suggests that even the most tradition-bound sports leagues recognize the need to join the digital broadcast world. And as young viewers continue to flee cable TV, the content shift to digital will accelerate.

COVID-19's Impact on Sports Media

The 2020 COVID-19 pandemic resulted in massive reductions in live sports events due to shortened seasons, cancelled games and league suspensions. With few exceptions, media companies offering significant sports programming content suffered major losses during the last nine months of 2020. Overall losses for the year across all forms of sports media advertising in the United States totaled nearly $5 billion. While substantial, the declines were not nearly as catastrophic as widely predicted early in the pandemic.

As the pandemic's severity heightened in late March 2020, media research firms began predicting huge losses in sports advertising revenues. eMarketer.com estimated that $10 billion in ad buys would vanish over 2020's first six months. Kantar Media projected the loss of the U.S.-based NCAA basketball tournament and NBA and NHL playoffs would "obliterate" as much as $2 billion in spending (43). In May 2020, ESPN predicted the prolonged absence of sports events would "erase at least $12 billion in revenue" (44). ESPN estimated lost U.S. TV revenues would amount to $2.2 billion, and the forecast seemed optimistic; sports media companies saw ad revenues tumble in April and May 2020.

During the first half of 2020, actual losses were considerable as major sports leagues cancelled or postponed play. The absence of the 2020 NBA playoffs, normally held in May, resulted in ad revenues for Disney's ABC and ESPN declining 45.5%; WarnerMedia's TNT saw ad revenues fall by 39.6%. ESPN lost more than $450 million in 2020's second quarter, while Turner Sports lost $150 million over the same three-month period. Due to a shortened MLB regular season and NASCAR's early season suspension, Fox reported that its linear broadcast TV networks lost $250 million in the quarter. From April to May, ESPN, Turner Sports and Fox reported a combined decline of $850 million in ad revenues. Despite the return of Major League Soccer, July's MLB All-Star Game and the NBA, ESPN ad revenues were down significantly in 2020's third quarter (45).

While almost all sports media companies lost revenue even as leagues resumed play during the last half of 2020, some suffered more than others. Traditional TV sports broadcasters were hardest hit. Major national broadcast and cable networks like Fox Sports and ESPN lost billions in ad revenue dollars during 2020's last three quarters. RSNs also suffered. The Sinclair Broadcast Group purchased 21 RSNs and the Fox College Sports channel from Fox in late 2019. The group took a $3.2 billion loss in 2020 due almost entirely to the RSNs' inability to overcome pandemic-related disruptions (46). Broadcasting trade publication TV News reported that broadcast and cable networks lost more than $3 billion in TV "sports ad dollars" due to COVID-19 cancellations from mid-March to July (47), and their real losses may have exceeded the estimate.

COVID-19 did less damage to streaming services like ESPN+ and DAZN. The platforms' lost ad revenues depended on their live sports content percentage. Sports heavy outlets like DAZN suffered some losses, while standalone sports streaming services featuring niche content, such as Fite TV or VSiN, saw minimal disruptions.

Overall, digital sports advertising was the only media segment that increased revenues in 2020, growing a healthy 15% from $1.32 billion in 2019 to $1.54 billion in 2020 (48). The increase reflects the migration of ad dollars from major broadcast networks during the pandemic to digital platforms providing engaging, non-traditional sports content on eSports and fantasy sports platforms.

The $1.5 billion in total ad sales revenue generated by U.S. digital sports media services represent only 8% of the $18.7 billion received by traditional broadcast organizations in 2020. However, national cable networks like ESPN continued to hemorrhage subscribers during the COVID-19 pandemic, while many streaming services increased subscriptions. ESPN lost 4.5% of its subscribers in 2020's first quarter, and eMarketer.com projects 6 million more American households to have abandoned cable by the end of 2020 (43). Meanwhile, Disney's sports streaming service ESPN+ exceeded pandemic-era expectations, adding more than 4 million new subscribers by year's end.

Fubo TV, which includes ESPN, FS1, FS2, NBCSN, the Olympic Channel, the Big10 Network, the NFL Networks and all major non-cable broadcast channels, saw its subscriptions increase by 73% in 2020 (49). The streaming service gained a net 92,000 subscribers in the fourth quarter, up 237% year-over-year. The internet media service reported $218 million in revenues for the year.

In fact, the sports advertising market did plummet 84% during the 2nd quarter of 2020, from $1.4 billion to $222, million year-to-year (50). Ad spending on NFL, NASCAR, NBA, MLB and NHL bounced back strongly over the last half of the year, with 3rd and 4th quarter spending increases of 59% and 9.5, respectively. Nielsen Sports reported that overall sports media advertising sales totaled $20.2 billion in 2020, $18.7 billion spent on traditional broadcast and cable networks and $1.5 on digital platforms (*Figure 3.17*) (48). The loss of $4.3 billion from 2019's near-record $24.5 billion in total ad sales represented a decline of 17.6 percent.

FIGURE 3.17
COVID-19 Impact Heat Map (U.S. billions)

U.S. Sports Media	2019	-50%				0%				50%	2020	2020
Segments	*(billions)*										*(billions)*	*% Change*
Sports Media Advertising	$23.2			-19.4%							$18.7	-19.4%
Sports Media Subscriptions	$15.3				-1.6%						$14.9	-1.6%
Digital Sports Advertising	$1.3						15.4%				$1.5	15.4%
TOTAL	$39.8			-11.8%							$35.1	-11.8%

The heat map in *Figure 3.17* shows COVID-19's impact on U.S. sports media companies' three primary revenue sources. The map indicates losses of 50% to gains of 50% for the virus-disrupted 2020 calendar year relative to revenues generated prior to the pandemic. The graphic shows that U.S. sports media operators lost $4.7 billion dollars in 2020, a year-to-year decline of 11.8%.

Traditional broadcast and cable networks accounted for almost all (95.7%) of the ad spending losses. Linear TV sports media advertising declined $4.5 billion, a drop of almost 20% in 2020. Subscription revenues declined less than 2% during 2020. The modest loss was largely the result of strong gains in paid subscriptions to digital streaming services (ESPN+, Fubo TV). This increase offset the continued erosion of subscribers from cable television networks (ESPN).

The widespread revival of league play and major sporting events around the world in 2021 has stimulated a robust uptick in sports media advertising sales. With Major League Baseball and National Football League back in full swing in 2021 and with both the National Basketball League and National Hockey Leagues planning to resume full schedules for the 2021-22 seasons, prospects for a full recovery are optimistic. The cause for optimism in the United States stems from the expectation that 70% of U.S. adults will have had at least one COVID-19 shot by July 4, 2021 (51).

The promising impact of live sports on media advertising was evidenced with the return of two marquee events in spring of 2021, the U.S. collegiate basketball championship, "March Madness" and the Masters golf tournament. Both events attracted large TV audiences – the Masters final round was the most-watched round of golf since Tiger Woods won in 2019 (52).

Following record-breaking television ad sales, the chief revenue officer for Turner Sports proclaimed, "This is the best year we've ever had" (53).

Even as the leagues continue to grapple with the double-barreled challenges of aging fan bases and ever-diminishing attention spans, the upper crust aren't in a hurry to abandon TV.

Anthony Crupi, Sportico

In the United States, the major beneficiaries of the return of live sports have been national broadcast networks. Even with younger viewers flocking to digital platforms, the overwhelming reach of traditional television is still attracting the dominant share of advertising spending. "While digital is growing, the traditional TV ecosystem is still incredibly rich and incredibly broad" stated Hans Schroeder, head of NFL Media (54). The NFL's $113 billion investment ensures a "rich" future over the next 10 years for its traditional broadcast partners (ABC, CBS, Fox, NBC and ESPN). According to Schroeder, "The reach of linear TV is impossible to duplicate" … noting that the NFL delivers 200 million viewers a year (54). The promise of the return of live sport also resulted in all of the other major North American professional leagues negotiating generous long-term agreements with their traditional media partners.

The prospect of live sports returning to a pre-pandemic state of play in 2021 and 2022 are less certain in other regions of the world. A third surge of the pandemic across Europe forestalled hopes of allowing fans back into stadiums in Italy, France and Germany at the end of the 2020-21 season. The slow rollout of vaccines across most of Europe may jeopardize the return of fans for the 2021-22 season. As of May 15, 2020, less than 15% of the population in four of Europe's leading soccer nations had been fully vaccinated: Spain 14.9%, Italy 14.2%, France 13.4% and Germany 10.8%. As a result, La Liga, Seria A, Ligue 1 and the Bundesliga all face strict COVID-19 restrictions and the real prospect of games without fans for the 2021-2022 season.

Another year without matchday revenues would have severe financial repercussions for each of these leagues. The impact would be even more devastating in that the media rights deals signed by four of the five top soccer leagues going into the 2021-2022 season are worth less than in 2019 (55). Unlike in North America, "the market for live (TV) rights in Europe peaked in 2018" (56). The economic downturn during the pandemic squeezed all of the league's principal broadcast partners. As a result, all sought substantial reductions in new rights fee extensions.

The large financial commitment by DAZN's plus the extension of Sky Sports existing rights agreement has resulted in the Bundesliga experiencing the lowest reduction of any of the European leagues signing new deals. The German league's $5.1 billion, 4-year media rights package represents only a five percent annual deduction from the previous agreement.

The French Ligue 1 is in the most financially vulnerable position after its nearly billion dollar, 4-year agreement with Mediapro collapsed in April 2020. The deal lasted just four months resulting in the league's loss of $662 million in television money for the 2020-21 season. Its would be replacement, Canal+ backed out of its television rights agreement early in 2021. In announcing the abrupt decision, the Canal+ President declared that "no broadcaster has been able to turn a profit on rights for many years and the days of subsidizing Ligue 1 were over" (57). The French league's financial crisis is "far from over." Over a good portion of 2020, the league and its clubs survived on bank loans guaranteed by the French government. In February 2021, the French Ligue de Football (LFP), the governing body of French football, requested a multi-million euro "emergency aid package" from the French government (58). Claiming the 'survival of professional football is at stake,' the rescue plan would distribute a yet-to-be disclosed amount to the leagues' 20 clubs. At the time of this writing, the LFP was still exploring option with government representatives.

In May of 2021, the English Premier League in an attempt to forestall a "hefty blow to the value of its rights fees" approached its broadcast partners (Sky, BT and Amazon) to extend the current rights agreements with similar terms (59). The proposal would provide the broadcasters with a slight discount in annual rights fee payments. The 3-year extension is reputed to be worth US$6.52 billion. If the Premier League is able to consummate this deal, its proactive initiative would result in the league suffering the smallest loss in rights fees of any of the top European leagues that have signed recent extensions.

While European clubs face continued economic stress into the 2021-22 season and the likelihood of another year of no or limited fans in attendance, India's Premier (cricket) League is in jeopardy of canceling all or part of its season.

India experienced a devastating virus outbreak in spring of 2021. In early May, the number of COVID-19 cases surpassed 20 million, with new cases averaging over 350,000 per day. Unfortunately, India's ability to combat the outbreak has been severely hobbled by persistent supply shortages. By the end of May only 3% of the nation's 1.3 trillion people had been fully vaccinated (60). The Indian Premier League, which had been operating in an NBA-like bubble, shut down completely, announcing it would suspend the 2021 season indefinitely due to the coronavirus (61). To date, there has been no announcement of a possible resumption of play. Given the severity of the crisis, it's quite likely that a suspension of play, including major tournaments, may extend into 2022. If so, it would disrupt the IPL's ability to meet its' obligations to Sky Sports which has exclusive rights to broadcast 60 matches as well as one of the world's top T20 tournaments through 2022 (57).

Finally, not even Australia's Down Under location shielded the country's major professional sports leagues from serious revenue losses during the pandemic. The government's strict lockdowns and quarantine controls resulted in shortened league schedules and "socially reduced crowds" (62). The "behemoth" of Australian sport, the wildly popular Australian Football League (playing Aussie Rules Football) lost $315 USD million in 2020, approximately one-third of its projected revenue. In June 2020, in the midst of the pandemic, the AFL agreed to revise its existing television rights deal and signed a three-year extension with its broadcast partners Seven West Media and Foxtel (63). The revised agreement reduced the current $312 USD million annual rights fee paid by the broadcasters to $270 USD million. The $42 USD million discount, roughly 13%, amounts to a rollback of $126 USD million in rights revenue over the three-year period.

The relentless coronavirus, coupled with the slow rollout of vaccines in many parts of the world, has led to considerable uncertainty as to when many countries will have the pandemic controlled sufficiently to invite fans back to crowded, mask-less stadiums and arenas. Current trends indicate the North America may reach that threshold more quickly than other regions of the world. Into the near future, at least, fan engagement with sport in most of the world will continue to depend on media.

References

We have added links to many references for direct and easy access. While we have tested each link, there are a few instances where the websites are no longer accessible. We will continue to monitor the accessibility of citation references and remove any links no longer active. In many instances the referenced data was purchased, this is noted.

1. Dennis R. Howard and John L. Crompton (2018). *Financing Sport* (4th edition), FIT Publishing.

2. Sources for Figure 3.1: Nielsen Sports Ad Intel (private source); *Home Truths – Annual Review of Football Finance 2020* (June 2020) Deloitte; *At the Gate and Beyond: Outlook for the Sports Market through 2023* (2019). PwC; *Changing the Game – Outlook for the Global Sports Market to 2015* (December 2015), PwC. (GSI Purchased Report)

3. Anthony Crupi, "NFL accounts for nearly three-quarters of the year's top 100 broadcasts," January 6, 2020. *Ad Age* (www.adage.com).

4. "Connected TV usage remains above pre-COVID-19 levels as traditional TV viewing normalizes," March 4, 2021. *Nielsen Insights* (www.nielsen.com). (GSI Purchased Report)

5. Jabari Young, "IF Comcast decides to sell regional sports networks, these buyers make the most sense," May 12, 2021. *CNBC* (www.cnbc.com).

6. Mike Ozanian, "New York Yankees buy back YES Network for $3.47 billion," March 6, 2019. *Forbes* (www.forbes.com).

7. Scott Moritz, "Sports rebates may return $1.1 billion to customers," December 2, 2020. *Bloomberg* (www.bloomberg.com).

8. Alister Taylor, "Why the sports broadcast model is now under threat," November 6, 2020. *MIDia* (www.midiaresearch.com).

9. Steve McCaskill, "Report: Fanatics could enter US regional Sports network market," October 12, 2021. *Sports Pro Media* (www.sportspromedia.com).

10. Lillian Rizzo, "NBCUniversal explores streaming its sports channels or selling them off," May 6, 2021. *The Wall Street Journal* (www.wsj.com).

11. Gavin Bridge, "The true cost to consumers of Pay TV's top channels, October 27, 2020. *Variety* (www.variety.com).

12. DecisionData Team June 22, 2020. REPORT: The average cable bill now exceeds all other household utility bill combined.

13. Darina Lynkova, "30+ cord cutting statistics {updated with 2021 trends]," February 17, 2021. *Review 42* (www.review42.com).

14. Jonathon Easton, "Pay TV revenues to fall to US$150 billion by 2025," May 28, 2020. *Digital TV* (www.digitaltveurope.com).

15. Audrey Schomer (April 24, 2020). The Sports Streaming Ecosystem: How sports are going over-the-top and eroding the last bastion of pay-TV, *Business Insider* (www.businessinsider.com).

16. Phil Nickinson, "ESPN Plus now has 12.1 million subscribers," February 2021. *Whattowatch* (www.whattowatch.com); Eric Fisher, (November 13, 2020). Disney continues to see growth in streaming services. Sportsbusiness.com; Amy Watson, (October 20, 2020).

17. Joe Lucia, "The yearly cost of ESPN+ for new subscribers is increasing to $59.99, effective January 8th," *Awful Announcing* (awfulannouncing.com).

18. Peter Kahn (July 20, 2019). Manny Pacquiao vs. Keith Thurman: How emerging platform Fite TV provides fans official interactive live stream, *Forbes* (www.forbes.com).

19. Al Walsh, "After years at SiriusXM, VSiN Betting is moving to iHeartRadio," January 4, 2021. Betting News (www.bettingnews.com).

20. Dade Hayes, "DAZN reactivates global expansion plan, updates strategy for sports streaming," October 28, 2020. Deadline

21. Press Release, "DAZN triples Bundesliga rights from 2021 in transformational agreement for Germany, Austria and Switzerland," June 22, 2020. DAZN (media.dazn.com).

22. Steve McCaskill, "DAZN: Serie A deal is a 'tipping point' for sports streaming," April 1, 2021. Forbes (www.forbes.com).

23. Tom Foster (October, 2017). They started with $10,000. Now they're taking on ESPN, Inc. (www.inc.com).

24. Phil Nickinson, "ESPN Plus now has 12.1 million subscribers," February 2021. Whattowatch (www.whattowatch.com).

25. "Top grossing sports apps worldwide for November 2019," December 27, 2019 Sensor Tower (www.sensortower.com).

26. Tom Dutton (February 8, 2019). Netflix of football: Premier League could launch live football streaming service and treble earnings, says Simon Jordan. Evening Standard (www.standard.co.uk).

27. Imagen Resources (2020). Direct-to Consumer trend pushing sports to go it alone, (imagen.io).

28. "Top 20 highest earning soccer YouTube channels," Data Wrapper (datawrapper.dwcdn.net).

29. John McCarthy (August 28, 2019). What Sky Sports gains from making Premier League highlights free on YouTube, The Drum (www.thedrum.com).

30. Inside World Football (July 11, 2020). "Sky Sports earns a $1m a month from YouTube, Liverpool are platform's leading club" (www.insideworldfootball.com).

31. Bob Adgate, "What you should know about Super Bowl LIV advertising and broadcast," January 27, 2020. Forbes (www.forbes.com).

32. Christina Gough, June 18, 2020). "Average cost 30-second advertisement Super Bowl US broadcast 2002-2020", Statista (www.statista.com). (GSI Purchased Report)

33. "Sports radio," May 14, 2021. Wikipedia (en.wikipedia.org).

34. Adam Platt (September 20, 2013). Sports radio's grand slam, Minneapolis Post (www.minnpost.com).

35. INSIDERADIO (February 21, 2018). Nielsen: Sports radio listeners are smart and well-heeled (www.insideradio.com).

36. Jeff Edelstein, "Sportsbook advertising is a total game-changer for radio stations," May 13, 2021. Sports Handle (www.sportshandle.com).

37. Blake Droesch (July 27, 2020). US Esports 2020: The pandemic puts the spotlight on a rising industry, eMarketer (www.emarketer.com).

38. Yorum Wurmser, "Mobile Trends 2019: 10 predictions for what marketers can expect, December 6, 2018. eMarketer (www.emarketer.com).

39. Pooja Kalloor (September 28, 2016). "How sports impact smartphone usage and mobile", Inmobi (www.inmobi.com).

40. Adam Flomenbaum, "Accenture Report: 87% of consumers use second screen device while watching TV, April 20, 2015. Lost Remote AdWeek (www.adweek.com).

41. Anthony Crupi, "Young audience flees TV, creating an uncertain future for sports," April 16, 2021. Sportico (www.sportico.com).

42. JohnWallStreet, "Sports fandom not decreasing in younger demographics," August 6, 2020. Sportico (www.sportico.com).

43. Meg James, "Coronavirus could wipe out $10 billion in TV ad spending," April 20, 2020, Los Angeles Times

44. ESPN Staff, "Sudden vanishing of sports due to coronavirus will cost at least $12 billion, analysis says," May 1, 2020. ESPN (www.espn.com).

45. Steven Impey, "State of the networks: How the US media giants fared during sport's hiatus," August 24, 2020. SportsPro Media (www.sportspromedia.com).

46. Holden Wilen, "Sinclair suffers $3.2 billion loss after writing down value of regional sports networks," November 4, 2020. Baltimore Business Journal (www.bizjournals.com).

47. John Consoli, "TVN focus on advertising – Nets look to recoup lost sports revenue," August 13, 2020. TVNews (tvnewscheck.com).

48. Total Ad $$ spent on Sports TV (2005 to 2020) and Total Ad $$ spent on sports digital (2016 to 2020), purchased from Nielsen Sports, May 11, 2020. (GSI Purchased Report)

49. Todd Spangler, "Fubo TV subscribers up 73% in 2020, Net loss balloons to $570.5 million," March 2, 2021. Variety (www.variety.com).

50. Karlene Lukovitz, "After strong second 2H, Q1 sports ad spend down 28% YoY," April 22, 2021 Digital News Daily Media Post (www.mediapost.com).

51. Nandita Bose and Jeff Nelson, "Biden aims for 70% of U.S. adults to get one vaccine dose by July 4," May 4, 2021. Reuters (www.reuters.com).

52. Anthony Crupi, "Masters draws largest audience in two years as young stars fill Tiger void," April 13, 2021. Sportico (www.sportico.com).

53. Alex Werpin, "Will sports TV advertising return to pre-pandemic form," April 24, 2021. Hollywood Reporter (www.hollywoodreporter.com).

54. Anthony Crupi, "Sports TV endures as networks hold line and streaming grows," April 23, 2021. Sportico (www.sportico.com).

55. Matt Slater, Premier League increases solidarity payments to renew Sky, BT and Amazon TV deal, May 12, 2021. The Athletic (www.theathletic.com).

56. Matt Slater, "Premier League TV rights: Has the bubble burst? February 24, 2021. The Athletic (www.theathletic.com).

57. Bobby McMahon," How Ligue 1's dream TV deal turned into a financial nightmare," January 18, 2021. Forbes (www.forbes.com).

58. "French soccer asks for state aid to bail out Ligue1 Clubs," February 10, 2021. Sports Business Journal (www.sportsbusinessjournal.com).

59. Tom Bassam, "Report: Premier League in private rights talks with Sky, BT and Amazon," April 21 2021. Sports Pro (www.sportspromedia.com).

60. "Our World Data: COVID-19 vaccinations by location," May 15, 2021 (ourworldindata.org).

61. Chris Bengel, "Indian Premier League: Cricket season suspended indefinitely due to increase of COVID-19 cases," May 4, 2021. CBS Sports (www.cbssports.com).

62. David Mark, "How coronavirus killed the golden goose of sport and how each code picked up the pieces," September 25, 2020. ABC Australia (www.abc.net.au).

63. Max Mason, "Seven and Foxtel lock in revised AFL deals," June 11, 2020. Financial Review (www.afr.com).

SPORTS ENTERTAINMENT
CHAPTER 4

Extending Sports Enjoyment

Through its Sports Entertainment core area, the Best-Howard Model (*Figure 4.1*) examines the ways fans engage the sport industry through mostly virtual experiences. Betting online, participating in or viewing esports competitions, joining a fantasy sports league and playing sports video games with friends all can be accomplished on various electronic devices, allowing easy and around the clock fulfillment.

Sports fans around the world spent $14 billion in 2020 on sports memorabilia from trading cards to game-used items, such as balls and jerseys. U.S. collectors accounted for nearly half that amount, spending $6.4 billion on sports collectibles. The value of cards and iconic sports merchandise has appreciated so rapidly over the past decade that some collectors view sports memorabilia as investment grade assets. Spurred by the rapid expansion of online platforms, the sports trading market is projected to reach 67 million collectors globally within the next three to five years.

In addition, sports fans have been entertained by reading books and specialty magazines and watching sports-themed movies for generations. Netflix now features an entire genre of sports movies, which the video streaming platform breaks down into themed categories, including dramas, documentaries, comedies, baseball movies, etc. In 2019, sports enthusiasts spent $15 billion worldwide to read sports books and watch sports movies. The Best-Howard Model also recognizes an increasingly popular sports engagement dimension, social dining experiences in sports-themed environments. Restaurant Business magazine recently recognized sports bars as a standalone industry category. In 2019, total sports bar sales reached $10 billion in the United States alone.

Sports Entertainment Segments

SPORTS BETTING	FANTASY SPORTS	ESPORTS	SPORTS VIDEO GAMES	MOVIES / COLLECTIBLES	SPORTS BARS
Sportsbooks, On-line/mobile In-venue, in-game.	DraftKings, FanDuel, DFS.	Leagues/Teams. Tournaments, Streaming platforms	Sports games sales, game publishers	Sports movies/ books, cards, merchandise, Online platforms	

A section of this chapter is devoted to providing an in-depth examination of the performance of each of the six segments, detailing spending trends over the past decade and projections for future growth. The final section of the chapter assesses the impact of the COVID-19 on each segment and the prospects for recovery for those segments adversely impacted by the pandemic.

FIGURE 4.1
The Best-Howard Model

$2.3 Trillion (Worldwide)

Domains (U.S. billions)

FAN ENGAGEMENT	SPORTS PRODUCTS	SPORTS PARTICIPATION
$586.3 (25.3%)	*$968.1 (41.8%)*	*$762.4 (32.9%)*

Core Areas (U.S. billions)

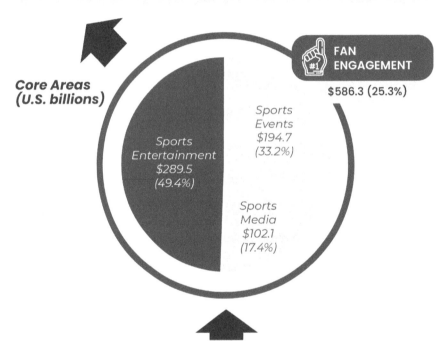

FAN ENGAGEMENT
$586.3 (25.3%)

Sports Entertainment $289.5 (49.4%)

Sports Events $194.7 (33.2%)

Sports Media $102.1 (17.4%)

Segments (U.S. billions)

Sports Entertainment Segments	Revenues	Percent
Sports Betting	$ 233.9	80.8 %
Fantasy Sports	$ 18.6	6.4 %
Esports	$ 1.0	0.3 %
Sports Video Games	$ 13.4	4.6 %
Movies & Collectibles	$ 12.6	4.4 %
Sports Bars	$ 10.0	3.5 %
TOTAL	**$ 289.5**	**100.0 %**

Copyright Best-Howard Model 2022. All Right Reserved.

The Best-Howard Model's Sports Entertainment core area accounted for nearly $290 billion in consumer spending in worldwide in 2019 (*Figure 4.2*). Sports gambling yields over three-fourths of all sports entertainment revenues globally. The recent legalization of sports betting in the United States ensures the segment's sustained growth. While the $13.1 billion wagered in the United States accounted for only 5.6% of all worldwide sports betting in 2019, the country only began legalizing the practice in May 2018. As more U.S. states allow sports gambling over the next decade, forecasts estimate revenues will grow exponentially. Canada also recently passed federal legislation authorizing sports betting across all provinces. North America's contribution to the worldwide sports wagering handle (i.e., the gross amount wagered) will likely exceed $100 billion by 2030.

FIGURE 4.2
U.S. and Global Sports Entertainment Revenues (U.S. billions)

REVENUES ($ Billions)	U.S.	Global	U.S %	U.S.	Global	U.S. %	U.S.	Global	U.S. %	U.S.	Global
Segment	2010	2010	2010	2015	2015	2015	2019	2019	2019	CAGR	CAGR
Sports Betting	$ --	$ 228.3	-- %	$ --	$ 216.8	-- %	$ 13.1	$ 233.9	5.6 %	-- %	0.24 %
Fantasy Sports	$ 4.6	$ --	-- %	$ 7.6	$ 13.0	5.5 %	$ 8.5	$ 18.6	45.7 %	6.3 %	7.43 %
Esports	$ --	$ --	-- %	$ 0.11	$ 0.33	33.0 %	$ 0.29	$ 0.98	30.5 %	22.2 %	27.0 %
Sports Video Games	$ --	$ --	-- %	$ 2.00	$ 8.25	24.4 %	$ 3.3	$ 13.4	24.6 %	13.3 %	12.9 %
Movies & Collectible	$ --	$ --	-- %	$ 5.66	$ 13.6	41.6 %	$ 5.9	$ 12.61	46.8 %	1.04 %	-2.07 %
Sports Bars	$ 7.69	$ --	-- %	$ 8.10	$ 8.10	100 %	$ 10.0	$ 10.0	100 %	2.66 %	2.66 %
TOTAL	**$ --**	**$ --**	**-- %**	**$ 23.5**	**$ 260.1**	**-- %**	**$ 41.1**	**$ 289.5**	**14.7 %**	**15.0 %**	**2.71 %**

Sports Betting

"In time, the expansion of legal wagering will drive fan engagement and in turn viewership and will become a growth category for sports advertising at both the national and local levels."

Eric Shanks, Head of Fox Sports, May 2019

Estimating the true magnitude of how much is wagered on sports presents challenges. According to one recent industry publication:

"It is important to recognize that the overall size of the sports betting market is difficult to estimate because regulations and record-keeping are inconsistent. There is no definitive resource, from nation to nation, that researchers can rely on. Records are too disparate to paint an entirely accurate picture" (1).

To make a credible sports wagering revenue estimate, the Best-Howard Model relies on two reputable statistical data firms, Statista and IBISWorld. However, each firm measures and reports annual sports betting revenues differently. Statista reports the actual amount wagered on sports annually, known as the handle (2). IBISWorld reports net total sports betting revenues, in which the analyst deducts the amount kept by gambling operators (e.g., casinos and online betting services) after paying winners (3). The result, known as the hold, amounts to about 7% of total wagered revenues (4).

In *Figure 4.3*, the Best-Howard Model transforms IBISWorld's net annual revenue figures into gross estimates by including the standard 7% hold. In 2019, the global handle totaled $233.9 billion.

FIGURE 4.3
Global Sports Betting Gross Revenues, 2010–2019 (U.S. billions)

	2010	2011	2012	2013	2014	2015	2016	2017	2018	2019	2020
Handle	$ 228.3	$ 227.2	$ 229.3	$ 231.5	$ 227.9	$ 216.8	$ 220.3	$ 228.9	$ 230.7	$ 233.9	$ 217.0 [1]

'COVID-19 impact discussed in last section of this Chapter

The model does not provide a historical perspective on U.S. sports gambling because the country did not legalize the practice until 2018, when its Supreme Court ruled states had the authority to sanction and regulate sports betting. Prior to the ruling, only Nevada allowed the practice. By the end of 2019, just 19 months after the ruling, U.S. bettors wagered $17.6 billion on sports (5). Eight states legalized sports betting by the end of 2018; 14 did so by the end of 2019. With as many as 30 states projected to legalize sports betting within the next few years, analysts forecasted robust growth, ranging from a conservative $100 billion estimate (6) to an optimistic $287 billion (7) by 2025.

The $217 billion global sports betting estimate in 2020 accounts only for bets placed legally. Prior to U.S. legalization, millions of Americans—an estimated 28% of adults—bet on sports illegally (6). U.S. federal law makes it a crime to participate in illegal betting; however, the internet has for decades allowed offshore sportsbooks in countries like Panama and Antigua to flourish. The sportsbooks target gamblers around the globe but emphasize North America, where sports betting has been largely prohibited. In Canada, online sports gambling has long been considered a legal gray area. But analysts estimate Canadians spend $7.8 billion annually on illegal sports betting, with an additional $3.1 billion in wagers placed with offshore sportsbooks (8).

In November 2020, the Canadian federal government introduced legislation to legalize sports gambling, including online betting on all events except horseracing. Analysts suggest the legislation was an effort to "stem the tide of wagered money moving offshore" (9, 10).

Both international bookmaking activities and unreported wagering via sports pools (e.g., for the NCAA March Madness basketball championship) and fantasy leagues make the U.S. betting market difficult to estimate. Estimates of the U.S. handle range from $80 billion to $380 billion (8). While substantiating the United States' illegal gambling figure is impossible, the 2020 legal sports betting estimate of $21.5 billion clearly underrepresents the full extent of sports gambling in the country.

U.S. SPORTS BETTING. With a few exceptions, the United States banned sports wagering in 1992 with the passage of the Professional and Amateur Sports Protection Act (PASPA). The law exempted a few states with established sports lotteries, as well as licensed sportsbooks in Nevada. Sportsbooks, derived from the gambling term bookmaker, allow gamblers to wager on many competitions, including in football, basketball, boxing and horseracing. After PASPA's adoption, Americans wanting to bet on sports had three options: travel to a casino in Nevada, engage with a local bookmaker or use an offshore website (1).

"The love affair with sports in the United States is a perpetual and immovable force with a new, natural and perhaps more powerful teammate in gambling."

PwC Outlook for Sports Market in North America through 2023

Shortly after PASPA's passage, several U.S. states, led by New Jersey, challenged the law. In 2014, New Jersey legalized sports betting at casinos and racetracks. Facing several court challenges and pushed by all four major sports leagues—"hell-bent on stopping sports gambling from expanding beyond Nevada"—New Jersey's sports betting bill was brought before the U.S. Supreme Court (11). On May 14, 2018, the court ruled 7-2 that the national sports betting ban was unconstitutional. The ruling upheld New Jersey's argument that state legislatures, not the U.S. Congress, had the power to license sports gambling. The decision granted states the right to choose whether to legalize sports gambling and in what form.

Less than two years after PASPA's repeal, 21 states and Washington D.C. (about 30% of the U.S. population) had fully implemented live sports betting (12). Three other states had passed laws legalizing sports gambling. U.S. voters approved all six sports gambling measures on ballots in November 2020. In 16 other states, bills legalizing some form of sports betting had been proposed by the end of 2020. Analysts forecast the number of states authorizing sports gambling would grow to 30 by the end of 2021 (13).

The COVID-19 pandemic provided considerable momentum for sports betting laws. The coronavirus's economic impact prompted state legislatures to seek new tax revenue sources. From June 2018 through October 2020, state and federal taxes on sports betting produced $257 million in new revenues. Statista provides a state-by-state rundown of sports betting tax rates on page 16 of the report, "Sports Betting in the United States" (2).

U.S. states have taken diversified approaches to legalized sports wagering. Some have limited bets to in-person action at casino sportsbooks, while others allow multiple betting options at land-based casinos, racetracks, retail sportsbook locations and online outlets. The Action Network provides a detailed report on sports gambling in all 50 states (13) and summarizes the opportunities offered in the states with legalized betting:

- Physical (in-person) sportsbooks only—Arkansas, Delaware, New York and North Carolina.

- Full mobile betting with multiple options—Colorado, Illinois, Indiana, Iowa, Michigan, New Jersey, Nevada, Pennsylvania, Tennessee and West Virginia.

- In-person online betting—Mississippi and Montana.

- One mobile betting option—New Hampshire (DraftKings), Oregon (state lottery), Rhode Island (William Hill) and Washington D.C. (GambetDC).

FIGURE 4.4
The Capital One Arena Sportsbook

Washington D.C.'s Capital One Arena, home of the U.S. National Hockey League's Capitals and National Basketball Association's Wizards, features an in-house sportsbook. The multi-level entertainment space (*Figure 4.4*) offers "a full-service sportsbook, with 12 ticket windows, 10 self-service kiosks, two VIP areas and one large private dining/event space" (14). Fans have access to live gameday action via a jumbotron, updated game scores from a 1,500-square-foot wraparound LED screen and premium culinary offerings. William Hill operates the facility year-round.

Capitals and Wizards owner Ted Leonsis believes "the gamification of all sporting events is a very, very positive development, especially for the fans." Click on the video in *Figure 4.5* to hear Leonsis talk about the future of sports betting.

FIGURE 4.5
Capital One Arena's Full-Service Sportsbook

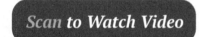 

Source: https://www.youtube.com/watch?v=KvVIYwzFkxo

Other team owners and venue operators in states with legalized sports gambling plan to enhance the fan experience by offering in-venue betting. At the PPG Paints Arena in Pittsburgh, the NHL's Penguins will open the BetRivers Sportsbook Lounge in 2021. A recently opened $2 billion stadium in Las Vegas, home of the National Football League's Raiders, was unable to showcase its first-ever sportsbook in an NFL stadium during the 2020 season due to the COVID-19 pandemic. The sportsbook is expected to open during the 2021 season. And in the near future, venerable Wrigley Field, home of Major League Baseball's Chicago Cubs, will be the first MLB venue to offer an on-property sportsbook.

It is highly likely that dedicated in-venue sports betting will become an increasingly prominent feature of sports venues as more states adopt legalized gambling. The opportunity to wager during a game will provide one more compelling reason for fans to attend live sporting events. In addition to spending time (and money) in the sportsbook entertainment lounge, fans will have the ability to place bets online throughout the game from their own seats. And, postgame the sportsbook offers more opportunities for betting and a chance for fans to either celebrate or drown their sorrows – all of which provide teams with a new and robust income stream.

ONLINE/MOBILE BETTING. Online/mobile sports betting has become the dominant platform in U.S. states where it is offered. Statista reports that 84% of all 2019 sportsbook bets in New Jersey were placed online (2). The ease and convenience of wagering from home or on a mobile device was particularly attractive during the 2020 COVID-19 pandemic. Several analysts at the time predicted mobile sports betting would claim 75% to 80% of all U.S. wagering activity over the succeeding five years.

Online sports betting's explosive growth has not been limited to the United States. Online gambling's worldwide market value is forecast to double to $92.9 billion by 2023 (2).

The ubiquity of smartphones and apps allowing easy access to lotteries, weekly jackpots, casino games, poker and live sports wagering, including on horseracing, have contributed to mobile betting's soaring popularity.

While as much as 80% of U.S. sports betting occurs online, only 10 U.S. states offer full online wagering. Many legislatures face pressure to protect and enhance established physical casino operators. According to one analyst, the lawmakers "have an overwhelming desire to 'bring people into those facilities'" (15). Several states have therefore limited sportsbooks to brick-and-mortar properties (*Figure 4.6*). But, as a Sportradar U.S. senior executive observed, "The audience who bets online or through a mobile app isn't necessarily interested in going to a casino or retail sportsbook" (15).

FIGURE 4.6
Expansive Sportsbook in Major U.S. Casino

Establishing online betting has been challenging in U.S. states with strong Native American Indian casino presences. Tribal gambling operations are a prominent part of the American industry, and in many states, tribes are the dominant gaming stakeholder. In 2020, American Indian tribes operated 501 casinos in 29 states. Annual revenues topped $32 billion, accounting for 43% of net U.S. revenues (16). In Arizona, Minnesota and Washington, tribes concerned about competition have pushed against gambling legalization. Tribal leaders believe mobile betting erodes their market share. Consequently, the Action Network forecasts that "full online sports betting will not come to many states for a long time" (13).

Legal online sports wagering may therefore be limited to 15 U.S. states for the foreseeable future. And while mobile betting will dominate the sportsbook share in those states, sportsbooks in commercial casinos across the United States, including those operated by Indian tribes, will receive a substantial portion of the handle. Statista reports bettors wagered $13.04 billion on sports in U.S. casinos in 2019 (17).

THE SPORTS GAMBLING ECOSYSTEM.

With some prognosticators estimating that sports betting could soon reach $287 billion, stakeholders are lining up to take advantage (7). The stakeholders include leagues (e.g., the NFL, NBA, MLB and NHL) sports media companies (e.g., ESPN and Fox Sports) and gambling operators (e.g., FanDuel, DraftKings, Caesars and MGM). Representatives of each group recognize that forming mutually beneficial partnerships with others in the sports gambling ecosystem is critical.

Opportunistic sports media companies have recently begun partnering with sports betting operators. ESPN has signed two long-term deals with Caesars Entertainment, along with its sports betting partner William Hill, and DraftKings. The agreement grants each partner co-exclusive access to ESPN's website, mobile app and digital network. Caesars and DraftKings will be able to advertise and provide direct links to their sportsbooks. The stock market quickly responded to the deals, with shares of DraftKings increasing by 17% and Caesars increasing by 7% following the announcement (18).

While the rights fees paid by DraftKings and Caesars Entertainment to ESPN has not been publicly reported, agreements struck by other major media companies (e.g., between NBC Sports and Points Bet and CBS Sports and William Hill) have been reported as "eight to nine-figure deals" (19). It's likely that ESPN's rights fee would be higher. Most analysts suggest media-betting operator partnerships are mutually beneficial. Media companies are rewarded financially and, as one analyst suggested, serve as funnels to drive enthusiastic sports fans—40% of whom bet on sports in 2020—to the sports betting apps of their respective partners.

The Big Four North American professional sports leagues, all of which battled legalizing sports betting "as an existential threat," now stand to be its greatest beneficiaries. According to research by Nielsen Insights for the American Gambling Association, the NFL, NBA, NHL and MLB will earn a combined $4.23 billion annually from legal sports gambling (20). The new revenues will come from direct spending by the gaming industry on television ads, sports gambling data and sponsorships, as well as from what Nielsen labels "fan engagement revenues" generated from bettors' increased consumption of league media and products (21). According to a Nielsen-conducted NFL study, the football league will be the biggest beneficiary, receiving $2.3 billion of the $4.23 billion total. The share aligns with data indicating bettors wager more on the NFL than any other sports league. An estimated 33.2 million American adults planned to bet on NFL games in 2020 (22). Next in line is MLB, projected to receive $1.1 billion, followed by the NBA at $585 million and NHL at $216 million.

One lucrative revenue source for leagues is selling the right to distribute data to sportsbooks. Data firm Sportradar has secured exclusive agreements with all four major North American sports leagues to sell official game information to casino and sportsbook operators. The NHL's partnership with Sportradar is estimated at $250 million over 10 years (23). Through the terms of the agreement, Sportradar gathers league data and distributes it to clients like FanDuel and MGM Entertainment. The data includes not only basic statistical information like goals and assists, but also advanced statistics like slapshot velocity and skater speed. The dynamic data is used both to enhance game telecasts and engage bettors. "It's all part of a league-wide push to give teams, fans and betting houses more information about its games," according to one analyst (24). The NFL's deal with Sportradar is reputed to be worth at least $250 million and "one of the biggest in company history," according to news outlet Bloomberg (25).

Leagues and teams have aggressively pursued partnerships with gambling companies, and the response has been favorable. Casino operators and online sports betting companies like FanDuel and DraftKings have spent significant amounts with leagues and teams to use their official trademarks on their platforms and gain access to Sportradar's licensed data. Most of the deals are multi-year agreements worth millions to tens of millions.

The NFL has been slow to engage with sports gambling. But after approving the Raiders' move to Las Vegas in 2018, the league has softened its stance. According to an NFL spokesperson, "What has not changed is our relentless protection of the integrity of the game. These new [gambling] partnerships have no impact on the play on the field" (26). In January 2019, the NFL signed a non-gambling deal with Caesars Entertainment.

The partnership would offer fans hospitality and entertainment at Caesars properties but not be connected to betting. By May 2020, the league voted to allow team owners to sign partnership deals with sports betting operators. The Denver Broncos signed three new deals, one with Betfred Sports to operate an in-stadium sportsbook lounge, another with retail bookmaker BetMGM Sportsbook, which opened a full-service sportsbook in nearby Saratoga Casino Black Hawk, and the third with FanDuel for exclusive advertising rights, including in-stadium signage.

The COVID-19 pandemic appears to have had a major impact on the NFL's decision to embrace sports gambling. Team owners facing substantial losses during 2020 sought new revenue sources, and several NFL teams established partnerships with casinos and online sportsbook operators. The New York Jets, Detroit Lions, Tennessee Titans and Las Vegas Raiders partnered with BetMGM, the Dallas Cowboys teamed with WinStar World Casino (*Figure 4.7*), the Baltimore Ravens signed an agreement with Caesars and the Philadelphia Eagles began working with DraftKings.

FIGURE 4.7
Dallas Cowboys Owner Jerry Jones Announces First NFL–Casino Partnership

In April 2021, the NFL signed its' first-ever league wide sports gambling deal reputed to pay the league "just shy of $1 billion" (27). The 5-year multiparty agreement expands Caesars Entertainment as the league's Official Casino Sponsor and adds DraftKings and FanDuel as Official Sports Betting partners. In announcing the deal, the NFL stated, " … all three partners will have exclusive ability to leverage NFL marks within the sports betting category and activate around retail and online sports betting. They will also engage with fan through NFL-themed free-to-play games" (28). The NFL also recently expanded its gambling presence globally, naming 888sport its official betting partner in the United Kingdom and Ireland and BetCris its partner in Latin America (29).

The following are the current betting partners of the major North American professional sports leagues:

- NBA: MGM Resorts, DraftKings, BetStars, FanDuel, William Hill, FoxBet, Francaise des Jeux (France's leading lottery operator).

- NFL: Caesar, DraftKings, FanDuel, FoxBet, 888sport (UK), BetCris (Latin America), Genius Sports

- MLB: MGM Resorts, FanDuel, DraftKings, Fox Bet.

- NHL: MGM Resorts, FanDuel, William Hill.

- MLS: MGM Resorts.

- PGA: DraftKings.

- UFC: Fox Bet.

- NASCAR: Wynn Resorts.

FIGURE 4.8
Legal Gambling's Impact on Sports Viewing

- **79%** *of current and potential gamblers plan to watch more live sports on TV*

- **63%** *said they would watch a greater variety of sports*

- **60%** *said they would watch sports they didn't follow before*

- **42%** *of those who watch sports wager on games, betting $82 per wager*

Beyond the financial benefits, leagues and teams have found sports betting deepens fan engagement. As shown in *Figure 4.8*, legalized sports gambling will likely benefit all sports ecosystem stakeholders as it changes fans' viewing behavior (30). Not only does betting on game outcomes increase media viewership, the practice increases viewing intensity level. North America's NBA now allows fans to stream the fourth quarter of a game for $1.99 (7). The opportunity not only appeals to fans with limited time, but it is also particularly attractive to gamblers interested in final outcomes.

Ultimate Fan Engagement: In-Game Micro-Betting

Simplebet has introduced automated, machine learning software enabling sports micro-betting. The technology allows fans to place bets in seconds, creating the opportunity to wager on every pitch in a baseball game, down in a football game and shot in a basketball game. The dynamic, in-play platform chops three-hour games into thousands of discrete occurrences: Will the next pitch be a ball or strike? Will the batter swing or miss? The frequency of the occurrences in baseball games—300 pitches, 75 at bats—allows fans to engage with games every 30 seconds in a uniquely absorbing manner.

Simplebet launched its micro-betting product with FanDuel during the 2020 NFL season. The FanDuel app began offering fans free "Play Action," giving players 1,000 betting tokens per quarter, with the option of risking 100 tokens per bet. For example, the following odds might be posted after a 4-yard run gives the Chicago Bears a first down at the Detroit Lion's 35-yard line:

How Will the Bears' Drive End?	*Odds*
• Touchdown	2.66
• Punt	47.00
• Field Goal	4.27

In the unlikely event that the Bears punt, the bettor would be rewarded 47 tokens for every 1 wagered.

During the first three weeks of the NFL season, fans placed more than 900,000 total wagers on the FanDuel platform (31). Simplebet CEO Chris Bevilacqua reported that the average user bet 71 times during a game and 25% of FanDuel Play Action users stayed on the app for one hour or more (32).

The NBA's Simplebet partnership debuted with the start of the 2020-2021 season, providing another opportunity to evaluate and enhance the micro-betting platform. Simplebet has plans to extend its technology to many other sports. The firm has a licensing deal with MLB and expects future partnerships with the NHL, PGA and tennis and soccer properties. Some have suggested Simplebet's offering is the ultimate fan engagement product, and in its free-to-play entertainment mode, it has proven successful in immersing fans in games.

What's next? FanDuel and other sports gambling operators are likely to begin offering real-money micro-betting. Simplebet is licensed in several states and expects to be in every legal online betting jurisdiction by 2021. Extending its reach would be a critical step in receiving regulatory approval for live, real-money wagering. Simplebet also recently signed a long-term deal with Sportradar, ensuring the platform access to the robust database necessary to run its betting models. If and when micro-betting becomes a legal opportunity, it will have an enormous impact on the volume and amount of money bet on sports. Chris Bevilacqua believes that "70% of all betting will in time become in-play," of which micro-betting will account for a substantial share (32).

SPORTS BETTING AROUND THE GLOBE. While legal sports betting is still in its infancy in the United States, it is well established in most world regions. Market research firm Technavio expects the global sports gambling market to expand at an accelerated annual growth rate of 10% from 2020 to 2024 (33). Applying the year-to-year growth to 2019's $233.9 billion handle results in an increase of $142.8 billion in sports wagering worldwide to $376.7 billion by 2024. Online betting will account for most of the growth, with the biggest contribution coming from the rapidly expanding U.S. market.

Countries in every world region offer legal, government-regulated sports betting. Listed in *Figure 4.9* are some of them.

In-depth information on the sports betting format allowed in each country

Scan to *Visit Legal Sports Betting*

Source: https://www.legalsportsbetting.com/

FIGURE 4.9
Notable Countries Offering Legal Sports Betting

The types of government-regulated sports gambling options available worldwide ranges widely, from horseracing only in Argentina to almost every sport in Australia. Several African countries, including Ghana, Nigeria and South Africa, permit gambling on almost all sports both at betting parlors and online. Nigeria bans sports betting ads on television and radio, while South Africa requires every broadcast advertisement to be accompanied by a service message offering help for gambling addiction. Analysts estimate that $4.2 billion is wagered annually on sports in Ghana, and billions are wagered in South Africa (34).

India, like several other countries, provides no national governing policy on gambling formats. Each of the 29 Indian states has the authority to permit gambling. Many states in India ban sports betting. Thirteen states have legalized lotteries, horseracing is confined to 10 racetracks and three states operate casinos. Retail sportsbooks are illegal in all states. Despite these limitations, sports gambling has become increasingly popular in India. While online sports betting is not legal, Indians are not prohibited from placing bets on sites outside of India (35). Millions are taking advantage of this opportunity. One survey reported that 40% of the people who use the internet in India do so for gambling. It is estimated that Indians spend US$60 billion annually betting on sports, with $48 billion of that total being wagered on cricket (36). Given that most of that money flows to out of the country, there has been a growing push for India to broadly legalize sports gambling to both "curb match-fixing" and generate new tax revenues (36).

While Legal Sports Betting recognizes China as the "country that invented gambling," the country has increasingly restricted the practice during its last 70 years of communist rule (37). In fact, the Chinese government permits only government-regulated lotteries. Many Chinese gamblers wager on sports like European soccer and American basketball through online sportsbooks, usually legal operators in Hong Kong and Macau. But the Chinese government can block access to the platforms at any time. China is potentially the most lucrative sports gambling nation in the world. Many of its 1.7 billion people already wager online, despite the government-imposed barriers.

The United Kingdom has the most well-established, robust legal sports betting industry of any nation in the world. Legal gambling has existed in Great Britain since 1960. The industry currently encompasses all sports, has more than 10,000 retail betting outlets and offers many sophisticated online gambling platforms. Most major U.K. soccer clubs have established partnerships with gambling firms like William Hill, which operate onsite betting parlors and dispatch roaming cashiers throughout stadiums during matches. The most current published figure on the U.K. sports betting handle is the Gross Gambling Yield from April 2016 to May 2017 at US$20.3 billion (38). Applying a conservative compound annual growth rate of 9%, the figure exceeded US $26 billion by the end of 2020.

While sports gambling likely occurs in every world country, the scope of legal opportunities varies widely. The United States is striving to accommodate sports betting's tremendous popularity despite disagreement on whether and in what forms it should be legal. Whatever the government regulations, sports betting demand cannot be suppressed. More and more countries, states and cities are recognizing that passing legislation authorizing sports betting allows them to both regulate the practice and financially benefit. All evidence suggests sports gambling will continue to be the fastest growing global sports industry segment into the foreseeable future.

Fantasy Sports

Source: BCC Research

Within the Fan Engagement Best-Howard Model domain, fantasy sports provide a unique experience, allowing fans to own, coach and manage virtual sports organizations. What began as a hobby among a few friends has grown into a nearly $20 billion global business played by more than 60 million people in the United States and Canada. In 2019, an estimated 19%, or 45.9 million, Americans participated in fantasy sports (39).

Fantasy sports involve players assembling virtual teams by selecting real professional athletes in an online auction or draft. Team performance is based on how the individual athletes perform during real-game competition. For example, in an NFL fantasy league, the scoring system might be based on offensive statistics like passing touchdowns, field goals kicked and rushing yards, as well as defensive performance metrics like number of sacks, interceptions and fumble recoveries. League standings are based on head-to-head team matchup results or the total points each team compiles.

FIGURE 4.10
North American Fantasy Players, 2005–2020 (U.S. millions)

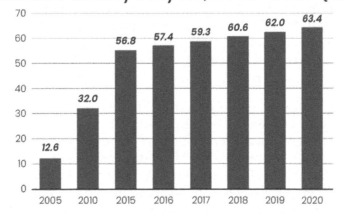

The Best-Howard Model offers a more in-depth overview of fantasy sports in the United States and Canada than other regions due to the availability of credible data. A Fantasy Sports & Gaming Association (FSGA) study shows the industry's impressive growth in North America over the last 15 years (*Figure 4.10*).

In one decade, the number of U.S. and Canadian fantasy participants nearly doubled, from 32 million in 2010 to an estimated 63.4 million in 2020 (39). The FSGA report reveals that among U.S. and Canadian fantasy sports participants:

- 81% are male, 19% are female.
- 50% are between 18 and 34 years of age (an average of 37.7 years).
- 50% have a college degree or higher.
- 47% earn more than $75,000 annually.
- 66% say football is their favorite sport.
- 61% say they watch more televised sports since joining fantasy leagues.
- Players age 18 and over spend $653 on average per year to participate.

While the socioeconomic descriptors the FSGA report provides are substantiated in other findings, the spending figure requires clarification. Applying the $653 annual average spending to the 63.4 million estimated to have played fantasy sports in 2020 yields a total spending figure of $41.4 billion. The figure more than doubles spending estimates of other reputable industry analysts. The FSGA notes its summary is synthesized using several research studies, "each with a slightly different cross-section of subjects." The spending respondents therefore appear to include those identified as "serious fantasy players or sports bettors." The Best-Howard Model assumes that the inclusion of players inclined to spend more than casual participants accounts for an exaggerated spending average. Using a median estimate moderates the inflation bias. Still, many fantasy players are working professionals earning above the national average, and to achieve an average spending level of $653 per player, many must invest thousands of dollars per year.

The Best-Howard Model can find no credible estimate of global fantasy sports participants, but evidence suggests some countries' participation is growing faster than that in the United States. In India, fantasy players increased from 2 million in June 2016 to about 100 million in 2020, a 25-fold jump in three years (40). Several factors have propelled the exponential growth: 1) The proliferation of affordable smartphones and high-speed internet, 2) court rulings affirming fantasy gaming's legality and 3) new professional sports leagues (e.g., for soccer, hockey, badminton, volleyball and kabaddi) creating more opportunities for fans to engage in fantasy leagues. One recent forecast predicts 150 million people in India will play fantasy sports by 2022 (41). Given the country's increasing availability of affordable digital devices, the prediction may be conservative. The number of internet subscribers in India grew from 368 million in 2016 to 560 million in 2018 and 639 million in 2020, more than double the 281 million U.S. internet users in 2020.

Fantasy sports are also popular across Europe. As in sports betting, the United Kingdom has Europe's most sizeable fantasy market. The estimated participant number is 8 to 10 million, with 3.5 million alone on the Fantasy Premier League game site (42). In 2019, the site reached an additional 6.3 million users around the world. Fantasy association football platforms are the centerpiece of gaming in football-centric nations. Italy has an estimated 8 million users for Fantasy Serie A, also known as Fantacalcio. In Spain, Comunio is the leading fantasy league.

FIGURE 4.11

Fantasy Sports Community Mondogoal Owner Shergul Arshad Discusses Gaming Issues

Source: https://www.lawinsport.com/topics/features/item/the-growth-of-daily-fantasy-sports-betting-and-the-legal-issues-it-faces-an-interview-with-shergul-arshad

Some European countries struggle to accommodate the market demand for fantasy sports due to gambling license requirements. Within the European Union, gaming licenses are subject to domestic law. Some countries, like Germany, Spain and France, impose strict licensing requirements on sports betting and fantasy sports. For an overview of the issues, see the interview with Shergul Arshad, who recently launched daily fantasy sports community Mondogoal, in *Figure 4.11* (43).

Daily fantasy sports (DFS) have also accelerated the industry's growth. Unlike traditional fantasy games, which stretch across entire seasons or tournaments, DFS allows users to compete against others on a daily basis for cash prizes. According to IBISWorld, the real money involved in DFS has "revolutionized the way fantasy sports are played" (44). In the traditional fantasy sports model, pooled league entry fees are paid by participants and distributed to winners on an informal basis. Typically, a voluntary league commissioner distributes the winnings according to an agreed-upon formula (e.g., winner takes all or top three to five in league standings).

> *"There is a big difference, as daily fantasy sports offer an alternative to sports betting, and there is much more of a personal attachment and sense of accomplishment with fantasy when a person constructs their own team and backs it with their own money as opposed to simply betting on a team to win" (42).*

In contrast, private gaming companies conducting DFS games offer fans the opportunity to compete in thousands of contests per day across every major sports property, from North America's NFL to the WNBA. DFS uses a pay-to-play model in which contestants submit an entry fee to compete, and winners receive a share of the pool. Contestants choose a sport, then build a player roster. Typically, contestants select players from a pool established by the game operator and must complete their lineup under a given salary cap (e.g., $50,000). They can then choose the type of contest in which they would like to compete, including "50/50" (top 50% win cash), "head to head" (winner takes all), "friends only" (private league of known players) and contests among only experienced daily players with higher entry fees and prize pots.

FIGURE 4.12
Fantasy Sports Operators Enhance Fan Engagement

In events like the FSGA Experts League Drafts, key fantasy sports industry stakeholders collaborate to host attractive fan engagement events. In the Experts League, FSGA and FanDuel co-produce a series of mock NFL drafts, each featuring 16-rounds of picks by draft experts. More than 50 leading fantasy football and betting pundits provide players with analysis and insights on their selections. The five-day event is livestreamed by Fantasy Alarm and aired on Sirius XM Fantasy Sports Radio. The mock draft event is timed as a prelude to the NFL season start. It provides millions of fantasy league players and bettors exposure to a network of websites offering DFS resources. For example, Rotowire.com provides NFL fantasy participants with a "Football Draft Kit" of in-depth player stats, position rankings, injury updates and insights on underrated players and top rookies.

FSGA provides a similar Experts League Draft event for Major League Baseball fantasy players. The opportunity to showcase FSGA members serving fantasy sports enthusiasts has proven popular.

As in sports gambling, traditional and online media companies dedicated to serving fantasy sports enthusiasts have proliferated. ESPN offers fantasy sports programs like The Fantasy Show and Daily Wager, SiriusXM offers a 24/7 station dedicated exclusively to fantasy sports, and numerous online fantasy sports sites like Fantasy Alarm and ProPlayers offer in-depth player performance data and advice on roster choices for a fee.

FanDuel and DraftKings dominate the U.S. DFS market. Both ventures entered the space around 2010 to create compressed fantasy sports league platforms to expand and enhance the gaming experience. Backed by millions of dollars in venture capital and aggressive promotional campaigns, the two firms quickly achieved their goals. By 2015, both were valued at $1 billion and controlled 90% of the market (45).

Despite its immediate popularity, daily fantasy gaming has faced legal challenges. While 1999's Gambling Prohibition and Enforcement Act deemed playing fantasy sports for money legal in the United States, several states have banned it as a form of unregulated gambling. The 1999 law determined fantasy sports were essentially games of skill, "where all winning outcomes reflect the relative knowledge and skill of participants…and no winning is based on the point spread," but several states view it as a "disguised" form of gambling (46). Currently, six states have banned all DFS forms. Others have restricted the types of daily fantasy gaming allowed and prohibit certain operators from offering DFS platforms. By 2021, Arizona, Hawaii, Alabama, Iowa, Idaho, Montana, Louisiana, Nevada and Washington had banned one or more fantasy sports platforms, such as DraftKings, Yahoo, FanDuel or Fantasy Draft.

Update on DFS's legality in the United States

Scan to Visit Legal Sports Report

Source: https://www.legalsportsreport.com/daily-fantasy-sports-blocked-allowed-states/

"A clear signal as to how the fantasy sports industry identifies itself was made when the leading trade group, the Fantasy Sports Trade Association changed its name to the Fantasy Sports & Gambling Association. As stated by the organization's president, 'this shift is really tied to the remarkable crossover between fantasy players and sports bettors.'"

Eric Fisher, Sports Business Journal, January 2019

Fantasy sports platforms' legality are ambiguous in many Asian countries, including Japan, Indonesia, Malaysia, Pakistan, Taiwan and Vietnam.

An overview of the global fantasy sports market and more detailed insights on DFS in specific regions and countries

Scan to See Fantasy Sports Market Size & Share

Source: https://www.alliedmarketresearch.com/fantasy-sports-market-A06468

FIGURE 4.13
Fantasy Sports Revenues, 2010–2020 (U.S. billions)

Revenue	2010	2011	2012	2013	2014	2015	2016	2017	2018	2019	CAGR	2020
Global	$ --	$ --	$ --	$ --	$ --	$ 13.0	$ 13.9	$ 15.0	$ 16.8	$ 18.6	7.4 %	$ 17.9
U.S.	$ 4.6	$ 5.1	$ 5.3	$ 5.4	$ 5.6	$ 7.6	$ 7.6	$ 7.7	$ 8.1	$ 8.5	6.3 %	$ 7.8
% U.S.	$ --	$ --	$ --	$ --	$ --	58.5 %	54.7 %	51.3 %	48.2 %	45.6 %	--	43.6 %

Accelerated by DFS and online accessibility, U.S. and global fantasy sports spending grew quickly from 2015 to 2019. As shown in *Figure 4.13*, U.S. revenues increased from $7.6 billion in 2015 to $8.5 billion in 2019 (44). Consumer spending on fantasy sports worldwide, driven largely by India's explosive growth, increased at an even faster rate. By 2019, global spending on fantasy sports reached an estimated $18.6 billion (45).

COVID-19 made 2020 a difficult year for fantasy sports, particularly in the United States where many professional leagues suspended play early in the year and shortened their seasons. The U.S. National Collegiate Athletic Association also canceled major events, such as the popular men's national basketball championship tournament. IBISWorld estimates fantasy sports revenues fell 8.4% to $7.8 billion in 2020 (44). Global fantasy sports revenues declined moderately during 2020, falling only 3.7% to $17.9 billion due in large part to India's surge in participation.

A report published by the Federation of Indian Fantasy Sports (FIFS) reported gross fantasy revenues at $340.5 million in 2020, an increase of more than 150% over the $130.5 million gross revenues in 2019. The incredible popularity of fantasy sports in India—FIFS claims "a 2,500% spike in the number of fantasy sport users in the past decade"—has analysts projecting gross revenues in India will reach $ 3.7 billion by 2024 (47). KPMG expects the Indian Premier Fantasy League to be worth $1 billion by 2022 (48).

One market research firm projects the global fantasy sports market to grow to $48.6 billion by 2027, expanding at a cumulative annual growth rate of 13.9% (45). DraftKings and FanDuel are expected to be at the forefront of the expansion. DraftKings' revenues are projected to increase by as much as 45% to between $750 and $850 million by 2021. FanDuel outperformed DraftKings in 2020, becoming the first online sportsbook to exceed $1.1 billion in gross gaming revenue. The return of live sports across all major sports in North America and Europe, coupled with continued legal betting expansion across the U.S., will push growth further. And DraftKings is expected to expand its operations globally, with its DFS platform currently available in eight countries, including India, the United Kingdom, Germany, Ireland and Austria.

Esports

"Esports revenue having passed the [$1 billion] mark in 2019...will achieve growth at a level unseen in almost any other media and entertainment category."

PwC Global Entertainment & Media Outlook, 2020

Esports, derived from the phrase electronic sports, is a non-traditional form of sports competition in which players compete by playing primarily combat video games like League of Legends, Dota 2 and Fortnite. PC Magazine refers to esports as "the video game industry's competitive player arm." Over the last decade, esports have become a global phenomenon; analysts estimate more than half a billion people viewed esports in 2020.

Competitive video gaming has evolved rapidly from casual events among recreational gamers in arcades to a global spectator sport in which professional esports teams compete in packed arenas for millions in prize money. Event organizers project gameplay, accompanied by lively commentary, on huge screens before enthusiastic audiences and stream the events for millions of digital viewers.

While the first video game tournament dates to the 1970s, it wasn't until the development of the internet, PCs and gaming consoles in the 1990s that gamers around the world could compete. Companies like Nintendo and Blockbuster began sponsoring gaming tournaments with cash prizes. The first official esports tournament was held in 1997 and attracted 2,000 participants. Over the following two decades, competitive gaming exploded. Video technology became less costly, making gaming more accessible to broad audiences. At the same time, developers began producing games intended to be esports products.

Now, millions of players compete recreationally, and the most talented emerge as professional gamers capable of earning millions of dollars in esports tournaments around the world.

Mimicking traditional sports, esports gaming companies have formed competitive leagues. The most prominent major franchise leagues are the Call of Duty League, League of Legends Championship Series and Overwatch League (OWL). A unique feature of esports is that the major leagues are "owned by the game makers themselves" (49). Activision Blizzard owns and operates the OWL and has established franchises in 10 major world cities, including San Francisco, Paris and Seoul. Franchises have reportedly sold for $30 million to $60 million.

Owning an esports team does not require high entry fees, but annual operating costs can run above $10 million. The average OWL franchise player roster has 12 team members. The league has established a minimum salary of $50,000, and top players earn up to $300,000 (49). Teams invest significant amounts in player development. The top teams provide players with high-end training facilities and coaching and the latest PC hardware.

In addition to sponsoring teams, a growing number of esports companies enter teams in international tournaments, such as the League of Legends World Championship, The Fortnite World Cup and The International. The tournaments attract as many 80,000 spectators and award sizeable monetary prizes. The 2019 International Dota 2 World Championship prize pool totaled $35 million, the largest to date. The events' streaming audiences are far larger than their live audiences. According to Esports Charts, the 126 hours of the 2020 League of Legends Tournament produced record-breaking viewership statistics: 3.9 million peak viewers, 1.1 million average viewers and 139.9 million hours watched (50).

As shown in *Figure 4.14*, the number of people playing and/or viewing esports around the world more than doubled to nearly half a billion from 2015 to 2020 (51). The rapid growth occurred despite the cancellation of several 2020 tournaments due to COVID-19.

FIGURE 4.14
Esports Viewers Worldwide, 2015–2020, 2023 (millions)

BENCHMARKS	2015	2016	2017	2018	2019	2020	CAGR	2023
Total Audience (Gamers & Viewers)	226	281	335	395	454	495	17.0%	646
Esports Enthusiasts	115	121	143	173	201	223	14.2%	295
Occasional Viewers	111	160	192	222	245	272	18.8%	351

Sources: Newzoo, Global Esports Market Reports, 2016-2020, Statista

Forecasts indicate continued exponential growth. The number of players and viewers is expected to grow by 151 million to nearly 650 million by 2023. The increase will likely accelerate as access to mobile gaming expands across emerging markets in the Middle East,

Africa and Southeast Asia (52). *Figure 4.15* shows Americans' esports engagement. A recent survey found "over a quarter of America is more interested in esports than either traditional sports or streaming films and TV" (53).

FIGURE 4.15
American Esports Engagement

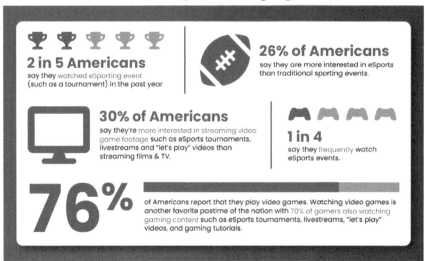

Analytics firm Newzoo differentiates esports audiences by their engagement level. *Figure 4.14* segments audiences into "esports enthusiasts," those who watch professional esports content more than once a month, and "occasional viewers," those who watch professional esports content less than once a month. Enthusiasts represent a large (45%) and stable portion of the total 2020 audience of 223 million. Twitch, a popular streaming platform for video game viewers, attracted four million unique viewers per day during February 2020. Twitch is designed specifically for gamers and allows viewers to watch others play games, stream esports tournaments and engage in a community forum through chat rooms and watch parties. The site's monthly average viewership exceeds a half a billion, more concurrent viewers than that of CNN, Fox News and ESPN (54). While Amazon-owned Twitch accounts for two-thirds of all esports viewers, YouTube has grown its share to 24%. In 2020, the two streaming platforms accounted for nearly 96% of the total esports viewing market. By 2023, analysts expect Twitch to attract 3.2 million average concurrent viewers and YouTube to draw 2.3 million (55).

FIGURE 4.16
Esports Audience Viewership Demographics

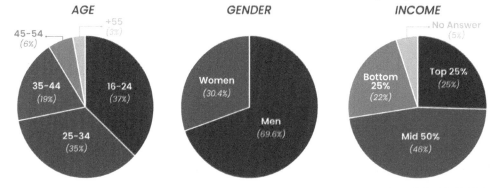

As shown in *Figure 4.16*, almost three-quarters of those attending or watching livestreamed esports tournaments in 2019 ranged from 16- to 34-years-old (56). The younger generations grew up with video gaming as prominent and accessible aspects of their lives. Only 3% of the esports audience in 2019 was above 55. Nevertheless, the young demographic is largely financially stable, with 25% saying they are in the top 25% income category globally. In the United States, 61% of esports viewers earn more than $50,000 per year (57).

Men account for 70% of those who play and/or watch esports competitions. However, women have increased participation, growing from 23.9% of watchers in 2016 to 30.4% by the end of 2018 (58). In the two succeeding years, women likely increased their share of watchers. According to NBC News interviews (see *Figure 4.17* for video), women may now account for 40-50% of all gamers.

FIGURE 4.17
The For the Women Gaming Summit

The esports industry is booming, and it's seeking female applicants

Source: https://www.nbcnews.com/know-your-value/feature/esports-industry-booming-it-s-seeking-female-applicants-ncna1143406

As shown in *Figure 4.17*, organizers launched the For the Women Gaming Summit to promote inclusivity in esports and integrate women into co-ed professional leagues and tournament teams. Another successful initiative was an international esports tournament series launched exclusively for women and culminating with the Dubai-based Girl Gamer Festival in 2020. The festival showcased the most talented all-woman teams from around the world. The video in Figure 4.18 highlights the Galaxy Racers, the first female esports team from the Middle East to compete in a global tournament.

FIGURE 4.18
The Galaxy Racers Compete in the Girl Gamer Festival World Championship

Middle East's first female esports team makes debut CNN

Source: https://www.youtube.com/watch?v=56sKeW1LjuQ

ESPORTS REVENUES. As esports audiences have grown, so have revenues. Spending on esports by gamers, fans and companies around the globe more than tripled from 2015 to 2019. As shown in *Figure 4.19*, revenues rose from $325 million in 2015 to $958 billion in 2019, increasing at a compound annual rate of 27% (52, 59). In October 2020, Newzoo released a revised 2020 revenue forecast, reducing its original yearly estimate from $1.1 billion to $950 million due to "almost no in-person attendance" at many esports events due to COVID-19 (60). Global esports revenues are projected to climb from a conservative estimate of $1.6 billion to as high as $1.8 billion by 2023. In 2020, China surpassed the United States as the largest esports market, with total revenues of $385 million compared to $253 million. China now accounts for 35% of all global esports revenues. The esports boom in China is projected to propel spending to $540 million in 2023.

FIGURE 4.19
Global Esports Revenues & Prize Money, 2015–2020, 2023 (U.S. millions)

	2015	2016	2017	2018	2019	2020	CAGR	2023
Total Revenues	$ 325	$ 493	$ 776	$ 906	$ 958	$ 950	27.0%	$ 1.60
Esports Events	112	424	588	737	885	--	67.7%	--
Total Prize Money	$ 71m	$ 93m	$ 116m	$ 159m	$ 247m	$92m	36.9%	--

1 Figures are estimates.

The number of esports matches and tournament events quadrupled from 112 in 2015 to 885 in 2019. Esports competitions declined dramatically in 2020 due to COVID-19 cancellations, and the prize pool plummeted, falling from a high of $247 million in 2019 to $92 million. The most notable cancellation erased a $40 million prize pool for Dota 2's The International. Despite lingering pandemic-based uncertainty, game developers planned a full 2021 tournament schedule. As one tournament CEO stated, "we completely pivoted our business to go fully digital" (61). Faced with the prospect of empty arenas, prominent game producer Blast planned to expand its partnership with the British Broadcasting Corporation. In 2020, the prominent U.K. public service broadcaster produced 120 hours of Blast's Counter Strike events on its iPlayer digital platform. Blast anticipated its global lineup of television and online partners would reach more than 150 million households in 2021.

FIGURE 4.20
Global Esports Revenue Streams, 2017–2020 (U.S. millions)

REVENUE SOURCES	2017	2018	2019	2020	CAGR	2023
Sponsorship / Advertising	$422	$533	$646	$637	14.7%	$824
Media Rights	$95	$161	$251	$185	24.9%	$506
Merchandise & Ticket	$64	$96	$105	$122	24.0%	$129
Game Publishing Fees	$116	$116	$95	$116	0%	$116
Digital & Streaming Ads	$NA	$NA	$28	$40	42.9%	$114
TOTAL	**$697**	**$906**	**$1.13b**	**$1.10b**	**16.5%**	**$1.69b**

The revenue sources shown in *Figure 4.20* focus exclusively on income generated by competitive esports gaming events. The approach mirrors that of traditional professional sports leagues, which report revenues from game and tournament spectators (e.g., ticket and merchandise sales) and sponsorship and media rights fees paid by companies to promote their brands or broadcast events. Since 2014, Newzoo has reported annual global esports revenue figures. The firm's data is widely cited and serves as the primary source for market profiles published by Statista, Forbes magazine and other global publications. Figure 4.20 draws from Newzoo reports from 2017 to 2020 and its 2023 forecast (52, 59).

Newzoo's strictly events-revenue definition excludes several operational expenditures used in estimating the economic value of major professional leagues, such as the NFL and Premier League. The Newzoo definition notably excludes player costs, a prominent component of league and team valuations. The top esports teams invest significantly in player development and compensation. Prominent esports organization Team Liquid provides its team members with training facilities, coaching, PC hardware and annual salaries from $100,000 to $200,000. The team also shares tournament prize money with its members. With many esports companies fielding several teams, overall annual player compensation, training, housing and travel costs can amount to millions of dollars.

While accounted for as expenditures, investments in talent are integral to the revenue streams in *Figure 4.20*. The contrast between Newzoo's focus solely on event revenues and China's leading esports company Tencent's approach to measuring esports revenues highlights the difference. Tencent's Penguin Intelligence reports China's esports revenues reached $1.9 billion in 2019 (62), twice Newzoo's total global esports revenue estimate of $951 million for the same year. The discrepancy results from Tencent using a revenue figure including income generated by tournaments, sponsors and media rights, as well as money earned by players and teams.

A recent International Journal of Esports paper makes a case that Newzoo's approach undervalues esports (63). The article, by Joseph Ahn and colleagues, uses Collis's Entire Esports Ecosystem model as its measurement framework (64). The model identifies six overlapping sectors (*Figure 4.21*) to represent the esports ecosystem. The categories include: 1) Teams, Professionals and Streamers, 2) Game Publishers, 3) Streaming Platforms, 4) Physical Products, 5) Leagues and Tournaments and 6) Digital Tools.

FIGURE 4.21
Total Estimated Global Esports Ecosystem Revenues, 2019 (U.S. billions)

SECTORS	REVENUES	%
Game Publishers	$15.85	63.7
Teams, Professionals, Streamers	$4.20	16.9
Streaming Platforms	$2.41	9.7
Physical Products	$1.42	5.7
Digital Tools	$0.84	3.4
Leagues and Tournaments	$0.14	0.6
TOTAL	**$24.86**	**100%**

The network includes the contribution of all principal agents, from producers to consumers. It captures game publisher revenues from firms like Epic Games, which produces Fortnite, including from download and physical copy sales and subscriptions, as well as player and video game streamer salaries, advertising and subscription revenues generated by platforms like Twitch and YouTube and sales revenues realized by firms selling gaming products (e.g., GameSensei).

As shown in *Figure 4.21*, Ahn and colleagues' model produces a larger economic estimate of the global esports market than other methods. The aggregated contribution of all sectors totals $24.9 billion, 25 times larger than the Newzoo estimate of $1.1 billion. While the researchers describe the limitations of their estimation methods, they offer compelling rationale for their model and methodology.

While Newzoo's events-only methodology is narrow, the Best-Howard Model uses the figures because they are the best available estimate of global esports revenues and provide annual income figures over an extended period. While arguably incomplete, the Newzoo measurement captures data on esports' core competitive dimension. Subsequent editions of The Sports Industry may draw on work inspired by Ahn and associates and adopt a broader valuation perspective, similar to those used by Forbes, PricewaterhouseCoopers and Deloitte in measuring well-established sports industry sectors like the four major North American leagues and five elite European soccer leagues.

The Newzoo esports revenue source breakdown (*Figure 4.20*) shows that the largest share of event income comes from companies promoting their brands through sponsorships and advertising and from rights fees for streaming (e.g., on Twitch) and broadcasting (e.g., on ESPN2) esports competitions. In 2020, brand sponsorships, advertising and media rights accounted for nearly 75% of global esports revenues. About one-quarter of annual revenues come from esports fans buying tickets and merchandise while attending competitive events.

Esports competitions' large live and streaming audiences have attracted growing corporate investment. Brand spending on sponsorships directly with leagues, teams and players, including advertising, totaled $634 million in 2020. Sponsorship income declined slightly from the $646 million spent in 2019 due to COVID-19-related tournament cancellations. Forecasts project that global sponsorship and advertising support will recover quickly, reaching an estimated $824 million by 2023. According to one analyst, consumer brands are investing more to reach esports audiences because they allow them to "reach a demographic that's been increasingly beyond their grasp" (57).

The esports audience, largely millennials and teens, is more inclined to purchase sponsors' products when endorsed by an esports athlete, team or league. In a recent study comparing attitudes toward sponsors between esports enthusiasts and general sports fans, esports fans said they were more than twice as likely to support their favorite team sponsor "no matter what," think more highly of companies sponsoring their favorite teams and "buy [the] brands" worn by their favorite teams (57).

Endemic sponsors like computer hardware companies have for years actively sponsored esports teams and leagues. Recently, non-endemic companies like Coca-Cola, Mercedes-Benz, T-Mobile, Red Bull, Gillette, Wendy's and Marvel Comics have become engaged sponsors. Over the last five years, Coca-Cola signed a multi-year agreement to be the eNASCAR virtual racing series title sponsor, sponsored the League of Legends World Championships and became the OWL's official beverage (65). As shown in *Figure 4.22*, Coca-Cola has increased its brand presence by hosting viewing parties for major esports events.

Disney-owned Marvel Comics has extended its partnership with Team Liquid through 2022, a

FIGURE 4.22
Coca-Cola Hosting On-Air Esports Watch Parties

strategic alliance featuring co-branded merchandise. The initial rollout included Team Liquid members wearing Marvel-themed jerseys inspired by comic heroes Captain Marvel and Iron Man at prominent events. In October 2020, IBM signed its first esports sponsorship deal, becoming the presenting partner for the OWL Grand Finals. The agreement allows the company to promote its analytic capabilities and highlight IBM Watson's artificial intelligence via live and in-broadcast predictive analysis. While the fees paid by Marvel and other major esports sponsors have not been released, analysts believe the agreements range from $5 million to $10 million. Coca-Cola reportedly invested $5 million in both its eNASCAR and OWL sponsorships (65).

Reports indicate media rights are the fastest growing revenue source for esports organizations. PricewaterhouseCoopers projects the revenues will reach $506 million by 2023, doubling the $251 million spent in 2019 (66). Amazon's Twitch signed a two-year, $90 million deal in 2018 to become the official OWL streaming platform. The agreement with Overwatch publisher Activision Blizzard allowed Twitch to broadcast all regular OWL matches during the 12-week regular season and post-season contests. In 2020, Activision Blizzard signed a multi-year deal with Google, giving YouTube exclusive broadcast rights to all the game publisher's sports leagues. While the agreement's value has not been made public, analysts speculate it is worth more than $100 million. As one YouTube executive said, "YouTube provides gamers and their passionate fans with the most popular video gaming platform in the world" (67). Analysts expect the competition between Amazon and Google to push esports media rights revenue levels beyond current forecasts for 2023. Microsoft's Mixer has also recently begun to compete for esports streaming market share.

Considerable uncertainty remains about live esports events in many parts of the world. Revenues from tournament ticket and merchandise sales may decline. The 2021 esports schedule is robust, but live audience attendance is not assured. Online team, league and tournament merchandise sales, however, flourished in 2020, covering ticket sales losses to drive a revenue increase from $95 million in 2019 to $112 million in 2020. Fees paid by game publishers to host events have remained stable, as reflected in the $116 million dollar estimate for 2020.

Newzoo recently recognized revenues from advertising on streamed esports events as a separate income source. While the smallest income stream at $40 million in 2020, digital and streaming sales are likely to be the fastest growing revenue source in the years ahead, according to Newzoo (52), as brands realize young esports audiences are moving away from traditional television to social media and streaming platforms.

While esports revenues surpassing $1 billion dollars in 2020 might seem inconsequential compared to the overall $160 billion global video gaming industry, publishers see esports as vital to sales. According to Newzoo, competitive gaming is "bringing back millions of lapsed gamers…whose passion is reignited by viewing other players and worldwide championships" (68). Global viewership is expected to double to more than 650 million by 2023, and game producers are investing more resources in esports. In 2015, Electronic Arts (EA) Sports established a competitive games division. Wanting to bring preeminent competitive experiences to the world, EA began developing competitive platforms for their suite of sports games: Madden NFL, FIFA, NHL and UFC.

Esports and North America's Professional Sports Leagues. Esports are dominated not by sports-focused games but combat platforms like Fortnite and League of Legends. However, publishers like EA Sports have begun to push their popular games onto the esports tournament landscape. EA's 2019 Madden 19 Championship Series culminating event, the Madden NFL 19 Bowl, generated 2.5 million views on Twitch, and its ESPN2 broadcast reached 805,000 viewers (69). The combined digital and linear broadcast produced a 208,000 average per-minute audience. The Madden 21 Championship series prize pool grew to $1.4 million (70).

EA Sports' FIFA Global Series soccer game has brought the world's most popular sport into mainstream esports gaming. Some of the world's best players like Tekkz and teams like FaZe Clan and Fnatic now compete for top championships. In 2020, EA Sports established another competitive format for its FIFA 21 launch, the eChampions League.

EA Sports has also moved to bring its competitive games to a broad, mainstream audience. As described by senior vice president Todd Sitrin, the target is an audience "that are not all video game players," and the approach involves "the use of people famous for something [other] than esports" (71). The company has launched esports tournaments with star NFL and Premier League athletes competing in Madden NFL or FIFA Global. And popular celebrities have competed among one another and against professional football and soccer players. The events include play-by-play commentary from both competitors and announcers. EA Sports announced its Madden 20 Celebrity Tournament, featuring athletes (e.g., DeAndre Hopkins), ESPN talent (e.g., Katie Nolan) and famous celebrities (e.g., Snoop Dogg), with a bracket reveal show on ESPN2, and all elimination matches aired on ESPN Esports, Twitch and YouTube. The week-long event culminated with a championship on ESPN2.

Major North American sports properties are embracing partnerships with producers like EA Sports. The NFL, NASCAR, NBA and MLS recognized that the Madden NFL, NBA 2K, FIFA Global and eNASCAR iRacing Series games provided their fans a way to stay connected during the COVID-19 pandemic. Leagues also recognize that video games and esports can reach young audiences. Almost all professional sports leagues have aging fan bases: The average NASCAR fan is 58-years-old, and not far behind are MLB and the NFL, with fans averaging 57- and 50-years-old (72). The average esports fan is 26-years-old.

NASCAR has committed to drawing elementary- and middle school-age children to racing. As part of its Acceleration Nation program, the league created lesson plans for science teachers using the aerodynamics of stock cars to teach the concepts of drag, downforce and aero balance to students in grades five through seven. eNASCAR's Ignite Series targets 13- to 16-year-olds, providing young gamers the opportunity to compete virtually on any track using "the unparalleled simulation experience on NASCAR's iRacing platform." NASCAR hopes the program will provide aspiring racers a platform to showcase their talent and launch racing careers.

> *"If there's a country fit for esports, then it is China. The country now boasts a gaming population of over 500 million with 26% of internet users watching esports monthly—that is more than double the level in the U.S."*

> **Tom Elsden, Business Director, Sports Insights Consultancy**

CHINA'S ESPORTS BOOM. China has assumed a dominant presence in global esports. The country's huge and passionate fanbase has embraced esports and built a total viewing audience of 160 million, almost three times larger than the 57 million esports viewers in North America (73). Newzoo estimates China's 2020 esports revenues at $385 million, compared to $286 million in North America. The country's esports boom has occurred despite the Chinese government long banning video games.

China took a dramatic turn on esports in 2016, becoming the first nation to recognize esports as an "official profession." The Ministry of Education of the People's Republic of China began listing "esports management" as a major curriculum specialization, stimulating the launch of courses and diploma programs throughout the country.

A look at China's online esports viewing patterns compared to other markets

Scan to Read the Article

Source: https://www.ibc.org/china-dominates-global-esports-consumption/5341.article

Since then, no government has supported esports more (73). In addition to investing hundreds of millions of dollars, the Chinese state government has called on technology companies like Tencent and Alibaba to lead the country to the top of the esports global market. Tencent, which produces League of Legends, announced in 2017 it would invest $15 billion to develop China's esports market.

With strong state support, major Chinese cities have invested millions in esports infrastructure, competing to become "the esports capital" of the world (74). Hangzhou has invested $315 million to vie with Shanghai as the global esports hub. With a population of more than 10 million, the city recently opened "esports town," a government-operated complex dedicated to esports (*Figure 4.23*). The complex's centerpiece is a 56,000-square-foot arena for esports competition that includes 21 VIP suites, player lounges and a flagship store for the hometown LGD Gaming team, which competes in the Tencent League of Legends Pro League. LGD Gaming and Allied Esports, which specializes in building esports venues, have established corporate headquarters in the complex. Allied Esports also constructed the HyperX Esports Arena in Las Vegas, expected to include an esports academy, office park, hotel and hospital by 2022. Hangzhou will host the Asian Games in 2022, expecting competitive esports to be included as a medal event for the first time.

FIGURE 4.23
Esports Town in Hangzhou, China

While China leads the world in investment and viewers, esports' popularity has also grown in other parts of the world. The rapid penetration of smartphones in developing countries has helped create vibrant esports markets, particularly across the Asia-Pacific region in Vietnam, Thailand and the Philippines. Esports players and viewers are growing at double-digit annual rates in India, Japan (24% compound annual growth) and Latin America (17.9%), with mobile games like Garena Free Fire and PUGB Mobile leading the way. Mobile esports gaming has largely displaced PC/console esports in India and Thailand.

Sports Video Games

"Games are playing a pivotal function in society as a pillar of entertainment, social connection and relief, improving the quality of life for millions during the COVID-19 pandemic."

2020 Newzoo Global Games Market Report

Aided by the growth of esports over the five years prior to 2020, the broader video game market flourished. In 2020, worldwide video game and hardware sales totaled $174.9 billion (75, 76). The U.S. accounted for 24% of global spending, with game sales revenues of $41.4 billion (77). China led the world in 2020 sales at $44.1 billion. The two markets accounted for almost half the nearly $175 billion spent on video games in 2020.

The $175 billion global spending figure represents a $15.6 billion increase over Newzoo's early-2020 forecast of $159.3 billion (78), despite the initial estimate being made prior to the COVID-19 pandemic being fully understood. Extended stay-at-home restrictions made video gaming an attractive entertainment option and avenue for safe social interaction. As shown in *Figure 4.24*, 2.69 billion people worldwide identified as "gamers" by the end of 2020, up 135 million from the previous year (79).

While some may play fewer video games when the COVID-19 threat subsides, most analysts predict continued growth. Newzoo forecasts the number of gamers will increase to more than 3 billion in 2023, with global spending reaching $217.9 billion (76).

FIGURE 4.24
Active Video Gamers Worldwide, 2015–2023 (billions)

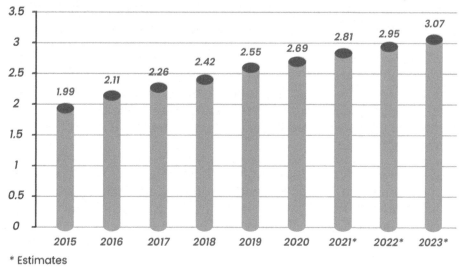

* Estimates

China is home to the world's largest gaming population, with an estimated 665 million players in 2020. The number represents one-quarter of the world's gamers and more than triples the estimated 200 million American gamers in 2020.

Figure 4.25 focuses on the amount consumers spend on sports video game content. In determining the data, the Best-Howard Model makes two adjustments based on credible industry reports. First, the model calculates game content's share of overall spending. Content includes the amount consumers spend on physical and online purchases and downloads, as well as in-game spending. The model removes costs associated with hardware (e.g., consoles and tablets) and accessories (e.g., headsets and controllers), as the devices can be used for non-sports play. According to sales data from IBISWorld, physical and online game content software accounts for 82.5% of total market sales (77). Of the estimated $174.9 billion consumers spent on video games in 2020, $144.3 billion was used to buy game content (76).

FIGURE 4.25
Consumer Spending on Sports Video Game Content, 2015–2020, 2023 (U.S. billions)

Sports Video Content Spending	2015	2016	2017	2018	2019	2020	CAGR	2023*
Global	$8.25	$9.76	$11.1	$12.7	$13.4	$16.0	14.2%	$19.9
United States	$2.0	$2.1	$2.3	$2.8	$3.3	$3.8	13.8%	$4.7

* Estimates

Second, the Best-Howard Model calculates the spending portion dedicated to sports-themed games. The video games industry identifies sports as one of many specialty genres, along with action, shooter and strategy. According to a 2021 Statista report, 11.1% of all U.S.-distributed video games were sports-themed, such as Madden NFL, FIFA 20 and Rocket League (79). The

Best-Howard Model applies the 11.1% sports category share to the total video games spending estimate to calculate the annual games revenues shown in *Figure 4.25*. For example, the $16 billion sports content figure represents 11.1% of the $144.3 billion spent by global consumers across all game genres in 2020. That year, worldwide gamers spent $37.5 billion on action games, $30 billion on shooter games and $16 billion on sports games, the fourth ranked genre.

Worldwide and U.S. sports games sales grew at annualized rates of 14% from 2015 to 2020. The U.S. share remained stable at around 24% over the five-year period. In 2020, the United States accounted for $3.8 billion of the world's $16 billion in sports-themed video game sales. The popularity of two games, NBA 2K and Madden NFL, largely propelled U.S. sales. As shown in Figure 4.26, the two games were ranked second and third on the 2019 list of the best-selling video games in the United States (80).

A third sports game, FIFA 2020, also appears on the U.S. top-15 list. The FIFA soccer series is the most popular sports game in the world. Since its first release in 1993, the annual series has sold 325 million copies worldwide, ranking it fifth in total video game sales across all genres (80,81). The game's popularity endures, as the October 2020 FIFA 21 release led to the sale of 1.5 million copies in one month, breaking the record of 1.2 million copies set by FIFA 20 (82).

Both the Madden NFL and NBA 2K game series are also listed among the top-20 all-time best-selling video games globally (*Figure 4.26*). Since the release of the first Madden NFL in 1988, the EA Sports product has sold more than 130 million units, placing it 15th overall. Sega has sold 116 million copies of NBA 2K since 1999, ranking the game 18th overall. Like FIFA 21, both the Madden 21 and NBA 2K21 releases set sales records. Madden 21 sold 20% more copies in its first week than the previous year's edition, and NBA 2K21 sold 8 million copies in the first five months after its September 2020 release, despite a price hike to $70 (83).

FIGURE 4.26
U.S. Top Selling Video Games, 2019

RANK	TITLE	PUBLISHER	GENRE
1	Call of Duty: Modern Warfare	Activision Blizzard	First-person shooter
2	NBA 2K20	Take 2 Interactive	Sports
3	Madden NFL 20	EA Sports	Sports
4	Borderlands 3	2k Games	Action / Role-playing
5	Motal Kombat 11	Warner Bros.	Fighting
6	Star Wars Jedi: Fallen Order	Electronics Arts	Action / Adventure
7	Super Smash Brothers	Nintendo	Fighting
8	Kingdom Hearts III	Square Enix	Action / Role-playing
9	Tom Clancy's The Division 2	Ubisoft	Action / Role-playing
10	Mario Kart 8	Nintendo	Action / Adventure
11	Grand Theft Auto V	Rockstar Games	Action / Adventure
12	Red Dead Redemption II	Rockstar Games	Action / Adventure
13	Minecraft	Mojang	Sandbox, survival

| 14 | FIFA 20 | EA Sports | Sports |
| 15 | Anthem | Electronic Arts | Action / Role-playing |

EA Sports has been successful largely due to FIFA and Madden NFL. The company's 2020 year-end financial report revealed its net revenues across all sports games reached a record $1.59 billion. It was the third consecutive year in which EA Sports game sales profits exceeded $1 billion. EA Sports' 2020 total net revenues topped $5.5 billion, with $2.7 billion realized from players purchasing in-game content (84). Video games are a staple entertainment option for billions around the world. In 2020, an estimated 2.7 billion people played video games. "Gamers" are spending more time and money than ever before on this largely home entertainment leisure activity. In 2020, global consumers spent a record $175 billion purchasing video games and hardware. The growth has been accelerated by shelter-at-home restrictions imposed by the coronavirus pandemic. The ability of millions of people in emerging nations to increasingly gain access to gaming on mobile devices has led analysts to predict gamers to exceed 3 billion by 2023. Already in 2021, more people are playing video games on their smartphones than on any other device.

While action-adventure games are the most widely popular around the globe, several sports-team video games are among the top sellers worldwide. FIFA, featuring elite association football leagues and teams from around the world, is the 5th highest selling game of all time. In the U.S., the globe's second largest games market, two sports titles – NBA 2K and Madden NFL - ranked 2nd and 3rd in overall sales in 2019. These widely popular games account for a significant share of the $16 billion game enthusiasts spent on sports-games worldwide in 2020. American consumers spent $3.6 billion, just about 24% of the world's total. Forecasts predict sustained sports game sales growth, with annual growth rates around 14% globally and in the United States.

Sports Movies, Books & Memorabilia

The sports movies, books and memorabilia segment of the Best-Howard Model's Sports Entertainment core area is often overlooked due to an absence of credible data. Despite the challenges, the model provides reasonable estimates of consumer spending in the three categories. As shown in *Figure 4.27*, the model omits global books and memorabilia spending figures for 2010 due to the absence of data. Global book sales are also omitted for 2015, 2019 and 2020.

FIGURE 4.27
Sports Movies, Books & Memorabilia Revenues, 2010, 2015, 2019, 2020 (U.S. billions)

REVENUES	U.S.	Global	% U.S.	U.S.	Global	% U.S.	U.S.	Global	% U.S.	U.S.	Global	% U.S.
Sub-segments	2010	2010		2015	2015		2019	2019		2020	2020	
Movies	$0.25	$0.91	27.0%	$0.81	$3.16	26.5%	$0.16	$0.61	26.2%	$0.07	$0.27	25.9%
Books	$0.46	--	--	$0.47	--	--	$0.55	--	--	$0.59	--	--
Memorabilia	--	--	--	$4.40	$10.00	44.0%	$5.40	$12.0	45.0%	$6.40	$14.0	45.7%

While collecting sports memorabilia (e.g., trading cards, player jerseys and sneakers) has been a popular pastime for decades, the practice has more recently transitioned into an asset-classed investment. Its rapid emergence as a multi-billion dollar industry has resulted in more credible revenue data reporting. Thus, the Best-Howard Model incorporates 2015, 2019 and 2020 sports memorabilia spending figures.

Even with the omission of global book revenues, the three Sports Entertainment segments combined to account for $14 billion in global consumer spending in 2020, driven largely by a surge in the collectibles market.

SPORTS MOVIES. Over the last decade, going to the cinema has been popular among hundreds of millions of individuals worldwide. In 2019, global consumers spent an-all time high of $42.4 billion buying tickets to watch movies. Spending $11.4 billion, the United States accounted for the second largest share of box office revenues, following Asia-Pacific countries at $17.8 billion (85). China, South Korea, Japan and India all have vibrant movie markets, with India's Bollywood producing more films per year than both China and the United States.

Unlike other Sports Entertainment segments, the movie theater business was devastated by the COVID-19 pandemic (*Figure 4.28*). Global box office revenues plummeted 72% in 2020, with actual losses greater than $30 billion (86).

According to a PricewaterhouseCoopers report, the U.S. theater market was also projected to contract severely, with revenues falling 66% from 11.4 billion in 2019 to $3.9 billion in 2020 (87).

FIGURE 4.28
Theaters Around the Globe Closed Due to the 2020 COVID-19 Pandemic

Figure 4.29 estimates the amount consumers spend directly on sports films. The data are provided by IMDb (i.e., the Internet Movie Database), which furnishes cumulative U.S. and worldwide box office revenues for each film categorized as a sports movie. The figures also capture how much moviegoers spend on food and beverages in theaters. According to IBISWorld, concessions account for 30% of total theater revenues (88). While theater operators share box office receipts with film producers and distributors, they claim 100% of food and beverage revenues (89).

How did sports-themed movies fare over the decade prior to 2020? *Figure 4.29* shows they account for a small portion of total consumer spending in worldwide movie theaters. On average, movies featuring sports competition, athletes and/or teams accounted for just more than 2% of all global box office revenues during the 10-year period. In 2015, the biggest year of the decade, sports films grossed about $2.35 billion, or 6% of global ticket sales.

FIGURE 4.29
Worldwide Movie Theater Spending, 2010–2019

YEAR	Global All Movies Box Office	Global Sports Movie Box Office	Sports % of Total Box Off	Food/Bev Sales at Sports Movies	Total Sports Movie Revenues
2019	$42.2 B	$470 M	1.1%	$140.1 M	$610.1 M
2018	$41.8 B	$610 M	1.5%	$181.8 M	$791.8 M
2017	$40.9 B	$729 M	1.8%	$217.2 M	$946.2 M
2016	$39.3 B	$928 M	2.4%	$276.5 M	$1.20 B
2015	$39.1 B	$2.35 B	6.0%	$702.1 M	$3.06 B
2014	$36.4 B	$600 M	1.6%	$178.8 M	$788.8 M
2013	$35.9 B	$1.06 B	2.9%	$314.7 M	$1.37 B
2012	$34.7 B	$380 M	1.1%	$113.2 M	$694.7 M
2011	$32.6 B	$822 M	2.5%	$245.0 M	$1.07 B
2010	$31.6 B	$702 M	2.2%	$209.2 M	$911.2 M
TOTAL	$374.5 B	$8.65 B	2.3%	$2.58 B	$10.08 B

Table figures compiled from IMDbPro data

More than half was attributable to the blockbuster Furious 7 (identified as "sport: motor racing" by most classification organizations), which grossed more than $1.5 billion after its 2015 release, making it the sixth highest all-time grossing film according to Box Office Guru.

Several other sports films have been box office successes. The Karate Kid, released in 2010, grossed $359.1 million, and the Indian film Dangal drew $303.7 million in receipts. Dangal is the story of a father training his daughters to wrestle in the Commonwealth Games; it was the most successful of the more than 25 sports films produced in India over the decade prior to 2020.

While sports films account for a modest portion of global film revenues, consumers spent an estimated $10 billion from 2010 to 2019 buying tickets and concessions for movies like Ford v. Ferrari (motor racing), Everest (mountain climbing) and 42 (baseball). None have reached the potential of sports films like the Rocky franchise, the renown boxing films that grossed more than $1.7 billion and spun off two other successful movies, Creed and Creed 2, with gross earnings of more than $300 million worldwide.

"Over the 12 to 24 months, there is going to be a lot of bankruptcies."

Brent Truman, Texas Association of Motion Media President

Analysts have found it difficult to predict the coming decade for the film industry. The 2020 COVID-19 pandemic was a financial catastrophe. While major U.S. movie chains like AMC and Regal have secured capital to hold off bankruptcy, many independent operators have closed their doors. Will moviegoers continue to stay home? During the pandemic, homebound families took advantage of movie streaming platforms like Netflix, Amazon Prime and Peacock. Since some U.S. movie theaters began reopening in late August 2020, audience response has been underwhelming. A survey conducted by Morning Consult found only 22% of American consumers felt comfortable returning to theaters (90).

The number of theater-production sports films declined sharply in 2019. More than one-third of all sports films released that year were documentaries, and half were made for or by streaming platforms, such as Heart of Gold (HBO), QBall (Netflix), Maradona (HBO) and Inside Game (Amazon Prime). Given the theater industry's uncertain future, the trend is likely to continue. Risk averse studios will continue to focus on proven blockbuster franchises like Warner Bros.'s Wonder Woman and Disney's Marvel films. Only 10 sports films have entered the top 350 grossing films of all-time, and it's unlikely major studios will make investing in new, unproven sports-themed movies a priority in the near future. Budget-friendly, human interest sports films produced for streaming platforms should prevail over the next several years.

> *"It's an extremely difficult time for sports books, extremely hard time to break through...What was the last really, really successful sports book?"*
>
> *Joe Posnanski, Sports Columnist & Author*

SPORTS BOOKS. While the book publishing industry has been resilient in the face of challenges since 2000, sports book sales have plummeted in the United States. One columnist referred to the prolonged decline as a "10-year batting slump" (91). Statista recently reported the narrow category of "sport and recreation" titles has fallen to 1% of all trade book sales, down from 3% in 2013 (92).

Trade magazine Publishers Weekly includes sports as part of its "health/fitness/medicine/ sports" category. Using the publications wider lens, sports-related book sales escalate dramatically. As a subset of adult nonfiction, wellness and sports-themed books were consistently among the top five best-selling subcategories from 2016 through 2018 (the latest reported figures). The 22.5 million books sold in 2018 topped business/economics, history/law/ politics, biography/memoirs and other prominent adult nonfiction subcategories, and health/ fitness/medicine/sports books annually account for 8% of the total adult nonfiction books purchased in the United States on average (93).

Because the Best-Howard Model encompasses health and fitness activities, sports medicine and other dimensions, the model uses the broader Publishers Weekly framework to estimate annual consumer spending on sports books. The model therefore employs the 8% average share of total nonfiction books sold from 2010 to 2020 to estimate the sales revenue figures reported in *Figure 4.30*.

FIGURE 4.30
U.S. Health, Fitness, Medicine and Sport Book Sales Net Revenue, 2010–2020 (U.S. millions)

YEAR	2010	2011	2012	2013	2014	2015	2016	2017	2018	2019	2020
Net Revenue	$460.8	$415.2	$430.4	$407.2	$397.6	$447.2	$469.6	$494.4	$548.0	$549.6	$592.8

Health/fitness/medicine/sports book revenues reached an all-time high in 2020, with estimated net sales of $592.8 million. The figure represents the largest annual increase in overall print book sales in the previous 10 years. Sales increased 8.2% in 2020, with total units sold hitting 751 million. The result comes despite retail bookstores being severely impacted by the COVID-19 pandemic. Bookstore sales fell by more than 33% in March 2020 (94). However, demand surged in June as many consumers increased their online purchases. Some analysts estimated Amazon's market share increased by 50% to 70% over pre-COVID-19 levels (95). Big box stores like Walmart and Target were also beneficiaries; designated as essential services, they remained open and provided another convenient outlet for book buyers.

The Best-Howard Model uses net revenues in *Figure 4.30*. All book sales information is reported in net revenues, in which the costs of goods sold (e.g., printing and shipping) are subtracted from gross revenues. All other model areas rely on the full or actual amount consumers spend on sports products or services. The model does not report worldwide sports book sales revenues due to a lack of credible data. Statista has published research dossiers providing detailed book sales information for several European countries (e.g., book sales in Spain reached $2.86 billion in 2019), but no data specific to sports book sales (96).

> *"The value of cards has risen so rapidly that stock market investors have begun to buy trading cards as an alternative to equities, pumping up prices for the cardboard commodity."*
>
> *Robert Channick, Chicago Tribune*

SPORTS MEMORABILIA. The sports memorabilia market soared over the decade leading to 2020 and grew into a multi-billion-dollar industry. The value of collectibles like cards, sneakers and jerseys appreciated rapidly, and some collectors now view sports memorabilia as an asset class for investment (97).

With more than 200 million worldwide collectors, the general collectibles market is estimated to be worth $370 billion (98). The largest market shares are claimed by classic cars, militaria and books, each valued at more than $15 billion. While not as large as the most popular categories, sports memorabilia are an increasingly prominent focus for collectors. SportsMemorabilia.com values the 2020 global sports memorabilia market at $14 billion (*Figure 4.31*), with licensed collectible merchandise accounting for $12 billion and autographed memorabilia accounting for $2 billion (99). Total worldwide sports memorabilia sales are projected to top $15 billion in 2021. Forbes reports the amount U.S. collectors spent on sports collectibles in 2018 was $5.4 billion (100). Given the surge in sports collectible sales in 2020, the Best-Howard Model estimates U.S. spending will have reached $6.4 billion.

FIGURE 4.31
Sports Memorabilia Revenues, 2010, 2015, 2019, 2020 (U.S. billions)

REVENUE $ MILLIONS	U.S.	Global		U.S.	Global		U.S.	Global		U.S.	Global	
	2010	2010	%U.S.	2015	2015	%U.S.	2019	2019	%U.S.	2020	2020	%U.S.
Sports Memorabilia	NA	NA	NA	$4.4	$10.0	44.0%	$5.6	$12.4	45.0%	$6.4	$14.0	45.7%

According to the CEO of the fastest growing online collectors' platform, "We expect the sports collectibles business to become an even bigger force in the industry in [the] years to come" (101). The optimism is based on a forecast suggesting the overall sports trading cards and memorabilia market could reach 67 million people. One in three general collectors either currently owns or has previously owned at least one sports collectible.

The commercial market for all collectibles has evolved from small stores and trade shows dominating trading to almost all transactions taking place online. Major platforms like eBay and specialty sites like Boxes and Collectibles.com now attract millions of sports memorabilia enthusiasts. A recent Forbes study reports that eBay alone generated $84 billion in gross merchandise volume (GMV) worldwide related to memorabilia transactions in 2017 (100). The study estimates that 43% of the GMV—$36 billion—came from U.S. collectors. The researchers suggest that 13% of the total transactions were for sports merchandise, amounting to $10.92 billion globally and the U.S. share totaling $4.68 billion.

In the United States, demand is high for trading cards and game-used items, such as balls and jerseys. Michael Jordan collectibles remain popular, with two of the NBA great's 1986 Fleer rookie season basketball cards selling for $738,000 each at a 2021 auction (102), an autographed 1997 Upper Deck card going for $1.44 million and a pair of game-worn sneakers fetching $615,000. Vintage memorabilia attract even higher sale prices. In January 2021, a mint-condition 1952 Mickey Mantle baseball card sold for a record $5.2 million, topping Babe Ruth's 1920 baseball jersey, which sold for $4.415 million (*Figure 4.32*). Not far behind was the $4.33 million paid for the Rules of Basketball, written by the game's supposed inventor James Naismith in 1891. The highest sports collectible sale price to date is $38.1 million for the 1962 Ferrari 250 GTO driven by some of the world's most iconic drivers in the European GTO series in the 1960s.

FIGURE 4.32
Mickey Mantle Rookie Card Sells for $5.2 Million

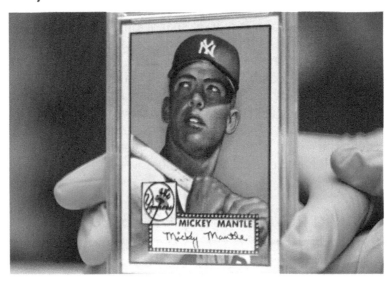

Industry analysts attribute the COVID-19-era collectibles surge to "investors, collectors sitting at home...with nothing else to do" (103). The record $5.2 million paid for the Mickey Mantle card was preceded by the online sale of an autographed Mike Trout rookie card in August 2020—the height of the pandemic—for $3.9 million. The promise of financial rewards is driving new baseball trading card demand to outstrip supply. According to an influential sports memorabilia broker, "new cards are immediately worth three to 10 times the retail price in the secondary market, if they are sold unopened...preserving their value." (103).

Most analysts are optimistic about sports collectibles' sustained growth. Solomon Engel, co-founder of online memorabilia trading site Boxes, says, "From the data we see on a daily basis, it's only a matter of time before the collectible market passes the $400 billion mark, and sports collectibles will be a very big part of that" (101).

Sports Bars

Sports bars are one of the great social fixtures of modern America. They provide a communal space where fans can gather and cheer for their favorite teams—or increasingly the teams they bet on—while enjoying food and beverages with friends and family. Staple features include large screen televisions, sports memorabilia, casual food (e.g., burgers, wings and fries), beer and a relaxed atmosphere. Many early sports bars, such as Hooters and The Tilted Kilt, catered to men. Hooters is still the second largest sports bar chain on the Restaurant Business Top 500 list (104). In 2019, the restaurant's 341 locations generated $858 million in total sales. Foodservice industry analytics company CHD-Expert finds most restaurants classified as sports bars in the United States are small, local establishments with annual revenues less than $500,000 (105).

Since 2000, sports bars have evolved from offering several standard definition televisions and a few beers on draft to being more family-friendly establishments with "bright, cheerful and sophisticated interiors with higher-end menus" (105). Recent innovations include segregated spaces for dining and watching games. The diversified approach appeals to families and women without losing bar- and sports-focused patrons. High definition television technology has enhanced the viewing experience. Now, U.S.-based fans can watch five or more NFL games simultaneously on a Sunday on multiple big screen monitors, which appeals to fantasy sports league enthusiasts and bettors invested in multiple games. Buffalo Wild Wings recently signed a deal with MGM Resorts International to bring sports betting to selected locations in U.S. states where gambling is legal (106).

In 2019, roughly 95,000 sports bars and grills operated in the United States (107). Over the previous decade, sports-focused restaurants came to account for one-third of the bar and nightclub industry's total revenues. While no reliable estimate of the number of Canadian sports bars is available, an internet search reveals they are plentiful across the nation's 10 provinces.

A broader search finds sports-themed bars and pubs in many other countries. However, no entity in the nations offers credible data on the number and sales revenues of sport bars as a food and beverage industry segment. In the United Kingdom, sports/social pubs are identified as a segment of "drink-led" pub or public establishments (108, 109). In 2019, 24,313 sports/social pubs operated across Great Britain. It is not clear how many of the establishments are tied directly to sports viewing in the North American tradition, but many are similar, such as the Sports Bar & Grill chain across London and the United Kingdom's Famous Three Kings pub (*Figure 4.33*).

FIGURE 4.33

Sports Fans at the United Kingdom's Famous Three Kings Pub

As in Canada and the United Kingdom, sports bar-explicit data is not available around the globe. While sports-themed establishments are ubiquitous, the Best-Howard Model limits its measure to the United States due to the lack of credible financial data. Information provided by IBISWorld and food industry sources like Restaurant Business and Full Service Restaurant News allows the model to provide estimates of the number and annual revenues of U.S. sports bars. Restaurant Business, the industry's leading magazine, publishes an annual report of the highest grossing restaurant chains. One of the categories used to differentiate the dining establishments listed is sports bars. The 2020 Restaurant Business report lists 10 sports bar chains among the 250 largest U.S. foodservice companies. Leading the way is Buffalo Wild Wings at number 22 with 1,206 locations and $3.7 billion in revenues. The other top-100 sports bars are Hooters (number 56), Dave & Busters (number 78) and Miller's Ale House (number 98). The 10 top-250 companies operate 2,191 sports bars and produce $6.8 billion in total sales.

Several smaller chains, like Arooga's Grille House & Sports Bar with 18 locations (nine company owned), and the Stacked Pickle with 10 locations in Indiana, are important industry players. While franchise operators account for the greatest number of locations and dominant sales revenue share, thousands of small to medium-sized independently owned and operated sports bars operate in towns and neighborhoods across the United States.

IBISWorld provides annual revenues generated by the U.S. bar and nightclub sector over the decade prior to 2020 (110). The report includes sports bars as part of the food and service industry sector. In reporting the IBISWorld data, Statista specifically mentions Buffalo Wild Wings' substantial $3.7 billion contribution to the $30.4 billion total bar and nightclub revenues in 2019.

Figure 4.34 shows sports bar sales figures progressively increased from $8.1 billion in 2015 to a high of $10.0 billion in 2019. The Best-Howard Model uses the revenue figures provided by Restaurant Business and IBISWorld to estimate that sport bars account for one-third of all bar and nightclub sales revenues in the United States.

Sports bars suffered greatly due to COVID-19. One estimate projected almost 30,000 sports bars would close due to the 2020 pandemic (107). The Best-Howard Model's assessment is not as severe. However, the model estimates that revenues fell considerably in 2020 as many bars were forced to close for several months and others closed permanently. Using IBISWorld's projection of COVID-19's impact on the bar and nightclub industry (110), the model estimates U.S. sports bar revenues fell 27% in 2020 to $7.37 billion.

FIGURE 4.34
Annual U.S. Sports Bar Revenues, 2010–2021 (U.S. billions)

	2010	2011	2012	2013	2014	2015	2016	2017	2018	2019	2020	2021
Bars & Nightclubs	$23.3	$23.8	$24.3	$23.9	$23.7	$24.5	$26.8	$28.4	$29.5	$30.4	$22.3	$25.8
Sports Bars	$7.69	$7.85	$8.02	$7.89	$7.81	$8.10	$8.88	$9.38	$9.74	$10.0	$7.37	$7.95

While many analysts project a healthy bar and nightclub sector rebound in 2021, the Best-Howard Model offers a cautious view of how quickly fan-centric sports bars can bounce back. As one sports bar owner wondering whether to reopen during the pandemic said, "We don't know what the future holds. Will people ever want to be wedged into a sports bar again?" (111).

IBISWorld forecasts bar and nightclub sector revenues to hit $25.8 billion in 2021, a jump of nearly 16%. Given the persistence of the COVID-19 infection over 2021's first quarter, the Best-Howard Model defers most of the recovery to the second half of the year and estimates U.S. sports bar revenues to grow to $7.95 billion in 2021, an increase more in line with pre-pandemic annual growth rates.

COVID-19's Impact on Sports Entertainment

The pandemic had a differential impact across the six Sports Entertainment segments in the Best-Howard Model. The variation in revenue gains and losses displayed in *Figure 4.35*'s heat maps highlight the effect of thousands of games and events being cancelled and postponed around the world.

The segments most dependent on live events were hardest hit. Sports bars and pubs were devastated. Not only were they deprived of their primary attraction, televised sports, but many were forced to close for months due to public health concerns even after live sports returned. Many were unable to reopen. U.S. sports bars suffered more than $2.6 billion in losses in 2020, a year-to-year decline of 26%.

Global spending on sports betting, fantasy sports and esports all declined in 2020. COVID-19's rapid spread barred fans for months from games to bet, athletes to select for fantasy league rosters and esports tournaments to attend or stream. The relatively modest losses in fantasy play and esports reflects a strong recovery as many countries relaxed pandemic restrictions during the second half of 2020 and the two segments rebounding quickly by delivering services online. Fans facing shelter-in-place restrictions or reluctant to socialize could engage in both activities from their homes or smartphones as sports leagues and events resumed. India reported a drastic increase in esports participation and sales during the pandemic as gaming "became a primary source of entertainment for youth" (112). Call of Duty and Dota 2 experienced 50% increases in hours played.

Sports gambling's significant decline of nearly $17 billion around the world in 2020 largely resulted from widespread casino closures. Casinos throughout Europe shut down in mid-March as the coronavirus spread across the continent.

The famed Casino de Monte-Carlo closed for three months. The venue reopened in June in compliance with strict hygiene measures and reduced hours and capacity limits. Macau,

FIGURE 4.35
COVID-19 Impact Heat Map (U.S. billions)

Global Sports Entertainment	2019	Growth	2020	-50%	0%	50%	2020	2020
Segments	(billions)	Rate	Forecast				(billions)	% Change
Sports Betting	$233.9	6.0%	$248.1		-7.2%		$217.0	-7.2%
Fantasy Sports	$18.6	7.0%	$19.9		-3.7%		$17.9	-3.7%
Esports	$0.98	30.6%	$1.28		-0.1%		$0.95	-0.1%
Sports Video Games	$13.4	12.7%	$15.1		19.4%		$16.0	19.4%
Movies, Books, Mem.	$12.8	--	--		13.2%		$14.3	13.2%
TOTAL	$279.5	--	$284.4		-4.8%		$266.2	-4.8%

Global figures unavailable for sports bars.

U.S. Sports Entertainment	2019	Growth	2020	-50%	0%	50%	2020	2020
Segments	(billions)	Rate	Forecast				(billions)	% Change
Sports Betting	$13.1	6.1%	$13.9			64.1%	$21.5	64.1%
Fantasy Sports	$8.4	7.1%	$9.0		-2.4%		$8.2	-2.4%
Esports	$0.29	27.6%	$0.37		0.0%		$0.29	0.0%
Sports Video Games	$3.3	2.1%	$3.37		15.1%		$3.8	15.1%
Movies, Books, Mem.	$5.9	--	--		18.6%		$7.0	18.6%
Sports Bars	$10.0	0.9%	$10.1	-26.0%			$7.4	-26.0%
TOTAL	$41.0	--	$36.7		17.6%		$48.2	17.6%

often cited as the "gambling capital of the world," suffered huge pandemic losses. With the early COVID-19 outbreak in nearby mainland China, Macau closed its casinos temporarily in February 2020 and imposed cross-border travel restrictions and compulsory quarantines on inbound visitors. When casinos were allowed to reopen, capacity was restricted to 50%. From February through August of 2020, Macau casino revenues plummeted 82% compared to the same six-month period in 2019 (113). Casino sportsbook closures also had a severe impact on gambling in the United States. In Nevada, home of nation's gambling hub, Las Vegas, gaming revenues fell 36% from a near-record $12 billion in 2019 to $7.7 billion in 2020 (114).

Like fantasy and esports providers, however, sports betting services quickly pivoted to online platforms. The result for U.S. gambling revenues was a 64% increase in 2020. By the end of the year, evidence indicated the COVID-19 pandemic had precipitated a monumental shift toward mobile sports betting in the United States, and as much as 80% of all sports betting now occurs online. Worldwide, online gambling revenue is forecast to double to $93 billion by 2023 (1).

Unlike Great Britain, which legalized sports gambling in 1960, the U.S. Supreme Court granted American states the right to offer legal sports betting in 2018. By June 2021, nearly two dozen states and the District of Columbia passed legislation allowing some form of sports betting.

1 Just prior to the release of this edition of The Global Sport Industry, the American Gambling Association (AGA) reported sports betting revenues in the U.S. achieved a record high in 2021. Fueled by the opening of seven new commercial sports betting markets in Arizona. Connecticut, Louisiana, Maryland, South Dakota, Virginia and Wyoming, the sports handle reached $57.2 billion, a 165 percent increase over 2020. AGA forecast continued healthy growth for sports gambling in 2022.

https://www.americangaming.org/new/2021-commercial-gaming-revenue-shatters-industry-record-reaches-53b/

Daily fantasy sports sites and apps are legal and operating in all but eight states (13). The United States accounts for a small portion of total worldwide sports gambling, just $21.5 billion of the 2020 global handle of $217 billion, but analysts project U.S. sports gambling revenue will grow exponentially to more than $100 billion by 2025.[1] The growing demand is propelled by professional sports leagues' embrace of sports betting, and recent studies suggest more than 40% of those who watch sports wager on games, nearly 80% are more likely to watch an entire game if they have a bet on the outcome (115, 116) and, of critical importance to media partners, 61% of those placing bets report greater interest in commercials during telecasts (117). The timing of the United States' abrupt change in sports gambling policy largely insulated the sector from COVID-19, and gambling in many forms will be an increasingly prominent part of fan engagement globally in the post-pandemic world.

The only Sports Entertainment segment not impacted directly by live sports' COVID-19-driven disappearance was sports books, movies and memorabilia. However, some of the sub-segments fared better than others. The widespread closure of theaters devastated the movie industry as 2020 box office revenues plummeted 72% worldwide and 66% in the United States. Over the decade prior to the pandemic, sports-themed movie revenues accounted for only 2%, or $1 billion, of average annual worldwide box office receipts. U.S. studios released only one sports film in 2020, The Way Back starring Ben Affleck, which grossed a modest $14.7 million in the United States and Canada. Like the industry at large, global sports film revenues fell from $610 million in 2019 to less than $270 million in 2020.

While sports films crashed, the sports memorabilia market (e.g., trading cards, sneakers, jerseys) flourished during the pandemic. Global sales grew 14.3% to a record $14 billion in 2020. U.S.-based sports memorabilia sales reached a record high of $6.4 billion, accounting for almost half the worldwide total. What began in the 1970s as a small market has evolved into an international online exchange with many transactions occurring on expanded online trading platforms, which now engage close to 70 million participants. Trading cards were highly coveted during the COVID-19 pandemic, with 23 of the 24 most expensive sports trading cards of all-time being sold since February 2020. One analyst suggested, "The demand for rare [sports trading] cards, especially basketball right now, is just like the demand for fine art" (117).

The COVID-19 pandemic remained a serious threat to sports' full reopening in many world regions well into 2021. India, ravaged by another coronavirus wave, postponed its cricket-focused Premier League indefinitely. Several European soccer leagues faced no or restricted fan attendance for the 2021-22 season. North American sports leagues were more optimistic. COVID-19 vaccination rates were projected to reach 70% by July, meeting a federal government threshold to allow teams to return to full stadiums and arenas.

Regardless of in-person sports attendance, sports industry projections are optimistic for entertainment segments engaging with fans/consumers primarily online. Esports and fantasy sports emerged from the pandemic with record levels of participation globally and in the United States. Live sports events in most world regions, even without fans, should provide sufficient inventory for fantasy sports play and betting to thrive. With more than 3 billion people worldwide expected to actively play video games by 2023—a majority on their smartphones—double digit growth is projected for video game sales over the three to five years post-pandemic.

Considerable uncertainty remains regarding sports bars' recovery given their dependence on in-person service. However, the pre-pandemic popularity of such fan-centric establishments suggests pent-up demand should result in a healthy recovery for sports bars able to reopen when fans are allowed to return.

References

We have added links to many references for direct and easy access. While we have tested each link, there are a few instances where the websites are no longer accessible. We will continue to monitor the accessibility of citation references and remove any links no longer active. In many instances the referenced data was purchased, this is noted.

1. Alice Hancock, "A bet on the sports gambling gold rush," October 15, 2109. The Big Read Gambling Industry

2. "Sports Betting in the United States," 2020. Statista Dossier Plus on Sports Betting. (GSI Purchased Report)

3. Shawn McGrath, "Global Sports Betting & Lotteries," November 2020. IBISWorld (my.ibisworld.com). (GSI Purchased Report)

4. Legal Sports Report, "US Sports Betting Revenue and Handle," March 2020. Legal Sports Report (www.legalsportsreport.com).

5. Bob Woods, "Making a Wager? Half of Americans live in states soon to offer sports gambling," July 10, 2019. CNBC Gaming Reports Inc. (www.cdcgamingreports.com).

6. "Economic Impact of Legalized Sports Betting," (May 2017). Oxford Economics American Gaming (www.americangaming.org).

7. "Deloitte's sports industry starting lineup – Trends expected to disrupt and dominate 2019," (2019), Deloitte Development LLC

8. "Canada's Govt. single-event sports betting bill filed, praised by the Score," November 27, 2020. YOGONET Gaming News (www.yogonet.com).

9. "Canadian Govt. to introduce single sports betting bill," December 8, 2020. YOGONET Gaming News (www.yogonet.com).

10. JohnWallStreet, "Bell Media, Rogers Corp. and The Score best positioned to dominate Canadian sports betting market, December 2, 2020. Sportico

11. Josh Kosman, "Supreme Court lifts federal sports ban on sports gambling," May 14, 2018. New York Post (nypost.com).

12. Sergei Klebnikov, "DraftKing's founders say profitability depends on rollout of States legalizing sports betting," June 11, 2021. Forbes (www.forbes.com).

13. Ryan Butler, "Where is sports betting legal? Projections for all 50 states," May 5, 2021. Action Network (www.actionnetwork.com).

14. Jon Sorenson, "First look inside new sports Book at Capital One Arena" October 15, 2020. NovaCaps (novacapsfans.com).

15. Corey Leff, "Despite overwhelming evidence that mobile sports betting is the future, states continue to pass legislation without option," February 5, 2020. Sportico (www.sportico.com).

16. "Indian Casinos: American Indian Casinos in 501 Gaming Locations," (2020). 500 Nations (500nations.com).

17. S. Lock, "Sports betting handle in commercial casinos in the U.S. 2018-2019," June 18, 2020. Statista (www.statista.com). (GSI Purchased Report)

18. Jesse Pound, "DraftKings surges after announcing ESPN deal," September 14, 2020. CNBC (www.cnbc.com).

19. Evan Novy-Williams, "ESPN links marketing deals with Caesars, DraftKings as sports betting spreads," September 14, 2020. Sportico (www.sportico.com).

20. "How much does the NFL stand to gain from legal sports betting," October 18, 2018. American Gaming Association (www.americangaming.org).

21. Nielsen NFL Study. *American Gaming* (www.americangaming.org).

22. "Americans' 2020 NFL betting plans," September 9, 2020. *American Gaming Association* (www.americangaming.org).

23. "Sportradar said to win NHL gambling data rights, complete U.S. sports sweep," August 16, 2020. *Sportico*

24. Thomas Barrabi, "With NHL deal, Sportradar hits sports betting grand slam, August 17, 2020. *FoxBusiness* (www.foxbusiness.com).

25. Dustin Gouker, "The NFL's big betting deal with Sportradar: Question and Answers," August 12, 2019. *Legal Sports Report* (www.legalsportsreport.com).

26. Arnie Stapleton, "The NFL is now betting big on once-taboo gambling industry," September 4, 2020. *Aol* (www.aol.com).

27. Eben Novey-Williams, "NFL inks nearly $1billion in betting deals with DraftKings, FanDuel and Caesars," April 15, 2021. *Sportico* (www.sportico.com).

28. "NFL announces tri-exclusive official sports betting partners," April 15, 2021. *NFL* (www.nfl.com).

29. Brad Allen, "The NFL keeps profiting from sports betting, adds 888sport as official UK partner," (September 10, 2020). *Legal Sports Report* (www.legalsportsreport.com).

30. Jon Lafayette, "Legal gambling could spur bettors to watch more TV," June 8, 2018. *Broadcasting + Cable* (www.nexttv.com).

31. Matt Rybaltowski, "Simplebet appears ready to transform In-game sports betting through innovative artificial intelligence platform, October 20, 2020. *SportsHandle* (www.sportshandle.com).

32. SBJ Unpacks podcast - The Road Ahead: Simplebet's Chris Bevilacqua, #187, December 17, 2020

33. "Sports betting market by platform and geography – Forecast and analysis 2020-2024," April 2020. *Technavio* (www.technavio.com).

34. "Which countries allow gambling on sports? Assessing the impact of betting around the world," May 16, 2019. *ESPN* (www.espn.com).

35. Web Desk, "3 reasons why sports betting is on the rise in India,' February 9. 2021. *The Week* (www.theweek.in).

36. "India pushes for legal betting sites," December 4, 2020. *EIN Presswire* (www.einnews.com).

37. "Legal Sports Betting in China," January 6, 2021. *Legal Sports Betting* (www.legalsportsbetting.com).

38. S. Lock, "Gambling Industry in United Kingdom (UK) – Statistics & Facts," November 17, 2020. *Statista* (www.statista.com). (GSI Purchased Report)

39. "Industry Demographics," December 27, 2020. *Fantasy Sports & Gaming Association* (www.thefsga.org).

40. Corey Leff, "India's Daily Fantasy Sports market is fertile for VC investment and continued growth," October 12, 2020. *Sportico* (www.sportico.com).

41. "Insights from BCC Research: Fantasy Sports: Market Trends you Need to Know," *BCC Research* (blog.bccresearch.com).

42. "Can Daily Fantasy Sports be a success in the UK? *Stats Perform* (www.statsperform.com).

43. "The growth of daily fantasy sports betting and the legal issues it faces: an interview with Shergul Arshad". *LawInSport* (www.lawinsport.com).

44. Kush Patel, "Fantasy Sports Services," June 2020. *IBISWorld* (my.ibisworld.com). (GSI Purchased Report)

45. "Fantasy Sports Market," 2021. *Allied Market Research* (www.alliedmarketresearch.com).

46. Ryan Chase, "Legality," June 22, 2020. *Daily Fantasy Café* (www.dailyfantasycafe.com).

47. IBEF Blog, "India has a huge potential for fantasy sports," January 5, 2021. *India Brand Equity Foundation* (www.ibef.org).

48. Venkat Ananth, "Fantasy sports in India gaining fast popularity on the back of the IPL," October 17,

2020. _The Economic Times_ (economictimes.indiatimes.com).

49. Robert Capps, "How to make billions in E-sports," February 16, 2020. _The New York Times Magazine_, pp. 46-51, 58-59. (www.nytimes.com).

50. "2020 World Championship [Worlds 2020] detailed viewers stats". _Esports Charts_ (www.escharts.com).

51. Christina Gough, "Expected global eSports audience numbers 2018 to 2023, by type," December 2, 2020. _Statista_ (www.statista.com); A.J. Willingham, "What is eSports? A look at an explosive billion-dollar industry," August 27, 2018. _CNN_ (www.cnn.com). (GSI Purchased Report)

52. "2020 Global Esports Market Report," _NewZoo_ (www.newzoo.com).

53. Trevor Wheelwright, "2021 eSports Report," February 21, 2021. _Reviews_ (www.reviews.org).

54. Hayden Taylor, "Twitch surpasses CNN and MSNBC with record-breaking viewership," February 14, 2018, _Games Industry Biz_ (www.gamesindustry.biz).

55. "Esports in N. America: Entering the major leagues," July 17, 2019. _Canaccord Genuity_ (www.strivesponsorship.com).

56. Christina Gough, "Share of internet users who watch esports tournaments worldwide as of July 2019, by age," October 26, 2020. _Statista_ (www.statista.com). (GSI Purchased Report)

57. "Esports graduates to the big leagues," July 23, 2018. _Deloitte_ (www2.deloitte.com).

58. Sean Takahashi, "Interpret: Women make up 30% of esports audience, up from 6.5% from 2016," February 21, 2109. _Venture Beat_ (www.venturebeat.com).

59. Christina Gough, "eSports market revenue worldwide from 2018 to 2023," October 13, 2020. _Statista_ (www.statista.com). (GSI Purchased Report)

60. Remer Rietkerk, "Covid-19 continues to impact the Esports market: Newzoo revises its Esports revenue forecast, October 7, 2020. _Newzoo_ (www.newzoo.com).

61. Ed Dixon, "'The bang for buck is so much greater': Blast's Robbie Douek evaluates esports' 2021 prospects," February 2, 2021. _SportsPro Media_ (www.sportspromedia.com).

62. "China esports market to hit $1.9 billion in 2019," 2019 Report, _Sports Business_ (www.sportbusiness.com).

63. Joseph Ahn, William Collis and Seth Jenny, "The one-billion dollar myth: Methods for sizing the massively undervalued esports revenue landscape," October 4, 2020. _International Journal of Esports_ (www.ijesports.org).

64. William Collis (2020). The Book of Esports. Rosetta Books

65. Dianna Christie, "Coca-Cola becomes title sponsor of NASCAR's esports race," February 7, 2020 _Marketing Dive_ (www.marketingdive.com); Ben Fischer, "Coca-Cola signs multiyear deal with Activision Blizzard, OWL," February 8, 2019. _Sports Business Journal_ (www.sportsbusinessjournal.com).

66. Andy Fahey, "Monetising esports via multiple revenue streams," January 14, 2020. _PwC_ (www.pwc.com). (GSI Purchased Report)

67. Kevin Webb, "YouTube just scored a major victory in its battle with Amazon's Twitch for esports supremacy, thanks to the company behind 'Call of Duty,' January 24, 2020. _Business Insider_ (www.businessinsider.com).

68. "2017 Global Esports Market Report," _NewZoo_ (www.newzoo.com).

69. Wyatt Fossett, "It has been a banner year for the EA Sports American football franchise's competitive scene, and it ended in a brilliant display of skills that shattered previous Madden viewership numbers " May 3, 2019. _Twin Galaxies_ (www.twingalaxies.com).

70. Hrithik Unnikrishnan, "EA Madden NFL 21 announces revamped championship series," August 8, 2020. _Essentially Sports_ (www.essentiallysports.com).

71. SBJ Unpacks, "The Road Ahead: Sports Video Games with Todd Sitrin of EA Sports," _Podcast SBJ Unpack 65_ (podcasts.apple.com).

72. Jay Busbee, "Study: NASCAR fans are oldest TV viewers; NBA, soccer are the youngest," June 17, 2107.

Yahoo Sports (sports.yahoo.com).

73. Yang Yue, & Wang Rui, "Development of E-sports industry in China: Current situation, Trend and research hotspot," November 26, 2020. *International Journal of Esports* (www.ijesports.org).

74. Tom Elsden, "Opinion – Five trends shaping the Chinese esports landscape," July 10, 2020. SP Smart Series. *SportsPro Media* (www.sportspromedia.com).

75. J. Clement, "Video game market value worldwide from 2012 to 2013," January 29, 2021. *Statista* (www.statista.com). (GSI Purchased Report)

76. "2020 Global Games Market Report," *Newzoo* (resources.newzoo.com).

77. Dan Cook, "Video Games in the US," December 2020. *IBISWorld* (my.ibisworld.com). (GSI Purchased Report)

78. Tom Wijman, "Global Game Revenues Up an Extra $15 billion this Year as Engagement Skyrockets," November 4, 2020. *Newzoo* (www.newzoo.com).

79. J. Clement, "Genre breakdown of U.S. video games in 2018," January 29, 2021. *Statista* (www.statista.com). (GSI Purchased Report)

80. "Video game charts, Game sales, Top Sellers," March 5, 2021. *VGChartz* (www.vgchartz.com).

81. Jeff Grubb, "2019's top-selling games of the year," January 16, 2021. *Venture Beat* (www.venturebeat.com).

82. J. Clement, "First month digital sales of FIFA 20 and FIFA 21 worldwide as on November 2020," January 21, 2021. *Statista* (www.statista.com). (GSI Purchased Report)

83. Mark Lurgis, "NBA 2K21 sells 8 million copies despite $70 price tag," February 9, 2021. *The Gamer* (www.thegamer.com).

84. "The Mind-Blowing Figures Behind EA Sports' Net Revenue from Ultimate Team," May 2020. *Sport Bible* (www.sportbible.com).

85. Julia Stoll, "Global box office revenue 2004-2019, by region," January 13, 2021. *Statista* (www.statista.com). (GSI Purchased Report)

86. Naman Ramachadran, "Global Cinema Industry set to lose $32 billion in 2020, says Omida Report. *Variety* (www.variety.com).

87. Greorg Szalai, "Global cinema revenue to drop 66 percent in 2020 amid pandemic: Forecast," September 3, 2020. *The Hollywood Reporter* (www.hollywoodreporter.com).

88. Anna Miller, "Movie Theaters in the US," September 2020. *IBISWorld* (my.ibisworld.com). (GSI Purchased Report)

89. Mark Young, et. al., "The Business of Selling Movies," June 7, 2007. Strategic Finance.

90. Sarah Whitten, "Movie theaters in jeopardy as studios move blockbusters to 2021, audiences stay at home," September 29, 2020. *CNBC* (www.cnbc.com).

91. Dennis Tuttle, "Once-reliable US sports publishing market hits heavy decline," December 18, 2019. *Sports Business* (www.sportbusiness.com).

92. Amy Watson, " U.S. book industry – statistics & facts, November 10, 2020. *Statista* (www.statista.com). (GSI Purchased Report)

93. "Book Market in the U.S.," 2020. *Statista* (www.statista.com). (GSI Purchased Report)

94. Alexandra Alter, "Coronavirus shutdowns Weigh on Book Sales, May 19, 2020. *New York Times* (www.nytimes.com).

95. Kate Knibbs, "The coronavirus pandemic is changing how people buy books,", April 27, 2020. *Wired* (www.wired.com).

96. Statista Research Department, "Book Market in Europe – Statistics & Facts," June 25, 2018. *Statista* (www.statista.com). (GSI Purchased Report)

97. Dan Weil, "The market for sports memorabilia continues to score big." December 15, 2019. *Wall Street Journal* (www.wsj.com).

98. "The Financialization of Everything," July 20, 2020. *John Street Capital* (john-street-capital.medium.com).

99. "19 sports memorabilia industry statistics and trends," 2021. 19 Sports Memorabilia. *Brandon Gaille* (www.brandongaille.com).

100. David Seideman, "Tech Entrepreneur determines first estimate of U.S. sports memorabilia market: $5.4 billion," September 18, 2018. *Forbes* (www.forbes.com).

101. Darren Heitner, "Playing Ball in the Multi-Billion dollar sports collectible market, *Forbes* (www.forbes.com).

102. Darren Rovell, "Rovell: Pair of Michael Jordan Rookie Cards sell for Record $738K Each," January 31, 2021. *Action Sports* (www.actionnetwork.com).

103. Robert Channick, Baseball cards are booming during the pandemic, with long lines, short supplies and million-dollar sales, February 12, 2021. *Chicago Tribune* (www.chicagotribune.com).

104. "Top 500 Chains," *Restaurant Business* (www.restaurantbusinessonline.com).

105. Lisa White, "Sports bars hit a homerun," June 1, 2018. *Foodservice* (fesmag.com).

106. Thomas Barrabi, " Buffalo Wild Wings tackles sports betting with MGM Resorts deal, September 5, 2019. *Fox Business* (www.foxbusiness.com).

107. Khristopher Brooks, "A very different Super Bowl for sports bars: "If I break even, I'm happy," one owner says," February 5, 2021. *CBS News* (www.cbsnews.com).

108. "Market Growth Monitor: Quarterly review of GB pub, bar and restaurant supply," August 2019. *Alix Partners* (www.alixpartners.com).

109. "Market Recovery Monitor: Review of GB pub, bar and restaurant supply" March 2021. *Alix Partners* (www.alixpartners.com).

110. Brigette Thomas, "Bars & Nightclubs in the US," December 2020. *IBISWorld* (my.ibisworld.com). (GSI Purchased Report)

111. Kelly Cohen, "How sports bars have struggled to stay open during the pandemic," January 26, 2021. *ESPN* (www.espn.com).

112. Suraj Iyer, "How eSports has grown in India amid the lockdown imposed due to COVID-19," June 20, 2020. *The Bridge* (thebridge.in); Aahana Mehrotra and Pratyush Pandey, " India: Impact of Covid-19 on The Business of Sports." December 2020. *Mondaq* (www.mondaq.com).

113. Hong-Wai Ho, "COVID-19 pandemic: Impact and implications for Macau casinos," October 20, 2020. *Gaming Law Review*: Vol. 24, No. 8 (www.liebertpub.com).

114. Ed Komenda, "When will Nevada tourism rebound? 'It's going to be a while.' Here's what needs to happen," December 15, 2020. *Reno Gazette Journal* (www.rgj.com).

115. Gavin Bridge, "Survey: Legalization of sports gambling could lead to increased sports viewing," July 3, 2019. *Variety* (www.variety.com).

116. "Have sports viewership and sports betting been impacted by the pandemic? The Harris Poll, October 23-26, 2020. *The Harris Poll* (theharrispoll.com).

117. Chris Bengel, "LeBron James card sells record $5.2 million, tying record mark for most expensive sports card," April 27, 2021. *CBS News* (www.cbsnews.com).

PART III:
Sports Products

Sports Products allow athletes to engage in sports and outdoor recreation activities with enhanced enjoyment, performance and safety.

Consider the product-intensive sport of pole-vaulting. Pole-vaulting requires tremendous strength, speed and agility. But to successfully vault over a crossbar, athletes depend on various specialized sports products:

• **Sportswear:** Shoes and apparel impact speed, which accounts for 67% of the height pole-vaulters achieve.

• **Sports Equipment:** The pole, running surface, pole box and landing pads enhance performance and safety.

• **Sports Health and Wellness:** Sports medicine, therapy and nutrition impact pole-vaulter performance and alleviate injury.

SPORSTWEAR

SPORTS EQUIPMENT

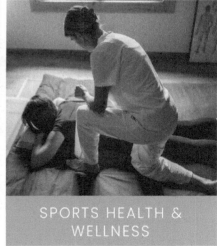

SPORTS HEALTH & WELLNESS

Since 1850, pole-vaulters have set 105 world records (*Figure I*). Innovations in footwear, apparel, poles, running surfaces, pole boxes, landing pads, sports medicine, therapy, nutrition and science-based training have influenced each world record.

The first pole-vault world record was recorded in 1850, with a height of 10 feet 4 inches. Armand Duplantis set the latest record in 2020 at 20 feet 3 inches. Pole-vaulters today are certainly better trained than they were 170 years ago, but Sports Products have played an indisputable role in the steady improvement of the sport's world record (1).

FIGURE I
Pole Vault World Records

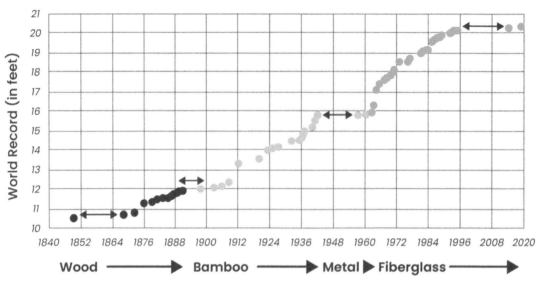

Figure II shows pole-vault material's evolution, from wood to bamboo around 1900, then to metal from 1945 to 1960, and finally to fiberglass. While analysts often focus on pole material, speed during the run-up is the primary driver of pole-vault height. The run generates kinetic energy, which is transferred to the pole, then to the athlete. Pole-vaulters have achieved faster speeds with lighter poles, improved running surfaces, engineered running shoes and advanced apparel.

FIGURE II
Pole-Vault Product Innovations

POLE VAULT ERA YEARS	1850–1998	1899–1944	1945–1960	1961–2020
World Records	24	27	2	52
Height Change	10'4" to 11'10.5"	11'11" to 15'7.25"	15'8" to 15'9"	15'10" to 20'3"
Pole Material	Wood	Bamboo	Metal	Fiberglass
Running Surface	Ground	Cinder	Asphalt	Plastic
Pole Box	None	Wood	Metal	Angled
Landing Area	None	Sand or Sawdust	Piled Foam	Foam Pad
Shoe Upper	Cow Leather	Calf or Elk	Kanagroo	Polymers
Shoe Sole	No Spike	Spike	Short Spike	Matrix Polymer
Apparel	Cotton & Wool	Cotton & Silk	Cotton & Poly	Polymer

An improved pole box helped pole-vaulters achieve a better entry angle and energy transfer. Landing surface innovations reduced injuries and enhanced athlete confidence. In total, the world records in *Figure I* resulted from a combination of elite athlete performance and innovations in sportswear, equipment and health.

Pole-vaulting is hardly alone in its dependence on high performance products and gear. The Sports Products domain of the Best-Howard Sports Industry Model accounts for all products used in all sports. In 2019, Sports Products revenues were $940 billion worldwide. The United States accounted for 40.4% of global sales. The Sports Products domain is built around the three core areas shown in *Figure III*: Sportswear, Equipment and Health & Wellness.

FIGURE III
Sports Products 2019 Revenues

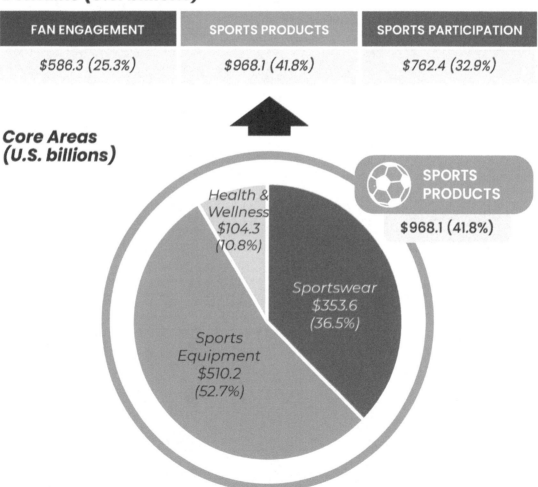

Copyright Best-Howard Model 2022. All Right Reserved.

Part III of The Sports Industry examines each of the Sports Products core areas. To learn more about them, watch the video of sports gear guru Matt Powell, vice president of NPD Group, in *Figure IV* (2). Powell is a recognized authority on sports product sales.

FIGURE IV
Sports Products 2019 Revenues

Source: https://www.youtube.com/watch?v=PlVviHVNN9c

SPORTSWEAR

CHAPTER 5

Sport, Athleisure & Work

Sportswear's unique contribution to the $2.3 trillion worldwide sports industry is found in its broad reach to consumers. An essential part of the sports products domain, sportswear's influence extends well beyond sports. Sportswear defines many sports and fitness activities, while also providing a specific fashion identity along with everyday comfort at home and at the workplace.

Figure 5.1 shows sportswear segments ranging from sport/outdoor fitness to fashion, workwear and leisure wear. While sportswear for sports and outdoor activities makes up roughly 20% of sales in the U.S., the largest American sportswear segment is athleisure at 60%. Athleisure is a style of clothing that is comfortable and suitable for sports, but also fashionable and casual enough to wear for other activities. Workwear, a fast-growing segment, makes up roughly 20% of sales in the U.S.

By 2028, the global athleisure market size is anticipated to reach $549.4 billion, with an estimated compound average growth rate of 8.6% (1). In 2020, athleisure sales were estimated to make up roughly 60% of global sportswear sales at $211 billion. Sportswear sub-segments in *Figure 5.1* will be discussed in this chapter. Global and U. S. Sales for each segment, from 2010 to 2019, will also be discussed, along with growth rates and strategic insights into sub-segment trending. The impact of Covid-19 on sportswear sales in 2020 is presented in the last section of this chapter.

FIGURE 5.1
Sportswear Consumer Segments

	TEAMS	INDIVIDUALS	OUTDOOR
SPORTS & OUTDOOR	Baseball Basketball Soccer	Golf Running Tennis	Hiking Winter Sports Water Sports
	FITNESS	**STREETWEAR**	**LEISURE**
ATHLEISURE	Yoga Group Fitness Aerobics	Lifestyle Fashion Athletic	Comfort Fit Ease to Use
	MEDICAL	**SERVICE**	**BUSINESS**
WORKWEAR	Health Care Lab Work Vet Services	Trade Workers Hospitality Food Service	Tech Workers Business Casual Office Staff

Overall sportswear is 36.5% of the Sports Product Domain as shown in *Figure 5.2.* In 2019, sportswear revenues were derived from the three-sportswear sub-segments, as illustrated in *Figure 5.1.* In 2019, athletic footwear and apparel accounted for 97.6% of all sportswear revenue. Wearable technology is relatively new but growing at a high rate worldwide.

FIGURE 5.2
The Best-Howard Model's Sportswear Core Areas

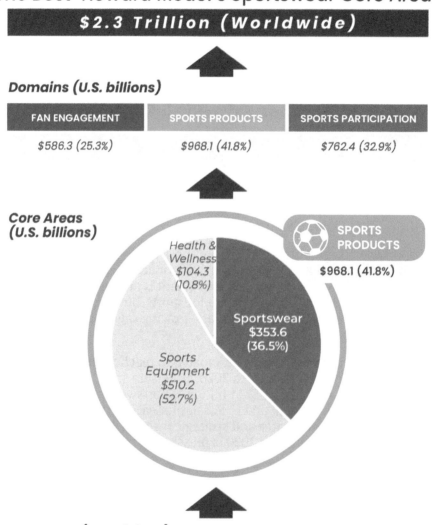

Sportswear Segments	Revenues	Percent
Footwear	$ 140.0	39.6 %
Apparel	$ 205.1	58.0 %
Wearables	$ 8.5	2.4 %
TOTAL	$ 353.6	100.0 %

Sportswear goes beyond the realm of athletics, extending into fitness, fashion, everyday leisure and workwear. However, most sportswear innovations are derived from the unique challenges faced by elite athletes. Thus, when designing sportswear for competitive athletes, designers must first observe how such athletes challenge their bodies to such an exceptional degree. This data is then used to better understand the attributes necessary to make sportswear that remains secure to bodies throughout intense performance, all while providing comfort, durability and reliability. Designers also conduct in-depth interviews with athletes to gain further insight into their past experiences with sportswear and developments they hope to see in the future.

The process of obtaining an "Athlete Insight" helps uncover athletes' frustrations with the current market of sports products, thereby identifying benefits athletes want but cannot achieve in current products. With careful athlete insight, sportswear developers often create new products that better meet athlete needs and contribute to higher levels of performance, safety and comfort.

Key takeaways from an "Athlete Insight" interview with Raevyn Rogers, a five-time NCAA champion and Nike-sponsored professional runner (2) are presented in *Figure 5.3*. Rogers explained her needs in three categories: Function and Fit, Comfort and Feel and Performance. Brands that met her expectations in all three categories earned Rogers' trust. Without brand trust, the potential for a "flow experience" would not be possible. A flow experience occurs in a high-stakes competition when the athlete loses self-consciousness; one's experience of time passing considerably slows down, evoking elated feelings of self-accomplishment (3). Thus, successful performance of sportswear must fit like a second skin, operate gracefully without requiring input from the wearer and remain in place under the harsh demands of athletic activity.

FIGURE 5.3
Athlete Insight & Brand Trust

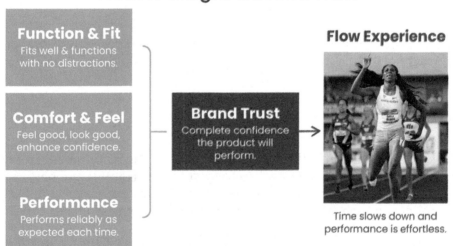

Function & Fit
Fits well & functions with no distractions.

Comfort & Feel
Feel good, look good, enhance confidence.

Performance
Performs reliably as expected each time.

Brand Trust
Complete confidence the product will perform.

Flow Experience

Time slows down and performance is effortless.

Sportswear allows us to engage with recreational activities in a way that enhances both physical performance and safety. Yet, sportswear also needs to fit well while looking good. A poorly designed shoe heel will eventually lead to foot injuries, whether you are a professional basketball player or a middle manager. In this sense, sports products are not just for elite athletes. Rather, only 7% of all sports products is purchased for professional use (4). Only 15% of sports shoes and just 25% of sports apparel are purchased for sports use (5). At their core, sportswear products fulfill the following needs:

• **Function & Performance:** This varies by sport, recreational activity and everyday use. What do I need from the sportswear I choose?

• **Comfort & Fit:** Comfort and fit will drive purchase and re-purchase, whether the apparel is destined for elite athletes, sports enthusiasts, casual users of sportswear, or for those whose job requires them to be constantly on their feet (waiters, nurses, etc.).

• **Fashion & Style:** Sportswear allows sports fans to express their team loyalty while providing non-sports consumers an opportunity to make a personal statement through their choice of street-fashion.

Sports & Outdoor

Sportswear is comprised of sports footwear, apparel and wearables. "Sports consumers" have always been a core focus for the sportswear industry, making up its primary focus group for many years. Today, these buyers are still the primary focus for most sportswear companies, even though this category of consumer only contributes less than 25% of global sales. Why?

These athletes provide the laboratory to study user needs and product performance. Companies seek to improve their products by meeting the most demanding needs of professional and amateur athletes. As shown in *Figure 5.4*, the range of needs of the different segments of sportswear.

FIGURE 5.4
Sportswear Needs-Based Segments

PURCHASE CONSIDERATIONS	SPORTS & OUTDOOR	ATHLEISURE			WORKWEAR	
		FITNESS	STREETWEAR	LEISURE	LABOR	OFFICE
Performance	✗	✗			✗	
Function	✗	✗	✗	✗	✗	✗
Fit	✗	✗	✗	✗	✗	✗
Comfort	✗	✗	✗	✗	✗	✗
Fashion	✗	✗	✗	✗		✗

Perhaps, more so than not for any other sportswear product, the requirements for elite women's swimsuits are critical, especially as they relate to fit, function, comfort and performance. For these athletes, their swimsuits are like "second skins," in which every aspect of the product plays a role in building up the athletes' trust and confidence in the swimsuit itself.

To illustrate this point further, consider Katie Ledecky, shown in *Figure 5.5*, is winner of 5 Olympic gold medals and 15 World Championship gold medals, the most in history for a female swimmer. Even an exceptional athlete as Katie Ledecky needs a swimsuit that can deliver on each requirement. It typically takes 20 painstaking minutes to put on the delicate, lightweight, compression-fabric swimsuit that women competitors wear. Because a competitive swimmer wants a suit that fits perfectly over the unique contours of her body, function and fit can be challenges. Straps, cuts and seams are all potential points of discomfort and even hindrances to her hydrodynamics. Once these concerns are resolved, the swimmer can be confident that they are utilizing apparel designed to work in tandem with her body, to perform at a high level.

FIGURE 5.5
Swimsuit Requirements – Competitive Woman Swimmers

Function & Fit
• Lightweight
• Repels Water
• Desired Fit

>

Comfort & Feel
• Soft and Comfortable
• Breaths
• Feels and Looks Good

>

Performance
• Does Not Ride
• Anti-Pilling
• Minimum Drag

>

After considering function and fit, the swimsuit for competitive swimmers, a suit performs well if it does not ride up during competition, the fabric does not pill and create drag and the suit repels water so that it remains lightweight. Once a suit has earned a swimmer's trust, the swimmer can more easily enter the psychological state of supreme confidence necessary for the flow experience.

Athleisure

This term describes sportswear used for exercise and casual wear. However, many consumers also wear sportswear for everyday comfort and fashion. This large and trendy segment of the sports apparel market has been around since the 1920s, developed originally around tennis and its accompanying fashion sense (6). Tennis outfits in the 1920s were functional, comfortable and fashionable. The tennis headscarf influenced many covers of Vogue, as women wore these scarves for fashion, not to excel at tennis. Likewise, V-neck tennis sweaters, polo shirts and casual tennis trousers found their way into country club fashion and casual sportswear (*Figure 5.6*).

FIGURE 5.6
Tennis Sportswear in the 1920s

This category of sportswear is the largest consumer segment shown in *Figure 5.7*, and it includes three sub-segments (7). Each sub-segment is discussed in the following sections to illustrate how the lifestyle of each sub-segment created a unique set of needs

FITNESS, FUNCTION & FASHION: Fitness and fashion meet in the core segment of athleisure apparel. Athleisure apparel is a fabricated style of hybrid clothing typically worn during athletic activities and in other settings, such as the workplace, school and other casual, social occasions. This segment was largely influenced by the emergence of LuluLemon in 1997 and similar companies that designed sportswear using the fashion sense of Yoga (particularly its emergence in West Coast popular culture during the 1990s) as its aesthetic foundation.

This style combines stretchy nylon with subdued colors and soft textures, thereby creating a more uniform yet sleeker look than the technicolor extravaganza of the Aerobic exercise scene of the 1980s. This new Yoga style of athletic clothing fueled growth in the athleisure fitness and lifestyle market. Typical outfits included yoga pants, tights, sneakers, leggings and shorts that "looked like athletic wear" and were characterized as "fashionable, dressed up sweats and exercise clothing." By the end of the 20th century and into the 21st, Gym clothes made their way out of the gym and are still now becoming a larger part of people's everyday wardrobes than ever before. This turn in everyday fashion is communicated well in *Figure 5.7*, which depicts the athleisure trends that have influenced streetwear fashion.

FIGURE 5.7
Athleisure – Function, Fashion & Fun

Streetwear- Fashion & Comfort: The sportswear needs of the "Streetwear Consumer" are primarily focused on function, comfort and fashion with the emphasis on fashion. Street wear style emerged from New York City's Hip Hop culture of the late 1970s, from the early 1980s LA surf and skateboard culture, and from the Japanese punk and hip-hop culture in the 1990s. Sportswear brands Schott NYC, Dr. Martens, Kangol, Fila and Adidas have become an important part of street wear fashion in major cities.

Sportswear commonly centers on "casual, comfortable pieces such as jeans, T-shirts, baseball caps and sneakers." Due to their common components, their relative value derives from intentional product scarcity. In doing so, enthusiasts follow particular brands and try to obtain limited edition releases. In the 2000s, the advent of "Bling" culture saw established luxury brands make inroads into the market, with Burberry, Gucci and Fendi making appearances in hip-hop videos and films. The most popular shoe of this era was the Nike Air Force 1.

In the 2010s, some street wear brands were coveted, as much as the historically elite fashion brands. Complex Magazine named Stussy, Supreme and A Bathing Ape as the top street wear brands. Many went on to collaborate with high fashion brands, such as Louis Vuitton, Fendi, Commes des Garcons and Dior. The Figure 5.8 video offers a look at current trends in street wear fashion.

Leisure Lifestyle- Function & Comfort: The "Leisure Segment" quickly adopted the comfort and ease of use (functionality) of less expensive sneakers, sweatpants, T-shirts and hoodies in the mid-1970s. Everyday people who were not necessarily athletes or sports enthusiasts found comfort in sportswear at prices they could afford. This segment grew as millions of consumers transitioned from everyday shoes to sneakers and from weekend jeans to more comfortable sweatpants and shorts. The "Leisure Consumer" continues to drive enormous growth worldwide.

FIGURE 5.8
Athleisure – Sportswear Fashion Streetwear Trends

Source: https://www.youtube.com/watch?v=YcMGCIhDa58

Workwear

The choice of sportswear in the workplace is a derivative of athleisure. The function and comfort offered by sportswear was quickly adopted among those in the labor force who spent most of their workday on their feet. *Figure 5.4* shows this portion of the workplace as physical work.

A more recent trend is sportswear worn in the "business" workplace. For many years, computer programmers working long hours have shown a preference for the comfort of sportswear. More recently, "business-casual," a trend dating back to the 1990s, began to include sneakers, sports shirts and other more fashionable sportswear. Each of these workplace markets is different in needs and product usage. For that reason, each will be explained in more detail.

Work – Comfort & Performance: A decade ago, denim workwear uniforms were common. Today, sportswear is increasingly popular among workers in the service industries, the health care sector, electricians and plumbers, independent contractors, delivery services and a variety of broadcasting companies.

Due to innovations in textiles and technology, improvements in functionality have led to garments and footwear that are more breathable, lightweight and waterproof. The new design enhances performance by allowing the consumer to carry out every day work activities with greater ease and comfort.

For example, the U. S. Market for Nurses' Footwear is approximately $1 billion in annual sales, dominated by sneaker brands that focus on athletes and by fashion sneaker brands with a focus on style. Until BALA came forward, no manufacturer had produced footwear designed specifically for nurses. When it came to discerning female sizes, most major footwear brand designs just shrunk down their male sizes to fit assumed specifications. On the other hand, BALA takes a "Her First" approach, using female foot morphology, as illustrated in *Figure 5.9.* The video highlights the athletic performance of this sneaker designed specifically to accommodate both the female body and the work environment that nurses encounter every day.

FIGURE 5.9
Footwear Designed for Nurses

BALA'S NURSING SHOE

- **Fit:** Optimized for nurses.

- **Comfort:** Enhanced by inner bootie.

- **Safety:** Fluid Protection, easy to clean & breathable.

- **Performance:** Provides support through the arch.

Source: https://www.youtube.com/watch?v=LaspI2miNqQ

Office – Fashion & Comfort: Business casual started in the 1990s, and it evolved into sportswear casual in today's workplace. By 2020 this clothing category was increasingly accepted in the business workplace. Prior to the COVID-19 pandemic, sneakers and more upscale sports apparel were already working their way into the offices of corporate America. The pandemic led to many employees working from home, making the preferred business attire sneakers, slippers, shorts, sweats and tops that looked good enough for a waist-up Zoom meeting.

In luxury department stores, such as Neiman Marcus, sneakers now account for 50 percent of the men's shoe business. Executives in Silicon Valley almost exclusively wear high-priced sneakers—including Lanvin, Common Projects and Louis Vuitton high-top sneakers (8). Styles, colors and fabrics suggest a stronger emphasis on fashion than functionality. Advances in fabric and production technology will enable yoga pants to be totally acceptable when America returns to the office. Brands working in this category include Epoque Evolution, Veilance and Rhone. Who knows what the future workplace will look like? We can safely bet it will accommodate more home office hours, causing the dividing line between business attire and sportswear to further disappear.

Sportswear Revenues

Sportswear includes footwear, apparel and wearables. In 2019, the Pre-COVID-19 global sales were $353.6 billion. U. S. Sales were 36.8% of this total at $130.1 billion (*Figure 5.10*). Pre-pandemic global sales of sportswear were growing at 4.6% from 2010 to 2019 (9). The United States rate of growth for the same period was 7.4%. As a result, the percent of sales that occurred in the U. S. grew from 28.9% in 2010 to 36.8% in 2019.

FIGURE 5.10
Sportswear Revenues – Global vs U.S. (billions)

YEAR	2010	2015	2019	CAGR
Global	$235.5	$296.2	$353.7	4.6%
United States	$68.0	$98.2	$130.1	7.4%
% United States	28.9%	33.2%	36.8%	-

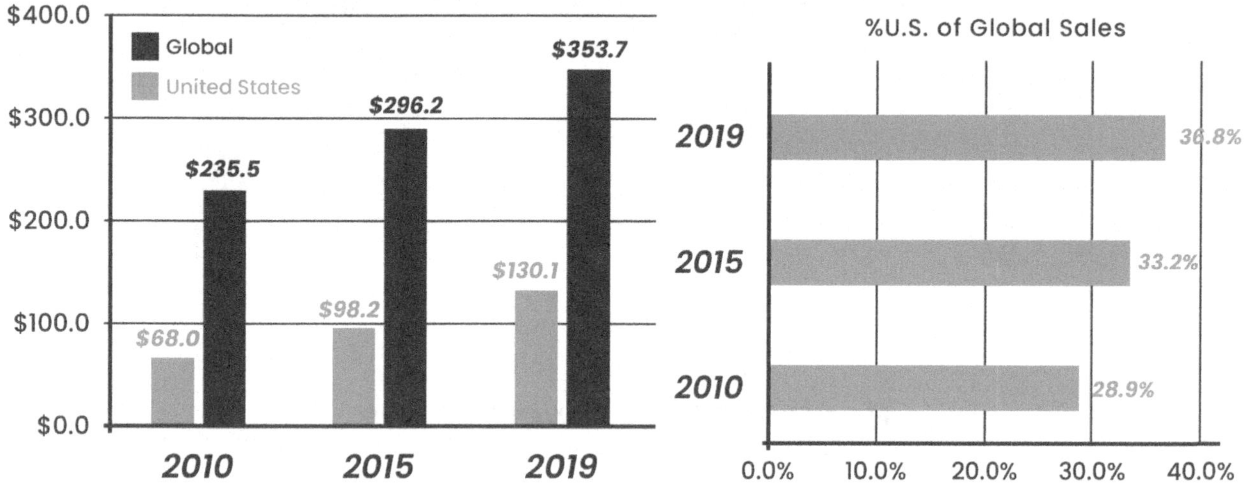

Sportswear Consumer Economics

When we look at sportswear sales per household, we can see how enormous the U. S. Market is with respect to the average global consumer. The average U. S. household spent $1078 in 2019, the year before the Covid-19 Pandemic (*Figure 5.11*). The 2019 global average was $167 per household. If the U.S. is removed from the global average, the rest of the world produces sportswear sales of $112 per household.

Why is this important? U. S.-based businesses seeking to sell their products globally may have to adjust their designs to fit a country's lifestyle and cultural preferences, as well as adjust the price of their sportswear. If the average cost of sportswear spent by an entire household in many countries is $112, that same household does have many options when it comes to buying sportswear at U. S. prices. Using household and consumer spending data, produced by Oxford Economics (10), we gained some additional sportswear sales insights (*Figure 5.11*).

In 2019 the average U. S. household spends $112,353 on consumption. This is almost 7 times the expenditure of the average household for the rest of the world. U. S. Sportswear sales were almost 1% of consumer spending in 2019. Consumer spending on sportswear globally was .74%. The U. S. market has more money to spend and U.S. consumers spend at a higher rate than the global average. The percent of consumer spending on sportswear has increased over the last 10 years, and it can be expected to continue to increase as consumers bring more sportswear into their lives at the gym, home, around town and at work.

FIGURE 5.11
Sportswear Sales and Buying Economics (billions)

Geographic Scope	Sportswear Sales	Household (millions)	Sportswear Sales per HH	Consumer Spending per HH	% Sportswear of Consumer Spending
Global	$353.6	$2,118.8	$167	$22,489	0.74%
U.S.	$130.1	$120.7	$1,078	$112,353	0.96%
Rest of World	$223.5	$1,998.1	$112	$17,061	0.66%

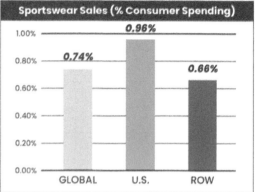

Regional Sportswear Sales

While the summary data in *Figure 5.11* illustrates how much larger the U. S. market is in total sales per household than the rest of the world, *Figure 5.12* provides a more complete view of sportswear spending by global region. In Chapter 11 we will expand this analysis to the top 10 sports countries in the world. Chapter 12 will examine the 50 cities that spend the most on sportswear.

Europe and Asia-Pacific regions accounted for nearly 50% of worldwide sales in 2019 (11) as shown in *Figure 5.12*. Latin America, Middle East and Africa made up 13.7% of global sportswear sales in 2019. North America contributed 37% of worldwide sportswear sales in 2019. Sportswear sales per household again show how much different North America is from other regions. Even in Europe it would take almost 4 households at $229 each in sportswear sales per household to equal one North American household's spending of $962. There are clearly more households in the Asia-Pacific region (52.6% of the world) but household spending in sportswear in that region is only $79, just 9% of the average household spending in North America.

It is also interesting to examine differences in sportswear purchases by region. In Latin America roughly 62% of the $134 average spent per household on sportswear sales is on sports footwear and 38.5% on sports apparel. At the other extreme, in North America 33% of sportswear sales consists of footwear, and 67% on apparel.

Figure 5.13 shows global and North American sportswear sales from 2010 to 2019. Sales in North America grew at a 6.3% rate during this period, while global sales grew by 4.6%. Global sales occurring in North America increased from 29,2% to 36.8%. This growth will important strategic implications over the next five years. North America can be expected to continue to grow as a percentage of global sales. Therefore, North America is a key market for companies outside the region who hope to expand their global share of sportswear sales.

FIGURE 5.12
Regional Revenues & Socio-Economics

REGION	Sportswear Sales (bil.)	Sportswear % Global	Percent Apparel	Percent Footwear	Population (mil.)	Percent Population	Households (mil.)	Percent Households	Sportswear Sales/HH
North America	$130.8	37.0%	67.1%	32.9%	367.8	4.9%	135.9	6.3%	$962
Europe	$82.4	23.3%	61.5%	38.5%	916.7	12.1%	359.7	16.7%	$229
Asia-Pacific	$91.9	26.0%	52.6%	47.4%	4,108.4	54.2%	1157.4	53.8%	$79
Latin America	$25.7	7.3%	38.5%	61.5%	657.1	8.7%	191.3	8.9%	$134
Mid East-Africa	$22.8	6.4%	58.8%	41.2%	1525.5	20.1%	308.9	14.3%	$74
Total/Average	$353.6	100.0%	59.6%	40.4%	7575.5	100.0%	2153.3	100.0%	$164

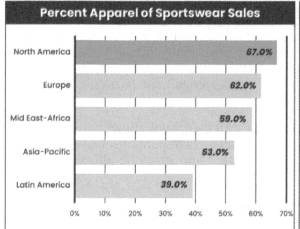

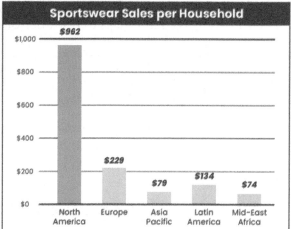

FIGURE 5.13
Sportswear Sales – Global vs. North America (billions)

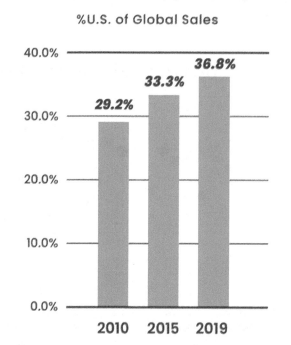

Sportswear sales are shown in *Figure 5.14* in three segments to better illustrate size and growth rates globally. Because the U.S. is such a large market, U. S. sales and growth rates for these three segments of sportswear are delineated.

• **Footwear**—includes purchases by the millions of people who wear running shoes for work (nurses, bartenders, service industry personnel), those who wear sport shoes as streetwear (often style-specific to cities) and a wide range of footwear from casual shoes to hiking shoes and boots, including ski boots and other sport-specific footwear.

• **Apparel** -includes specialized clothing, such as swimsuits, wetsuits, ski apparel and gymnastic leotards, as well as everyday sports apparel, streetwear, fashion and sports apparel appropriate for work. Also included are accessories such as hats, socks, gloves and scarfs.

• **Wearables** – includes digital products by performance athletes, sport enthusiasts, walkers and those engaged in fitness to track performance and health-related metrics.

Sportswear for professional and amateur sports and for recreational sports offers consumer benefits designed to optimize performance in their sport or recreational activity. Shoes specifically designed for baseball, track and basketball are designed to be particularly effective for the particular kinds of movements used in each sport.

In addition to functionality, sportswear is also a fashion statement that allows consumers to project a desired look. Sportswear is also a big part of fan engagement. Professional and college teams provide sportswear, featuring team colors, logos and jersey numbers for fans to choose from.

Sportswear Sales Seasonality

Figure 5.14 shows the U. S. quarterly sales of sportswear from 2015 to 2019. This sales trend depicts an overall growth rate of 7.6%. The variation around the third trend line is due to seasonal effects of U. S. consumers buying of sportswear (14). Seasonal influence is estimated with the seasonal indexes shown. Winter season U.S. sales are 20% below the yearly average and have a seasonality index of .80 (the average winter sales divided by average sales for a year).

FIGURE 5.14
United States Sportswear Seasonality (billions)

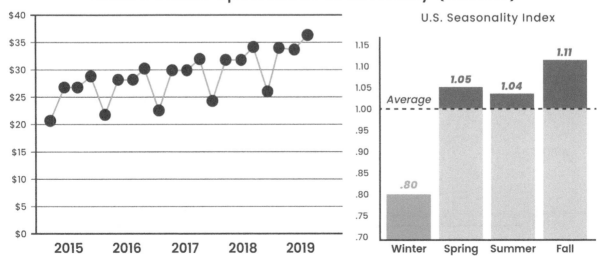

In the spring and summer, U. S. sales of sportswear are 4% to 5% higher than average. In the fall, sportswear sales are 11% above average, due to back-to-school buying and purchases related to college, professional sports and holiday buying. The biggest adjustment to sportswear sales happens when sales go from 11% above average in the fall quarter to 20% below average in the winter quarter (*Figure 5.14*). The steep drop in sales creates an important challenge for production and supply chain management, as there is a 31% swing in average sales from fall to winter. Of course, we would expect the effects of seasonality are likely to be different across the world based on differences in climate, consumer lifestyles, and buying power. Also, different sports have a seasonality which also impact these seasonal averages.

Sports Footwear

Worldwide sales of sports footwear grew 5.3% from $88 billion in 2010 to $140 billion in 2019. U. S. sales were 23% of global sales in 2010 and grew to 28.2% of worldwide sales in 2019. U. S. sales grew at a rate of 7.7% per year, as shown in *Figure 5.15*. The data presented in *Figure 5.15* was obtained from the 2020 Euromonitor as referenced earlier (12).

FIGURE 5.15
Sport Footwear Sales (billions)

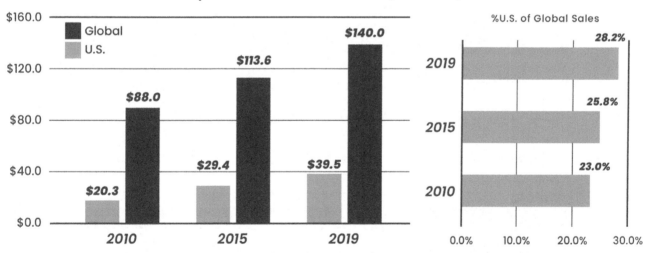

Sports footwear covers a wide range of shoes for different sports and outdoor recreation activities. *Figure 5.16* illustrates both the breadth of uses and U. S. revenues for four sub-segments of sport footwear (15). Fitness footwear was the largest sub-segment. The percent of footwear sales associated with athleisure is about 42% of total U. S. sports footwear sales.

What makes this core area unique is that the sales of this sportswear go beyond athletes. Millions use sports footwear as everyday wear for the sake of comfort. Not included in these tables is the sports footwear purchased by service industry workers and tradespeople like nurses, painters, retail workers, delivery people and restaurant and hospitality workers who wear these shoes.

FIGURE 5.16
U.S. Sport, Fitness and Outdoor Footwear (millions)

TEAM SPORTS	2010	2015	2019	CAGR
Baseball/Softball	$219.0	$287.1	$296.2	3.2%
Basketball	$721.3	$966.1	$1,006.5	4.2%
Cheerleading	$62.3	$86.0	$89.7	4.3%
Football	$102.3	$128.3	$132.1	3.0%
Soccer	$195.7	$234.0	$239.9	2.5%
Volleyball	$32.6	$35.8	$36.3	1.4%
Total	**$1,333.2**	**$1,737.3**	**$1,800.8**	**3.4%**

INDIVIDUAL SPORTS	2010	2015	2019	CAGR
Bowling	$54.0	$57.5	$57.8	0.5%
Cycling	$59.3	$76.2	$78.7	3.3%
Golf	$207.9	$249.9	$257.0	2.9%
Tennis	$403.7	$472.2	$485.1	2.7%
Track	$39.8	$51.2	$52.7	2.9%
Skateboarding	$220.5	$256.2	$261.7	2.1%
Track	$8.6	$7.9	$7.8	-0.9%
Total	**$993.8**	**$1,171.1**	**$1,200.8**	**2.1%**

FITNESS	2010	2015	2019	CAGR
Aerobics	$294.2	$292.6	$294.6	0.7%
Cross Training	$2,121.3	$2,644.8	$2,734.5	3.4%
Sneakers	$3,576.6	$4,411.7	$4,592.8	4.1%
Jogging/Running	$2,316.4	$3,215.0	$3,345.0	4.0%
Trail Running	$30.2	$37.8	$39.1	3.3%
Walking	$4,256.3	$5,465.9	$5,690.4	4.1%
Total	**$12,595.0**	**$16,067.8**	**$16,696.4**	**3.2%**

OUTDOOR RECREATION	2010	2015	2019	CAGR
Boat/Deck	$275.5	$353.9	$365.3	3.2%
Hiking	$988.8	$1,380.1	$1,449.4	5.0%
Hunting	$249.3	$278.2	$283.8	2.0%
Sport Sandals	$568.6	$589.9	$595.7	1.0%
Water Sports	$50.3	$56.4	$57.7	2.3%
Total	**$2,132.4**	**$2,658.5**	**$2,751.9**	**2.9%**

The workwear sub-segment of sports footwear is large and growing. While hard to measure, we know that service industry workers and tradespeople often wear sneakers (*Figure 5.17*). For example, of the 5 million nurses working in the U.S., about 67% wear running shoes at work. The average purchase is 1.5 pairs per year, which equates to 3.75 million pairs of running shoes per year for the U. S. nursing community alone.

Of course, sneakers and some high-end sports apparel have made their way into the business world. As dress for the workplace became more casual, so did the increased appearance of sneakers and polo shirts. For example, sneakers now account for 50% of the men's shoe business at Neiman Marcus. Execs in Silicon Valley now almost exclusively wear high-priced sneakers like Lanvin and Common Projects, both sold by Neiman Marcus. Silicon Valley is the birthplace of the casual work wardrobe. So, it's no surprise that its leaders are dressing down, and sneakers have become a cornerstone of workplace casual style. According to data from The RealReal, Louis Vuitton's high-top sneaker has become a top-seller in the San Francisco area. (18).

As the casualization of the workplace continues, we should expect these more expensive sneakers to grow in popularity (17). Designer sneakers sold in platforms like The RealReal start at just over $200 and can go to over $300 per pair. Those who can afford that cost consider it a small price to pay to look good.

FIGURE 5.17
Workwear – Comfort, Function and Performance

| Bartenders | Nurses | Painters | Delivery Drivers | Servers |

The hospitality sector employs an estimated 12 million workers who are on their feet for long hours (16). A Portland company (Mise) has created a shoe specifically designed for use in the hospitality industry, and it has tested its prototype with more than 100 chefs. Their product is a "performance sneaker for the kitchen." It's a shoe designed from the ground up to meet the needs of service industry professionals.

The combination of sports footwear for sports, outdoor recreation, leisure and work creates a wide range of sports footwear designs, styles, and performance. *Figure 5.18* categorizes 2019 worldwide and U. S. sales by three categories. Performance and sports inspired footwear are the two dominant use categories with outdoors represented in about 13% of total worldwide sales. The U. S. accounts for 28.2% of worldwide sports footwear overall but this percent jumps to 36% for performance footwear. Sports inspired footwear in the U. S. is growing at 8.2%, a higher rate than other categories in the U. S. or worldwide sales for men in 2019 but down from 50% in 2016.

FIGURE 5.18
Sports Footwear Segments – 2019 (billions)

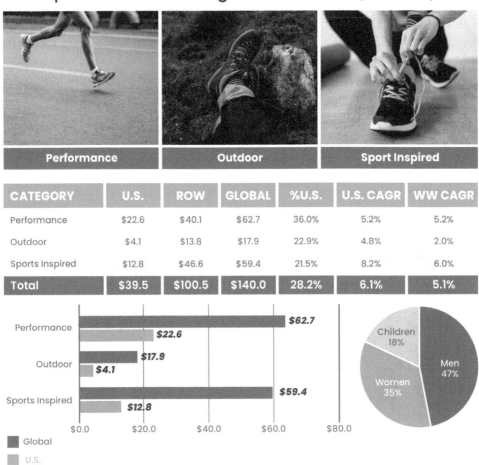

CATEGORY	U.S.	ROW	GLOBAL	%U.S.	U.S. CAGR	WW CAGR
Performance	$22.6	$40.1	$62.7	36.0%	5.2%	5.2%
Outdoor	$4.1	$13.8	$17.9	22.9%	4.8%	2.0%
Sports Inspired	$12.8	$46.6	$59.4	21.5%	8.2%	6.0%
Total	$39.5	$100.5	$140.0	28.2%	6.1%	5.1%

Women's sports footwear represented 35% of worldwide sales in 2019, up from 30% in 2016. Children's footwear sales declined from 20% in 2016 to 18% in 2019. These are big changes in a short period of time. As leisure and work wear usage increases, we can expect the women's percentage to increase. As youth participation in sports declines, we can expect the children's percentage to decrease.

While there are many different types of sport footwears that contribute to sales revenues, the running shoes is the leading category, as it is currently stands as the industry with the most amount of innovation in its field. However, running shoes are used as streetwear, workwear and for everyday leisure. Hence, consumer needs for running shoes can vary based on consumer use and lifestyle.

Running is Back: There are 621.2 million runners worldwide, driving sales of $11.56 billion in running gear (19). The U. S. is home to 60 million people engaged in running; Europe has 59.4 million; the Asia-Pacific region has 295 million, and Africa has 113 million runners. North America makes up 42% of the total sales of the running shoe market.

Running in China had been growing in popularity even before COVID-19. (*Figure 5.19*). There are now over 1 million marathon runners and over 100 marathons per year in China. This uptick has made running one of the most important sports for the Chinese, as 44% of sports-playing Chinese count running among their main activities (20).

With COVID-19, the U. S. has also seen a resurgence in running and walking. Both fitness activities typically take place outside, thereby allowing participants to maintain social distancing. Before COVID-19, approximately 50% of the U. S. population included walking or running as a routine recreational activity. With the arrival of COVID-19, that number rose to 63% (21). We will address the impact of COVID-19 on sports footwear revenues at the end of this chapter.

FIGURE 5.19
Running Growing in China

Sports Apparel

Sports apparel sales of $205.1 billion made up 58% of total sportswear sales in 2019. From 2010 to 2019, the worldwide sales of sports apparel grew 3.5% per year. U. S. sales were 35.5% of global sales in 2010 and increased to 40.4% in 2019. This increase was achieved with a growth rate of 5.9% (*Figure 5.20*) and was undoubtedly due to the growth in the athleisure market and to everyday use of sports apparel in the U. S. market. This trend is likely to spread to other parts of the world and should continue to fuel good growth in the sales of sports apparel. The data presented in *Figure 5.20* was obtained from the 2020 Euromonitor as referenced earlier (12).

FIGURE 5.20
Sports Apparel (billions)

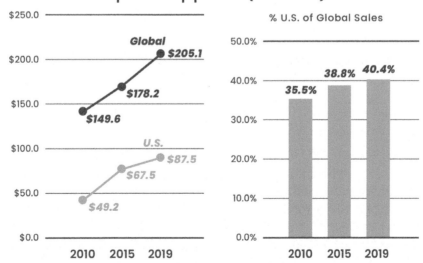

Sports apparel created for sports, outdoor recreation, leisure and work has led to a wide range of sports footwear designs, styles and performances. *Figure 5.21* categorizes 2019 worldwide and U.S. sales by three categories. As shown, performance and sports-inspired footwear are the two dominant use categories with outdoors represented in about 16% of worldwide sales. Overall, the U. S. accounts for 42.7% of worldwide sports apparel sales, but this percentage jumps to 51.9% for performance footwear. Sports inspired apparel in the U.S. is growing at 8.5%, which is a higher rate than other categories in the U. S. or worldwide.

FIGURE 5.21
Sports Apparel Use Segments- 2019 (billions)

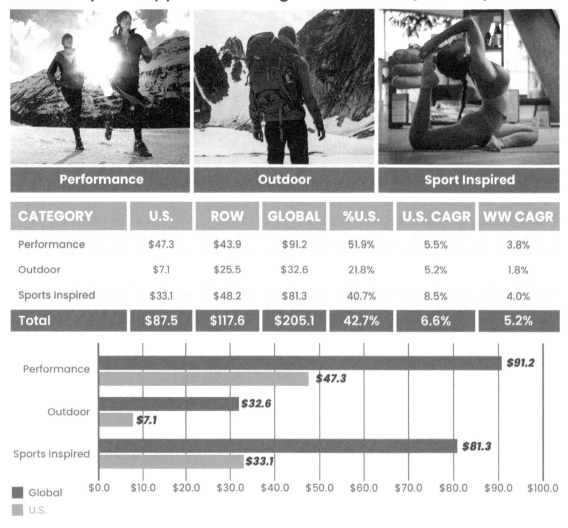

CATEGORY	U.S.	ROW	GLOBAL	%U.S.	U.S. CAGR	WW CAGR
Performance	$47.3	$43.9	$91.2	51.9%	5.5%	3.8%
Outdoor	$7.1	$25.5	$32.6	21.8%	5.2%	1.8%
Sports Inspired	$33.1	$48.2	$81.3	40.7%	8.5%	4.0%
Total	$87.5	$117.6	$205.1	42.7%	6.6%	5.2%

Figure 5.22 shows U.S. sales for 30 different kinds of sport use categories from 2012 and 2019 (15). While most readers might not be surprised to see golf as the top sales category, many would not have assumed that swimming would come in second. Camping apparel sales might also be higher than expected. However, we would expect walking, running, jogging club, gym and studio fitness to be stronger in sales than camping. The top five categories of sports apparel accounted for almost 50% of U. S. sales in 2019. Many of the categories were 1.5 to 2% of total sales, while several categories made up under 1% of total sales.

FIGURE 5.22
U.S. Sport, Fitness and Outdoor Apparel (millions)

TEAM SPORTS	2010	2015	2019	CAGR
Baseball	$361.0	$344.7	$341.9	−0.8%
Basketball	$325.5	$323.4	$323.6	0.1%
Cheerleading	$277.5	$282.0	$282.9	0.3%
Football	$270.5	$214.9	$208.6	−2.9%
Ice Hockey	$140.3	$140.5	$140.5	0.0%
Lacrosse	$64.6	$64.9	$65.0	0.1%
Soccer	$337.1	$382.5	$389.4	1.8%
Softball	$262.5	$313.9	$321.1	2.3%
Volleyball	$115.1	$98.6	$96.6	−2.0%
Total	**$2,154.1**	**$2,165.4**	**$2,167.5**	**0.1%**

INDIVIDUAL SPORTS	2010	2015	2019	CAGR
Bicycle Riding	$654.6	$737.7	$753.9	2.2%
Bowling	$404.2	$332.1	$322.4	−2.9%
Golf	$1,370.7	$1,677.2	$1,715.6	2.3%
Gymnastics	$163.8	$185.4	$188.7	1.8%
Swimming	$1,268.7	$1,626.7	$1,678.5	3.2%
Tennis	$205.3	$192.7	$191.0	−0.9%
Wrestling	$48.7	$50.6	$51.2	1.1%
Total	**$4,116.0**	**$4,802.4**	**$4,896.1**	**2.0%**

FITNESS	2010	2015	2019	CAGR
Aerobic Exercising	$738.8	$843.1	$860.4	2.0%
Walking	$1,155.9	$1,219.2	$1,231.4	1.0%
Excercising with Equipment	$1,069.9	$1,105.7	$1,113.6	0.7%
Jogging/Running	$933.8	$1,159.4	$1,194.2	3.0%
Weightlifting	$484.7	$481.3	$483.8	0.5%
Gym/Club/Studio	$1,033.0	$1,090.9	$1,102.7	1.1%
Yoga	$229.0	$340.1	$358.7	5.5%
Total	**$5,645.1**	**$6,239.7**	**$6,344.8**	**1.6%**

OUTDOOR RECREATION	2010	2015	2019	CAGR
Backpacking/Camping	$306.2	$326.9	$331.0	1.3%
Camping	$1,474.7	$1,475.3	$1,473.6	−0.1%
Fresh Water Fishing	$592.9	$528.5	$521.5	−1.3%
Saltwater Fishing	$223.5	$224.8	$225.1	0.1%
Hiking	$259.3	$278.3	$284.2	2.1%
Bow & Arrow Hunting	$59.1	$60.1	$60.3	0.3%
Firearms Hunting	$340.9	$337.0	$336.2	−0.2%
Total	**$3,256.5**	**$3,230.9**	**$3,231.9**	**0.0%**

Figure 5.23 provides a view of how worldwide sports apparel sales are categorized. Upper garments represented 48% of sales in 2019, while undergarments were roughly 41% of sales. Hats were 8.2% of sales, while other sports apparel were 2.9% of sales. Shown in *Figure 5.23* are global sports apparel sales from 2015 to 2019 (11).

FIGURE 5.23
Global Sports Apparel Sales (billions)

Like sports footwear, sports apparel is made up of a diverse category of products that include a wide range of use, including sports, fitness and casual wear. Sports apparel is an important part of this area. In many countries, the annual spending on sports apparel is much higher than footwear. This is especially true in countries with higher household consumer spending, such as the United States, England and Germany. This phenomenon will be discussed with more detail in Chapter 11.

Sports Wearables

The global sports technology market is projected to reach a market size of $40.2 Billion by 2028 (22). This growth can be attributed to increasing adoption of advanced technologies for a range of sports-related applications. Around the globe, athletes, teams and fans are taking a more technologically advanced approach for improving training and performance.

This new approach can most directly be tied to the emergence of fitness watches. These watches use apps that can be downloaded to a mobile device to track distances traversed by the wearer. These apps can perform various functions, such as allowing the user to set fitness goals, track caloric intake and record progress. They can be personalized for workout plans and often incentivize users. The benefits of fitness go on and on, but you need consistency and discipline to stick with a fitness routine long enough to reap those benefits. That's where technology can help. The right app can act as a virtual personal trainer or training partner to keep you motivated and accountable.

Wearable Technology uses sensors to exchange data when connected to the internet. Several categories of wearables are shown in *Figure 5.24*, along with the different ways wearable apps can be acquired. Products like Activity Tracking devices detect, analyze and transmit information concerning body signals, such as vital signs and/or ambient data, which allow immediate biofeedback to be transmitted back to the wearer. The five major wearable categories are summarized below (23):

- **Watches:** Within the watch, there is a fitness tracker which monitors and tracks fitness-related metrics, such as distance walked or run, calorie consumption and, in some cases, heartbeat.

- **Wrist Activity Trackers:** The wrist activity tracker is a type of wearable tech with many uses. Most of these track daily steps taken, calories burned, heart rate (provided a monitor is worn), sleep accumulation and sleep quality. The daily activity total can be adjusted based on personal fitness goals.

- **Posture Enhancers:** Poor posture is the root cause of many injuries and problems, from low-back pain and hip discomfort to carpal tunnel syndrome. The enhancer is a tiny sleek pin fastened to a shirt or jacket, making it both a posture coach and activity tracker in one. Any time you slouch forward (while standing, walking or just sitting), a gentle vibration reminds the wearer that they are slouching.

- **Eyewear:** With computerized sunglasses, the sum of one's workout history is on display without having to reference information culled from activity tracking devices. Using the wearer's pre-determined heart rate, different color-coded lights appear in the lower part of one's field of vision to communicate to the wearer if they are working too hard, not hard enough or just right.

- **Smart Clothing:** One of the newest areas of the wearable tech world is that of "smart fabrics." Going far beyond reflective safety capabilities, semiconductor technology has made it possible for simple articles of clothing, such as a T shirt, to monitor heart rate.

FIGURE 5.24
Wearable Sport Products

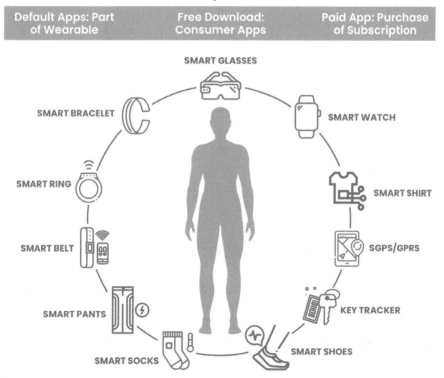

Wearables make up a relatively new segment of the sportswear market. As shown in *Figure 5.25* it had global sales of $.3 billion, growing 41.8% to $8.5 billion by 2019 (25). The U. S. market for wearables was 41.2% of global sales in 2015 at $.9 billion, growing 46% to $3.8 billion by 2019 (24). In 2019, the U. S. sales of wearables grew to 36.5% of global sales. Clearly the U. S. market is ahead of the world in adopting this health-related sportswear product. We can expect that other economically developed countries will follow and global growth rates will increase over the next five years.

FIGURE 5.25
Sports Wearables (billions)

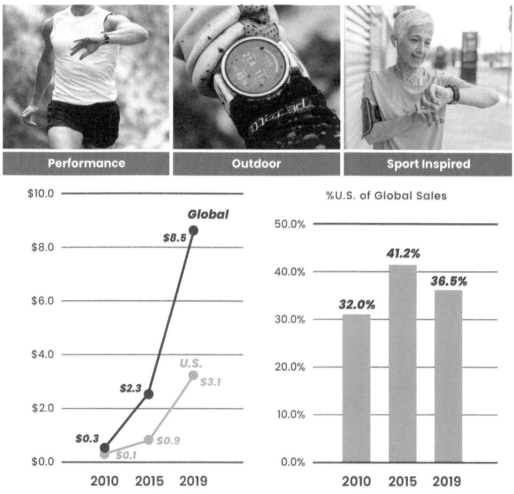

Sportswear Brands

Manufacturers in this sector of the sports domain have built up tremendous brand recognition. Nike and Adidas are among the top 100 brands in value and are recognized and sold around the world. Together these two brands have a retail sales market share of 27.6%, more than a quarter of global sales (26). These brands and the 17 others shown in *Figure 5.26* make up 50% of global sportswear sales. Many more brands with much smaller market share make up the remaining 50% of global sales.

FIGURE 5.26
Sportswear Brand Global Market Share

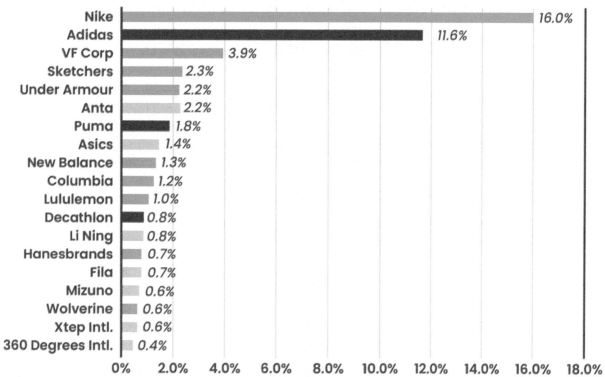

Brands highlighted in red are from Asia: four from China, three from Japan and one from South Korea. Companies, such as VF Corp and Wolverine, have acquired many familiar brand names. Shown below are several less recognizable sportswear companies that have either developed or acquired more well known brands. As shown, these multi-brand companies are located around the world. In 2020, AmerSports from Finland was acquired by Anta, a Chinese company that is one of the top 10 companies within the sportswear brand global market share (*Figure 5.26*). In many instances, the goal of a new brand is to be acquired by a larger company in order to provide the owners and stockholders a large return on their investment.

- *VF Corporation (U.S.):* Altra, Eagle Creek, Eastpak, Icebreaker, Kipling, JanSport, Lucy, North Face, Reef, Smartwood, Timberland, Vans.

- *Wolverine World Wide (U.S.):* Merrell, Saucony, Keds, Stride Ritem, Hush Puppies.

- *AmerSports (Finland):* Arc'teryx, Atomic, Mavic, Precor, Salomon, Suunto, Wilson.

- *JD Sports (U.K.):* Chausport, Sprinter, Getthelabel, Kooga, KukriSports, Source Lab, Scotts, Tessuti, Clogs, Nicholas Deakins, Blacks, Millets, Tiso, Ultimate Outdoors.

- *Vista Outdoor (U.S.):* Federal Premium, CamelBak, Champion, Savage Arms, Bushnell, CampChef, Primos, Bell, Giro, Blackhawk.

- *Decker Outdoor (U.S.):* Teva, Hoka One One, Sanuk, Ahnu and UGG.

- *Fenix Outdoor (Switzerland):* Fjällräven, Tierra, Primus, Han Wag, Grunton, Royal Robbins.

• *LaFuma (French):* Millet, Elder, Oxbow.

• *Pentland Group (U.K.):* Boxfresh, Catreberry, Ellesse, Endura, KangaRoos, Lacoste, Miltre, Red or Dead, Seaves, Speedo.

COVID-19's Impact on Sportswear

The COVID-19 pandemic turned the world upside down. Trends from historical and economic data used in the past to forecast sportswear revenue have been rendered meaningless. Once the COVID-19 pandemic took hold of the world in 2020, hopes for continual growth in the industry were dashed. *Figure 5.27* shows the estimated damage to sportswear revenue from 2019 to 2020 (26). The pandemic altered the global sports industry in ways we never could have predicted.

FIGURE 5.27
COVID-19 Impact Global Sportswear Revenues

FOOTWEAR: DOWN -15.4% | APPAREL: DOWN -15.1% | WEARABLES: UP 31.0%

GLOBAL SPORTSWEAR HEAT MAP: The 2020 pre-COVID-19 forecast of global sportswear revenues (*Figure 5.28*) is based on growth generated from prior years and on 2019 revenues. However, the impact of COVID-19 significantly decreased sales figures. Overall, sales worldwide were down 14% (9). While footwear and apparel were each down 15%, wearables grew by 35%. This contrast may be partially due to a higher level of interest in health and exercise during the 2020 pandemic. As shown in *Figure 5.28*, that forecast fell far short because of the disruptive impact that the COVID-19 pandemic had on 2020 sales.

FIGURE 5.28
Global Heat Map – Sportswear (billions)

Global	2019	Growth	2020	-50%				0%			50%		2020	2020
Segment	(billions)	Rate	Forecast										(billions)	% Change
Footwear	$140.0	6.4%	$149.0			-15.4%							$118.5	-15.4%
Apparel	$205.1	6.7%	$218.8			-15.1%							$174.1	-15.1%
Wearables	$8.5	5.4%	$9.0								35%		$11.1	31.0%
TOTAL	$353.6	6.6%	$376.9			-14%							$303.7	-14.1%

U.S. SPORTSWEAR HEAT MAP: Taking the impact of COVID-19 into account, 2020 U.S. sportswear sales decreased to $105.4 billion (28). This is a 19% decrease from 2019's actual sales of $130.8 million and a 15.9 decrease from the previous forecast for United States sportswear sales. The heat map shown in *Figure 5.29* represents the impact on 2020 sportswear segment sales.

FIGURE 5.29
United States Heat Map – Sportswear (billions)

United States	2019	Growth	2020	−50%			0%			50%	2020	2020
Segment	(billions)	Rate	Forecast								(billions)	% Change
Footwear	$39.5	6.4%	$42.0			−21%					$31.3	−20.8%
Apparel	$87.5	6.7%	$93.4			−20%					$70.0	−20.0%
Wearables	$3.1	5.4%	$3.3							32%	$4.1	32.3%
TOTAL	$130.1	6.6%	$138.7			−19%					$105.4	−19.0%

In 2019 U. S. sports footwear sales were $39.5 billion and forecasted pre-COVID-19 to grow 6.4 percent to $42 billion in 2020. The COVID-19 sports footwear sales by Euromonitor (9) for 2020 was $31.3 billion. As shown in our heat map this is a 20.8% decrease in U. S. sports footwear sales when compared to actual sales of $39.5 billion in 2019. U.S. sports apparel revenues were down a similar percent while wearables increased during the 2020 pandemic by almost a third.

References

We have added links to many references for direct and easy access. While we have tested each link, there are a few instances where the websites are no longer accessible. We will continue to monitor the accessibility of citation references and remove any links no longer active. In many instances the referenced data was purchased, this is noted.

1. Athleisure Market Size Worth $549.41 Billion By 2028 | CAGR 8.6%. PR Newswire (www.prnewswire.com).

2. Damian Vaugh, Roger Best and Robin Vieira, "Flow Experience and Sports Products", (Nov. 23, 2017). University of Oregon (business.uoregon.edu).

3. Csikszentmihalyi, Mihaly. Flow: The Psychology of Optimal Experience. New York: Harper Perennial, 1990.

4. "Update COVID-10 Outbreak-Global Sportswear Industry Market Report – Development Trends, Threats, Opportunities and Competitive Landscape in 2020," p. 34, Absolute Reports (2020)

5. Matt Powell, "Sports Industry Recap," (Sept. 23, 2020), NPD presentation to University of Oregon, Sports Product Management Program.

6. "Athleisure Will Be an $83B Market By 2020, But Only the Strongest Will Survive," BoxFox (boxfox.co).

7. Tsapovsky, Flora (22 June 2020). "Once a WFH Staple, Athleisure Gets Down to Business". WIRED. Condé Nast: Athleisure. Wikipedia (en.wikipedia.org).

8. "Designer Sneakers: Why Men Are Ditching Dress Shoes for Them". The Wall Street Journal (www.wsj.com).

9. "Global Sportswear Revenues 2019" Euromonitor International: (2021). Passport Database, Historical/Forecast: Market Size, World Sportswear. (GSI Purchased Report)

10. Oxford Economics, (2020), "Population and Socio-Economic Statistics," (GSI Purchased Report)

11. Sports Apparel Revenues, 2010, 2015 and 2019 Global and 2010, 2015 and 2019 U.S., Euromonitor International, Passport Database, Historical/Forecast Market Size (July 8, 2019). Please note: 2010 and 2015 figures were derived based on CAGR estimates from 2019-2012. (GSI Purchased Report)

12. Sports Footwear Revenues, 2010, 2015 and 2019 Global and 2010, 2015 and 2019 U.S., Euromonitor International, Passport Database, Historical/Forecast Market Size (July 8, 2019). Please note: 2010 and 2015 figures were derived based on CAGR estimates from 2019-2012. (GSI Purchased Report)

13. "U.S. Sportswear Revenues 2019" Euromonitor International: (2021). Passport Database, Historical/Forecast: Market Size, World Sportswear. (GSI Purchased Report)

14. Richard Lipsey, The Sporting Goods Industry: Practices and Products," McFarland & Co., May, 2006. p. 31

15. THE SPORTING GOODS MARKET: 2019 EDITION (ISSN: 0193-8401) Copyright 2019 National Sporting Goods Association (NSGA) - CATEGORY: ATHLETIC & SPORTS FOOTWEAR (GSI Purchased Report)

16. "Meet Mise, a shoe startup aiming to change the game for chefs, bartenders and baristas," October 27, 2021. The Business Journals (www.bizjournals.com).

17. "Designer Sneakers: Why Men Are Ditching Dress Shoes for Them". The Wall Street Journal (www.wsj.com).

18. "Sneakers are the new status symbol at work — and they're killing an office staple". Business Insider (www.businessinsider.com).

19. *A. Emmanuel, Globally, how many people practice running (as a sport), and what is the global market size for this sport? Feb, 5, 2017.* <u>AskWonder</u> *(askwonder.com).*

20. *"These are the Most Popular Sports in China"* <u>Ispo</u> *(www.ispo.com).*

21. *"Sports Footwear in World", Passport, (May 2020).* <u>University of Oregon</u> *(uoregon.edu). (GSI Purchased Report)*

22. *Sports Technology Market Size to Reach USD 40.22 Billion by 2028 | Rapid Adoption of Technologically Advanced Solutions for Urgent Need For Recovery Across The Sports Industry will Proper Industry Growth.* <u>Globe Newswire</u> *(www.globenewswire.com).*

23. *Close to body' wearables, Insulin pump patches are 'On the body' smart wearables."* <u>Apparel Resources</u> *(apparelresources.com).*

24. *Global Sports Wearables Revenues, 2010, 2015 and 2019 Global, and U.S. Sports Wearables Revenues, 2010, 2015 and 2019 Global.* <u>Statista</u> *(www.statista.com). (GSI Purchased Report)*

25. *"U.S. Sports Wearable's & Apps Revenues 2012" THE SPORTING GOODS MARKET: 2019 EDITION (ISSN: 0193-8401) Copyright 2019 National Sporting Goods Association (NSGA) -CATEGORY: ATHLETIC & SPORTS EQUIPMENT (GSI purchased report), Revenue of digital fitness and well-being devices in the United States from 2017 to 2025, by segment (in million U.S. dollars).* <u>Statista</u> *(www.statista.com). (GSI Purchased Report)*

26. *Roger Best, Dennis Howard, Ofuma Eze-Echesi, and David Borlack, "COVID-19 Impact on 2020 U.S. Sportswear Sales, December 2, 2020.* <u>University of Oregon</u> *(uoregon.edu).*

27. *"Global Sportswear Segment Revenues 2021" Euromonitor International: (2021). Passport Database, Historical/Forecast: Market Size, World Sportswear. (GSI Purchased Report)*

28. *"U.S. Sportswear Segment Revenues 2021" Euromonitor International: (2021). Passport Database, Historical/Forecast: Market Size, World Sportswear. (GSI Purchased Report)*

SPORTS EQUIPMENT
CHAPTER 6

Sports, Fitness and Recreation

Equipment is essential to all sports. Athletes doubled the world pole-vault record from the 1850s to 2000s in part due to continuous equipment improvement, as poles moved from wooden construction to fiberglass. Equipment plays an equally defining role in many other sports, as well as fitness and outdoor recreation activities.

Fitness machines continue to evolve, and wearables allow consumers to closely monitor their health and exercise. Likewise, equipment for camping, snow sports, hunting and fishing, water sports and equestrian activities enhances performance, safety and activity enjoyment.

The Best-Howard Sports Industry Model also includes recreational vehicles, such as campers, motor homes, ATVs, jet skis, golf carts and snowmobiles, in its accounting of the Sports Equipment core area. Many other industry models neglect the segment (*Figure 6.1*). The Sports Equipment core area is encompassed by the Best-Howard Model's Sports Products domain. It represents 52.7% of the domain's $988.4 billion in revenues. (*Figure 6.2*)

FIGURE 6.1
Sports Equipment Segments

SPORTS & FITNESS	OUTDOOR RECREATION	RECREATION VEHICLES
• Team Sports • Individual Sports • Fitness & Exercise	• Camping & Hiking • Fishing & Hunting • Water, Snow & Equestrian	• Campers & Trailers • Snowmobiles & Jet Skis • ATVs & Golf Carts

FIGURE 6.2
The Best-Howard Model's Sports Equipment Core Area

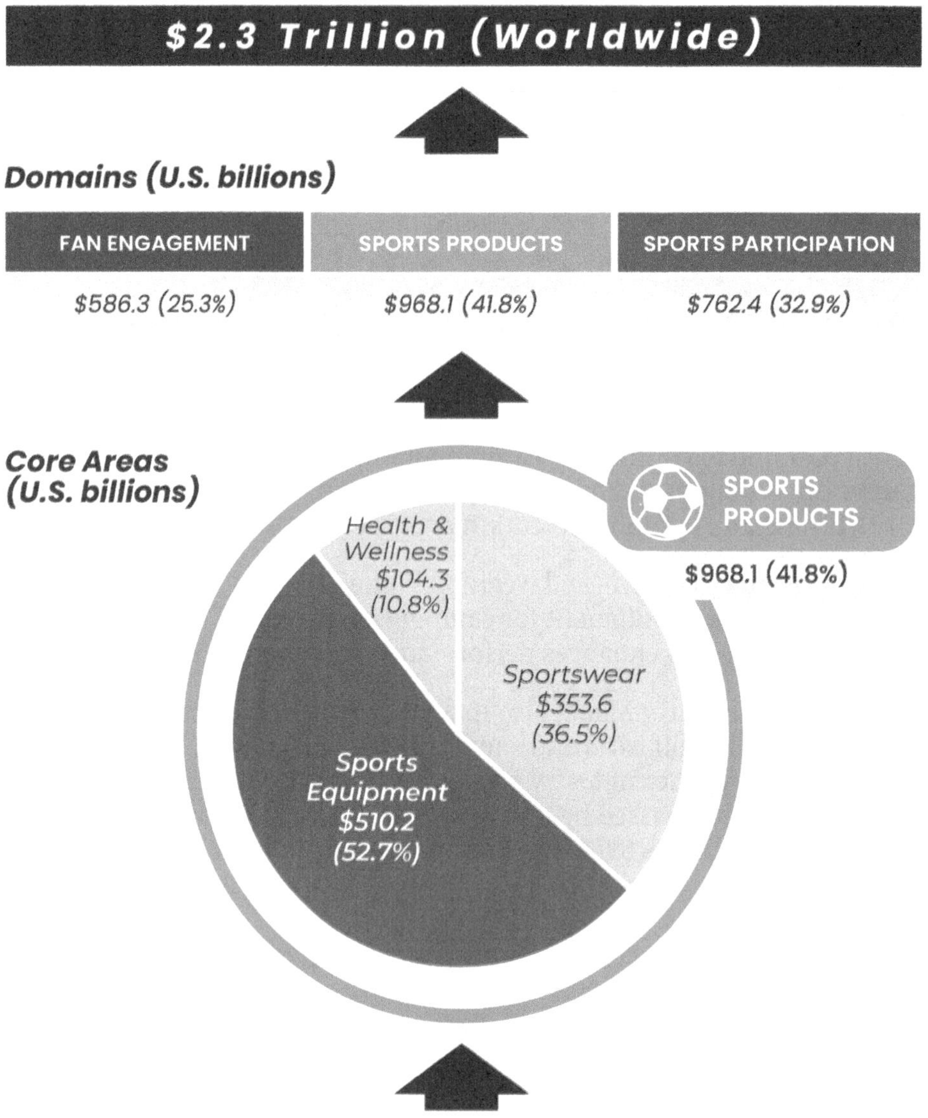

$2.3 Trillion (Worldwide)

Domains (U.S. billions)

FAN ENGAGEMENT	SPORTS PRODUCTS	SPORTS PARTICIPATION
$586.3 (25.3%)	*$968.1 (41.8%)*	*$762.4 (32.9%)*

Core Areas (U.S. billions)

SPORTS PRODUCTS
$968.1 (41.8%)

Health & Wellness
$104.3
(10.8%)

Sportswear
$353.6
(36.5%)

Sports Equipment
$510.2
(52.7%)

Segments (U.S. billions)

Sports Equipment Segments	Revenues	Percent
Sports & Fitness	$ 126.2	24.7 %
Outdoor Recreation	$ 231.5	45.3 %
Recreational Vehicles	$ 152.5	29.9 %
TOTAL	**$ 510.2**	**100.0 %**

Copyright Best-Howard Model 2022. All Right Reserved.

The model further divides Sports Equipment into three segments (*Figure 6.2*):

• **Sports & Fitness:** Equipment needed to play and practice a sport; fitness equipment used for exercise and conditioning.

• **Outdoor Recreation:** Equipment used in camping, hunting and fishing, water sports, snow sports and equestrian sports.

• **Recreational Vehicles:** Motorized equipment like campers, trailers, motor homes, snow-mobiles, jet skis, motocross bikes and off-road ATVs.

Worldwide Sports Equipment core area revenues were $510.1 billion in 2019. *Figure 6.3*'s global and U.S. segment sales breakdowns provide a strategic look at 2010 to 2019 growth rates. The U.S. percentage of global sales during the period grew from 26.6% to 39.1%. The increase makes the United States an increasingly important market for both domestic and foreign companies hoping to grow their global sales.

FIGURE 6.3
Sports Equipment Segment Sales (billions)

REVENUES	U.S.	GLOBAL		U.S.	GLOBAL		U.S.	GLOBAL
Segments	2010	2010	% U.S.	2019	2019	% U.S.	CAGR	CAGR
Sports & Fitness	$ 20.4	$ 91.3	22.3 %	$ 35.8	$ 126.2	28.4 %	6.4 %	3.7 %
Outdoor Recreation	$ 40.1	$ 186.4	21.5 %	$ 100.9	$ 231.4	43.6 %	10.8 %	2.4 %
Recreational Vehicles	$ 37.8	$ 91.9	41.1 %	$ 62.5	$ 152.5	41.0 %	5.7 %	5.8 %
TOTAL	$ 98.3	$ 369.6	26.6 %	$ 199.2	$ 510.1	39.1 %	8.2 %	3.6 %

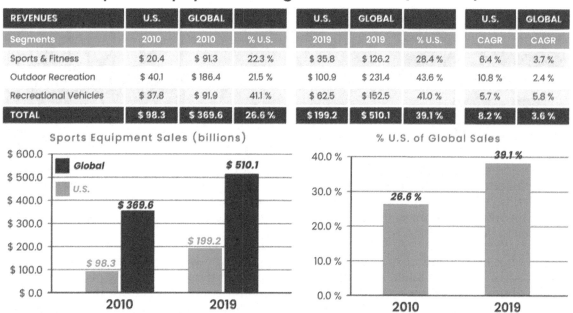

While the 2020 COVID-19 pandemic hurt many sports industry sectors, some Sports Equipment manufacturers performed well. Exercise bike makers like Peloton and Echelon saw increased sales as household consumers purchased large amounts of fitness equipment and enrolled in at-home workout programs. Described as the "Netflix for Fitness," Peloton made it possible to join instructor-led workouts without setting foot in a gym.

Both exercise bike companies offer classes at $39 per month, but the average Peloton bike costs $2,245, while an Echelon bike averages $1,639 (1). Peloton sales grew from $434.5 million in 2018 to $1.83 billion in 2020 (2). And while Peloton subscription sales increased 100% during the pandemic year, growing from 511,200 in 2019 to 1.09 million in 2020 (*Figure 6.4*), COVID-19 severely hampered gym revenues.

FIGURE 6.4
Peloton Products & Subscriptions (millions)

PERFORMANCE	2018	2019	2020	CAGR
Products	$ 354.2	$ 733.8	$ 1,462.2	103 %
Subscriptions Sold	$ 80.3	$ 181.1	$ 363.7	113 %
Total Revenue	$ 434.5	$ 914.9	$ 1,825.9	105 %
Subscriptions	245,600	511,200	1,091,100	111 %
Revenue/Customer	**$ 326.95**	**$ 354.26**	**$ 333.33**	**1.0 %**

Sports & Fitness Equipment

Sports equipment, often known as sporting goods, denotes the products facilitating athletic performance. Sports equipment varies in use from allowing part of an activity's performance to facilitating entire sports; it includes protective equipment and items like balls, nets and helmets. Over time, sports equipment has evolved as activities have come to require more protective gear to prevent injuries (3).

The sports and fitness segment of the Best-Howard Model's Sports Equipment core area also includes equipment used for exercise and training. Both households and gyms/clubs purchase the equipment, which includes stationary bikes, treadmills, elliptical/cross training machines, free weights, rowing machines, lifting machines, Pilates apparatuses and accessories ranging from gloves to belts, benches, ropes, poles and bars.

Equipment has been a part of sports from its beginnings, whether the activity involved a javelin, chariot or soccer ball, and much has changed over the years. For example, *Figure 6.5* shows the evolution of the baseball glove. Athletes played baseball without gloves from 1840 to 1870. Once gloves were introduced, producers continuously innovated new materials, technologies and designs. Manufacturers today provide baseball gloves for the position-specific skills of infielders, outfielders, first basemen and catchers.

FIGURE 6.5
Baseball Glove Evolution

| **1840-1870** | **1870-1880** | **1880-1950** | **1950-1980** | **1980-Present** |

The sports and fitness segment of the Sports Equipment core area was $126.2 billion worldwide in 2019 (4). The segment's sales grew at 3.7% per year from $91.3 billion in 2010. As shown in *Figure 6.6*, the United States represented 28.4% of global sales in 2019. U.S. sales grew at a higher rate after 2010 (6.4%), when their percent of global sales was 22.3%. In other words, the U.S. market not only produces more sports and fitness equipment sales than all other countries, the market is also growing at a faster rate than all other countries.

FIGURE 6.6
Sports & Fitness Equipment Sales (billions)

REVENUES	U.S.	GLOBAL		U.S.	GLOBAL		U.S.	GLOBAL
Segments	2010	2010	% U.S.	2019	2019	% U.S.	CAGR	CAGR
Sports & Fitness	$ 20.4	$ 91.3	22.3 %	$ 35.8	$ 126.2	28.4 %	6.4 %	3.7 %

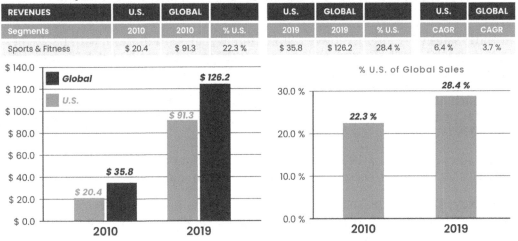

To better understand sports and fitness equipment sales, the Best-Howard Model examines U.S. sales in the segment individually for selected team sports, individual sports and fitness equipment. (Global sales data is not available.)

Team Sports

Using wholesale equipment sales for the United States from Statista, the Best-Howard Model we can report U.S. sales for the five major sports shown in *Figure 6.7* for 2010 and 2019. Baseball/softball produced the most sales in 2019 at $600 million; ice hockey produced about half the number at $279 million. The biggest gains in sales from 2010 to 2019 were in basketball ($107 million increase) and soccer ($103 million increase). Sales growth in the other three sports was modest.

FIGURE 6.7
U.S. Teams Sports Equipment Wholesale (millions)

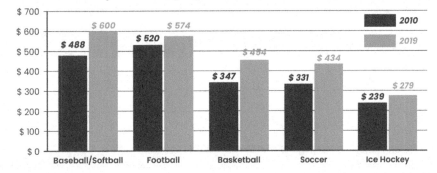

Volleyball had wholesale equipment sales of $84 million in 2019 (5); lacrosse had $102 million (6). Sales grew at 4.6% for volleyball and 5.4% for lacrosse. The two sports are growing faster in wholesale equipment sales than the top five major sports shown in *Figure 6.7*. COVID-19's impact on the team sports in 2020 is discussed at the end of this chapter.

Figure 6.8 offers a detailed look at equipment sales for the five major sports in *Figure 6.7*. Summarized below are the important strategic insights for each of the sports.

- **Baseball/Softball:** The largest sport category at $600 million in 2019, with 63.7% of the sales in bats and gloves/mitts. Bat sales (2.6%) grew a slightly faster rate than other products, except for protective/other equipment (3.1%) (7).

- **Football:** Sales were slightly lower than baseball's, at $574 million, with 62.2% being in protective gear. Overall, the growth rate from 2010 to 2019 was low at 1.1%, well below the sports and fitness segment overall at 6.4% (8).

- **Basketball:** At $454 million in 2019 and growing at 3% per year, basketball sales remained an important part of U.S. team sports equipment. Basketballs accounted for almost 51% of sales in 2019 (9).

- **Soccer:** Sales ($434) in 2019 and growth (3%) were comparable to basketball. Uniquely, 62% of sales was in other/accessories, while 30% was in balls (10).

- **Ice Hockey:** This was the smallest of the major sports in 2019, with U.S. wholesale equipment sales of $179, 42% of which were in in protective gear. Hockey is a highly regional sport and growing slowly at 1.7% per year (11).

FIGURE 6.8
U.S. Teams Sports Equipment Wholesale (millions)

Baseball/Softball	2010	2015	2019	CAGR	% 2019
Bats	$ 181	$ 191	$ 228	2.6 %	38.0 %
Gloves & Mitts	$ 129	$ 152	$ 154	2.0 %	25.7 %
Baseballs	$ 41	$ 47	$ 51	2.5 %	8.5 %
Batting Gloves	$ 35	$ 37	$ 40	1.5 %	6.7 %
Softballs	$ 30	$ 31	$ 32	0.6 %	5.3 %
Protective / Other	$ 72	$ 81	$ 95	3.1 %	15.8 %
TOTAL	**$ 488**	**$ 538**	**$ 600**	**2.3 %**	**100.0 %**

Football	2010	2015	2019	CAGR	% 2019
Balls	$ 87	$ 90	$ 88	0.2 %	15.4 %
Protective	$ 327	$ 337	$ 357	1.0 %	62.2 %
Other / Accessories	$ 106	$ 119	$ 129	2.2 %	22.4 %
TOTAL	**$ 520**	**$ 547**	**$ 574**	**1.1 %**	**100.0 %**

Basketball	2010	2015	2019	CAGR	% 2019
Basketballs	$ 162	$ 183	$ 231	4.0 %	50.9 %
Backboards	$ 155	$ 182	$ 181	1.7 %	40.0 %
Other / Accessories	$ 30	$ 36	$ 42	3.6 %	9.2 %
TOTAL	$ 347	$ 401	$ 454	3.0 %	100.0 %

Soccer	2010	2015	2019	CAGR	% 2019
Balls	$ 111	$ 127	$ 131	1.8 %	30.2 %
Protective Gear	$ 29	$ 32	$ 34	1.7 %	7.8 %
Other / Accessories	$ 191	$ 242	$ 269	3.8 %	62.0 %
TOTAL	$ 331	$ 401	$ 434	3.0 %	100.0 %

Ice Hockey	2010	2015	2019	CAGR	% 2019
Skates	$ 60	$ 65	$ 73	2.1 %	26.0 %
Sticks	$ 66	$ 64	$ 66	0.0 %	23.7 %
Protective Gear	$ 89	$ 102	$ 115	2.9 %	41.2 %
Other	$ 24	$ 25	$ 25	0.5 %	9.0 %
TOTAL	$ 239	$ 257	$ 279	1.7 %	100.0 %

Lacrosse, with 2019 sales of $102 million and growing at 5.4% per year, is an emerging sport in the United States. It is played primarily in Europe, China, Japan, Southeast Asia and India. In 2017, there were more than 873,294 players in the United States and more than 36,000 at the college level (12). This included 62% male and 38% female players. The highest level of female participation, 43.6%, was among U.S. high school players. Lacrosse's increased growth rate has been driven by parents and players drawn to its relative safety contact sports.

Individual Sports

Many sports are played individually against other players. Golf, tennis, archery, skateboarding and bicycling are predominantly outdoor individual sports, while billiards, bowling and darts are played indoors. *Figure 6.9* shows 2010 and 2019 U.S. wholesale equipment sales for five major individual sports equipment categories.

As shown, bicycles and golf achieved more than $2 billion in annual sales in 2019, while the other three sports had sales well below $1 billion. Growth in the categories from 2010 to 2019 was low, ranging from -1% to 1%. Outlined below is a summary of each of the individual sports' equipment sales.

FIGURE 6.9
U.S. Individual Sports Equipment Wholesale (millions)

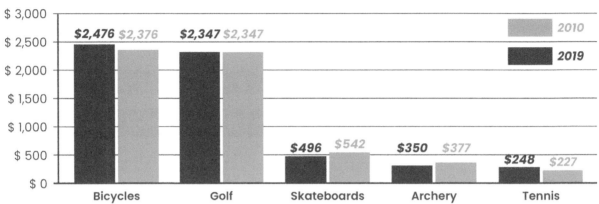

• **Bicycles:** The $2.4 billion market declined in sales by an average of -.5% per year, as shown in *Figure 6.9*; 91% of the sales where in bikes but varied by type, with mountain bikes at 53%, road bikes at 37% and electric bikes at 7% of sales (13)

• **Golf:** The $6.65 billion global golf equipment market grew by 2.2% worldwide in 2019 (14). North America has the world's highest concentration of golfers; Europe and the Asia-Pacific region have relatively high concentrations (15). As shown in *Figure 6.9*, U.S. golf wholesale equipment sales did not grow from 2010 to 2019 (16).

• **Skateboards:** The 2019 global skateboard market was $2 billion and growing at 3.1% per year (17). As shown in *Figure 6.10*, streetboards are the sport's largest product segment, accounting for 50.8% of 2019 revenues. The United States constituted 29.2% of 2019 world-wide skateboard sales of $541.7 billion; growth was at 1% per year (18).

• **Archery:** The global archery market reached a value of $3.21 billion in 2019 and grew at 5% per year from 2014 to 2019 (19). Archery's growth as a recreational sport has been due to increased participation among women and other demographics outside the traditionally male dominated sport. As shown in *Figure 6.9*, 2019 U.S. archery equipment sales were $377 million (20).

• **Tennis:** The United States has about 17.7 million tennis players. The 2019 global tennis equipment market was valued at approximately $800 million and growing at 2% per year (21). U.S. wholesale tennis equipment sales were $227 in 2019 and declining at a rate of 1% per year (22). While in 2019 the United States was 28.5% of the global market, its share was projected to decline (23).

FIGURE 6.10
U.S. Individual Sports Equipment Wholesale (millions)

Bicycles	2010	2015	2019	CAGR	% 2019
Bicycles	$ 2,307	$ 21,183	$ 2,159	-0.7 %	90.9 %
Helments	$ 269	$ 210	$ 217	2.8 %	9.1 %
TOTAL	**$ 2,476**	**$ 21,393**	**$ 2,376**	**-0.5 %**	**100.0 %**

Golf	2010	2015	2019	CAGR	% 2019
Clubs	$ 1,232	$ 1,103	$ 1,211	-0.2 %	51.6 %
Balls	$ 623	$ 599	$ 634	0.2 %	27.0 %
Other / Accessories	$ 492	$ 499	$ 502	0.2 %	21.4 %
TOTAL	$ 2,347	$ 2,200	$ 2,347	0.0 %	100.0 %

Skateboards	2010	2015	2019	CAGR	% 2019
Streetboard	$ 260.1	$ 268.8	$ 275.4	0.6 %	50.8 %
Cruiser	$ 102.3	$ 111.6	$ 114.8	1.3 %	21.2 %
Long Board	$ 95.5	$ 104.8	$ 112.5	1.8 %	20.8 %
Other	$ 38.4	$ 38.7	$ 39.0	0.2 %	7.2 %
TOTAL	$ 496.3	$ 523.9	$ 541.7	1.0 %	100.0 %

Archery	2010	2015	2019	CAGR	% 2019
Equipment	$ 350	$ 382	$ 377	0.8 %	100.0 %
TOTAL	$ 350	$ 382	$ 377	0.8 %	100.0 %

Tennis	2010	2015	2019	CAGR	% 2019
Rackets	$ 106	$ 93	$ 89	-2.0 %	39.0 %
Balls	$ 81	$ 92	$ 77	-0.5 %	34.1 %
Other	$ 61	$ 66	$ 61	0.0 %	26.9 %
TOTAL	$ 248	$ 251	$ 227	-1.0 %	100.0 %

Fitness Equipment

Fitness equipment includes any machine or device allowing physical exercise to manage bodyweight, improve physical stamina or develop muscular strength. Global fitness equipment demand has increased due to growing consumer health and obesity awareness and exercise requirements for medical treatments. A surge in gym memberships, in-home equipment sales, urban populations and government initiatives to promote healthy lifestyles also have promoted fitness equipment adoption. The most commonly used fitness equipment includes treadmills, elliptical/cross training machines, stationary bicycles, weightlifting machines and strength building machines.

The Best-Howard Model breaks the fitness equipment market into cardiovascular training, strength training and other equipment. Cardiovascular training equipment is sub-segmented into treadmills, ellipticals, stationary bikes, rowing machines and others. The global home market for fitness equipment users is about 36% of the total. Health clubs and gyms make up

43% of worldwide fitness equipment users. Other segments constitute 21% of the market and include hotels, corporate offices, hospitals, medical centers and public institutions. In the United States, health clubs account for 60% of fitness equipment sales, households account for 26% and other segments account for 14%.

The 2019 global fitness equipment market was $11.5 billion and projected to grow at 3.5% per year (*Figure 6.11*) The cardiovascular training segment led sales with 55% of the global market (24). North America was the largest regional market with more than 60% of global sales (25). The Asia-Pacific region was estimated to grow most rapidly, at 7.6% annually for several years.

FIGURE 6.11
Global Fitness Equipment Wholesale (millions)

FITNESS EQUIPMENT	2010	2015	2019	CAGR	% 2019
Cardiovascular Machines	$ 5,300.0	$ 5,834.7	$ 6,300.0	1.9 %	54.8 %
Strength Training	$ 3,804.5	$ 4,125.1	$ 4,400.0	1.6 %	38.3 %
Other	$ 522.6	$ 662.6	$ 800.0	4.6 %	7.0 %
TOTAL	**$ 9,627.1**	**$ 10,622.4**	**$ 11,500.0**	**3.5 %**	**100.0 %**

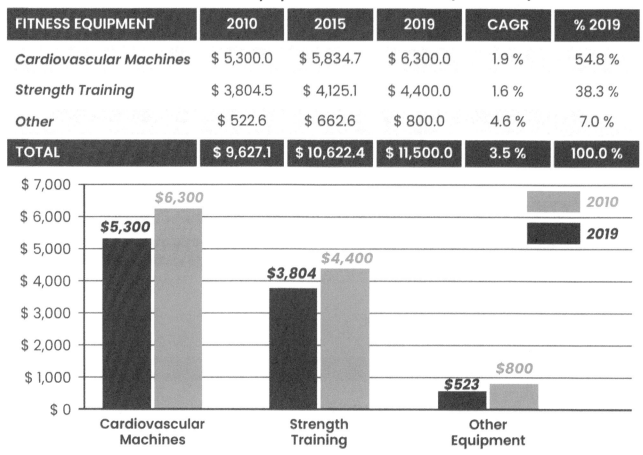

U.S. wholesale fitness equipment sales were $6.9 billion in 2019 and growing at 1.8% per year, as shown in *Figure 6.12*. This was 62% of the global market. However, with the global market growing at 3.5% and the U.S. market growing at roughly half the rate, the country's percentage of global sales will likely decrease over the next several years.

Cardiovascular machines constituted 69.6% of 2019 U.S. sales at $4.8 billion. The equipment is large, complex and expensive. Overall, cardiovascular machine sales grew at 1.9% from 2010 to 2019. As shown, strength training and other equipment each represented about $1 billion in wholesale in 2010, with other equipment growing at a higher rate than the other two categories.

FIGURE 6.12
U.S. Fitness Equipment Wholesale (millions)

FITNESS EQUIPMENT	2010	2015	2019	CAGR	% 2019
Cardiovascular Machines	$ 4,040.2	$ 4,689.1	$ 4,791.2	1.9 %	69.6 %
Strength Training	$ 971.0	$ 1,026.1	$ 1,035.0	0.7 %	15.0 %
Other	$ 827.0	$ 1,014.4	$ 1,055.3	2.7 %	15.3 %
TOTAL	$ 5,838.3	$ 6,729.6	$ 6,881.5	1.8 %	100.0 %

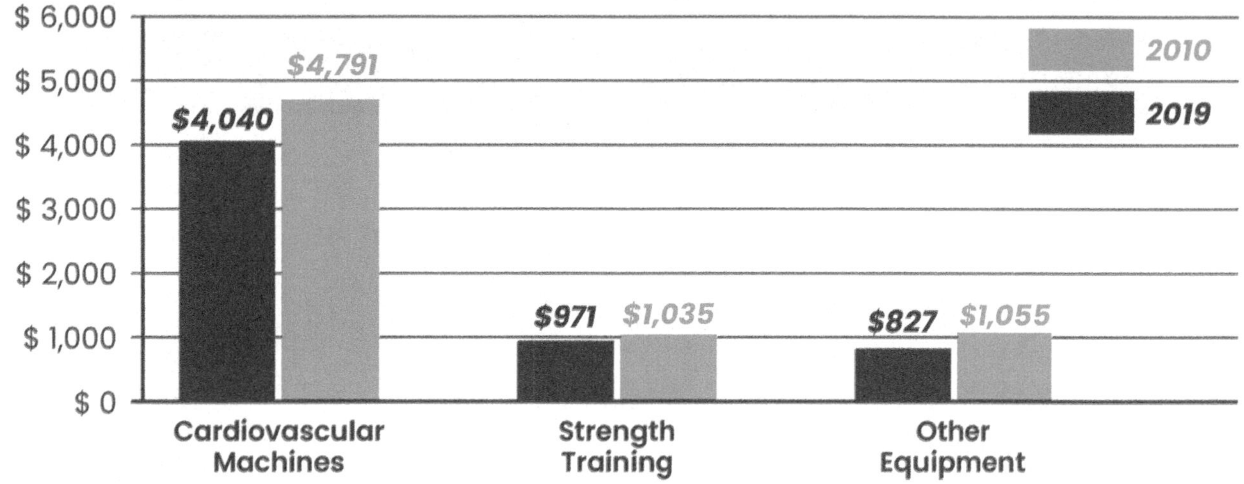

To better understand the fitness equipment market, the Best-Howard Model breaks the products into three categories (*Figure 6.13*), which are summarized below.

• **Cardiovascular Machines:** Cardiovascular machines constituted 69.6% of 2019 U.S. sales. Treadmills are among the largest, heaviest and most complex. In 2019, U.S. treadmill sales were $3.7 billion and growing at 21% per year. They made up 77% of cardiovascular machine sales. Overall, cardiovascular machine sales grew at 1.9% from 2010 to 2019.

• **Strength Training:** Strength training equipment sales made up about 15% of U.S. fitness sales in 2019 and close to 23% of worldwide sales. *Figure 6.13* illustrates the range of equipment included in the product segment. The largest sales were for multi-purpose gyms (33.4% of U.S. sales) and free weights (24.6% of U.S. sales). The two categories accounted for 58% of U.S. strength training equipment sales. Overall, the product segment was growing slowly at 0.7% per year.

• **Other Equipment:** Other fitness equipment, such as non-wearable fitness trackers and health monitors, produced $1.05 billion in 2019 sales (*Figure 6.13*). The category was growing at 4.6% per year in the United States. Yoga mats made up the remaining 16.7% of the category's sales and were growing at 1.5% per year (24).

FIGURE 6.13
U.S. Cardiovascular Equipment Wholesale (millions)

Cardiovascular Equipment	2010	2015	2019	CAGR	% 2019
Stationary Exercise Bicycles	$ 468.0	$ 535.1	$ 550.4	2.9 %	11.5 %
Treadmills	$ 3,096.3	$ 3,609.4	$ 3,686.9	2.1 %	77.0 %
Elliptical / Cross Trainers	$ 475.9	$ 544.6	$ 553.8	1.7 %	11.6 %
TOTAL	$ 4,040.2	$ 4,689.1	$ 4,791.2	1.9 %	100.0 %

Weight Conditioning	2010	2015	2019	CAGR	% 2019
Free Weights / Weight Sets	$ 212.3	$ 250.0	$ 254.9	2.0 %	24.6 %
Hand/Wrist/Ankle Weights	$ 101.1	$ 108.9	$ 110.5	1.5 %	10.7 %
Abdominal Exercisers	$ 39.4	$ 42.6	$ 43.3	1.5 %	4.2 %
Multi-Purpose Home Gyms	$ 380.9	$ 350.3	$ 345.3	−1.4 %	33.4 %
Exercise Balls	$ 75.0	$ 94.0	$ 97.9	4.2 %	9.5 %
Weight Benches	$ 102.0	$ 110.5	$ 111.3	0.8 %	10.8 %
Band / Spring Resistance	$ 60.3	$ 69.8	$ 71.8	2.9 %	6.9 %
TOTAL	$ 971.0	$ 1,026.1	$ 1,035.0	0.7 %	100.0 %

Other Fitness Equipment	2010	2015	2019	CAGR	% 2019
Fitness Trackers / Health Monitors	$ 666.3	$ 841.1	$ 879.4	4.6 %	83.35 %
Yoga Mats	$ 160.7	$ 173.3	$ 175.9	1.5 %	16.67 %
TOTAL	$ 827.0	$ 1,014.4	$ 1,055.3	2.7 %	100.0 %

Strength training equipment sales made up about 15% of U.S. fitness sales in 2019 and close to 23% of worldwide sales. *Figure 6.13* illustrates the range of equipment included in the product segment. The largest sales were for multi-purpose gyms (33.4% of U.S. sales) and free weights (24.6% of U.S. sales). The two categories accounted for 58% of U.S. strength training equipment sales. Overall, the product segment was growing slowly at 0.7% per year at the end of 2019.

Outdoor Recreation Equipment

Outdoor recreation offers consumers athletic enjoyment without competition, games with rules or an ultimate winner. Many outdoor recreational activities do, however, require high sport-competency levels. Outdoor activities can promote physical health, self-sufficiency, appropriate risk-taking, social ties and individual achievement (e.g., practicing, enhancing and challenging skills, testing stamina and endurance, and seeking adventure or excitement).

Global outdoor recreation revenues grew 6.1% from $189 billion in 2010 to $322 billion in 2019 (*Figure 6.14*). During the same period, U.S. outdoor recreation sales grew by 3.9% per year, resulting in the U.S. percentage of global sales decreasing from 38.7% to 32.1%.

FIGURE 6.14
Outdoor Recreation Sales (billions)

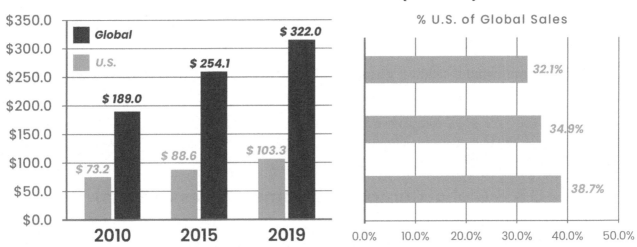

Each of the outdoor recreation sub-segments are important sources of global equipment sales. Equestrian, one of the world's oldest sports with competitions being part of the first Olympics, produced more than one third of 2019 sales (*Figure 6.15*). Water sports constituted about one fourth of global outdoor recreation sales. Surprisingly, wildlife watching was the third leading category. The remaining four sub-segments made up 24.1% of global sales.

The outdoor recreation segment includes the following sub-segments:

- **Camping:** The activity requires gear like tents, sleeping bags, stoves and coolers.

- **Fishing:** Recreational fishing, or sport fishing, requires rods, reels, lines, hooks, bait and lures.

FIGURE 6.15
Outdoor Recreation Sales (billions)

EQUIPMENT	U.S.	GLOBAL	% U.S.
Camping	$ 2.8	$ 11.4	24.6 %
Fishing	$ 4.6	$ 17.0	27.1 %
Hunting	$ 7.1	$ 35.10	18.0 %
Wildlife Watching	$ 12.1	$ 48.40	25.0 %
Snow Sports	$ 5.3	$ 11.10	47.7 %
Water Sports	$ 32.2	$ 84.40	38.2 %
Equestrian	$ 39.2	$ 114.8	34.1 %
TOTAL	$ 103.3	$ 322.2	32.1 %

% U.S. of Global Sales

- Equestrian: 35.6%
- Water Sports: 25.8%
- Wildlife Watching: 14.7%
- Hunting: 12.0%
- Fishing: 5.2%
- Camping: 3.5%
- Snow Sports: 3.4%

- **Hunting:** Hunting involves seeking, pursuing and killing wild animals and birds and is accomplished primarily with firearms, but it is also done with bows and arrows.

- **Wildlife Watching:** Enthusiasts observe animal species either for research or recreation; bird watching is the most common wildlife watching activity.

- **Snow Sports:** The category includes downhill and cross-country skiing and snowboarding.

- **Water Sports:** Water sports equipment has two major sub-segments—boats/boating equipment and activity-based equipment.

- **Equestrian:** Includes saddles, stirrups, bridles, halters, reins, girths, bits, harnesses, saddle pads, breastplates and more.

CAMPING: The 2019 global camping equipment market was $11.4 billion and grew 22.5% in 2020 (26) to $13.96 billion (*Figure 6.16*). Camping equipment sales growth was 6.7% from 2010 to 2019.

FIGURE 6.16
U.S. & Global Camping Equipment Sales (billions)

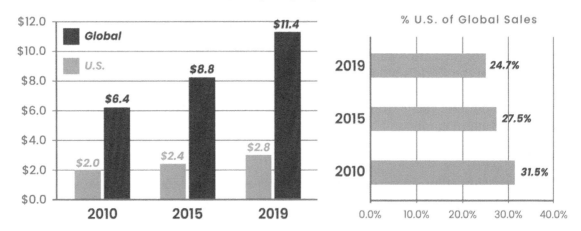

Global / U.S.

2010: U.S. $2.0, Global $6.4
2015: U.S. $2.4, Global $8.8
2019: U.S. $2.8, Global $11.4

% U.S. of Global Sales

- 2019: 24.7%
- 2015: 27.5%
- 2010: 31.5%

U.S. Camping Equipment Sales (millions)

EQUIPMENT	2010	2015	2019	CAGR	% 2019
Sleeping Bags	$ 370.0	$ 556.9	$ 653.4	6.5 %	23.2 %
Backpacks	$ 399.0	$ 577.9	$ 627.8	5.2 %	22.3 %
Cooler & Ice Chests	$ 279.0	$ 374.0	$ 600.0	8.9 %	21.3 %
Tents & Shelters	$ 269.0	$ 340.1	$ 368.7	3.6 %	13.1 %
Furniture	$ 216.0	$ 221.4	$ 247.6	1.5 %	8.8 %
Stoves & Fuels	$ 119.0	$ 145.1	$ 152.8	2.8 %	5.4 %
Jugs & Containers	$ 69.0	$ 79.6	$ 112.2	5.5 %	4.0 %
Others	$ 48.0	$ 50.3	$ 53.3	1.2 %	1.9 %
TOTAL	**$ 1,769.0**	**$ 2,345.3**	**$ 2,815.8**	**5.3 %**	**100.0 %**

Increasing recreational expenditures, changing lifestyles and rising outdoor recreation participation have driven camping equipment sales growth. The Best-Howard Model expects an aging population and early retirement to drive the industry further, as retired consumers have more time for outdoor recreation. Outdoor activities' health benefits will also affect the camping equipment market over the next decade, and despite challenges, the market is expected to grow over the model's forecast period (27).

North America, with the world's largest number of campers, dominates the global equipment market, and the activity is the region's third most popular form of outdoor recreation (26). Camping frequency among young people is leading the growing demand. U.S. camping equipment sales grew 3.8% per year from $1.7 billion in 2010 to $2.82 billion in 2019. In 2020, U.S. sales soared 31% to $3.7 billion (28). In 2019, U.S. camping equipment sales were 24.7% of global sales. The number increased to 26.4% in 2020, as the pandemic and consumers' desire to be outdoors and distanced from others created a sales surge.

Figure 6.16 provides a detailed look at U.S. camping equipment sales. Sleeping bags and backpacks constituted 45.5% of 2019 sales, while coolers and tents combined to add another 34.4%. The remaining equipment types were roughly 20% of 2019 sales. The fastest growing area was coolers at 8.9%, with sleeping bags growing at 6.5% and backpacks at 5.2% (28).

FISHING: Recreational fishing is one of the most popular outdoor recreation activities in the United States. In 2019, more than 50 million Americans engaged in freshwater, saltwater and fly fishing, marking the highest participation rate in over a decade. In line with global participation trends, the Best-Howard Model forecasts U.S. hobbyist fisherman numbers to increase, a development contributing to individuals' health and wellbeing but posing a challenge to regional ecosystems.

Global fishing equipment sales were estimated at $18 billion in 2020, up from pre-pandemic sales of $17 billion in 2019 and representing a 5.8% one-year increase in a market growing at 2.3% (29). The U.S. accounted for 27.1% of global sales. The U.S. recreational fishing equipment market was $4.6 billion in 2019 (30) and was estimated to be 11.3% higher in 2020 at $5.1 billion (*Figure 6.17*).

FIGURE 6.17
Fishing Equipment Sales (billions)

FISHING EQUIPMENT	2010	2015	2019	CAGR
Global	$ 13.9	$ 15.5	$ 17.0	2.3 %
U.S.	$ 3.3	$ 4.0	$ 4.60	3.8 %
% U.S.	23.7 %	25.8 %	27.1 %	

HUNTING: Many North American cultures view hunting and fishing as key to their identity, and hunting license sales help generate revenues for wildlife conservation and habitat management. The Best-Howard Model therefore expects the North American outdoor hunting equipment market to grow over its forecast period (31).

Hunting is a global sport, with equipment sales at about 18% for the Asia-Pacific and Middle East/Africa regions and 20% to 22% for North America, Europe and Latin America. The global hunting equipment market was $35.1 billion in 2019, having grown slowly at 1% per year from $32.1 billion in 2010 (32). The U.S. market represented about 20% of global equipment sales in 2019 and was growing at a rate of 3.8% per year (*Figure 6.18*).

FIGURE 6.18
Hunting Equipment Sales (billions)

HUNTING EQUIPMENT	2010	2015	2019	CAGR
Global	$ 32.1	$ 33.8	$ 35.1	1.0 %
U.S.	$ 5.0	$ 6.1	$ 7.1	3.8 %
% U.S.	15.5 %	18.1 %	20.2 %	

FIGURE 6.19
U.S. Hunting Equipment Sales (millions)

HUNTING EQUIPMENT	2010	2015	2019	CAGR	% 2019
Handguns	$ 1,182.2	$ 2,183.8	$ 2,364.3	8.3 %	33.2 %
Rifles	$ 1,448.6	$ 1,927.6	$ 2,003.6	3.9 %	28.2 %
Shotguns	$ 839.4	$ 1,113.7	$ 1,149.8	3.2 %	16.2 %
Air / Co² Pistols & Rifles	$ 280.0	$ 251.0	$ 247.5	-1.4 %	3.5 %
Paintball Guns / Packages	$ 141.7	$ 128.5	$ 126.9	-1.3 %	1.8 %
Ammunition	$ 1,019.8	$ 1,048.0	$ 1,053.7	0.5 %	14.8 %
Reloading Equipment	$ 165.5	$ 165.3	$ 165.3	0.0 %	2.3 %
TOTAL	$ 5,077.2	$ 6,817.9	$ 7,111.1	3.8 %	100.0 %

Hunting equipment includes many products (31), as shown in *Figure 6.19*. Handgun sales grew by 8.3% per year from 2010 to 2019 and accounted for 33.2% of U.S. sales by the end of the period. Rifles and shotguns accounted for 44.4% of 2019 U.S. sales. Rifle sales grew at an annual rate of 3.9%, and shotguns grew at 3.2% annually. U.S. ammunition sales for the firearms totaled more than $1 billion.

WILDLIFE WATCHING: According to some analysts, bird watching is America's fastest growing outdoor activity. One-third of the U.S. population age 16 and older watches wildlife, defined by the Best-Howard Model as closely observing, feeding and photographing wildlife, visiting parks and natural areas around the home because of wildlife's presence and maintaining plantings and natural areas around the home to benefit wildlife.

Wildlife watching activities are categorized as around (within 1 mile of) or away from (more than 1 mile from) the home. In the United States, 86 million residents (34% of the 16 and older population) participated in wildlife watching in 2019 (*Figure 6.20*) and spent $12.1 billion on it. People taking an interest in wildlife around their homes numbered 81.1 million, while those taking trips away from the home numbered 23.7 million. Around-the-home bird watchers averaged 96 days engaging in the activity. Away-from-home birders averaged 16 days (33).

FIGURE 6.20
U.S. Wildlife & Bird Watching (millions of watchers)

LOCATION	WILDLIFE	BIRDS ONLY	% BIRDS
Home	81.1	38.7	47.7 %
Away	23.7	16.3	68.8 %

Bird watching has become the number one hobby in the United Kingdom. Along with the Netherlands, Denmark, France and Sweden, the country is a top purchaser of bird watching equipment. U.K. consumers spent 12 times as much as those in the United States on bird watching gear. Consumers take an estimated 3 million international trips for the main purpose of bird watching (34).

The COVID-19 pandemic impacted wildlife watching equipment sales significantly. In 2020, U.S. sales increased an estimated 22%. The increase represents a $2.7 billion gain over 2019 U.S. equipment sales of $12.1 billion. Consumers stuck at home realized birding was easy to do while maintaining social distance. And compared to other types of wildlife watching, birding can more easily be done without traveling. Equipment for bird watching is expensive and includes binoculars, books, birdseed and feeding apparatuses. People just discovering bird watching must purchase their first feeder sets, binoculars and field guides (35).

WATER SPORTS: The water sports sub-segment of outdoor recreation implements boats and other equipment. Global water sports equipment sales were $84.3 billion in 2019, with the market growing at 5.9% per year from 2010 to 2019, and the United States represented 38.2% of global sales (*Figure 6.21*). During the same period, the U.S. water sports equipment market grew by 8%. The Best-Howard Model projects U.S. sales will continue to grow faster than global sales and eventually reach 40% of the total market.

FIGURE 6.21
Water Sports Equipment Sales (billions)

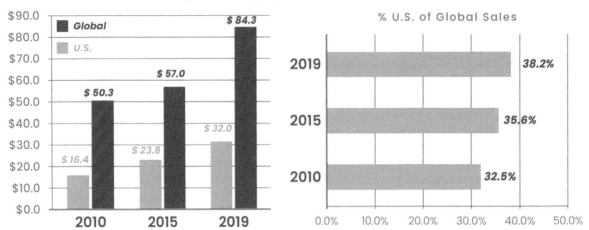

The Best-Howard Model breaks the water sports category into sales derived from 1) recreational boats and 2) equipment. In the boat market, consumers have come to a growing consensus regarding the benefits offered by integrated technologies, and manufacturers are increasingly offering artificial intelligence and smart sensors to provide users features like GPS tracking, automatic controls and smart-connect. The Best-Howard Model expects the technologies to improve boat safety and security and fuel market growth.

The 2020 global leisure boat market was valued at $41.1 billion. It is expected to expand at a CAGR of 4.5% from 2021 to 2028. Consumers' rising disposable incomes and flourishing tourism sectors in emerging economies like Brazil and China will be key factors accelerating the market's growth (36).

U.S. recreational boat demand was $16.6 billion in 2019 and growing at 8.4% per year. As shown in *Figure 6.22*, powerboats constituted 54.5% of sales and were growing at 11.2% prior to the COVID-19 pandemic (37). Increases in disposable income and personal consumption expenditures, particularly on durable and recreational activity goods, were key drivers of U.S. boat sales growth from 2010 to 2019.

FIGURE 6.22
U.S. Recreational Boats & Equipment Sales (millions)

EQUIPMENT	2010	2015	2019	CAGR	% in 2019
Powerboats	$ 3,480	$ 5,907	$ 9,021	11.2 %	54.3 %
Personal Watercraft	$ 340	$ 510	$ 706	8.4 %	4.2 %
Other Boats (*)	$ 475	$ 545	$ 607	2.8 %	3.7 %
Propulsion Systems	$ 1,572	$ 2,252	$ 3,002	7.5 %	18.1 %
Boating Accessories	$ 2,147	$ 2,720	$ 3,287	4.8 %	19.8 %
TOTAL	$ 8,014	$ 11,934	$ 16,623	8.4 %	100.0 %

North American recreational boat, engine and marine accessory merchandisers report that new powerboat retail unit sales in the U.S. increased by about 12% from 2019 to 2020. More than 310,000 new powerboats were sold in 2020, levels the industry has not seen since before the 2008 recession (37).

The water sports equipment sub-segment includes items required for swimming, such as suits, goggles, caps, accessories and footwear. The global demand for the equipment was $43.2 billion and growing at 7.2% in 2019 (38). Swim fins, masks and goggles made up 25.6% of 2019 global sales (*Figure 6.23*), and the sub-segments grew at more than 10% per year from 2010 to 2019.

Increased water sports participation rates across all age groups has led to countries establishing water sports facilities around the globe. In recent years, governments have actively promoted water sports to increase tourism revenues. With the growing inclination toward recreational water sports, the Best-Howard Model expects the segment's gear and equipment market to grow significantly over the next four years.

FIGURE 6.23
Global Water Sports Equipment Sales (billions)

EQUIPMENT	2010	2015	2019	% in 2019	CAGR
Swimwear	$ 8.4	$ 8.9	$ 9.3	21.6 %	1.1 %
Swim Fins	$ 1.2	$ 2.4	$ 4.2	9.8 %	14.7 %
Masks & Goggles	$ 2.3	$ 3.9	$ 5.9	13.7 %	10.9 %
Buoyancy Devices	$ 2.2	$ 3.8	$ 5.9	13.7 %	11.6 %
Swim Watches	$ 3.2	$ 4.1	$ 5.1	11.8 %	5.2 %
Life Jackets	$ 2.9	$ 3.6	$ 4.2	9.8 %	4.3 %
Helmets	$ 1.7	$ 2.1	$ 2.5	5.9 %	4.9 %
Other	$ 4.5	$ 5.2	$ 5.9	13.7 %	3.2 %
TOTAL	$ 26.5	$ 34.2	$ 43.2	100.0 %	7.2 %

North America represented the largest global water sports equipment market in 2019, largely due to the region's increasing adoption of healthy lifestyles. However, the coronavirus pandemic crippled the market. Many water sports locations and recreation centers were closed, and travel restrictions further limited demand. The Best-Howard Model projects it will take time for the segment to return to pre-pandemic sales levels. The 2008 recession saw sales drop 50%, and 10 years passed before U.S. boat sales recovered (39).

SNOW SPORTS: Increasing participation rates in outdoor activities like skiing, is due to government initiatives to encourage participation and growing ski resort numbers are some of the factors driving ski gear and equipment sales globally. In recent years, women have begun participating in snow sports in larger numbers worldwide. As a result, manufacturers have introduced ski gear and equipment designed specifically for women (40).

Global snow sports equipment sales were $84.3 billion in 2019 and grew at 5.3% per year from 2010 to 2019 (41). U.S. snow sport equipment sales were 38.2% of global sales in 2019 at $32 billion (42) and growing at 7.7% per year. The U.S. percentage of global sales grew from 40.7% in 2010 to 47.7% in 2019 (*Figure 6.24*).

FIGURE 6.24
Snow Sports Equipment Sales (billions)

Europe has long been the world's premier destination for skiers/snowboarders, with well-reputed resorts dotted across the Alps and Pyrenees mountains. The rest of the world has responded, however, and the United States now has the most skier visits per season worldwide. The world's best skiing conditions are found in North America and the northern parts of Europe and the Asia-Pacific region (60).

Ski equipment demand is likely to boom in the Asia-Pacific region after China hosts the 2022 Winter Olympics. North America, Europe and China have the highest level of snow sport equipment sales (43). Shown in *Figure 6.25* are the 2019 global unit sales for major snow equipment products (44). Alpine boots and skis accounted for 47.8% of worldwide units sold. Cross-country boots and skis account for 23.6% of all units sold, and 700,000 snowboards were sold in 2019, roughly 5% of worldwide unit sales.

FIGURE 6.25
Snow Sports Equipment Sales (units billions)

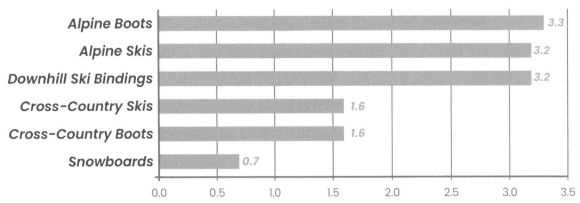

While the 2018 and 2019 snow sports seasons were the most successful in 20 years, the 2020 COVID-19 pandemic damaged winter sports severely. Ski resorts, hotels, bars and tourism operators all were affected, as were their suppliers. The Best-Howard Model believes the industry will have to adapt to survive and will take at least two to three years to reach pre-COVID-19 levels (43).

EQUESTRIAN: Equestrian equipment is used in horse-based sporting activities and is specifically manufactured for riders and equines. More than 16 million consumers engage in equestrian worldwide, with more than 2 million U.S. participants, a number likely to rise. Shown in *Figure 6.26* (45) is the percentage of global equestrian equipment demand around the world (46).

FIGURE 6.26
Global Equestrian Equipment Percent Sales

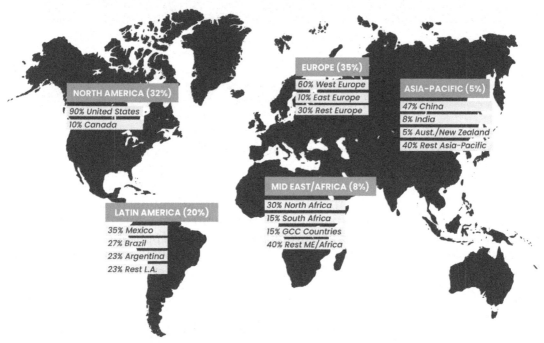

Global equestrian equipment sales were $114.8 billion in 2019 and growing at 6.2% per year. U.S. equipment sales were 34% of global sales at $39.1 billion and growing by 4.3%. The U.S. percentage of global sales declined from 40.1% in 2010 to 34.1% in 2019 (*Figure 6.27*). The Best-Howard Model forecasts the trend will continue in the near future.

FIGURE 6.27
Equestrian Equipment Sales (billions)

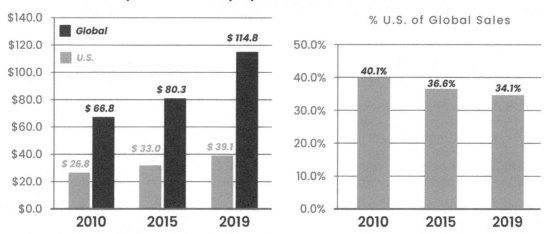

Figure 6.28 divides 2019 global and U.S. equestrian equipment sales into four categories. The three main categories—racing, showing and recreation—were roughly equal worldwide and in the United States, with the U.S. percentage of global sales at 34% across all categories (46).

FIGURE 6.28
Equestrian Equipment Sales (billions)

USE	Racing	Showing	Recreation	Other	Total
Global	$ 31.6	$ 31.8	$ 35.2	$ 16.3	$ 114.9
U.S.	$ 10.8	$ 10.8	$ 12.0	$ 5.5	$ 39.1
% U.S.	34.2 %	34.0 %	34.1 %	33.7 %	34.0 %

New technologies enable horse trainers and owners to take accurate measurements of their animals' health, and such smart equestrian equipment has had a major impact on the market. Enthusiasts and professionals alike are drawn to the devices, which can provide metrics to improve training methods. For example, advanced synchronicity systems allow sensors in reins to measure riders' contact with their horse at every instant. Connected equipment can also measure and record horses' horizontal and vertical jump height, breathing rate, calories burned, minimum and average speeds and overall health. Mobile applications can continuously stream, monitor and analyze all the information. Coaches can provide accurate assessments and correct horse and rider imbalances. The Best-Howard Model projects increasing demand for the advanced equestrian equipment in coming years.

Recreational Vehicles

The recreational vehicle segment of the Sports Equipment core area includes motorized transports used for sports, outdoor recreation and travel. One of the largest components of the segment is the RV industry. The segment is comprised of the following motorized vehicles:

• **RVs:** RVs are motor vehicles or trailers that include living quarters. RVs include motor homes, camper vans, caravans (also known as travel trailers and camper trailers), fifth-wheel trailers, popup campers and truck campers.

• **Recreational Boats:** The sub-segment includes motorized and non-motorized boats used for water sports and fishing. Motorboats are fitted with inboard or outboard engines.

• **All-Terrain Vehicles:** An all-terrain vehicle (ATV) is a motorized, off-highway craft with four tires, a seat straddled by the operator and handlebars for steering control.

- **Jet Skis:** Jet Ski is the brand name of a personal watercraft manufactured by Kawasaki. The term is used generically to refer to any type of personal recreational watercraft.

- **Golf Carts:** The sub-segment includes small, motorized carts used primarily to carry golfers and their equipment.

- **Snowmobiles:** A snowmobile is a motorized vehicle designed for winter travel and recreation on snow and ice. Most snowmobiles are driven on open terrain or trails.

The global recreational vehicle market was $58.2 billion and growing at 7.1% per year in 2019 (*Figure 6.29*). The U.S. constituted 42.9% of global sales at $24.9 billion and had an annual growth rate of 8.2% (47).

FIGURE 6.29
Recreational Vehicle Sales (billions)

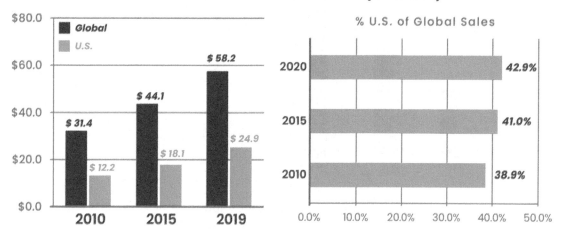

Figure 6.30 offers more perspective. RVs made up 73% of global segment sales in 2019, with 42% occurring in the United States. Adding Canada, the percentage was more than 44% of worldwide sales.

FIGURE 6.30
2019 Global Recreational Vehicle Market Segments

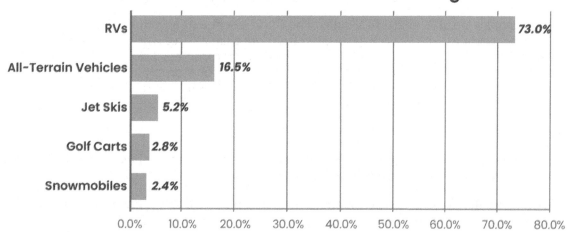

RVS: The millennial population, especially in the United States, has exhibited increasing demand for camping and outdoor recreational activities. The number of U.S. households taking up camping increased by 1.4 million in 2019. The growing numbers have contributed to demand for RVs, and RV rental businesses have also boosted the market. Growing numbers of peer-to-peer rental services have driven popularity among young adults.

Global RV sales were $42.5 billion and growing at 7% per year in 2019 (47), as shown in *Figure 6.31*. The U.S. market was 46.5% of 2019 worldwide sales of $19.8 billion. From 2010 to 2019, the U.S. market grew at a higher rate (8.5%) than the global market and gained a larger share.

FIGURE 6.31
Recreational Vehicle Sales (billions)

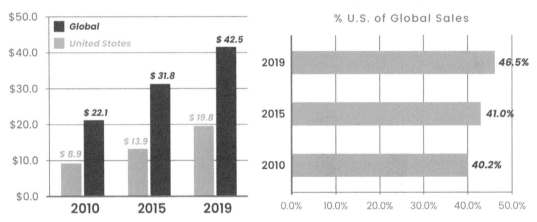

The RV market is further broken down into motorhomes and towables. Motorhomes are grouped into three classes:

• **Class A (40%):** The motorhomes have strong, heavy-duty frames. Class A frames are built on commercial truck or motor vehicle chassis.

• **Class B (12%):** Class B motorhomes look like large vans and are commonly known as camper vans. They offer standing-room cabins.

• **Class C (48%):** Class C motorhomes are a compromise between Class A and B; they are built on cabin chassis but feature over-cab sleeping areas.

Motorhomes made up 50% of 2019 RV sales. The Class A segment accounted for more than 40% of global revenues, and Class B accounted for more than 12% of worldwide revenues while experiencing the fastest growth in the segment. Class B motorhomes are typically affordable to maintain and offer better fuel economy than their larger counterparts. The versatile and affordable Class C segment is expected to reach more than $13 billion in sales by 2025. However, Class A vehicles are expected to continue dominating in terms of revenue (48).

Towable RVs represent 45% of total sales. Towable RVs come in three types:

• **Travel Trailer:** Travel trailers are connected to bumper-level hitches and pulled by pickup trucks and other vehicles with the required towing capacity.

• **Fifth Wheel:** Fifth wheel travel trailers connect directly to the vehicles towing them instead of via a bumper-level hitch.

• **Tent Trailer:** Pop-up campers, or tent trailers, are towed recreational vehicles that can be collapsed for storage and transport.

The rapidly growing demand for towable RVs is driven by their low cost compared to motorized RVs and absence of built-in engines and powertrains. Towable RVs allow customers to use an existing truck or van to tow them, significantly reducing on-the-road costs.

The North American RV market is the largest around the globe. More than 11% of American households own RVs, and more than 1 million U.S. households live in them full-time. RVs allow traveling at 20%-60% less cost, a primary factor driving their popularity among millennials (48).

RECREATIONAL BOATS: Global recreational (motorized and non-motorized) boat sales were $37.3 billion in 2019 (49). Global sales grew 2.9% per year from 2010 to 2019. U.S. recreational boat sales were 26.4% of the 2019 global number of $9.9 billion. As shown in *Figure 6.32*, the U.S. percentage of sales increased from 21.1% in 2010 due to its higher annual growth rate of 5.3%.

New powerboat unit sales in the U.S. increased by an estimated 12% from 2019 to 2020. More than 310,000 new powerboats were sold in 2020, levels not seen since the 2008 recession (37).

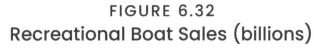

FIGURE 6.32
Recreational Boat Sales (billions)

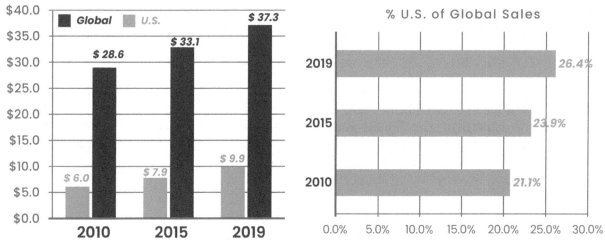

ALL-TERRAIN VEHICLES: ATVs are motorized, off-highway vehicles designed to travel on four low-pressure or non-pneumatic tires. ATVs are subdivided into two types as designated by manufacturers (50):

• **Type I ATVs:** Type I ATVs are used by single operators and not intended for passengers.

• **Type II ATVs:** ATVs in the second class are built for operators and passengers in designated seating positions.

ATVs come in various sizes to accommodate different age groups and speeds. The industry recommends all riders operate vehicles intended for their age. Youth model ATVs are designed for smaller hands and feet and travel at low speeds. The 2019 global ATV market was valued at $9.63 billion. From 2010 to 2019, the market grew by 5.6% (51). The United States accounted for 18.7% of 2019 worldwide sales. Growing at 5.1% per year, the U.S. ATV market decreased as a percentage of global sales from 19.6% in 2010 to 18.7% in 2019 (*Figure 6.33*)

FIGURE 6.33
All-Terrain Vehicle Sales (billions)

China's ATV market is forecast to expand at an 8.5% CAGR to $2.1 billion by 2027 (52). Japan and Canada each are forecast to grow at 3.1% and 5% over the 2020-2027 period. Within Europe, Germany is forecast to grow fastest at approximately 3.5%.

JET SKIS: Jet skiing is a popular recreational activity, as it does not require special training. The relatively low cost of entry and increase in jet ski equipment variety helped the market grow at close to 10% from 2012 to 2017. The market posted CAGR of 12.12% from 2017 to 2021 (53).

Global jet ski sales were $3.03 billion in 2019 and growing at 10% per year. The United States, followed by Europe, the Asia-Pacific region and the Middle East/Africa region, is the biggest market for the equipment. The U.S. market represented 40.7% of the global sales total of $1.2 billion in 2019 (*Figure 6.34*). However, with 8% annual growth, the U.S. market slipped from 49.6% of global sales in 2010. Three brands served the U.S. jet ski market in 2019—Sea Doo had a 55% market share, Waverunner retained 39% and Jet Ski had a 6% share (54).

FIGURE 6.34
Jet Ski Sales (billions)

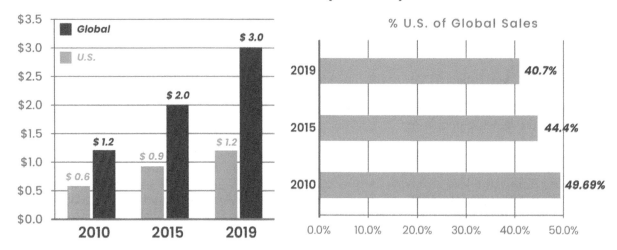

GOLF CARTS: Originally designed to carry golfers on courses, golf carts today are some of the most widely used vehicles in many industries. Available in various formats and sizes, the carts are powered by gasoline, solar power or electric power. The global golf cart market is anticipated to achieve a CAGR of 6.9% from 2020 to 2027.

As shown in *Figure 6.35*, the global golf cart market was $1.62 billion in 2019 and growing at 4.2% per year (55). In 2019, the U.S. market was $1.2 billion and 73.5% of worldwide sales. However, the U.S. market is growing more slowly at 3.9% than it is worldwide, and its percentage of global sales has decreased from 75.6% to 73.5%.

FIGURE 6.35
Golf Cart Sales (billions)

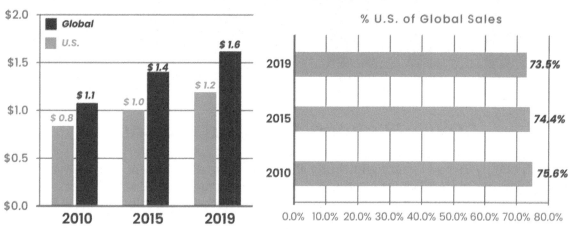

The global golf cart market is divided by product type, battery capacity, passenger capacity, length, application and region. The passenger capacity segment is subdivided into two-seat, four-seat and six-seat carts. Of the segments, two-seaters held the largest market share at about 44% in 2018. The two-seat segment is anticipated to grow at a compound annual rate of 6.3% through the Best-Howard Model's forecast period. The four-seat segment is anticipated to have the highest CAGR at 7.5%.

Based on region, the global golf cart market is segmented into North America, Europe, the Asia-Pacific region, Latin America, and the Middle East/Africa region. The Asia-Pacific market, which accounted for about 20% of the market share in 2018, is estimated to see a CAGR of 8.1% over the forecast period.

SNOWMOBILES: Recessions severely impact the global snowmobile market, as the vehicles cost thousands of dollars and access is limited to relatively affluent consumers. Also called power sleds or snow machines, snowmobiles can be easily operated on ice or snow and do not need proper trails or roads. Snowmobiling is a recognized sport with many passionate followers (56).

The 2019 global market for snowmobiles was $1.4 billion and growing at a rate of 1.2% per year. As shown in *Figure 6.36*, the United States contributed 65% of global demand in 2019. Because the U.S. market is growing at 1.7% per year, its percentage of global sales increased from 62.1% in 2010 to 65% in 2019. U.S. sales accounted for 41% of the global total that year, with Canada contributing 35%. Together, the countries accounted for 76% of global sales (57).

FIGURE 6.36
Snowmobile Sales (billions)

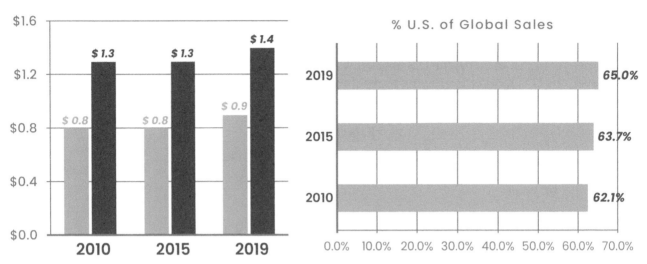

COVID-19's Impact on Sports Equipment

The 2020 COVID-19 pandemic significantly altered all Sports Equipment core area sales in 2020. Sports and outdoor activities offering social distancing saw 2020 sales increase. Sales in bicycling, golfing, camping and recreational vehicles soared, while equipment sales for football, baseball, soccer and equestrian decreased significantly.

Global Sports Equipment data for 2020 is difficult to obtain. However, U.S. wholesale revenues are available for most categories. Following is a look at the pandemic's effect on Sports Equipment revenues in the United States for 2020.

TEAM SPORTS EQUIPMENT: Many team sports shut down for much of 2020, dramatically affecting equipment purchases for baseball, football, ice hockey, lacrosse and soccer. The heat map presented in *Figure 6.37* provides a summary of major team sports equipment wholesale in the United States for 2019, pre-pandemic forecasts for 2020 and 2020 actual sales.

The pandemic produced significant sales declines in five of the seven team sports analyzed. Four sports had major declines from 21% to 28%. Only basketball and volleyball realized sales increases during the 2020 pandemic.

FIGURE 6.37

COVID-19's Impact on U.S. Team Sports Equipment Wholesale (millions)

TEAM SPORTS

U.S. Equipment Segment	2019 (billions)	Growth Rate	2020 Forecast	-50%	0%	50%	2020 (billions)	2020 % Change
Baseball/Softball	$600	2.3%	$613.8		-10.3%		$538	-10.3%
Basketball	$454	3.0%	$467.6			11.5%	$506	11.5%
Football	$574	1.1%	$580.3		-6.3%		$538	-6.3%
Ice Hockey	$279	1.7%	$283.7		-17.7%		$229	-17.9%
Soccer	$434	3.0%	$447.0		-8.3%		$398	-8.3%
TOTAL	$2,341	6.6%	$2,392.5		-5.6%		$2,209	-5.6%

The 36% increase in U.S. basketball equipment sales was despite a pandemic that shut down organized youth and young adult basketball for much of the year. In 2020, portable basketball system sales increased an estimated 69% over 2019. Sales of in-ground and mounted basketball systems increased 48%. The systems provided a fresh air solution for families seeking social distance, and at-home basketball systems became difficult to find at retail stores and online.

INDIVIDUAL SPORTS EQUIPMENT: Most individual sports are played outdoors and provide distance between competitors. The circumstances played a major role in how COVID-19 impacted the sports' equipment sales in 2020. As shown in the *Figure 6.39* heat map, outdoor sports equipment sales soared beyond forecasts. Indoor sports like bowling and billiards, however, saw equipment sales decrease (61). Bicycles were the biggest winner among individual sports in 2020. Cycling is an activity enjoyed by children, families, commuters, enthusiasts and mountain bikers.

FIGURE 6.38

COVID-19's Impact on U.S. Individual Sports Equipment Wholesale (millions)

INDIVIDUAL SPORTS

U.S. Equipment Segment	2019 (billions)	Growth Rate	2020 Forecast	-50%	0%	50%	2020 (billions)	2020 % Change
Golf	$2,347	0.0%	$2,347.0		19.0%		$2,794	19.0%
Bicycling	$2,359	0.5%	$2,370.8			101.5%	$4,753	101.5%
Archery	$377	1.7%	$383.4		2.1%		$385	2.1%
Tennis	$227	1.0%	$229.3		-0.9%		$225	-0.9%
Skateboarding	$542	0.9%	$546.9			26.0%	$683	26.0%
TOTAL	$5,852	0.4%	$5,877.4			51.0%	$8,840	51.0%

FITNESS EQUIPMENT: With health clubs and gyms closed in 2020, consumers turned to purchasing fitness equipment for home use from sports retailers, mass merchandisers and online sellers. As shown in the Figure 6.39 heat map, cardiovascular machine sales soared in the U.S. to an estimated 85% increase over 2019 sales (58), driven by digital exercise programs offered on treadmills, exercise bikes and performance bikes (62).

FIGURE 6.39
COVID-19's Impact on U.S. Fitness Equipment Wholesale (millions)

FITNESS

U.S. Equipment Segment	2019 (billions)	Growth Rate	2020 Forecast	-50%			0%		50%		2020 (billions)	2020 % Change
Cardiovascular Machines	$4,791	1.9%	$4,883							85.0%	$8,864	85.0%
Free Weights	$409	1.5%	$415							62.8%	$666	62.8%
Home Weight Machines	$345	-1.2%	$341						37.4%		$474	37.4%
Fitness Accessories	$1,055	4.2%	$1,099							44.8%	$1,528	44.8%
TOTAL	$6,600	2.1%	$6,738							74.7%	$11,532	74.7%

Strength training equipment sales grew by 63% during the 2020 pandemic. Likewise, other fitness equipment sales grew an estimated 50%, and it became difficult to locate free weights for purchase. Total U.S. fitness equipment sales were $5.3 billion more in 2020 than 2019.

OUTDOOR RECREATION EQUIPMENT: COVID-19 positively impacted sales in five of the seven outdoor recreation equipment categories shown in the *Figure 6.40* heat map. Equestrian and snow sports were shut down for much of 2020, leading to equipment sales decreasing by more than 50%. Because equestrian sales are more than one third of total sales, the entire segment was down 20% in 2020.

FIGURE 6.40
COVID-19's Impact on U.S. Outdoor Equipment Wholesale (billions)

OUTDOOR SPORTS

U.S. Equipment Segment	2019 (billions)	Growth Rate	2020 Forecast	-50%		0%		50%	2020 (billions)	2020 % Change
Camping	$2.8	5.3%	$2.97		-4.3%				$2.7	-4.3%
Fishing	$4.6	-4.3%	$4			10.9%			$5.1	10.9%
Hunting	$7.1	4.1%	$7		-4.2%				$6.8	-4.2%
Equestrian	$39.2	4.3%	$41	-59.9%					$15.7	-59.9%
Snow Sports	$5.3	2.8%	$5	-67.9%					$1.7	-67.9%
Water Sports	$32.2	8.7%	$35			10.9%			$35.7	10.9%
Wildlife Watching	$12.1	2.5%	$12			17.4%			$14.7	17.4%
TOTAL	$103.3	5.0%	$109	-20.7%					$82	-20.7%

The other three outdoor recreation areas experienced noteworthy increases over forecast equipment sales, and COVID-19 presented an opportunity for campers around the world.

U.S. camping equipment sales were up 31% in 2020 over 2019. The Best-Howard Model forecasts camping interest and camping equipment purchases to grow over the next five years (59). North America dominates the global camping equipment market (26).

RECREATIONAL VEHICLES: The COVID-19 pandemic positively impacted U.S. recreational vehicle sales in 2020, as the vehicles offered an outdoor experience with good social distancing. As shown in *Figure 6.41*, 2020 sales were 10% higher than those in 2019. Snowmobiles showed the segment's only decrease, as snowmobile parks were shut down for much of the season.

FIGURE 6.41
COVID-19's Impact on U.S. Recreational Vehicle Wholesale (billions)

RECREATIONAL VEHICLES

U.S. Equipment Segment	2019 (billions)	Growth Rate	2020 Forecast	-50%	0%	50%	2020 (billions)	2020 % Change
Motor Homes & Campers	$19.8	9.1%	$21.6		11.1%		$22.0	11.1%
Recreational Boats	$9.9	5.1%	$10.4		12.1%		$11.1	12.1%
All-Terrain Vehicles	$1.1	9.1%	$1.2		9.1%		$1.2	9.1%
Jet Skis	$1.2	8.3%	$1.3		8.3%		$1.3	8.3%
Golf Carts	$1.2	0.0%	$1.2		8.3%		$1.3	8.3%
Snowmobiles	$0.9	0.0%	$0.9	-11.1%			$0.8	-11.1%
TOTAL	$34.1	7.3%	$36.6		10.6%		$37.7	10.6%

Because of the COVID-19 outbreak, the global recreational vehicle market is expected to witness rapid growth, especially in North America and Europe. The vehicles provide a reliable, personal and socially distanced way to travel, and consumers are likely to continue finding them preferable to public transportation.

References

We have added links to many references for direct and easy access. While we have tested each link, there are a few instances where the websites are no longer accessible. We will continue to monitor the accessibility of citation references and remove any links no longer active. In many instances the referenced data was purchased, this is noted.

1. *Echelon Vs Peloton: How These Two Super Buzzy At-Home Bikes Actually Compare, March 2020.* Women's Health Magazine *(www.womenshealthmag.com).*

2. *Peloton 2020 Annual Report,* Yahoo *(finance.yahoo.com).*

3. *Sports Equipment,* Wikipedia *(en.wikipedia.org).*

4. *Global Sports Equipment Data: Size of the Global Sports Equipment Market 2012 to 2023.* Statista *(www.statista.com). (GSI Purchased Report)*

5. *Volleyball equipment wholesale sales in the U.S. from 2007 to 2020.* Statista *(www.statista.com). (GSI Purchased Report)*

6. *Lacrosse equipment wholesale sales in the U.S. from 2007 to 2020.* Statista *(www.statista.com). (GSI Purchased Report)*

7. *Baseball/softball sports equipment wholesale sales in the U.S. from 2007 to 2020.* Statista *(www. statista.com). (GSI Purchased Report)*

8. *Football equipment wholesale sales in the U.S. from 2007 to 2020.* Statista *(www.statista.com). (GSI Purchased Report)*

9. *Basketball sports equipment wholesale sales in the U.S. from 2007 to 2020.* Statista *(www.statista.com). (GSI Purchased Report)*

10. *Soccer equipment wholesale sales in the U.S. from 2007 to 2020.* Statista *(www.statista.com). (GSI Purchased Report)*

11. *Ice hockey equipment wholesale sales in the U.S. from 2007 to 2020.* Statista *(www.statista.com). (GSI Purchased Report)*

12. *Why Lacrosse Is the Sport Of Choice Of Today's Youth.* Army and Navy Academy *(armyandnavyacademy.org).*

13. *2020 US Bike Sales,* Dataintelo *(www.dataintelo.com).*

14. *Golf Equipment Market Size, Share & Trends Analysis Report By Product (Clubs, Gears, Footwear & Apparel, Balls), By Distribution Channel (Sports Goods Retailers, Online, Department & Discount Stores), And Segment Forecasts, 2019–2025.* Grand View Research *(www.grandviewresearch.com).*

15. *Global Golf Equipment Market - Growth, Trends.* Mordor Intelligence *(www.mordorintelligence.com).*

16. *Wholesale Sales of Golf Equipment in the U.S. from 2007 to 2020.* Statista *(www.statista.com). (GSI Purchased Report)*

17. *Skateboard Market Value Worldwide from 2018 to 2025 (in billion U.S. dollars).* Statista *(www.statista. com). (GSI Purchased Report)*

18. *Skateboard Market Size, Share & Trends Analysis Report By Product (Street Board, Long Board), By End User (Kids, Teenagers, Adults), By Region, and Segment Forecasts, 2019–2025.* Grand View Research *(www.grandviewresearch.com).*

19. *Archery Equipment Markets - Global Industry Trends, Share, Size, Growth, Opportunity and Forecasts, 2014-2019 & 2020-2025 - ResearchAndMarkets.com.* AP News *(www.apnews.com).*

20. *Archery Sports Equipment Wholesale Sales in the U.S. from 2007 to 2020.* Statista *(www.statista.com). (GSI Purchased Report)*

21. *Global Tennis Equipment Sales.* Dataintelo *(www.dataintelo.com).*

22. *Tennis Equipment Wholesale Sales in the U.S. from 2007 to 2020.* <u>Statista</u> *(www.statista.com). (GSI Purchased Report)*

23. *Wholesale sales of tennis equipment in the U.S. 2007-2019, Published by Statista Research Department, Nov 27, 2020.* <u>Statista</u> *(www.statista.com). (GSI Purchased Report)*

24. *Fitness Equipment Market by Type (Cardiovascular Training Equipment, Strength Training Equipment and Other Equipment) and End User (Home Consumer, Health Club/Gym and Other Commercial User): Global Opportunity Analysis and Industry Forecast, 2020–2027.* <u>Allied Market Research</u> *(www.alliedmarketresearch.com).*

25. *U.S. consumer fitness equipment wholesale sales from 2007 to 2020.* <u>Statista</u> *(www.statista.com). (GSI Purchased Report)*

26. *Global Camping Equipment Market - Growth, Trends, Covid-19 Impact, and Forecasts (2021–2026).* <u>Mordor Intelligence</u> *(www.mordorintelligence.com).*

27. *Growth Opportunities in the Global Camping Equipment Market.* <u>Lucintel</u> *(www.lucintel.com).*

28. *Camping equipment wholesale sales in the U.S. from 2007 to 2020.* <u>Statista</u> *(www.statista.com). (GSI Purchased Report)*

29. *Global Sports Fishing Equipment Industry.* <u>Globe Newswire</u> *(www.globenewswire.com).*

30. *Market size of the fishing sector in the United States from 2011 to 2020, with a forecast for 2021.* <u>Statista</u> *(www.statista.com). (GSI Purchased Report)*

31. *Hunting Equipment Market in the Americas - Size, Growth, Trends, and Forecast For 2019-2023.* <u>Technavio</u> *(www.technavio.com).*

32. *Global Hunting Equipment Market.* <u>Data Bridge Market Research</u> *(www.databridgemarketresearch.com).*

33. *National Survey of Fishing, Hunting, and Wildlife-Associated Recreation (2016),* <u>U.S. Fish & Wildlife Service</u> *(www.fws.gov).*

34. *Market Analysis of Bird-Based Tourism: A Focus on the U.S. Market to Latin America and the Caribbean Including Fact Sheets on The Bahamas, Belize, Guatemala, Paraguay.* <u>Responsible Travel</u> *(www.responsibletravel.org).*

35. *Birdwatching Is a Bright Spot in a Pandemic-Stricken Economy.* <u>Audubon</u> *(www.audubon.org).*

36. *Leisure Boat Market Size, Share & Trends Analysis Report By Type (New Leisure Boat, Used Leisure Boat, Monitoring Equipment), By Region (North America, Europe, Asia Pacific, South America, Middle East & Africa), and Segment Forecasts, 2021–2028.* <u>Grand View Research</u> *(www.grandviewresearch.com).*

37. *U.S. Recreational Boating Demand by Product: 2017-2022 (US $ mil).* <u>Freedonia Group</u> *(www.freedoniagroup.com).*

38. *Water Sports Gear Market by Product Type (Water sports Clothes, Swim Fins, Swim Mask & Goggles, BCD (Buoyancy Control Device), Watches, Life Jackets, Safety Helmets, and Others), Age Group (Kids, Adults, and Geriatric), and Distribution Channel (Specialty Store, Franchise Store, Online Store, Supermarket/Hypermarket, and Others): Global Opportunity Analysis And Industry Forecast, 2020–2027.* <u>Allied Market Research</u> *(www.alliedmarketresearch.com).*

39. *Global Water Sports Gear Market By Product Type (Clothes, Swim Fins, Swim Mask & Goggles, Buoyancy Control Device (BCD), Watches, Life Jackets, Safety Helmets, and Others), Age Group (Kids, Adults, and Geriatric), and Distribution Channel (Specialty Store, Franchise Store, Online Store, Supermarket/Hypermarket, and Others), Opportunity Analysis and Industry Forecast, 2020–2025.* <u>Market Data Forecast</u> *(www.marketdataforecast.com).*

40. *Global Ski Gear and Equipment Market (2020 to 2025) - Growth, Trends, and Forecast - ResearchAndMarkets.com.* <u>Businesswire</u> *(www.businesswire.com).*

41. *Sales of skis, snowboards and skiing equipment worldwide in 2019 (in million units),* <u>Statista</u> *(www.statista.com). (GSI Purchased Report)*

42. *Snow sports equipment wholesale sales in the U.S. from 2007 to 2020. Statista (www.statista.com). (GSI Purchased Report)*

43. *COVID-19 has crippled the winter sports industry – but a digital revolution will help it recover, February 19, 2021. The Conversation (www.theconversation.com).*

44. *Winter Sports Equipment. Statista (www.statista.com). (GSI Purchased Report)*

45. *Equestrian Equipment Market to Reflect Preeminence of Small Players Consolidating Domestic Presence. The Northwest Horses Sources (www.nwhorsesource.com).*

46. *Equestrian Equipment Market Forecast, Trend Analysis & Competition Tracking - Global Market Insights 2018 to 2028. Fact.MR (www.factmr.com).*

47. *Recreational Vehicle Market Size By Vehicle (Motorhomes [Class A, Class B, Class C], Towable RVs [Travel Trailer, Fifth Wheel, Tent Trailer]), By Fuel (Gasoline, Diesel), Industry Analysis Report, Regional Outlook, Growth Potential, Price Trends, Competitive Market Share & Forecast, 2020–2026. Global Market Insights (www.gminsights.com).*

48. *The global recreational vehicle market by revenue is expected to grow at a CAGR of over 7% during the period 2019-2025. PR Newswire (www.prnewswire.com).*

49. *Leisure Boats Market Size By Product (Bowrider, Catamaran, Cruiser, Pontoon, Yacht, Sailboat), By Type (Motorized, Non-Motorized), By Propulsion System (Diesel, Gasoline, Electric/ Hybrid, Sail Drive), Industry Analysis Report, Regional Outlook, Growth Potential, Price Trends, Competitive Market Share & Forecast, 2020–2026. Global Market Insights (www.gminsights.com).*

50. *"What is an ATV?" ATV Safety (atvsafety.org).*

51. *"All Terrain Vehicle Market 2020 to 2025" Businesswire (www.businesswire.com).*

52. *Global All Terrain Vehicle (Sport & Utility) Market Report 2020: Market Projected to Surpass $10 Billion by 2027 - ResearchAndMarkets.com. Businesswire (www.businesswire.com).*

53. *Global Jet Skiing Equipment Market 2017-2021. PR Newswire (www.prnewswire.com).*

54. *Global Jet Ski Equipment is Expected To Reach USD 4530 Million by 2022 Owing to Rise in Popularity of Jet Skiing as a Sport and Increase in Jet Skiing Championships & Tournaments Worldwide: Ken Research Industry Analysis. Open PR (www.openpr.com).*

55. *Global Golf Cart Market Study (2020 to 2027) - Players Include Autopower, Marshell Green Power & Speedways Electric Among Others. Globe Newswire (www.globenewswire.com).*

56. *New Snowmobile Sales Data for Winter of 2019-2020. Snow Mobile (www.snowmobile.org).*

57. *Snowmobile Market Forecast, Trend Analysis & Competition Tracking: Global Market insights 2017 to 2022. Fact.MR (www.factmr.com).*

58. *Fitness Equipment Market Size By Equipment (Cardiovascular [Elliptical Machines, Treadmills, Exercise Bikes, Climbers], Strength Training [Weightlifting, Weights, Barbells & Ladders, Extension Machines, Power Racks]), By End Use (Home, Health Clubs, Office, Hotel), Industry Analysis Report, Regional Outlook, Growth Potential, Price Trends, Competitive Market Share & Forecast, 2020–2026. Global Market Insights (www.gminsights.com).*

59. *Global Camping Equipment Industry Analysis 2020-2025 - Expected to Grow at a CAGR of 5%, with Europe Dominating Market Shares - ResearchAndMarkets.com. Businesswire (www.businesswire.com).*

60. *Ski Gear and Equipment Market - Growth, Trends, COVID-19 Impact, and Forecasts (2021–2026). Mordor Intelligence (www.mordorintelligence.com).*

61. *Billiards and Snooker Equipment Market - Growth, Trends, Covid-19 Impact, and Forecasts (2021–2026). Mordor Intelligence (www.mordorintelligence.com).*

62. *"COVID-19 Pandemic Fuels Bicycle Boom". Statista (www.statista.com). (GSI Purchased Report)*

SPORTS HEALTH & WELLNESS
CHAPTER 7

Medicine, Therapy & Nutrition

Sports and recreational activities lead to a variety of injuries and accidents. Professional, college and high school athletes, as well as sport enthusiasts and everyday participants, all experience health and wellness issues. Sports injuries range from simple strains to conditions requiring surgery. Sports therapy aids in injury recovery and prevention, and sports counseling addresses mental issues (*Figure 7.1*).

The Health & Wellness core area of the Best-Howard Model's Sports Products domain includes the sports medicine, wellness products, therapy and nutrition segments. The largest segment is nutrition, which includes sports drinks, energy bars and protein bars. Like Sportswear, the Health & Wellness core area attracts non-sports consumers.

The Health & Wellness segments presented in *Figure 7.1* are as follows:

• **Sports Medicine:** Medical treatment for sports injuries, including repairs, surgeries, recovery products, prescriptions, braces, walking boots and slings.

• **Wellness Products:** Products created for injury prevention, recovery and performance, as well as specialized products for para-athletes.

• **Sports Therapy:** Physical and mental therapy products, such as acupuncture, chiropractic treatment, massage, thermotherapy, cryotherapy and counseling.

• **Sports Nutrition:** Drinks for hydration, recovery and protein, nutritional supplements helping athletes perform better and sports bars for energy and protein.

FIGURE 7.1
Health & Wellness Segments

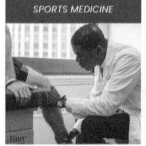

SPORTS MEDICINE | WELLNESS PRODUCTS | SPORTS THERAPY | SPORTS NUTRITION

Figure 7.2 shows where Health & Wellness fits into the Best-Howard Sports Industry Model. Of the $968.1 billion in sales making up the model's Sports Products domain, Health & Wellness contributes 10.8%. The revenues are derived from each of the core areas four segments, which are further divided into sub-segments.

FIGURE 7.2
Health & Wellness – Best-Howard Sports Industry Model

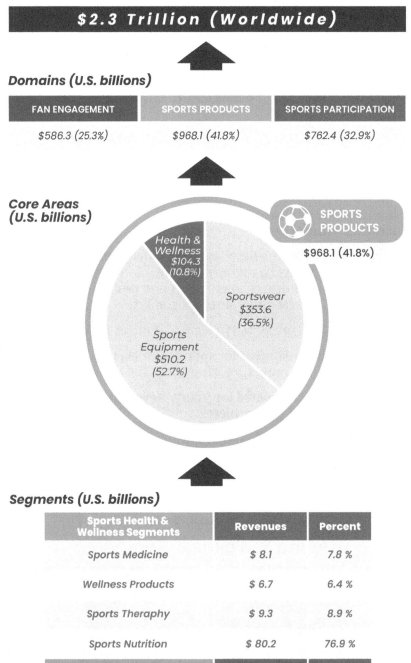

$2.3 Trillion (Worldwide)

Domains (U.S. billions)

FAN ENGAGEMENT	SPORTS PRODUCTS	SPORTS PARTICIPATION
$586.3 (25.3%)	*$968.1 (41.8%)*	*$762.4 (32.9%)*

Core Areas (U.S. billions)

SPORTS PRODUCTS
$968.1 (41.8%)

Health & Wellness $104.3 (10.8%)

Sportswear $353.6 (36.5%)

Sports Equipment $510.2 (52.7%)

Segments (U.S. billions)

Sports Health & Wellness Segments	Revenues	Percent
Sports Medicine	$ 8.1	7.8 %
Wellness Products	$ 6.7	6.4 %
Sports Theraphy	$ 9.3	8.9 %
Sports Nutrition	$ 80.2	76.9 %
TOTAL	**$ 104.3**	**100.0 %**

Copyright Best-Howard Model 2022. All Right Reserved.

Sports injuries are driven by participants' level of involvement in sports, exercise and active recreation. Countries with high numbers of participants in the activities experience more injuries than others. As shown in *Figure 7.3*, 2019 U.S. participation was at 19.3%, up from 18.5% in 2010, according to the U.S. Bureau of Labor Statistics (1). Male participation was higher, at 20.7%, than female participation at 18%. On average, Americans spent half an hour per day engaging in sports, exercise and recreational activities in 2019. According to a 2020 report on Japanese activity participation, staying healthy, losing weight and improving or maintaining physical strength were among the main reasons people exercised, worked out or engaged in sports (2).

FIGURE 7.3
U.S. Sports, Exercise & Recreational Activity Participation

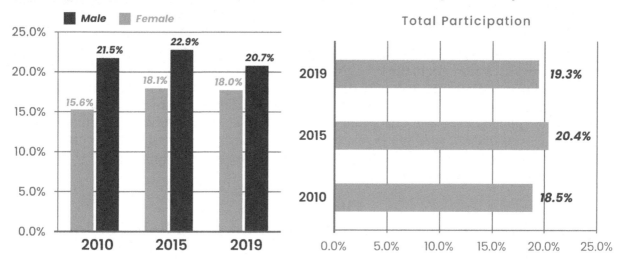

Sports Medicine

Sports participation is vital for a healthy lifestyle; it is good for the heart, respiration and building and maintaining muscular strength. But sports also have negative outcomes. These sports injuries most often occur with falls, muscle strains, and collisions with others.

A significant part of sports medicine involves treating injuries occurring at the professional and college levels. Modern teams work diligently to prevent injuries, condition their athletes and provide nutrition. The video presented in *Figure 7.4* provides a glimpse at a "day in the life" of a professional team's sports medicine doctor.

Sports injuries occur at all levels and during fitness, exercise and outdoor recreation activities. Participants at injury of risk include millions of youth, teens, young adults, adults and seniors. Exercise and organized sports' growing popularity have led to an increase in sports injuries, according to U.S. Department of Health and Human Services data (3):

- An estimated 8.6 million sports injuries occur each year.

- One-third of all sports injuries occur in sports facilities, on athletic fields or on playgrounds.

- Sprains and strains, followed by fractures, are the most common sports injuries.

FIGURE 7.4
A Day in the Life of a Professional Team's Sports Medicine Doctor

Source: https://www.youtube.com/watch?v=bebNvifQsJ4

High school athletes experience an estimated 2 million injuries, 500,000 doctor visits and 30,000 hospitalizations each year (4). In the U.S., about 30 million children and teens participate in some form of organized sports, and more than 3.5 million children aged 14 and younger are hurt playing sports or engaging in recreational activities (5). Sports and recreational activities contribute to approximately 21% of all traumatic brain injuries among American children. *Figure 7.5* presents an estimate of 2020 sports related injuries requiring a hospital visit for children aged 5 to 14. According to the U.S. Centers for Disease Control and Prevention, nearly half of sports injuries among children are preventable.

FIGURE 7.5
2020 Emergency Room Costs, Children Aged 5-14 (billions)

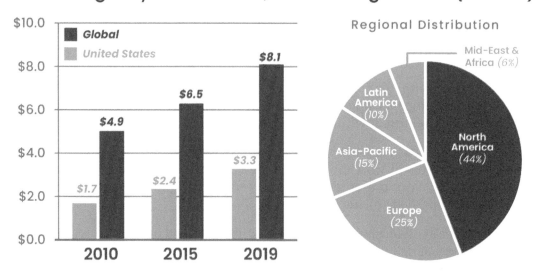

Globally, sports injuries have also increased due to a focus on healthy lifestyles and growing participation in athletics and fitness activities. Global sports medicine market revenues were $8.1 billion in 2019 and were expected to grow significantly over the next several years based on greater participation levels, a shift from reactive to preventative care and increased use of wearable devices that monitor athlete stress and fatigue (6). The market's 2020 revenues were expected to increase 7.4% to $8.7 billion. The growth represents an increased rate compared to the segment's 2010 to 2019 CAGR of 5.7%.

In 2019, the United States dominated the age 5 to 14 sports medicine market with $3.3 billion in revenues, which was 40.7% of global revenues, up from 34.7% in 2010. The change was due to the total U.S. market growing at 8.3% compared to worldwide growth of 5.7% (7).

North America accounted for 44% of global sports medicine revenues in 2019, with Europe comprising 25%. Treatment availability and advanced medical devices for orthopedic injuries were factors driving the sports medicine market at the time. By 2018, Stryker Corporation had installed more than 650 surgical robots around the world to perform more than 76,900 knee and hip replacement procedures.

The Best-Howard Model anticipates the Asia-Pacific region's sports medicine market will grow fastest during the model's forecast period, as countries like China, Japan and South Korea rapidly adopt treatments. The product approval process is less stringent in the countries, which facilitates medical devices' entry into their markets.

In 2019, the body reconstruction and repair sub-segment dominated the U.S. sports medicine market with a 39.2% revenue share (*Figure 7.6*). The segment includes surgical equipment, soft tissue repair equipment and bone reconstruction devices. Its large market share is attributed to growing fracture and ligament repair device use and adoption of arthroscopy devices in minimally invasive surgeries (8).

FIGURE 7.6
U.S. Sports Medicine Revenues (billions)

SPORTS MEDICINE	2010	2015	2019	CAGR	% Total
Reconstruction/ Repair	$ 0.70	$ 0.95	$ 1.21	6.3 %	36.3 %
Support & Recovery	$ 0.45	$ 0.58	$ 0.71	5.3 %	21.2 %
Monitoring & Evaluation	$ 0.34	$ 0.55	$ 0.81	10.1 %	24.2 %
Braces, Bandages, Wraps, etc.	$ 0.18	$ 0.35	$ 0.61	14.5 %	18.2 %
TOTAL	$ 1.67	$ 2.43	$ 3.34	8.3 %	100.0 %

The Best-Howard Model anticipates the accessories sub-segment, which includes braces, bandages, wraps, disinfectants and other products for treating minor sports injuries, will grow more quickly than any other segment for the next several years. The growing use of PRICE therapy—protection, rest, ice, compression, elevation—for immediate sports injury treatment is driving the segment's growth.

Knee applications dominated the sports medicine market in 2019. Knee injuries continue to surge as excessive running and jumping lead to joint wear. According to the British Journal of Sports Medicine, knee issues account for about 41% of total sports injuries. Advanced knee treatments include dry needling, soft tissue massage, osteopathic manipulation, platelet-rich plasma therapy and arthroscopic surgery. The Best-Howard Model expects knee injuries to grow at 8.9% in the years to come.

The 2020 COVID-19 outbreak upended many lives and businesses on an unprecedented scale. Many organized sports activities, including the 2020 Tokyo Olympics and Paralympics, were placed on hold or postponed. According to the CovidSurg Collaborative, a 120-country research initiative analyzing the pandemic's impact on surgeries, consumers canceled or postponed about 28.4 million elective surgeries in 2020, mostly during 12 weeks of peak hospital service disruption. CovidSurg estimates orthopedic procedures were the most affected, with 6.3 million orthopedic surgeries canceled worldwide over the 12 weeks. While the sports medicine market's growth halted due to the COVID-19 outbreak, the Best-Howard Model expects it to achieve a higher growth rate in 2021 than in pre-pandemic years.

Wellness Products

Wellness products assist in injury prevention and recovery, as well as impaired athlete sports participation. Its sub-segments include concussion products, orthopedic braces, orthotics, compression clothing, adaptive sports equipment and healthcare wearables.

SPORTS CONCUSSION PRODUCTS. Data suggests as many as 3.8 million concussions occur in the United States per year during competitive sports and recreational activities. As many as 50% of them go unreported. For children and teens, sports-related concussions can be especially traumatic (9):

- Sports and recreation-related concussions are a leading cause of traumatic brain injury emergency department visits among children and teens.

- Children and teens suffer approximately 70% of all sports- and recreation-related concussions addressed in emergency departments.

- Children have the highest rate of emergency department visits for traumatic brain injuries among all age groups.

Concussions can occur in all sports but are most frequent in football, hockey, rugby, soccer and basketball. The largest number of sports and recreation-related traumatic brain injuries among males occur during bicycling, football and basketball. *Figure 7.7* links to a video providing a history of football helmet technology aimed at preventing injuries and reducing concussions.

FIGURE 7.7
Football Helmet Technology & Concussions

Source: https://www.youtube.com/watch?v=W5slAfJ5S0Y

ORTHOPEDIC BRACES. Orthopedic braces aid in preventing injury during sports activities and reduce pain caused by medical conditions like osteoarthritis and tendonitis. Knee braces are the most common among the devices. The growing prevalence of anterior cruciate ligament (ACL) and posterior cruciate ligament (PCL) injuries, among others, has driven knee brace segment growth (10).

Braces can both support joints to prevent injuries and alleviate pain. They are used for fast post-surgery recovery and rehabilitation, particularly of knee joints. Manufacturers produce braces using a combination of metal, plastic, foam and elastic materials.

The global orthopedic brace and support market was $2.93 billion in 2019, up from $1.76 billion in 2010, a 5.8% CAGR (11). The increasing prevalence of orthopedic diseases and disorders, continuous product commercialization, greater product affordability and availability, rising sports and accident-related injuries and growing public awareness of preventive care have driven the market's growth.

As shown in *Figure 7.8*, four types of knee braces serve consumers' unique needs. Functional braces, primarily used for providing stability during rotation, have the largest market share. The braces are recommended after ACL and PCL injuries and for limiting additional injuries after ligament reconstruction. The types of knee braces are as follows:

- **Prophylactic:** Prevent knee injuries, often among athletes in high-risk sports.

- **Functional:** Support injured knees; used after surgery to help recover and rehabilitate ligaments.

- **Rehabilitative:** Support injured or surgically repaired knees and have carry-over effects from repeated wear, resulting in improved functional abilities and reduced pain after use is discontinued.

- **Unloader:** Provide stability, support and pain relief from osteoarthritis, which primarily affects only one side of the joint; transfer, or "unload," pressure from one side of the joint to the other.

FIGURE 7.8
Global Knee Brace & Materials Sales (billions)

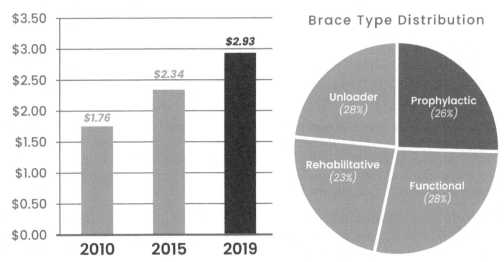

ORTHOTICS. Orthotic insoles are shoe inserts designed to cure and stabilize biomechanical misalignment of feet and lower limbs due to conditions like diabetes, plantar fasciitis, rheumatoid arthritis and foot deformity. The products serve the safety and comfort needs of athletes like football and hockey players, absorbing the shock of extensive foot activity.

The global orthotic insoles market was $3.62 billion in 2019, up from $2.02 billion in 2010, a 6.6% CAGR (*Figure 7.9*). The United States accounted for about 50% of the global market in 2010 but decreased to 48% in 2019 due to its slower growth rate of 6.3% (12). The Best-Howard Model expects the global and U.S. insole markets to continue to grow at similar rates.

Increases in sports activities and custom-made foot products have driven orthotic market demand. Custom-made orthotics require a complete foot structure evaluation and have clinically proven advantages in pain management and comfort over prefabricated products. End-users also increasingly demand 3-D printed orthotics, which are thinner than traditional products and provide increased gait efficiency and proprioception. As shown in *Figure 7.9*, polyethylene foams are used in about 50% of insoles; other materials range from 8.8% to 17.6% of the market (13).

FIGURE 7.9
Global & U.S. Insole & Materials Sales (billions)

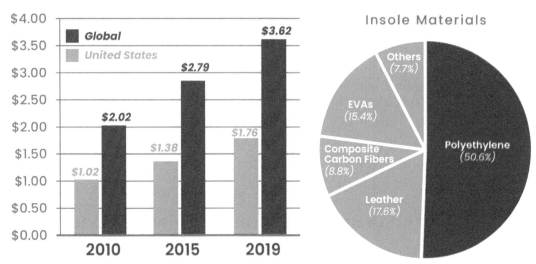

COMPRESSION CLOTHING. Sports compression clothing includes pants, shorts, shirts, socks sleeves and tops that improve performance during exercise and speed recovery afterward by aiding vascular circulation, thus increasing oxygen delivery to muscles and removing metabolic waste products like lactic acid.

Many consumers associate compression stockings with medical conditions among the elderly, such as varicose veins and swollen ankles. However, compression clothing is also beneficial for athletes. Professional athletes and Olympic gold medalists use compression socks and running sleeves to improve training and performance. Compression clothing can improve muscle recovery after fatiguing exercise like marathon training.

The overall sports compression clothing market was $2.9 billion in 2020 and is projected to grow at a 5.35% CAGR to $3.8 billion in 2025. North America and Europe account for more than 60% of sports compression clothing demand.

Adaptive Sports Products. Adaptive equipment is used in sports where the rules accommodate participants with physical differences or impairments. The most common adaptive sports are featured in the Paralympics and include track events, wheelchair tennis, wheelchair basketball, blind judo and sled hockey. Athletes also compete in adaptive surfing and skateboarding, wheelchair motocross, adaptive golf and other activities.

Adaptive sports and their athletes have inspired many technology improvements. 3-D printing has driven many prosthetics developments and made adaptive sports equipment less expensive and more accessible (14). However, the Best-Howard Model has not been able to obtain credible global or U.S. annual sales data for the sector.

As with all athletes, those with disabilities commonly suffer injuries. A 1992 survey indicated 32% of para-athletes sustain injuries resulting in missed competitions (15). Blind athletes' injuries are to the lower extremities more than 50% of the time. Overall, disabled athletes suffer injuries at a rate similar to that of athletes without disabilities.

The Paralympics' growth has driven adaptive sports participation and event numbers (16). The 2016 Paralympics in Rio de Janeiro attracted 1,147 athletes from 140 countries spanning five continents (*Figure 7.10*). Female Paralympics participation grew from 20% in 1976 to almost 40% in 2016.

FIGURE 7.10
Paralympics Country Participation & Medals Awarded

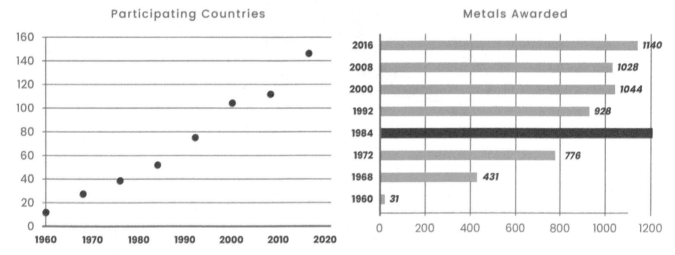

The 2016 Paralympics received 357 hours of television airtime, reaching a cumulative audience of 673 million people. The games' social media channels reached another 23.4 million. The 2020 Paralympics in Tokyo (held in 2021 due to the COVID-19 pandemic) featured several new events, including a mixed-class 4 x 100-meter relay involving two male and two female para-athletes.

HEALTHCARE WEARABLES. The growth of connected smart phones, mobile payment systems, accessibility among the aging population and general activity monitoring has driven market demand for wearable technology. Small sensor devices used for healthcare and medical purposes, often called wearable electronics, are expected to disrupt user habits, consumption patterns and existing business practices in the coming years. See *Figure 7.11* for examples.

Healthcare wearables can be classified in three categories:

• **Activity Trackers:** The main devices used in personal health and fitness management. One in 10 U.S. adults owns an activity tracker. Popular trackers include Fitbit, Apple Watch, Pebble+ and Jawbone. Fitbit is the market leader, shipping nearly 50% of all wearable bands.

• **GPS Monitors:** Used in recreational and competitive sports to deliver performance information. Garmin, one of the largest GPS navigation device providers, has developed several fitness-focused watches and bands for elite athletes and recreational sports enthusiasts.

• **Other:** Unique wearables used in areas outside consumers' typical understanding of personal health and fitness monitors. PosturePulse is a sensor-outfitted belt worn around the

FIGURE 7.11
Wearable Devices in Healthcare, Wellness & Fitness

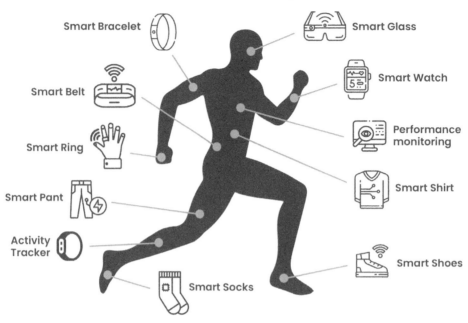

waist to monitor a user's spine position. The device vibrates when the user is in an improper posture for more than seven seconds. Lumo Lift is a similar device worn around the lower back that measures metrics like posture, steps taken and time spent sitting or sleeping (*Figure 7.12*).

FIGURE 7.12
Health Wearables & Smart Clothing

Worldwide demand for health and sports wearables was $9.94 billion in 2019. The market grew from $2.57 billion in 2010 at a rate of 16.2% per year (17). As shown in *Figure 7.13*, almost 58% of sales were for healthcare, with sports and fitness accounting for 42%. The Best-Howard Model therefore estimates the 2019 heath-related wearables market at $5.76 billion. In 2010, North America accounted for 48.8% of worldwide sales but decreased to 41.4% by 2019. The region's sales were $4.11 billion in 2019, up from $1.25 in 2010. North America's growth rate was slower, at 14.1%, than global growth of 16.2%, explaining the region's decreasing percentage of sales.

FIGURE 7.13
Healthcare/Sports & Fitness Wearable Sales (billions)

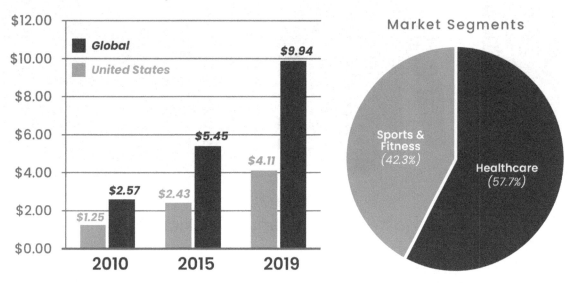

Clothing's core functionality has not changed substantially in thousands of years. But by fusing semiconductors with textiles, manufacturers have created a new generation of apparel intelligent enough to solve health problems and enrich long-term wellness. With seamless integration of technology and apparel, smart clothing can be fashionable, functional and comfortable. The clothing meets consumers' needs in sports, fitness, outdoor activities, leisure, home-wear and healthcare.

The BioMan t-shirt (*Figure 7.14*), for example, features ribbed sleeves measuring heart rate, skin temperature and respiration rate. The garment can be customized to measure skin moisture and physiological signals like electrocardiography, electroencephalography and electromyography.

Smart fabrics and interactive textiles allow personal health management through integration with networked mobile devices. They can integrate sensors/actuators, energy sources, processing capabilities and communications to enable safety, protection, emergency and healthcare applications. For instance, Google and Levi Strauss & Co. have collaborated to launch Project Jacquard, intended to incorporate touch-sensitive yarn into clothing (18).

Smart fabrics' application in sports and fitness overlaps with the healthcare industry (see *Figure 7.14*). Both industries measure similar features, though sports and fitness suppliers face fewer regulatory hurdles, as their offerings are not categorized as medical products. Manufacturers are therefore integrating smart fabrics into t-shirts, shoes, jackets, sports bras and other sportswear. Google and Apple have increased their investments in wearable technology, entering the fashion design field, and Nike and Google have launched a shoe capable of tracking real-time footprints using Google Earth. The shoe allows users to check their movements at any time and gather data for analysis (19).

FIGURE 7.14
Smart Fabric Sensors & Health Monitoring

FIGURE 7.15
Smart Fabric Revenues (billions)

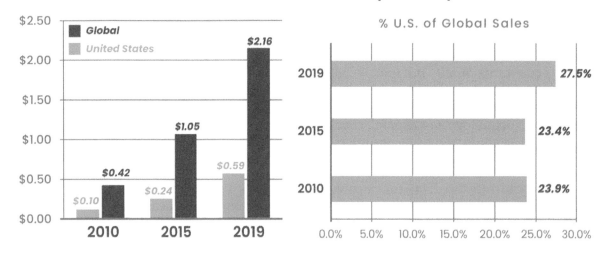

The global demand for smart fabrics was $2.16 billion in 2019. The market grew from $0.42 billion in 2010 at a rate of 19.9% per year (20). In 2010, the United States represented 23.9% of worldwide sales and increased to 27.5% by 2019. U.S. sales were $0.59 in 2019, up from $0.1 billion in 2010. The U.S. growth rate was faster, at 24.8%, than global growth.

Sports Therapy

Physical sports therapy can help athletes prevent injuries and recover from them. The market segment also includes psychological counseling. The relevant sports therapy sub-segments are as follows:

• **Chiropractic Therapy:** Specializes in preventing and caring for musculoskeletal injuries.

• **Therapeutic Massage:** Treats soft tissue aches, pain and injuries associated with recreational activities.

• **Sports Acupuncture:** Speeds healing, relieves pain and increases muscle strength and stamina; embraced by surfers, skaters, runners, baseball players, football players and Olympians.

• **Cryotherapy:** Uses ice to reduce Inflammation and pain due to injuries like strained ligaments and muscles.

• **Compression Therapy:** Relies on controlled pressure to the extremities to increase blood flow and lymphatic and vascular system efficiency.

• **Psychological Counseling:** Addresses athlete performance and wellbeing, as well as developmental and social aspects of sports participation; can also help obese people embrace physical activity and healthy diets.

CHIROPRACTIC THERAPY. Sports chiropractors specialize in musculoskeletal injuries, injury prevention and enhanced athlete performance (21). Chiropractic sports medicine is a relatively new subspecialty. Chiropractic care has existed for thousands of years, but it wasn't until 1980 that the first chiropractor was added to the U.S. Olympic medical team. Since then, spinal adjustments have become important medical treatments for athletes from recreational participants to professionals (22).

The U.S. National Football League reports 100% of its teams had a chiropractor on staff in 2020, up from 31% in 2002 (23). The average NFL team chiropractor performs 30-50 chiropractic treatments per week during football season. Major League Baseball also reports 100% of its teams had a chiropractor on staff in 2020, as do most National Basketball Association and National Hockey League teams, and 72% of PGA golfers received chiropractic care the same year.

The U.S. chiropractic market was valued at $13.5 billion in 2019 and growing at 4.32% per year (24). The Best-Howard Model cannot estimate what percentage of the overall chiropractic market is devoted to sports care but expects the segment to grow rapidly based on increased use in professional athletics.

THERAPEUTIC MASSAGE. Sports massage therapists help condition athletes' muscles at all competition levels. The trained wellness professionals identify their clients' frequency and types of physical activities and apply appropriate massage techniques to various muscle groups. Athletes employ sports massage therapists to condition their muscles prior to sporting events, as well as to help their bodies recover after strenuous training and performances (25).

Massage equipment is an important part of the Health & Wellness core area; 2019 global sales were $6.9 billion (26). North America represented 40.6% of global sales at $2.8 billion that year. While the Best-Howard Model cannot make a sales estimate for sports massage specifically, equipment sales are likely driven by the high concentration of sports enthusiasts in the United States and Canada.

The Asia-Pacific region's massage equipment sales are expected to expand at the fastest rate worldwide at 10.2% from 2019 to 2025. The growth is attributed to increasing awareness of fitness among millennials in countries like China and India.

Massage guns, also known as percussive massagers, were first launched in 2016 and rapidly gained popularity due to their ability to enhance muscle recovery. The devices work like foam rollers, releasing tight muscles and breaking up scar tissue. They can also be used before workouts to prepare muscles for stress. The guns send direct vibration through muscles, decreasing the body's saturated lactic acid levels after heavy workouts. Massage guns can increase blood flow, break up tension, decrease soreness and improve range of motion. They are popular among chiropractors, high-level athletes and other fitness enthusiasts.

The massage gun market has seen increased demand from professional athletes, gymgoers and individuals with chronic muscle pain. Customizable massage accessories fitting specific body areas and advanced sensors have also driven demand. The global market was valued at $267 million in 2019 and growing at 9.8% per year (27). North America, followed by Europe, dominates the global massage gun market, and the trend is expected to continue (28).

SPORTS ACUPUNCTURE. Sports acupuncture operates at three levels: addressing injuries, enhancing recovery and supporting performance. Each level has a unique set of treatment goals and its own sublevels, which also build on each other (29).

Acupuncture is the fastest growing sports therapy segment in North America, as increasing numbers of recreational and professional athletes seek new treatments for injury prevention and management (30). Surfers, skaters, runners, professional baseball and football players and Olympians have embraced acupuncture to speed healing, relieve pain and increase muscle strength and stamina.

The global acupuncture market was $32.2 billion in 2019 and growing at 14.5%, projected to reach $55.3 billion in 2023 (31). While the Best-Howard Model cannot estimate sports acupuncture's percentage of the overall market, it is growing at a faster rate than other segments.

CRYOTHERAPY. Cryotherapy uses ice to reduce inflammation and pain due to sports injuries like strained ligaments and muscles. The technique induces blood flow to injured areas and helps prevent bleeding and swelling. Cryotherapy is most effective immediately after injuries, while warm temperature therapies should be used only after inflammation has decreased.

The cryotherapy market is expected to grow from $206 million in 2019 to $319 million in 2024 at 9.1% CAGR (32). The Best-Howard Model cannot determine the percentage of the market devoted to sports treatment. Growing incidences of sports injuries, cardiac disease and cancers, as well as technological advancements, have driven cryotherapy market growth.

The European cryotherapy market has witnessed especially pronounced growth (33) due to rising sports injury cases and the invention of new cryotherapy applications. Analysts project Europe's cryo-chambers market will grow to more than $70 million by the end of 2024.

COMPRESSION THERAPY. Compression therapy devices help athletes and fitness enthusiasts quickly recover from workouts. Using pulsing technology, compression boots (*Figure 7.16*) function much like stretching and warming up the muscles before and after workouts. The boots repeatedly compress and decompress, encouraging blood flow.

By increasing blood flow to specific body parts, compression therapy devices encourage oxygen and nutrient delivery. Like cryotherapy, compression therapy has existed for decades. In addition to delivering oxygen, nutrients and hormones to every cell in the body, the circulatory system removes metabolic wastes like carbon dioxide and lactic acid, effectively flushing out toxins (34).

FIGURE 7.16
Compression Therapy Boots for Workout Recovery

PSYCHOLOGICAL COUNSELING. Psychological counseling can take a variety of forms for athletes (35). Applied sports psychology focuses on improving performance and endurance. Applied therapists motivate their clients to perform better, making use of meditation, visualization tactics and extrinsic and intrinsic rewards. Professional athletes seek applied psychologists' services when recovering from injuries or facing intense competition.

Clinical sports psychology combines mental health care and applied techniques. When athletes suffer from eating disorders, substance abuse or depression, their performance is affected. Clinical psychologists can help athletes overcome the conditions. The therapists can also address mental roadblocks to improve performance, such as helping a baseball player overcome a hitting slump or a runner regain confidence after an injury (36).

"An athletes' success is 80% mental…What separates the good from the great is between the ears, the way they talk to themselves, their inside communication. If they talk to themselves with a lot of respect, their self-image and esteem is higher. When my self-esteem is high, I have less doubts about my capacity of doing things." - Sports Psychologist Sylvain Guimond

Sports psychologist Sylvain Guimond suggests only 20% of an athlete's success comes from raw, physical talent (37). The remainder comes from mental resiliency. Guimond says as many as 50% of professional athletes suffer from performance anxiety, up from 10% in the early 2000s. With mental health issues, violence and activism in sports on the rise, more athletes and teams have begun seeking sport psychologists' expertise (38).

Psychologists can also assist individuals struggling with weight issues. An estimated 97 million U.S. adults, or more than six out of 10 men and women, are overweight or obese (39). In the United States, approximately 300,000 deaths per year are attributed to a combination of diet and physical inactivity, the two primary causes of obesity.

Sports and fitness psychology focuses on the intersection of sports science, medicine and mental health (40). Sports and physical activity promote health and prevent disease, yet only 23% of Americans exercise enough to obtain the benefits (41). Increasing activity through sports can help, but obesity's causes are complex and can be confounded by mental health and emotional wellbeing. Combining activity with sports psychology can be an effective approach.

Sports Nutrition

Sports nutrition is focused on the following categories of products:

• **Sports Drinks:** Specialty beverages focused on hydration, energy, focus, recovery and protein.

• **Performance Supplements:** Pills and powders used to build muscle, lose weight and improve endurance.

• **Energy & Protein Bars:** Foods supplying the body with protein and carbohydrates; critical for endurance athletes.

SPORTS DRINKS. Sports and energy drinks are rich in electrolytes, amino acids, vitamins, essential nutrients and carbohydrates. Athletes are routinely advised to consume energy drinks during and immediately after working out. Leading sports drink brands include Gatorade, Powerade, Accelerade and All Sport. Gatorade, owned by Pepsico and valued at $6.7 billion in 2019, is among the four most valuable sports brands in the world. Gatorade commanded 72% of the U.S. market in 2019 (42).

Energy depletion drinks focus on athlete deficiencies before and while they perform, when the body often requires an instant source of glucose. They also provide essential vitamins and electrolytes. Energy drinks can be isotonic, hypertonic, hypotonic or carbonated. Leading brands include Red Bull, Full Throttle, Monster Energy, Rockstar and Power Trip.

FIGURE 7.17
Sport Drink Revenues (billions)

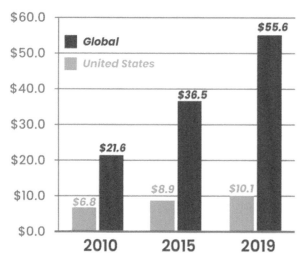

The global sports and energy drinks market value was estimated at $55.6 billion in 2019 (43). As shown in *Figure 7.17*, the global market was $19.4 billion in 2010 and grew worldwide at 11.1% from 2010 to 2019. The U.S. market is roughly 18% of the global market and grew at 5.8% per year from $6.8 billion in 2010 to $10.1 billion in 2019. The United States leads the sports and energy drinks market with a share of 38%. The U.S. market thrives due to elevated general consumption and sporting event sponsorship. An increasing number of consumers beyond sports now seek active lifestyles, and Europe is expected to emerge as the second largest market for sports and energy drinks.

PERFORMANCE SUPPLEMENTS. For many years, only bodybuilders trying to meet consumption needs efficiently thought about sports nutrition. Now, all types of athletes and fitness enthusiasts use sports nutrition to improve their abilities. Sports health products occupy two primary categories:

- **Dietary Supplements:** Ergogenic supplements matching performance goals with micro-nutrients or providing essential fatty acids lacking in the basic diet.

- **Sports-Specific Nutrition:** The basic diet of macronutrients athletes require.

With the rise of wellness culture, average consumers have begun seeking out sports nutrition solutions. Sports nutrition products have therefore expanded to help everyday athletes meet their needs. Marathon runners can use lightweight gels for a quick energy burst, boxers can increase post-fight recovery with simple supplements and weightlifters can use them to control their protein and carbohydrate intake.

We can expect the sports nutrition field to continue expanding rapidly.

The global sports nutrition market value was $15.6 billion in 2019 and expected to grow at 8.9% CAGR from 2020 to 2027 (44). Nutritional bars, dietary supplements and energy drinks all are in increasing demand. Rising disposable income, rapid urbanization and the growth of gyms and fitness centers endorsing nutrition products have positively influenced the market's growth.

As shown in *Figure 7.18*, the U.S. performance supplement market decreased from 52.9% of global sales in 2010 to 48.7% in 2019. The market grew at a 1% CAGR, more slowly than the global market's growth of 7.9%. In 2019, U.S. sales of performance supplements were $7.5 billion.

FIGURE 7.18
Performance Supplement Sales (billions)

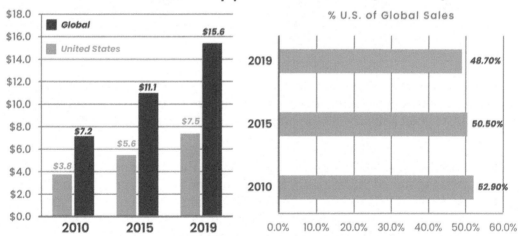

ENERGY & PROTEIN BARS. Although proper nutrition is important for all consumers' health and wellness, athletes have enhanced nutritional needs due to their physical output. Energy bars, often composed of cereals, include instant energy-providing nutrients like protein, carbohydrates, vitamins and minerals.

The energy bar market includes products designed to meet both daily and sports nutrition needs. Growing demand for functional foods, indulgences, meal replacements and on-the-go snacking have fueled the market's growth.

Global energy bar sales were $4.32 billion in 2019, up from $3.2 billion in 2010, with an annual growth rate of 3.8% (45). As shown in *Figure 7.19*, 2019 U.S. sales were $2.5 billion, up from $1.55 billion in 2010, an annual growth rate of 5.5%. In 2019, the U.S. market was about 58% of worldwide energy bar sales. While consumers involved in sports and outdoor activities constitute a large market segment, the Best-Howard Model cannot precisely estimate the segment's sales.

Data suggests consumers adjusting to new lifestyles during the 2020 COVID-19 pandemic began choosing convenient, healthy snacking options like energy bars in greater numbers. The demand for energy bars is consistently high in developed countries due to their convenience (46).

FIGURE 7.19
Nutritional Bar Sales

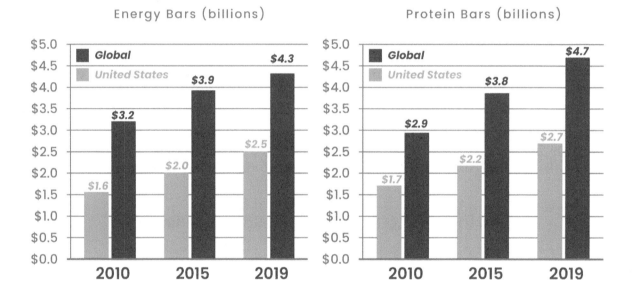

Nutritional bars providing a protein supplement have also attracted consumers desiring healthy, ready-to-eat foods, and manufacturers have responded. Manufacturers have increasingly offered snack bars that taste good and provide the protein sports and outdoor recreation enthusiasts desire.

Global protein bar sales were $4.7 billion in 2019 (47), and the market was growing at 5.5% per year. The U.S. market garnered 2019 sales of $2.7 billion and was also growing at 5.5% per year. However, the Best-Howard Model expects the COVID-19 pandemic to fuel the market's growth going forward. While sales were down about 10% from 2019 to 2020, the model suggests protein bar sales will grow at a faster rate than 5.5% in the coming years.

Worldwide Health & Wellness core area sales were $104.3 billion in 2019. U.S. sales were 41% of the global total, at $42.3 billion. Sales for the core area's four critical segments are shown in *Figure 7.20*. The global sports nutrition segment, at $8.2 billion, accounted for 77% of worldwide Health & Wellness sales. Sports medicine was estimated at 7.8%, wellness products at 6.4% and sports therapy at 8.9%. The sales estimates are likely underestimated, as the Best-Howard Model is forced to rely on incomplete data for the sports medicine and therapy sub-segments.

FIGURE 7.20

2019 Sports Health & Wellness Segment Sales (billions)

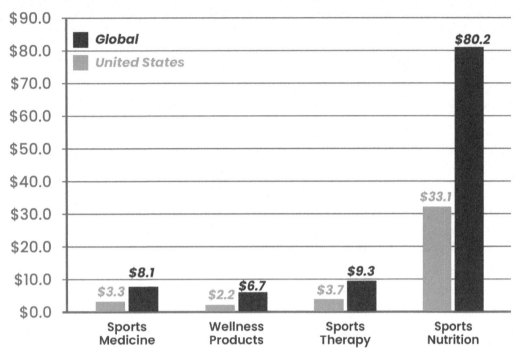

References

We have added links to many references for direct and easy access. While we have tested each link, there are a few instances where the websites are no longer accessible. We will continue to monitor the accessibility of citation references and remove any links no longer active. In many instances the referenced data was purchased, this is noted.

1. David Lange, Physical Activity - Statistics & Facts, Mar 16, 2021. Statista (www.statista.com). (GSI Purchased Report)

2. Lange

3. "Sports Injuries: Trends and Prevention," Cary Orthopaedics (www.caryortho.com).

4. StopSportsInjuries.com.

5. "How frequently do sports injuries occur?" Hopkins Medicine (www.hopkinsmedicine.org).

6. Sports Medicine Market Size, Share & Trends Analysis Report By Application (Knees, Shoulders, Ankle & Foot), By Product Type (Body Reconstruction & Repair, Body Support & Recovery), By Region, And Segment Forecasts, 2020 – 2027. Grand View Research (www.grandviewresearch.com).

7. Sports Medicine Market Size, Share & Trends Analysis Report By Application

8. "How frequently do sports injuries occur?"

9. "Concussion and Sports" Brainline (www.brainline.org).

10. Knee Braces Market Size, Share & Trends Analysis Report By Product (Prophylactic, Functional), By Application (Sports, Arthritis), By Delivery Channel (Hospitals, E-Commerce), And Segment Forecasts, 2019 – 2026. Grand View Research (www.grandviewresearch.com).

11. Orthopedic Braces & Supports Market by Product (Knee, Ankle, Hip, Spine, Shoulder, Neck, Elbow, Hand, Wrist), Category (Soft, Hard, Hinged), Application (Ligament (ACL, LCL), Preventive, OA), Distribution (Hospital) & Region - Global Forecast to 2025. Markets and Markets (www.marketsandmarkets.com).

12. Global Foot Orthotic Insoles Market to 2023 - Market to Reach Revenue of $4.58 Billion. PR Newswire (www.prnewswire.com).

13. Foot Orthotic Insoles Market Size, Share & Trends Analysis Report By Product (Polyethylene Foams, EVAs), By Application (Medical, Sports & Athletics), By Distribution Channel (Hospitals & Specialty Clinics), And Segment Forecasts, 2019 – 2026. Grand View Research (www.grandviewresearch.com).

14. "The Rise of Adaptive Sports" Sport Techie (www.sporttechie.com).

15. "Athletes with Disabilities, Injury Epidemiology in Athletes with Disabilities" Physiopedia (www.physio-pedia.com).

16. HISTORY OF PARA ATHLETICS. Paralympic (www.paralympic.org).

17. Mind Commerce, Connected Wearable Device Market in Healthcare, Wellness, and Fitness Market Outlook and Forecasts 2021 – 2028

18. Global Smart Fabrics Industry Report 2020-2025 - AIQ Smart Clothing, Interactive Wear, Ohmatex, Nike, Schoeller Textil, Sensoria, and Textronics are Dominating, May, 2020. PR Newswire (www.prnewswire.com).

19. Global Smart Textiles Markets Report 2020: U.S. Market is Estimated at $740 Million, While China is Forecast to Grow at 24.8% CAGR, September 30, 2020. Globe Newswire (www.globenewswire.com).

20. Market size estimate comparison for the global smart clothing/fabrics market from 2018 to 2025. Statista (www.statista.com). (GSI Purchased Report)

21. Sports Chiropractic: The Athlete's Secret Weapon. _The Joint Chiropractic_ (www.thejoint.com).

22. Chiropractic Sports Counsel, History. _Chiropractic Sports Council_ (www.acasc.org).

23. SPORTS CHIROPRACTIC: A WINNING SOLUTION FOR ATHLETES. _Palmer College of Chiropractic_ (www.palmer.edu).

24. U.S. Chiropractic Market Size, Share & Trends Analysis Report By Entity Type (Solo DC, DC Group), By Location Spread (West, South, Midwest, East), Vendor Landscape, And Segment Forecasts, 2018 – 2025. _Grand View Research_ (www.grandviewresearch.com).

25. What is a Sports Massage Therapist? _Sports Management Degrees_ (www.sports-management-degrees.com).

26. Massage Equipment Market Size, Share & Trends Analysis Report By Product (Chairs & Sofas, Handheld), By Application (Commercial, Home), By Region, And Segment Forecasts, 2019 – 2025. _Grand View Research_ (www.grandviewresearch.com).

27. Massage Guns Market, By End Users (Individuals, Athletes, Trainers, Chiropractors); By Region (North America, Europe, Benelux Union, Asia Pacific, Middle East & Africa, Latin America) – Global Insights, Growth, Size, Comparative Analysis, Trends And Forecast, 2019 – 2027. _Absolute Market Insights_ (www.absolutemarketsinsights.com).

28. Massage Guns Market: Global Industry Analysis 2015-2019 and Opportunity Assessment 2020-20. _Future Market Insights_ (www.futuremarketinsights.com).

29. The Sports Acupuncture Pyramid. _Valley Health Clinic_ (valleyhealthclinic.com).

30. Acupuncture for sports injuries growing in popularity. _Health Times_ (healthtimes.com.au).

31. Acupuncture Market In-Depth Analysis By Size, Share, Current Trends, High Cost of Treatment, Competitive Outlook and Global Market Opportunities From 2019 – 2023. _Medgadget_ (www.medgadget.com).

32. Cryotherapy Market by Product (Cryosurgery Devices, Localized Cryotherapy Devices, Cryosaunas), Application (Surgical Application, Pain Management, Health & Beauty), End User (Hospitals & Specialty Clinics, Spas) - Global Forecast to 2024, _Markets and Markets_ (www.marketsandmarkets.com).

33. _Cryo Action_ (www.cryoaction.com).

34. "What's a NormaTec? The compression therapy elite athletes love" _CNET_ (www.cnet.com).

35. "Is Sports Psychology a Growing Field?" _Online Psychology Degrees_ (www.online-psychology-degrees.org).

36. _American Psychological Association_ (www.apa.org).

37. _Montreal Gazette_ (www.montrealgazette.com).

38. _American Psychological Association_ (www.apa.org).

39. "Counseling for Physical Activity in Overweight and Obese Patients" _American Family Physician_ (www.aafp.org).

40. Sport / Fitness Psychology. _Good Therapy_ (www.goodtherapy.org).

41. "Sport Psychology Provides Integrated Treatment for Obesity" _Sport Psychology Today_ (www.sportpsychologytoday.com).

42. "Global Sports Drinks Revenues 2019," Sports Drinks (e.g. Gatorade) Global (2017):Mordor Intelligence: Sports Drink Market – Segmented by Type, Packaging and Sales Channel, and Geography - Growth, Trends, and Forecast (2018 - 2023). _Mordor Intelligence_ (www.mordorintelligence.com).

43. "USA Sports Drinks Revenues 2019," Sports Drinks (e.g. Gatorade) US (2020): Statista: Retail dollar sales of sports drinks in the United States from 2012 to 2019 (in million U.S. dollars). _Statista_ (www.statista.com). (GSI Purchased Report)

44. *Sports Nutrition Market Size, Share & Trends Analysis Report By Product (Drinks, Supplements, Foods), By Distribution Channel (Ecommerce, Bricks & Mortar), By Region, And Segment Forecasts, 2020 – 2027*

45. *Energy Bar Market Size 2021 with a CAGR of 3.8% , Top Companies data report covers, Market-specific challenges, Share, Growth, Trends, and Forecasts 2021–2025. WBOC (www.wboc.com).*

46. *ENERGY BAR MARKET - GROWTH, TREND AND FORECAST (2021 - 2026). Mordor Intelligence (www.mordorintelligence.com).*

47. *Protein Bar Market Size, Share & COVID-19 Impact Analysis, By Source (Plant-Based and Animal-Based), By Type (Sports Nutritional Bars, Meal-Replacement Bars, and Others), By Distribution Channel, and Regional Forecast, 2020-2027. Fortune Business Insights (www.fortunebusinessinsights.com).*

PART IV:
Sports Participation

Sports Participation, the third domain in the Best-Howard Sports Industry Model, captures active sports and recreational activity engagement by everyday people. Their engagement is driven by a range of motives: playing a game they love, sharing experiences with friends, improving health and fitness, and observing and interacting with the outdoor world.

Part IV of The Sports Industry explores each core area of the Sports Participation domain: Sports Recreation, Fitness & Exercise and Outdoor Recreation. Each chapter provides in-depth analysis of participation and spending patterns for the three to five segments comprising each core area (*Figure I*).

FIGURE I
Sports Participation Core Areas

CHAPTER 8
Sports Recreation

Outdoor Recreational Sports
Indoor Recreational Sports
Youth Sports

CHAPTER 9
Fitness & Exercise

Fitness Clubs
Exercise Studios
Coaches/Trainers
Specialty Gyms

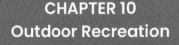

CHAPTER 10
Outdoor Recreation

Camping
Hunting/Fishing
Water Sports
Snow Sports
Equestrian

In examining the global sports industry's economic magnitude, the Best-Howard Model finds participation costs are universally ignored in existing estimates. Estimation efforts limit measurement to at most two dimensions of the model—Fan Engagement (event revenues from tickets, sponsorships, media rights and merchandise sales) and Sports Products (sportswear, equipment, and vehicles consumers buy to camp, golf, ski, etc.).

Missing in almost all available estimates are the direct costs paid by participants to engage in sports and recreational activities. The costs include user fees (e.g., golf greens fees, ski lift tickets), registration fees (e.g., for leagues), licenses and permits (e.g., for hunting, fishing or operating a pleasure boat), membership fees (e.g., for fitness or country clubs), rental fees (e.g., for recreational vehicles, jet skis or ski equipment) and trip-related expenses (e.g., for transportation and lodging).

FIGURE II
Sports Participation in The Best-Howard Model (U.S. billions)

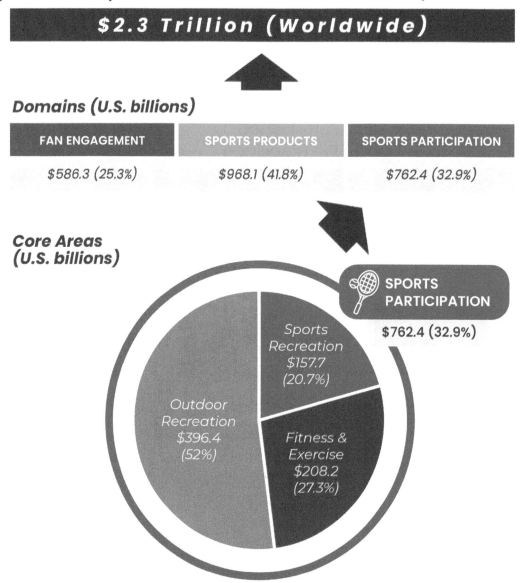

Copyright Best-Howard Model 2022. All Right Reserved.

The three Sports Participation-focused chapters of The Sports Industry captures all available data on how much participants spend in each of the fee and expense areas.

As highlighted in Best-Howard Model (*Figure II*), sports enthusiasts in the United States and around the world spend billions engaging in their favorite pastimes, from competing in recreational sports like golf and tennis, to enhancing their physical and mental wellbeing through yoga and martial arts classes, to camping, fishing, hunting and hiking. Americans spend lavishly across all three core areas, accounting for half the $144 billion spent on recreational sports globally in 2019 and more than a third of total fitness and exercise and outdoor recreation spending.

The Best-Howard Model estimates consumers worldwide spent $762.4 billion engaging in sports-related activities in 2019. U.S. participants accounted for about 38.9% of the total, or $296.7 billion.

SPORTS RECREATION

Segment	Revenues
Outdoor	$ 96.6
Indoor	$ 19.6
Youth	$ 41.4
TOTAL	**$ 157.7**

FITNESS & EXERCISE

Segments	Revenues
Health & Fitness Clubs	$ 96.7
Exercise Studios	$ 53.2
Coaches & Trainers	$ 19.1
Specialty Gyms	$ 39.2
TOTAL	**$ 208.2**

OUTDOOR RECREATION

Segments	Revenues
Camping	$ 41.6
Hunting & Fishing	$ 87.2
Snow Sports	$ 25.3
Water Sports	$ 25.0
Equestrian	$ 217.3
TOTAL	**$ 396.4**

Revenue totals across the Sports Participation domain's three core areas demonstrated healthy growth rates from 2010-2019 in the United States and globally. Outdoor recreation has become the dominant category due to the increased popularity of camping and caravanning and the inclusion of equestrian sports. Revenues related to purchasing and operating recreational vehicles and boarding, training, breeding and campaigning horses have increased dramatically in recent years, elevating total outdoor recreation spending to nearly $400 billion in 2019.

Each Sports Participation-focused chapter examines the differential impact of the COVID-19 pandemic on participation and spending levels. All seven activity segments in the Sports Recreation and Fitness & Exercise core areas suffered substantial losses in 2020 due to government-imposed closures. Conversely, all five Outdoor Recreation activity segments flourished as people around the world sought safe recreational environments. The Best-Howard model offers post-pandemic financial recovery forecasts for key activity segments.

Collecting credible data on participation spending is difficult. Hundreds of millions of people engage in the most popular sports around the globe, but the figures cited widely in the popular press often lack verifiable sourcing. For example, cricket's governing body launched a campaign "to celebrate the 460 million playing all forms of cricket around the world" prior to the sport's 2019 world championship (1). A comprehensive search found no credible source for the participation figure the International Cricket Council cited. Similarly, USA Volleyball once claimed without verification that 800 million people around the world play the sport, "making it the most popular participation sport" (2). The sport's international governing body, Fédération Internationale de Volleyball, states volleyball is "the fourth most popular sport globally, with more than 800 million fans and high participation across attractive markets"(3). One source estimates global volleyball participation at 998 million individuals (4).

Volleyball organizations are not alone in lacking data attribution and reporting varying participation numbers. Fortunately, multiple reputable publications provide credible figures on participation rates and spending across a spectrum of sports, fitness and recreation activities.

The Best-Howard Model relies on IBISWorld and Statista for much of its Sports Participation data. While the organizations aggregate data globally, their coverage is limited for some sports and world regions. Statista, for example, provides cricket participation data for only two countries, England (292,000) and Australia (541,000). Missing are figures on the leading cricket-playing countries in the world—India, Pakistan and Bangladesh—likely because accurate figures do not exist. IBISWorld provides extensive analyses of each industry sector; however, it focuses primarily on the U.S. sports market.

IBISWorld and Statista aggregate and report only data they retrieve. Thus, their emphasis on the United States reflects the country's credible sports participation and spending data. The reliable U.S. sports and recreation participation data is evident through all three Sports Participation chapters in The Sports Industry. Each chapter also draws on information from the U.S. Census Bureau, Bureau of Labor Statistics, National Park Service, U.S. Fish & Wildlife Service and U.S. Forest Service. Multiple U.S. nonprofit and private organizations, such as the Outdoor Industry Association, Aspen Institute and Sports Industry Association, provide detailed statistical reports on participation trends and spending patterns. Reputable American business and sports-specialty analysts, including Forbes magazine, PricewaterhouseCoopers, Sportico and the Sports Business Journal, are rich resources, as well.

The Best-Howard Model draws on credible global Sports Participation sources where available. Commercially produced reports (e.g., Laurent Vanat's 2020 International Report on Snow & Mountain Tourism and The Equine Industry: A Global Perspective) and data from international and national sports governing bodies and trade associations (e.g., The International Health, Racquet & Sportsclub Association) are critical. Wherever the Best-Howard Model is unable to source credible participation and/or spending data, NA (i.e., not available) is used.

References

We have added links to many references for direct and easy access. While we have tested each link, there are a few instances where the websites are no longer accessible. We will continue to monitor the accessibility of citation references and remove any links no longer active. In many instances the referenced data was purchased, this is noted.

1. World Cricket launches Criiio on the eve of the ICC Men's Cricket World Cup 2019. *ICC* (icc-cricket.com).

2. "International Volleyball Fact Sheet," *The Washington Post* (www.washingtonpost.com).

3. "FIVB partners with CVC Capital Partners to drive global growth of volleyball," January 1, 2021. *FIVB* (www.fivb.com).

4. "Top 10 most popular sports in the world by participation," 2017. *Pledge Sports* (www.pledgesports.org).

Indoor & Outdoor

Most people begin engaging in recreational sports at an early age through informal play in public playgrounds, parks, swimming pools and school gyms. Once introduced to the activities, many young people move on to participate in organized youth sports leagues sponsored by nonprofit organizations or government entities.

The Best-Howard Model's Sports Recreation core area presents data on recreational sports pastimes, highlighting the most popular activities and how often individuals participate in them (*Figure 8.1*). The model divides the activities into those played primarily outdoors versus indoors, further differentiating them as team or individual sports. The model also examines emerging trends and challenges in youth sports, a nearly $25 billion global industry segment.

The Best-Howard Model's Sports Recreation core area examines participation trends in each activity over the period from 2010 to 2019 and examines how much participants spend on them annually. The model considers COVID-19's 2020 impact separately.

Individuals spent more than $157 billion worldwide participating in recreational sports in 2019 (*Figure 8.2*). Americans accounted for slightly more than half the global total at nearly $80 billion. While all three segments highlighted in *Figure 8.2* grew steadily from 2010 to 2019, COVID-19 induced lockdowns resulted in significant financial losses for almost all recreational sports in 2020 (1).

While reliable data on popular recreation sport activities were obtainable for a number of countries (2), participation and spending figures were not available from many parts of the developing world. Some of the available data were dated. The most current study of sports participation in European nations was published in 2016. Eurostat found that 43% of the European Union population above 15-years-old reported "practicing sports or some physical activity at least once a week," in 2014 and "less than a third of the E.U. population attended a live sporting event in 2015" (3). The report provides active participation data by gender and age level for 27 E.U. nations.

Estimates of global soccer participation numbers range from 250 million to 270 million "actively involved" players. The sources for the most recent estimates are from two FIFA "Big Count" surveys released in 2001 and 2007 (4).

Due to these limitations, it is important to recognize that several of the global figures cited in this chapter could not be fully authenticated and should be viewed as "best estimates." Conversely, the annual participation and spending figures for the United States are drawn from several highly reputable sources and should be viewed as "best available" data.

FIGURE 8.1
The Best-Howard Model's Sports Recreation Core Area

$2.3 Trillion (Worldwide)

Domains (U.S. billions)

FAN ENGAGEMENT	SPORTS PRODUCTS	SPORTS PARTICIPATION
$586.3 (25.3%)	$968.1 (41.8%)	$762.4 (32.9%)

Core Areas (U.S. billions)

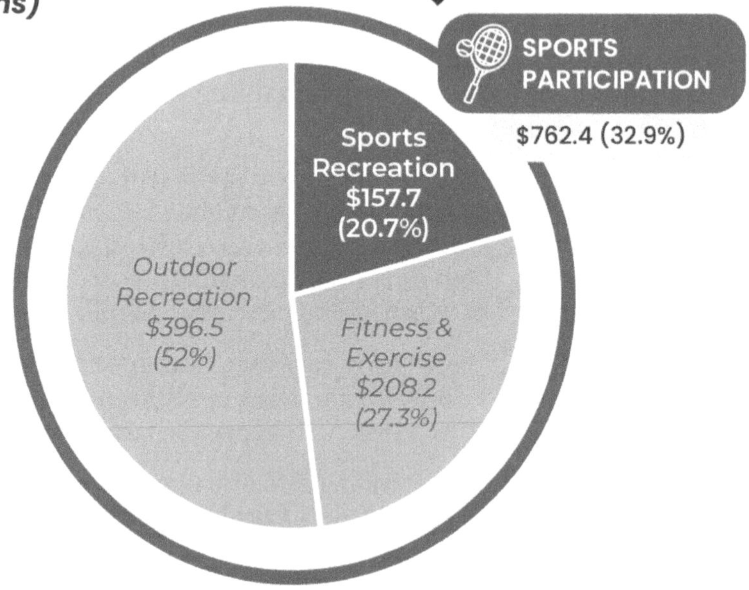

Sports Recreation $157.7 (20.7%)

Outdoor Recreation $396.5 (52%)

Fitness & Exercise $208.2 (27.3%)

SPORTS PARTICIPATION $762.4 (32.9%)

Segments (U.S. billions)

Sports Recreation Segments	Revenues	Percent
Outdoor	$ 96.6	61.3 %
Indoor	$ 19.6	12.4 %
Youth	$ 41.4	26.3 %
TOTAL	**$ 157.7**	**100.0 %**

Copyright Best-Howard Model 2022. All Right Reserved.

The Best-Howard Model's Sports Recreation participation trends analysis is therefore largely limited to U.S. data. The model relies primarily on data provided by The Sports & Fitness Industry Association (SFIA). SFIA collaborates with eight major industry trade associations to provide detailed annual reports on participation levels across 122 sports and recreational activities in the United States (5). SFIA's 2020 "Topline Report" provides the participation trends for key recreational sports from 2014 to 2019.

Fluctuating engagement levels have impacted the amount participants spend on recreation sports. In the absence of reliable global data, the Best-Howard Model's revenue analysis relies heavily on reputable U.S. data sources, including IBISWorld, Statista and relevant sports industry trade associations.

FIGURE 8.2
Total Sports Recreation Participation Revenues (billions)

REVENUE SOURCES	U.S. 2010	Global 2010	% U.S.	U.S. 2015	Global 2015	% U.S.	U.S. 2019	Global 2019	% U.S.	U.S. CAGR	Global CAGR
Outdoor Sports											
Golf Courses	$23.80	$45.81	51.9%	$24.10	$47.60	50.6%	$24.50	$50.01	49.0%	0.3%	1.0%
Recreational Sports (e.g., adult sports leagues, driving ranges, go-kart tracks)	$9.63	$24.87	38.7%	$13.11	$33.60	39.0%	$15.62	$40.20	39.9%	5.5%	5.5%
Organized Athletic Events (e.g., running, cycling)	$1.62	$4.03	40.2%	$1.93	$4.82	40.1%	$2.58	$6.42	40.2%	5.3%	5.3%
TOTAL	$35.05	$74.71	46.9%	$39.14	$86.02	45.5%	$42.70	$96.63	44.2%	2.2%	2.9%
Indoor Sports											
Indoor Swim Complexes[1]	$1.19	$3.05	39.0%	$1.39	$3.56	39.0%	$1.56	$4.01	38.9%	3.1%	3.1%
Bowling Centers	$3.62	$8.94	40.4%	$3.74	$9.18	40.6%	$4.18	$9.99	41.8%	1.6%	1.2%
Ice Rinks (e.g., leagues, tournaments, skating)	$0.65	$1.64	39.6%	$0.82	$2.07	39.7%	$0.91	$2.28	39.9%	3.8%	3.7%
Special Indoor Facilities (e.g., tennis, soccer)	$0.80	$1.94	41.2%	$1.22	$3.04	40.0%	$1.37	$3.34	40.0%	6.2%	6.2%
TOTAL	$6.26	$15.57	40.2%	$7.17	$17.85	40.2%	$8.02	$19.62	40.9%	2.8%	2.6%
Youth Sports											
Sports Camps	$5.61	$7.71	72.8%	$8.56	$11.81	72.5%	$9.92	$12.71	72.1%	6.5%	5.7%
Leagues	$6.90	$8.10	74.1%	$10.87	$14.69	74.0%	$19.20	$28.70	66.9%	12.0%	15.1%
TOTAL	$11.61	$15.81	73.1%	$19.43	$26.50	73.3%	$29.12	$41.41	69.6%	10.8%	11.3%
TOTAL REVENUE	$52.9	$106.1	49.8%	$65.74	$130.1	50.5%	$79.8	$157.7[2]	50%	4.7%	4.5%

Source: Revenues compiled from multiple sources listed as (1) in the References section below. [1] Includes both private and publicly operated pools; data do not distinguish between indoor and outdoor swim complexes. [2] Estimate

Team & Individual Outdoor Sports

Figure 8.3 presents the number of Americans 6 years and older annually participating in popular outdoor team and individual sports from 2014 to 2019 (5). The data distinguish between committed participants (i.e., "core") from those who participate less frequently. Core participants typically play on organized adult and/or youth sports teams and account for 40% to 60% of all participants in the eight outdoor sports listed in the figure.

FIGURE 8.3
U.S. Team & Individual Outdoor Sports Participation
(thousands of participants)

Activity (millions)	Definition	2014	2015	2016	2017	2018	2019	1-year change	3-year CAGR	5-year CAGR
TEAM SPORTS										
Baseball	Total 1+ times	13,152	13,711	14,760	15,877	15,877	15,804	-0.5%	2.3%	3.8%
	Core 13+ times	8,857	8,908	9,087	9,238	9,314	9,149	-1.8%	3.8%	0.7%
Basketball	Total 1+ times	23,067	23,410	22,343	23,401	24,225	24,917	2.9%	3.7%	1.6%
	Core 13+ times	15,746	15,636	14,957	14,856	14,890	15,248	2.4%	0.9%	-0.6%
Football (Flag)	Total 1+ times	5,508	5,829	6,173	6,551	6,572	6,783	3.2%	3.2%	4.3%
	Core 13+ times	2,669	2,724	2,924	2,979	2,999	2,989	6.2%	5.4%	6.0%
	Core 6-17yrs 13+	1,178	1,276	1,401	1,565	1,578	1,590	-0.3%	4.4%	6.3%
Football (Tackle)	Total 1+ times	5,978	6,222	5,481	5,224	5,157	5,107	-1.0%	-2.3%	-3.0%
	Core 13+ times	3,390	3,380	3,240	3,078	2,898	2,694	-7.1%	-6.0%	-4.5%
	Core 6-17yrs 13+	2,590	2,539	2,543	2,427	2,353	2,311	-1.8%	-3.1%	-2.2%
Lacrosse	Total 1+ times	2,011	2,094	2,090	2,171	2,098	2,115	0.8%	0.4%	1.1%
	Core 13+ times	1,032	947	938	1,030	1,061	1,094	3.1%	5.3%	1.3%
Rugby	Total 1+ times	1,276	1,349	1,550	1,621	1,560	1,392	-10.8%	-3.3%	2.1%
	Core 8+ times	440	431	460	524	562	557	-0.9%	6.8%	5.0%
Soccer (Outdoor)	Total 1+ times	12,592	12,646	11,932	11,924	11,405	11,913	4.5%	0.0%	-1.0%
	Core 26+ times	5,971	5,949	5,590	5,259	4,975	5,050	1.5%	-3.3%	-3.2%
Softball (Slo-pitch)	Total 1+ times	7,077	7,114	7,690	7,283	7,386	7,071	-4.3%	-2.7%	0.1%
	Core 13+ times	4,252	4,110	4,314	4,223	4,105	4,048	-1.4%	-2.1%	-0.9%
INDIVIDUAL SPORTS										
Bicycling (street/paved)	Total 1+ times	39,725	38,280	38,365	38,886	39,041	39,338	0.9%	0.9%	-0.2%
	Core 26+ times	20,456	19,435	19,121	18,654	18,264	18,592	1.8%	-0.9%	-1.9%
Golf (9/18 holes)	Total 1+ times	24,700	24,100	23,815	23,829	24,240	24,271	0.1%	0.6%	-0.3%
Golf (off-course)	Total 1+ times	5,362	6,998	8,173	8,345	9,279	9,905	6.7%	6.7%	13.5%
Skateboarding	Total 1+ times	6,582	6,436	6,442	6,382	6,500	6,610	1.7%	0.9%	0.1%
	Core 26+ times	2,700	2,569	2,487	2,411	2,511	2,345	-6.6%	-1.8%	-2.7%
Tennis	Total 1+ times	17,904	17,963	18,079	17,683	17,841	17,684	-0.9%	-0.7%	-0.2%

Figure 8.3 shows a slow, persistent participation decline for most mainstream outdoor sports from 2014 to 2019 in the United States. Lacrosse was the only activity displaying consistent growth on the three time comparisons displayed in the figure.

Core participation as a percentage of the total has also declined for team sports. Tackle football and soccer have driven the trend. Football had 700,000 fewer core participants in 2019 compared to 2014. The loss was greater for soccer, which had 920,000 fewer committed players (i.e., those participating in 26-plus times) in 2019 than it did in 2014. While total baseball and basketball participation grew during the same period, the sports' percentages of core participants declined significantly. The percentage of those playing baseball more than 13 times per year fell from 67% in 2014 to 58% in 2019. For basketball, the number declined from 68% to 61%, a loss of nearly 500,000 participants. The core segment's erosion has implications for many sports industry sectors, principally manufacturers, retailers, teams and leagues.

Apart from a 0.3% decline in young core participants in 2019, flag (or non-contact) football showed the highest annual growth rate from 2014 to 2019 for all (6%) and young core (6.3%) participants. Tackle football, the American sport's full contact version, suffered major declines, with a loss of 871,000 participants over the five-year measurement period. The number of youth (6-17 years of age) playing tackle football fell by 279,000 over the same period. Growing concern over tackle football's dangers, particularly its high concussion risk, has led many parents to keep their children out of the sport. A 2016 survey found 78% of U.S. adults do not think tackle football is appropriate for children before age 14 (6). In 2019, high school tackle football participation dropped to its lowest point since 2000 (7).

The National Football League has aggressively moved to expand opportunities for children to play flag football. The league's NFL Flag program provides a relatively safe way to learn the game's fundamental skills. The NFL believes the initiative can provide an attractive gateway for children to continue playing, "serving as a great entry point to the game of football" (8). Reliable data is not yet available to determine whether flag football's growing popularity will result in more high school students transitioning to tackle football.

Soccer, slow pitch softball and baseball all experienced moderate U.S. participant losses over the five-year period. Baseball lost 1.8% of core participants from 2018 to 2019; slow pitch softball lost 4.3% of total participants and 1.4% of core participants the same year. The one-year declines may prove to be an aberration, but given youth sports' widespread shutdown during much of 2020, it may be several years before analysts know if the sports will recover.

Rugby suffered extensive losses in 2019. The sport's ability to preserve many of its core participants in the United States moderated its 11% decline in overall participation.

FIGURE 8.4
Simulated Golf Courses Have Grown in Popularity

Overall U.S. individual outdoor sports participation also showed a pattern of decline from 2014 to 2019. While golf participation levels stabilized in 2018 and 2019, 429,000 fewer Americans played on regulation courses in 2019 than in 2014. However, increasing numbers of participants began playing golf in off-course settings, as driving ranges and golf entertainment venues (i.e., simulators, *Figure 8.4*) have grown faster than any other activity. In 2019, nearly 10 million people reported playing golf exclusively in off-course settings. The rapidly growing number of alternative golfers appears to have had little impact on traditional golf participation. However, golfers played a record number of rounds during the last half of 2020 as COVID-19 restrictions were relaxed.

U.S. tennis participation remained relatively stable during the period, although its rate of decline increased from a five-year average of 0.1% to 0.9% in 2019. The net result was 300,000 fewer Americans playing tennis in 2019 than in 2014. Skateboarding showed a modest increase (0.1%) in total participants over the five-year period. The sport lost 166,000 core participants (i.e., those skating 26 or more times per year) in 2019 but experienced a boom during the COVID-19 pandemic. The industry's trade association reported, "skateboarding popularity skyrocketed the moment we went into lockdown" (9). Analysts also expressed hope that skateboarding's first-ever appearance in the Olympics in 2021 would fuel further global growth.

Total global spending on outdoor sports and recreation activities amounted to $97 billion in 2019, accounting for more than 60% of all Sports Recreation spending (*Figure 8.5*). Americans contributed the largest share across all three activity segments, supplying nearly half the estimated world's golf total and 40% for both recreational sports and organized athletic events like marathons and cycling races.

FIGURE 8.5
Outdoor Recreational Sports Participation Revenues (billions)

OUTDOOR SPORTS	U.S. 2010	Global 2010	% U.S.	U.S. 2015	Global 2015	% U.S.	U.S. 2019	Global 2019	% U.S.	U.S. CAGR	Global CAGR
Golf Courses	$23.80	$45.81	51.9%	$24.10	$47.60	50.6%	$24.50	$50.01	49.0%	0.3%	1.0%
Recreational Sports (e.g., adult sports leagues, driving ranges, go-kart tracks)	$9.63	$24.87	38.7%	$13.11	$33.60	39.0%	$15.62	$40.20	39.9%	5.5%	5.5%
Organized Athletic Events (e.g., running, cycling)	$1.62	$4.03	40.2%	$1.93	$4.82	40.1%	$2.58	$6.42	40.2%	5.3%	5.3%
TOTAL REVENUES	$35.05	$74.71	46.9%	$39.14	$86.02	45.5%	$42.70	$96.63	44.2%	2.2%	2.9%

The total amount spent on golf (e.g., greens fees, cart rentals, lessons) was the single largest revenue expenditure among all sports recreation activities both globally ($50 billion) and in the United States ($24.5 billion). Yet golf exhibited the lowest revenue growth rate, at less than 1%, of all outdoor sports from 2010 to 2019. The modest spending growth coincides with a slight decline (0.3%) in the number of people playing golf from 2014 to 2019 (*Figure 8.3*). While 429,00 fewer people played golf over the period, the National Golf Foundation provides evidence that a small core of what it calls "20-percenters" sustained overall spending on the sport (10). The core group of 2.5 to 3 million golfers' increased spending on equipment and rounds played appears to have compensated for the declining number of overall golfers.

Adult recreational sports leagues are a critical part of the global community sports culture. Millions of adults pay to play in organized leagues, including for soccer, basketball, hockey, tennis, golf and volleyball in much of the world and American flag football and cricket in certain regions. League organizers in the United States and Canada include local governments, nonprofit organizations like the YMCA and churches.

In 2019, analysts estimated that 15,678,005 adult men and women played in at least one adult sports league in the United States. The average cost per team member ranged from $30 to $75, depending on sport and roster size. Each member typically contributes a pro rata share of the total team registration fee, which pays for referees and field/court equipment and maintenance. The fees accounted for a large share of the 2019 recreational sports segment's total revenues of almost $16 billion.

FIGURE 8.6
Organized U.S. Running Events

DISTANCE	RACES	TOTAL RUNNERS	REGISTRATION FEE RANGE [1]
5k (3.1 miles)	17,000	8.9M	$25–$50
10k (6.2 miles)	4,200	1.50M	$25–$75
8k (5 miles)	1,200	N.A.	N.A.
Half Marathon (13.1 miles)	2,800	1.79M	$65–$105
Marathon (26.2 miles)	1,100	427K	$125–$300 (big cities)
Other (e.g., fun runs, team relays, ultra-marathons)	4,100	4.92M	$25–$100 (local)
TOTAL	**30,400**	**17.62M**	

Sources: Running USA, 2020 U.S. Running Trends; Statista, Number of Running Events, 2016
[1] Race fee ranges are drawn from a national search of road race websites for all distances

Running events remain the most popular among all forms of organized recreational competition. In 2019, 17.6 million people registered for U.S. road races (11). *Figure 8.6* breaks road races down by distance. Close to 9 million runners participated in 17,000 5K races held in the in the United States in 2019, making the distance more popular than any other race length. Short races like 5Ks attract casual, recreational runners to the local community events, which often raise money for a cause or charity.

Worldwide organizers hold an estimated 2,500 to 4,000 marathons per year, with 1,100 taking place in the United States (12). More than 400,000 runners participated in a U.S. marathon in 2019. Small, local marathons typically held in support of causes or charities charge registration fees ranging from $25 to $100, with the fee often waived in lieu of a donation. International marathon competitions held in the world's biggest cities—Tokyo, London, Berlin and New York City—attract the world's best runners. The New York City Marathon, the world's largest marathon, receives nearly 100,000 entry applications. Organizers choose participants meeting certain eligibility criteria by lottery. In 2019, 53,627 runners finished the race (13). Its registration fee is $295, but the race's full expense can reach thousands of dollars, including travel and lodging. The cost of staging the event is estimated to exceed $50 million, with about 40% paying for city permits, police security and traffic control throughout New York's five boroughs.

While the United States' presence in high profile international bicycling road races like the Tour de France declined from 2010 to 2019, Americans participate in thousands of local and regional events annually. BikeReg.com lists 1,320 scheduled events from June 2021 through mid-2022, including Gravel Grinders, Cyclocrosses and Gran Fondo "Big Ride" races. Most are single-day events. Recreational races can cost as little as $10 to $25, with more competitive events running up to $150. A few demanding events, like the three-day, 350-mile Oregon Trail Grinder, cost as much as $1,100. Despite identifying thousands of U.S. cycling events, the Best-Howard Model finds information on the number of entrants and revenues collected insufficient to provide a credible total spending estimate for the subsegment.

Triathlons, multisport endurance races consisting of swimming, biking and running various distances, have become popular worldwide. The first modern triathlon was held in the United States in 1974. By the early 1980s, European organizers began holding triathlon competitions. In 1989, the International Triathlon Union formed as the sport's official governing body. The International Olympic Committee voted to include the triathlon in the Games in 1994. In 2000, 30 nations sent triathletes to compete in the Sydney Olympics.

Triathlon participation peaked at 2.5 million in 2015 but declined at an accelerating rate over the next four years, hitting a low of 2 million in 2019 (5). The sport suffered its largest single year loss in 2019, with 168,000 fewer participants than in 2018, a 7.7% drop. Analysts have suggested the decline is due to triathlons being "too hard and too expensive" (14). Road bikes alone often cost more than $1,000. The average 2019 race entry fee was nearly $185, with some being as high as $300. Including the cost of event travel and lodging, Triathlon Business International found the full commercial impact of the U.S. triathlon market was $2.8 billion in 2015 (15).

Prior to the COVID-19 outbreak, USA Triathlon sanctioned more than 4,300 events annually in the United States. Concerns about virus exposure led to many U.S. and European events being cancelled. While the number of cancelled or suspended 2020 triathlons is not available, race directors reported significant financial losses and concerns about their events' survival. As a result of widespread vaccination programs, however, analysts suggested the triathlon "racing landscape for 2021 [was] looking increasingly positive" (16). Many global events resumed by 2021, often under strict safety guidelines. The Hamburg World Triathlon conducted its race on a course closed to spectators. RacePlace listed 155 U.S. triathlons scheduled for June and July 2021 (17).

While events began to recover in 2021, the Best-Howard Model projects it will take several years to determine whether running, cycling and multisport endurance races will reach or exceed the $6.5 billion spent by global enthusiasts in 2019.

Team & Individual Indoor Sports

Figure 8.7 features participation numbers for popular indoor sports in the United States (5). The sports often are played in specialized facilities, such as bowling centers, ice rinks, gymnasiums or large multisport complexes. Indoor sports participation patterns from 2014 to 2019 are similar to those of outdoor sports. Only two team sports, indoor soccer and volleyball, experienced consistent gains in total participants over the period.

Gymnastics, ice hockey and swimming suffered significant declines from 2016 to 2019. During the period, 682,000 gymnasts, 547,000 swimmers and 340,000 hockey players left their sports. Youth sports participation declines have driven the dramatic erosion.

As for outdoor team sports, persistent core participant decline has significantly impacted five of the six indoor team sports examined and all three individual sports. In 2014, 10.8 million core

FIGURE 8.7
U.S. Team & Individual Indoor Sports Participation
(thousands of participants)

Activity (millions)	Definition	2014	2015	2016	2017	2018	2019	1-year change	3-year CAGR	5-year CAGR
TEAM SPORTS										
Gymnastics	1+ times	4,621	4,679	5,381	4,805	4,770	4,699	-1.5%	-4.3%	0.7%
	Core 50+ times	1,689	1,618	1,800	1,666	1,723	1,695	-1.6%	-1.9%	0.3%
Ice Hockey	1+ times	2,421	2,546	2,697	2,544	2,447	2,357	-3.7%	-4.4%	-0.4%
	Core 13+ times	1,292	1,326	1,344	1,317	1,342	1,317	-1.8%	-0.7%	0.4%
Racquetball	1+ times	3,594	3,883	3,579	3,526	3,480	3,453	-0.8%	-1.2%	-0.7%
	Core 13+ times	1,159	1,048	1,106	1,075	1,073	1,055	-1.7%	-1.1%	-1.6%
Soccer (Indoor)	1+ times	4,530	4,813	5,117	5,399	5,233	5,336	2.0%	1.5%	3.4%
	Core 13+ times	2,614	2,656	2,770	2,742	2,782	2,755	-1.0%	-0.2%	1.1%
Swimming (on a team)	1+ times	2,710	2,892	3,369	3,007	3,045	2,822	-7.3%	-5.6%	1.3%
	Core 50+ times	1,464	1,411	1,488	1,343	1,367	1,293	-5.4%	-4.5%	-2.3%
Volleyball (Court)	1+ times	6,304	6,423	6,216	6,317	6,317	6,487	2.7%	1.4%	0.6%
	Core 8+ times	3,545	3,575	3,364	3,378	3,450	3,525	2.2%	1.6%	-0.1%
INDIVIDUAL SPORTS										
Badminton	1+ times	7,176	7,198	7,345	6,430	6,337	6,095	-3.8%	-5.9%	-3.1%
	Core 13+ times	2,127	2,166	2,069	1,867	1,782	1,756	-1.4%	-5.3%	-3.7%
Bowling	1+ times	46,642	45,931	45,925	45,491	45,793	45,372	-0.9%	-0.4%	-0.5%
	Core 13+ times	10,851	10,382	10,059	9,603	9,439	9,212	-2.4%	-2.9%	-2.7%
Table Tennis	1+ times	16,385	16,565	16,568	16,041	15,592	14,908	-4.4%	-3.5%	-1.9%
	Core 13+ times	4,553	4,534	4,497	4,207	4,205	4,199	-0.1%	-2.2%	-1.6%

bowlers—those bowling 13 or more times per year—comprised 24% of all participants. The core dropped to 9.2 million, or 20% of the total, in 2019, a loss of 1.64 million. The high-frequency participants have traditionally accounted for a substantial share of league bowlers, who typically devote at least one night a week for up to 30 weeks competing on four or five-person teams against as many as 10 other teams. League play accounted for 35% to 40% of bowling center business in 2020, down from 75% in the late 1980s (18).

The rapid 5% annual decline of league bowlers has forced the industry to adapt. For the past several years, alleys have repositioned and rebranded themselves from strictly bowling establishments to "bowling-based entertainment centers" (19). While bowling remains their core product, the centers now feature activities like arcade lounges, laser tag, glow-in-the-dark miniature golf, karaoke, simulated golf and go-karts. They have also upgraded their food and beverage operations, with many providing full-service restaurants, bars and sports bars. The centers have transformed the sport itself, as well, offering glow-in-the-dark bowling. In what is also known as "cosmic" bowling, computer-enhanced lighting, lasers, strobe lights and throbbing music transform the experience into a virtual disco setting to attract younger, more diverse audiences.

Evidence suggests the repositioning effort has been effective. For an example of how the largest bowling center operator in the world transformed a dilapidated alley into the highest grossing "party bowling center" in the United States, see the interview with Tom Shannon, CEO of Bowlero Corporation (formerly known as Bowlmor), in *Figure 8.8.*

FIGURE 8.8
Interview with Bowlero Corporation CEO Tom Shannon

Bowlmor's CEO Tom Shannon on "Bloomberg Enterprise"

Scan to *Watch the Video*

Source: https://www.youtube.com/watch?v=4ekEgTqQkMQ

Indoor soccer has been a bright spot in the sector, with more than 8 million Americans playing in 2019. The sport's growth coincides with a decline in outdoor soccer participation. A modified version of indoor soccer known as futsal has become popular in many U.S. regions.

Despite flat to declining participation levels among almost all indoor recreational sports, the four venue categories shown in *Figure 8.9* grew revenues globally and in the United States from 2010 to 2019. Participants around the world spent nearly $20 billion on indoor sports activities in 2019, up 2.6% from $15.57 billion in 2010. Americans accounted for 40% of total global spending at $8 billion in 2019.

FIGURE 8.9
Indoor Recreational Sports Participation Revenues (billions)

REVENUE SOURCES	U.S. 2010	Global 2010	% U.S.	U.S. 2015	Global 2015	% U.S.	U.S. 2019	Global 2019	% U.S.	U.S. CAGR	Global CAGR
Indoor Swim Complexes[1]	$1.19	$3.05	39.0%	$1.39	$3.56	39.0%	$1.56	$4.01	38.9%	3.1%	3.1%
Bowling Centers	$3.62	$8.94	40.4%	$3.74	$9.18	40.6%	$4.18	$9.99	41.8%	1.6%	1.2%
Ice Rinks (leagues, tourneys, skating)	$0.65	$1.64	39.6%	$0.82	$2.07	39.7%	$0.91	$2.28	39.9%	3.8%	3.7%
Special Indoor Facilities (e.g., tennis, soccer)	$0.80	$1.94	41.2%	$1.22	$3.04	40.0%	$1.37	$3.34	40.0%	6.2%	6.2%
TOTAL	$6.26	$15.57	40.2%	$7.17	$17.85	40.2%	$8.02	$19.62	40.9%	2.8%	2.6%

[1] Includes both private and publicly operated pools; data do not distinguish between indoor and outdoor swim complexes

Specialized indoor sports facility revenues, spurred by the growing popularity of indoor soccer, grew at an annual rate of 6.2% from 2010 to 2019 both in the United States and globally. Indoor facilities' ability to offer year-around participation opportunities unaffected by weather offers a significant advantage.

Despite a downturn in overall hockey participation, rink revenues grew nearly 4% both in the United States and around the world. However, revenue growth rates fell significantly from 2010 to 2019. Globally, CAGR fell from 4.9% for 2010-2015 to 1.9% for 2015-2019. The U.S. revenue growth decline was more moderate, from 4.8% for 2010-2015 to 2.1% for 2015-2019. COVID-19 closures accelerated the downward trend in 2020.

Youth Sports

Global youth sports had grown into an estimated $41.4 billion industry by 2019 (*Figure 8.2*). Participants and their parents spent almost $29 billion of the amount on organized league fees, purchasing uniforms and equipment, and making travel arrangements for tournaments (20). Worldwide consumers spent an additional $12.7 billion sending children to sports camps and academies, where they receive skill instruction from experienced coaches and athletes. Youth sports camps range from casual day- or week-long sessions to high-intensity in-residence experiences costing thousands of dollars.

U.S. residents accounted for a dominant portion of the youth sports market in 2019, spending $29 billion. Two thirds of the total, $19.2 billion, comprised registration fees, equipment purchases and tournament travel expenses (transportation, food and lodging). Americans invested close to $10 billion in youth sports camps and personalized skills instruction in 2019 (21).

Because youth sports serve as a wellspring for adult participation, their growth is essential to the wellbeing of all individual and team sports. A 2020 ESPN study highlighted the importance of sustainable participation, asserting that the youth market is "the largest sports-revenue driver in the country" (22).

Data in *Figure 8.10* indicate that youth participation in many sports gradually declined between 2012 and 2019 (23). The most serious losses were among core, or high frequency, team sports participants. While the percentage of youth playing a team sport at least once during a year remained steady at about 60 percent, the proportion of more highly committed children, participating in team sports on a sustained basis, declined slightly from 41.4% in 2012 to 38.1% in 2019. Importantly, the total proportion of young children experiencing sport either individually or on a team at least once during a year remained constant at a healthy 70-plus percent over the entire decade.

FIGURE 8.10

Percentage of All Children Ages 6 to 12 Participating in Sports by Type

TYPE	2012	2013	2014	2015	2016	2017	2018	2019	1-Year Change	7-Year CAGR
Team Sport (1+ times)	60.5%	55.5%	56.2%	56.6%	56.5%	56.5%	56.2%	60.5%	7.6%	0.0%
Team Sport on a Regular Basis (core)	41.4%	41.1%	38.2%	38.6%	36.9%	37.0%	37.9%	38.1%	0.5%	-1.2%
Individual Sport (1+ times)[1]	52.9%	52.9%	50.8%	50.8%	49.8%	49.3%	48.2%	49.5%	2.7%	-0.9%
Team or Individual Sport (1+ times)	72.9%	72.7%	71.5%	71.7%	71.5%	71.8%	71.8%	73.2%	1.9%	0.06%

[1] Core participation levels vary by sport, as shown in Figure 8.3

The upturn in participation levels across all sport types in 2019 indicated the extended youth sports decline might have been over. However, the 2020 COVID-19 pandemic changed the industry's short-term outlook.

Research shows children drop out of organized sports at an early age (*Figure 8.11*). The Aspen Institute reports that youths quit regularly playing individual sports when they are 10.5 years old on average (24). The average length of participation across all sports is less than three years.

On average, young people stop playing soccer at 9 years of age, hockey, baseball, tackle football and softball at 10, and skiing/snowboarding and volleyball at 12. Before they reach high school, 70% of youths have dropped out of sports.

Multiple factors contribute to kids discontinuing organized sports. Common reasons given by young people include excessive pressure, poor coaching and being forced to specialize in one sport. Many children find appealing alternatives to sports. The Aspen Institute finds children spend increasing amounts of time on the internet. The U.S. Center for Disease Control and Prevention reports kids ages 11 to 14 spend an average of nine hours per day in front of a screen (25). Children's infatuation with video games led one youth sports league administrator to lament, "Technology can be a better babysitter than youth sports" (26).

FIGURE 8.11
Age When Children 3- to 18-Years Stop Regularly Playing Sports

SPORT	AVR. AGE OF LAST REGULAR PARTICIPATION	AVG. LENGTH IN YEARS OF PARTICIPATION
Baseball	10.5	3.3
Basketball	11.2	3.2
Bicycling	9.5	2.5
Cross Country	12.7	1.7*
Field Hockey	11.4	5.1
Flag Football	10.4	4.1
Tackle Football	11.9	2.8
Golf	11.8	2.8
Gymnastics	8.7	3.0
Ice Hockey	10.9	3.1
Lacrosse	11.2	2.2
Martial Arts	9.2	2.6
Skateboarding	12.0	2.8
Skiing/Snowboarding	12.1	4.3
Soccer	9.1	3.0
Softball	10.4	2.8
Swimming	10.2	3.2
Tennis	10.9	1.9
Track and Field	13.0	2.0*
Volleyball	12.3	2.0*
Wrestling	9.8	1.6
ALL SPORTS	**10.5**	**2.9**

* These sports have low average lengths of participation due to kids starting these sports later.

Many U.S. families say rising participation costs push them away from sports. A 2020 survey found a significant gap in sports participation rates between rich and poor households (24). According to the survey, three of 10 children in homes earning less than $25,000 did not participate at all, compared to one in 10 in households with incomes greater than $100,000. Children in the poorest homes are increasingly moving toward less physical activity through sports.

Figure 8.12 shows participation costs for the six most popular sports among U.S. youths. The Aspen Institute's 2019 study found families spent an average of $903 annually for one child to participate in an organized sport (24). As shown in the figure, annual costs vary widely by sport, from $427 for basketball to $2,583 for ice hockey. Basketball is the most affordable among the popular sports because equipment often includes only footwear and registration fees are limited to games played in free to low-cost public play spaces, parks and schools.

FIGURE 8.12
Annual Participation Costs for One Child in Popular Team Sports

SPORTS	Registration/Facility /Uniform	Equipment	Tournaments/ Travel	Lesson/Camps	Total Cost Per Prayer
Baseball	$166	$121	$175	$206	$660
Basketball	$86	$74	$144	$147	$427
Tackle Football	$91	$110	$83	$192	$485
Ice Hockey	$634	$389	$829	$691	$2,583
Lacrosse	$411	$280	$281	$299	$1,289
Soccer	$158	$125	$107	$139	$537

In addition to paying for youth sports leagues, a growing number of U.S. households spend hundreds or thousands of dollars to send their children to sports camps and academies. The camps provide skills development training for young people 10 to 19 years of age. They range from relatively inexpensive (e.g., less than $200 per week), non-residential, community or school-based camps to high-cost, elite camps providing overnight residential experiences with instruction from well-known coaches in specific competitive team sports like soccer, football, hockey and basketball. Prices can be as high as $2,000 for a week-long stay at an elite high school football camp. A girls' tennis camp offered by IMG Academy targeting elite-level prospects costs $3,800 for one week and $11,059 for three weeks, according to the organization's website. In 2019, U.S. youth sports camps generated $5.4 billion in revenues (21).

Families also invest in individual sports instruction, either at home or in specialized facilities. The demand for intensive, specialized one-on-one training sessions grew rapidly from 2010 to 2019 as parents sought to enhance their children's scholarship prospects in the face of rising U.S. college tuition costs. By 2019, spending on personal sports coaching had reached $1.98 billion, twice the $1.01 billion spent in 2010 (21).

Total global youth sports spending grew steadily between 2010 and 2019 both globally and in the United States (*Figure 8.13*). Worldwide spending grew from $15.8 billion in 2010 to an estimated $41.4 billion in 2019, a compound annual growth rate of 11.3%. Americans' investment of $29.12 billion in organized youth sports accounted for almost 70% of total global spending.

FIGURE 8.13
U.S. & Global Youth Sports Revenues (billions)

Youth Sports	U.S. 2010	Global 2010	% U.S.	U.S. 2015	Global 2015	% U.S.	U.S. 2019	Global 2019	% U.S.	U.S. CAGR	Global CAGR
Sports Camps, Individual Coaching	$5.61	$7.71	72.8%	$8.56	$11.81	72.5%	$9.92	$12.71	72.1%	6.5%	5.7%
Youth Sports Leagues	$6.90	$8.10	74.1%	$10.87	$14.69	74.0%	$19.20	$28.70	66.9%	12.0%	15.1%
TOTAL	$11.61	$15.81	73.1%	$19.43	$26.50	73.3%	$29.12	$41.41	69.6%	10.8%	11.3%

For youth sports revenues to grow despite substantial participation declines, those continuing to participate must bear rising costs. Rising costs, in turn, keep low income children from being able to participate. Evidence shows U.S. household income is already a serious barrier to youth sports participation levels, something the industry must address in the coming years.

COVID-19's Impact on Sports Reaction Activities

While global losses due to COVID-19 were significant across all three Sports Recreation segments, the absence of detailed information on subsegment activities like youth sports and specialized indoor facilities makes it impossible to analyze fully the pandemic's worldwide impacts. Credible U.S. data sources on all Sports Recreation segments allow a detailed comparison of 2019 and 2020 revenues. IBISWorld provides substantial data on outdoor and indoor sports, as do industry trade associations (e.g., the National Golf Foundation and Bowling Proprietors Association of America) and nonprofit support groups like the Endurance Sports Coalition and The Aspen Institute.

All three Sports Recreation segments in the Best-Howard Model suffered substantial revenue losses during the pandemic (*Figure 8.14*). After a decade of steady growth for all segments, COVID-19 significantly affected almost all activities in 2020.

FIGURE 8.14
COVID-19 Sports Recreation Heat Map (billions)

SPORTS RECREATION

Outdoor Sports	2019	Growth	2020	-50%	0%	50%	2020	2020
Segments	(billions)	Rate	Forecast				(billions)	% Change
Golf	$24.49	0.63%	$24.26		5.2%		$25.36	5.2%
Rec. Sports	$15.62	3.9%	$16.23	-22.1%			$12.16	-22.1%
Organized Events	$2.58	7.4%	$2.77	-39.0%			$1.58	-39.0%
Total	$42.69	1.3%	$43.26	-8.4%			$39.10	-8.4%

Indoor Sports	2019	Growth	2020	-50%	0%	50%	2020	2020
Segments	(billions)	Rate	Forecast				(billions)	% Change
Swim Complexes	$1.56	3.2%	$1.61	-19.2%			$1.26	-19.2%
Bowling Centers	$4.18	2.8%	$4.30	-24.2%			$3.16	-24.2%
Ice Rinks	$0.91	2.2%	$0.93	-6.5%			$0.85	-6.5%
Spec. Indoor Facilities	$1.37	2.9%	$1.41	-12.4%			$1.20	-12.24%
Total	$8.02	2.9%	$8.25	-19.3%			$6.47	-19.3%

Youth Sports	2019	Growth	2020	-50%	0%	50%	2020	2020
Segments	(billions)	Rate	Forecast				(billions)	% Change
Camps	$9.92	3.7%	$10.29	-10.0%			$8.93	-10.0%
Youth Leagues	$19.20	15.3%	$22.14	-49.4%			$5.76	-49.4%
Total	$29.12	11.4%	$32.43	-49.6%			$14.69	-49.6%
TOTAL	$79.83	5.1%	83.94%	-32.5%			$60.26	-32.5%

The transmissible virus led to a virtual shutdown of almost all sports recreation activities across the United States in mid-March. Closures and cancellations of organized events and indoor facilities persisted across the country for the rest of the year. Seven of the nine activities on the *Figure 8.14* heat map experienced double-digit percentage revenue losses. Four lost more than 20% of their 2019 revenues. The youth sports segment was hardest hit, with revenues falling nearly 50%. Only golf was able to produce revenue gains during the pandemic. The collective loss across all three Sports Recreation segments due to the COVID-19 pandemic amounted to $19 billion in 2020.

The surge in golf participation in late spring 2020 provided a lift for a sport that had experienced moderate but steady declines over most of the previous decade. Golf has historically struggled to attract young golfers to replace aging players leaving the game.

> *"As we learned more about the virus…one thing became more and more clear: golf had the potential to serve as an ideal quarantine outlet."*

National Golf Foundation

In early spring 2020, golf courses across the United States shut down. Many were closed or required to impose low capacity, social distancing restrictions. The National Golf Foundation estimated revenue losses of $1 billion during the shutdown (27). In late spring, many states relaxed their COVID-19-related golf course restrictions as they recognized the game inherently maintains distance among players, significantly reducing viral transmission risks.

The consumer response was overwhelming, as enthusiasts also recognized golf was one of a few safe sports available. The National Golf Foundation's COVID-19 tracking study reported U.S. golfers played 20.6% more rounds of golf in August 2020 than in August 2019 (28). Over the three-month summer period, golfers played 27 million more rounds than they did during summer 2019. The revitalization allowed the industry to overcome first half losses and realize a year-end revenue increase of $870 million.

All other outdoor recreational sports activities ended 2020 with losses greater than $1 billion. COVID-19 vaccines became available in December 2020, and many sports leagues and organized events remained dormant for most or all of the year. Revenues for organized sports events (e.g., marathons, triathlons) fell 39%; recreational league revenues dropped 22%. Indoor sports facilities also struggled. Both bowling and swim center operators suffered double-digit percentage losses, at 24% and 19% respectively.

COVID-19 impacted youth sports in both the United States and around the world. Wintergreen Research reported that global youth team, league and tournament sports revenues declined from $28.7 billion in 2019 to $6.7 billion in 2020 (29). In the United States, they fell nearly 50% from $29.1 billion in 2019 to $14.7 billion in 2020.

In a survey of 290 youth sports organizers conducted in late spring 2020, almost half of the respondents said their programs were "in danger of permanently shuttering due to the impact of COVID-19" (30). As one youth sports league CEO stated, "Canceled games and tournaments equals no income for organizers…Youth sports organizations' bank accounts are running dry" (31).

The PLAY Sports Coalition formed to address the serious challenges COVID-19 imposed. More than 1,500 local and national sports organizations and supporters petitioned the U.S. Congress in April 2020 to create a $8.5 billion "youth sports relief fund" to stabilize the industry (32). While a bipartisan group of congressmen announced support for the coalition's initiative, legislators had taken no action as of July 2021.

FIGURE 8.15

Key Findings from National Parenting Survey of COVID-19's Impact on Youth Sports Participation

- *Total hours spent playing sports per week dropped 48.5% from 13.6 to 7.2 hours.*

- *64% reported concern that their child would become sick by resuming sports.*

- *29% reported their child was no longer interested in playing organized sports after the COVID-19 shutdown.*

As many U.S. regions resumed youth sports in September 2020, The Aspen Institute surveyed parents about their expectations (33). All respondents had children who participated regularly in sports prior to the COVID-19 restrictions. The findings (*Figure 8.15*) revealed several challenges to a full and immediate recovery. Parents' most widely-held concern was the fear of illness for their child (64%) if they resumed sports. Of long-term concern, nearly one third of children said they were no longer interested in playing organized sports after the COVID-19 shutdown. It is too early to determine the extent to which pandemic-related health concerns will affect long-term youth sports participation.

Figure 8.16 shows data forecasting recovery prospects for several recreational sports (34). The 2019 revenues shown serve as pre-COVID-19 reference points; the 2020 figures represent the pandemic's financial impact on each sport. The numbers are compared with each sport's projected 2023 financial performance to assess: a) the extent to which each sport may recover from pre-COVID-19 levels and b) the rate at which each activity is expected to recover from losses incurred during the pandemic.

FIGURE 8.16

Selected U.S. Sports Recovery Forecast (billions)

ACTIVITIES	2019	2020	2021	2022	2023	2019-2023 CAGR	2020-2023 CAGR
Golf	$21.49	$25.36	$25.75	$25.88	$26.14	5.02%	1.01%
Organized Athletic Events (running, cycling)	$2.58	$1.58	$1.89	$2.02	$2.14	−4.57%	10.64%
Recreational Sports (adult leagues, driving ranges)	$15.62	$12.16	$13.00	$13.90	$14.23	−2.30%	5.38%
Bowling	$4.18	$3.16	$3.30	$3.46	$3.58	−3.80%	4.25%
Ice Rinks / Arenas	$0.91	$0.85	$0.87	$0.91	$0.93	0.54%	3.04%
Indoor Swim Centers	$1.56	$1.26	$1.26	$1.33	$1.38	−3.02%	3.08%

Because many U.S. states gradually relaxed COVID-19 restrictions in late 2020 and completely lifted them by July 2021, all examined sports are expected to show modest gains by the end of 2021 and healthy annual growth rates by 2023. Revenues for organized athletic events are forecast to recover most rapidly as runners, cyclists and triathletes flock back to competitive racing in 2021 and 2022.

Golf's 2020 gains are projected to settle into a modest annual growth rate of 1.01% through 2023. The conservative forecast is based on the National Golf Foundation's concern about new golfers continuing the sport. The foundation says retention has been "golf's Achilles heel for some time now" (28).

Bowling's post-COVID recovery has been buoyed by facilities transitioning to offering a range of entertainment options to attract broader, more diverse audiences. Bowlero, now the largest bowling center operator in the United States, has led the transformation. While bowling industry revenues are not projected to return to pre-COVID-19 levels by 2023, forecasts indicate they will eclipse $4 billion by the end of the decade.

References

We have added links to many references for direct and easy access. While we have tested each link, there are a few instances where the websites are no longer accessible. We will continue to monitor the accessibility of citation references and remove any links no longer active. In many instances the referenced data was purchased, this is noted.

1. Bridgette Thomas, "Golf courses & country clubs in the US," February 2021. *IBISWorld* (my.ibisworld.com); Thi Li, "Golf driving ranges & family fun centers,"February 2021; *IBISWorld* (my.ibisworld.com); Thomas Henry, "Go-Kart racing tracks," March 2020; *IBISWorld* (my.ibisworld.com); Dan Cook, "Athletic Event Organizers," November 2020; *IBISWorld* (my.ibisworld.com); Ryan Roth, "Swimming Pools," March 2021; *IBISWorld (my.ibisworld.com)*; Thi Li, "Bowling Centers in the US," February 2021; *IBISWorld* (my.ibisworld.com); Nick Masters, "Ice Rinks," October 2020; *IBISWorld* (my.ibisworld.com); Ryan Roth, "Indoor Sports Facilities Management," September 2020; *IBISWorld* (my.ibisworld.com); Claire O'Connor, "Sports Coaching in the US," March 2021; *IBISWorld* (my.ibisworld.com); Christine Gough, "Size of the youth sports market in the United States in 2017 and 2019," March 1, 2021; *Statista* (www.statista.com); Christine Gough, "Size of the youth sports market worldwide from 2018 to 2020," March 1, 2021; *Statista* (www.statista.com); "Global youth team, league and tournament sports market report 2020: Market size was $24 billion in 2018, $28.7 billion in 2019 but dropped to $6.7 billion in 2020 as result of the pandemic," November 19, 2020; and Research and Markets. *Globe Newswire* (www.globenewswire.com). (GSI Purchased Report)

2. "Australia's top 20 sports and physical activities revealed" April 2019. *Sport Australia* (www.sportaus.gov.au); "China - regular participation in sports, by type 2018". *Statista* (www.statista.com); "England: most participated sports". *Statista* (www.statista.com); "India - regular participation in sports, by type 2018". *Statista* (www.statista.com); "Japan: most common sports and physical activities to participate in 2020". *Statista* (www.statista.com). (GSI Purchased Report)

3. "Statistics on sport participation," *Eurostat, Statistics Explained* (ec.europa.eu).

4. "FIFA Big Count 2006: 270 million active in football". *FIFA* (www.fifa.com).

5. "SFIA Topline Report," February 2020, Sport & Fitness Association Sports, Fitness, And Leisure Activities Participation Report.

6. SI Wire, "Poll: Four out of five Americans oppose tackle football before age 14," July 20, 2016. *Sports Illustrated* (www.si.com).

7. Matthew Roy, "Tackle this: Decline in youth football participation raises questions about future," December 11, 2019. *Cronkite News* (cronkitenews.azpbs.org).

8. *NFL Flag* (nflflag.com).

9. Ruben Vee, "Why is skateboarding so popular? A new golden age," December 17, 2020. *Skateboarders HQ* (www.skateboardershq.com).

10. "Industry Update," June 2021. *National Golf Foundation* (www.thengfq.com).

11. "2020 U.S. Running Trends," Running USA 2020 *Running USA* (www.runningusa.org).

12. "I'm interested in reliable statistics about marathons," May 9, 2017. *Ask Wonder* (askwonder.com).

13. "New York City Marathon," *Wikipedia* (en.wikipedia.org).

14. Kelly O'Mara, "The truth about Triathlon participation in the United States," August 6, 2019. *Triathlete* (www.triathlete.com).

15. "US Triathlon market revenue hits the big time at US$2.8 billion," June 8, 2015. *Endurance Biz* (www.endurance.biz).

16. Michael Pavitt, "World Triathlon anticipates "hugely exciting" 2021 following successful events during

pandemic," November 15, 2020. *Inside the Games* (www.insidethegames.biz).

17. "RacePlace," July 1, 2021. Triathlon Race Calendar. *RacePlace* (www.raceplace.com).

18. "Bowling Today," April 2021. *BowlingSeriously* (www.bowlingseriously.com).

19. Sandy Hansell, "Overview of the bowling industry," Hansell & Associates. *CourseHero (www. coursehero.com)*.

20. "Global youth team, league and tournament sports market report 2020: Market size was $24 billion in 2018, $28.7 billion in 2019 but dropped to $6.7 billion in 2020 as result of the pandemic," November 19, 2020. Research and Markets. *Globe Newswire* (www.globenewswire.com).

21. Claire O'Connor, "Sports Coaching in the U.S.," March 2021. *IBISWorld* (my.ibisworld.com). (GSI Purchased Report)

22. ESPN Staff, "Sudden vanishing of sports due to coronavirus will cost at least $12 billion, analysis say," May 1, 2020. *ESPN* (www.espn.com).

23. "Youth Sports Facts: Participation Rates," Project Play 2021, *The Aspen Institute* (www. aspenprojectplay.org).

24. "Youth Sports Facts: Challenges," Project Play 2021, *The Aspen Institute* (www.aspenprojectplay.org).

25. "Screen time for kids; How much is too much? January 10, 2020. *OSF Healthcare* (newsroom. osfhealthcare.org)

26. Tom Farrey, "Project Play at five years: Progress, next steps," 2021. *The Aspen Institute* (www. aspenprojectplay.org).

27. "20 million rounds lost to Covid-19, Estimates the National Golf Foundation," June, 2020. *Asian Golf Industry Association* (agif.asia).

28. Dylan Dethier, New study shows shocking effects of coronavirus on the golf industry, September 25, 2020. *Golf* (www.golf.com).

29. 'Youth team, league, tournament sports: Market shares, strategies, and forecasts, COVID 19 and post-COVID 19, worldwide, 2021-2027," May 2021. Wintergreen Research, Inc. *Business Wire* (www. businesswire.com).

30. "Pandemic Trends," State of Play 2020, *The Aspen Institute* (aspenprojectplay.org).

31. Alex Silverman, "Organizers, parents concerned youth sports programs will fold due to COVID—19 pandemic," May 13. 2020. *Morning Consult* (www.morningconsult.com).

32. JohnWallStreet, "Youth sports coalition seeks $8.5 billion for COVID-related infrastructure, *Sport Hiatus* (sporthiatus.com).

33. "Covid-19 Parenting Survey," Project Play, September 20, 2020. The Aspen Institute. *Squarespace* (www.squarespace.com).

34. Sources for Figure 8.16: Dan Cook, "Athletic Event Organizers," November 2020. *IBISWorld* (my. ibisworld.com); Thi Li, "Golf Driving Ranges & Family Fun Centers," September 2021. *IBISWorld* (my. ibisworld.com); Thi LI, "Bowling Centers in the US," September 2021. *IBISWorld* (my.ibisworld.com); Nick Masters, "Ice Rinks in the US," October 2020. IBISWorld. Ryan Roth, "Swimming Pools in the US," March 2021. *IBISWorld* (my.ibisworld.com). (GSI Purchased Report)

FITNESS & EXERCISE
CHAPTER 9

Home & Gym

Fitness & Exercise, the second core area of the Best-Howard Sports Industry Model's Sports Participation domain (*Figure 9.1*), captures engagement in a range of health-related activities, from the ancient spiritual practice of yoga to new pursuits like CrossFit and bouldering.

FIGURE 9.1
The Best-Howard Model's Fitness & Exercise Core Area

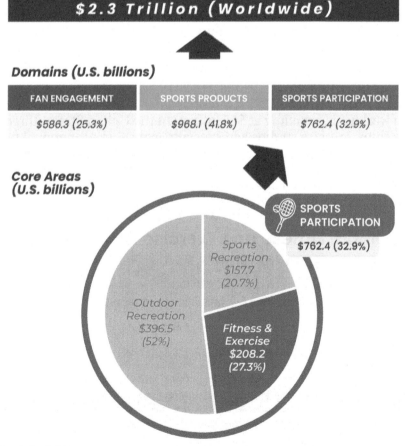

$2.3 Trillion (Worldwide)

Domains (U.S. billions)

FAN ENGAGEMENT	SPORTS PRODUCTS	SPORTS PARTICIPATION
$586.3 (25.3%)	$968.1 (41.8%)	$762.4 (32.9%)

Core Areas (U.S. billions)

SPORTS PARTICIPATION
$762.4 (32.9%)

Sports Recreation $157.7 (20.7%)

Outdoor Recreation $396.5 (52%)

Fitness & Exercise $208.2 (27.3%)

Segments (U.S. billions)

Fitness & Exercise Segments	Revenues	Percent
Health & Fitness Clubs	$ 96.7	46.4 %
Exercise Studios	$ 53.2	25.6 %
Coaches & Trainers	$ 19.1	9.2 %
Specialty Gyms	$ 39.2	18.8 %
TOTAL	**$ 208.2**	**100.0 %**

Copyright Best-Howard Model 2022. All Right Reserved.

The activities comprising the Fitness & Exercise core area are separated into four segments:

• **Health & Fitness Clubs:** Providers in the category offer a full range of services and amenities like exercise areas, fitness classrooms, athletic courts, swimming pools and spas, and food and beverage services.

• **Exercise Studios:** The category draws on the popularity of yoga and Pilates and focuses on teaching flexibility and joint mobility via certified teachers in small group settings.

• **Coaches & Trainers:** Close to 750,000 specialists, often called personal trainers, offer customized training programs to fitness and exercise enthusiasts. Fitness and health clubs often provide personal trainers to their members.

• **Specialty Gyms:** The category includes indoor specialty fitness and exercise activities, including traditional combat sports, martial arts and rock climbing. The segment has grown rapidly due to the popularity of high-intensity programs like CrossFit and climbing and bouldering centers.

People around the world pay a lot to stay fit (1). In 2019, worldwide spending across the four Fitness & Exercise segments totaled $208.2 billion (*Figure 9.2*). U.S. participants accounted for about one third of worldwide spending at $35 billion. In the United States, three of the four segments—health clubs, exercise studios and specialty gyms—grew at annual rates between 5% and 6.5% from 2010 to 2019. Revenues grew steadily around the world, particularly in the exercise studio and specialty gym segments. Yoga studios, martial art centers and CrossFit gyms worldwide expanded at a compound annual growth rate of 6.3%.

FIGURE 9.2
U.S. & Global Fitness and Exercise Revenues (billions)

SEGMENT	U.S. 2010	Global 2010	% U.S.	U.S. 2015	Global 2015	% U.S.	U.S. 2019	Global 2019	% U.S.	U.S. CAGR	Global CAGR
Health & Fitness Clubs	$20.3	$70.9	28.6%	$25.8	$81.2	31.8%	$35.0	$96.7	36.2%	5.60%	3.15%
Exercise Studios	$6.8	$28.9	23.5%	$10.0	$42.7	23.7%	$12.7	$53.2	23.9%	6.45%	6.29%
Coaches & Trainers	$7.8	$13.4	58.2%	$9.3	$16.8	55.4%	$10.3	$19.1	53.9%	2.82%	3.05%
Specialty Gyms	$5.2	$12.8	40.6%	$12.6	$28.9	43.6%	$16.4	$39.2	41.8%	5.41%	6.29%
TOTAL	**$40.1**	**$126.0**	**31.8%**	**$57.7**	**$169.6**	**34.0%**	**$74.4**	**$208.2**	**35.7%**	**6.38%**	**5.15%**

Sources: Revenues compiled from multiple sources listed as (1) in this chapter's references section

The COVID-19 virus, however, had a profound effect on all four Fitness & Exercise segments in 2020. U.S. health and fitness club revenues plunged 58% in 2020 (2). By early spring 2020, almost all health clubs, exercise studios and specialty gyms had closed. All the previous decade's gains evaporated, with revenue losses amounting to $20.4 billion by the end of 2020.

The Best-Howard Model analyzes the Fitness & Exercise core area using membership and participation data for each of the activities comprising the four segments and provides a detailed breakdown of how much consumers spent on them from 2010 to 2019.

The video shown in *Figure 9.3* provides a U.S. fitness industry overview, highlighting emerging trends like boutique, high-end fitness studios and the influence of technology (e.g., virtual reality and wearables) on the future of fitness participation.

FIGURE 9.3
The Future of Fitness

Source: https://www.youtube.com/watch?v=ziVYKYZ4ou8

Health and Fitness Clubs

Worldwide health club, athletic club and gym memberships have grown steadily over the past decade. In 2019, nearly 184 million people worldwide belonged to the clubs (*Figure 9.4*). The United States led the way, with 64.2 million Americans (about one in five adults) holding a membership in one of the country's 110,870 health and fitness clubs (3). Germany ranked second in 2019 with 11.7 million members. The United Kingdom (10.39 million), Brazil (10.33 million) and France (6.19 million) rounded out the top five.

Total global fitness club memberships increased by 55.8 million from 2010 to 2019, a compound annual growth rate of 3.7%. Most of the growth occurred over the last three years of the decade. More than 22 million, or 40% of the total membership increase, joined the market from 2016 to 2019. The period coincides with explosive fitness market growth in China.

China's rapidly growing fitness industry became a top-10 market in 2019. While commercial fitness clubs did not appear in China until the 1980s, the country's economic prosperity propelled annual membership and revenue growth rates of nearly 9% from 2015 to 2019. In just two years, health and fitness clubs in China nearly tripled, from 37,627 in 2017 to 97,746 in 2019 (4). In 2019, 4.5 million Chinese people spent $3.9 billion on memberships or pay-as-you-go fees at fitness and health clubs (4).

The United States accounted for more than one third (34.8%) of the 184 million worldwide health club memberships in 2019. Five European nations ranked among the top eight (*Figure 9.5*). Germany, the United Kingdom, France, Italy and Spain accounted for 39.3 million memberships, about 21.4% of the total.

FIGURE 9.4
U.S. & Global Health & Fitness Club Members (millions of members)

YEAR	UNITED STATES	WORLDWIDE	% U.S.
2019	64.2	184.6	34.8%
2018	N.A.	N.A.	N.A.
2017	60.9	174.1	35.0%
2016	57.3	162.1	35.3%
2015	55.0	151.5	36.3%
2014	54.1	144.7	37.4%
2013	52.9	138.8	38.1%
2012	50.2	131.7	38.1%
2011	51.4	129.4	39.7%
2010	50.2	128.8	39.0%

FIGURE 9.5
2019 Health & Fitness Club Memberships by Country
(millions of members)

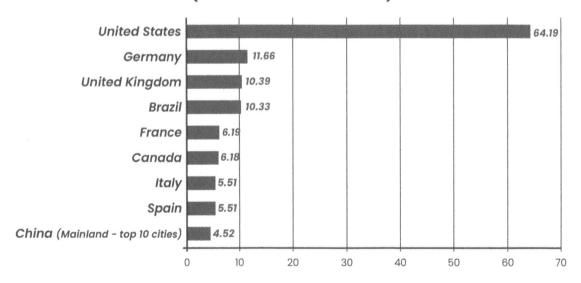

The United States' relatively modest health and fitness club membership growth rate from 2010 to 2019, at 2.5%, reflects the market's maturity. The emergence of boutique gyms and studios, such as Equinox, Pure Barre and Orangetheory Fitness, has propelled most of the U.S. fitness market's growth. The gyms offer small, class-focused workouts with high staff-to-member ratios. Orangetheory, for example, markets its "coach-inspired" workouts. Premium boutique gym memberships average $159 to $260 per month (5). While boutique gyms have grown in popularity, their high cost limits their appeal to a narrow market range.

Most of than 64 million Americans belonging to health and fitness clubs use moderately priced gyms like Gold's Gym, 24-Hour Fitness and LA Fitness. The large chain establishments offer many options, including individual exercise machines and equipment, group fitness classes (e.g., Zumba and spinning), personal training and amenities like locker rooms, swimming pools, and basketball and racquetball courts. Memberships in the high-volume, mass-market clubs are priced from $30 to $60 per month. The clubs often charge members an initiation fee, which may roll over to an annual fee, of $40 to $50.

The well-established health and fitness club segment accounts for the largest share of worldwide Fitness & Exercise core area spending. Health club members spent $96.7 billion in 2019, nearly half the $208 billion spent globally across all four Fitness & Exercise segments. The U.S. and European markets generate a dominant share of the revenues, as shown in *Figure 9.6* (6).

FIGURE 9.6
Global, U.S. & Europe Health Club Industry Revenues (billions)

YEAR	GLOBAL	UNITED STATES		EUROPE	
		$	% TOTAL	$	% TOTAL
2019	$96.7	$35.0	36.2%	$31.5	32.5%
2018	$94.0	$32.3	34.4%	$30.6	32.7%
2017	$87.2	$30.0	34.4%	$28.8	33.0%
2016	$83.2	$27.6	33.2%	$29.6	35.6%
2015	$81.2	$25.8	31.8%	$29.8	36.7%
2014	$84.3	$24.2	28.7%	$35.0	41.5%
2013	$78.2	$22.4	28.6%	$32.9	42.1%
2012	$75.5	$21.8	28.8%	$32.0	42.4%
2011	$72.6	$20.9	28.7%	$31.2	42.9%
2010	$70.9	$20.3	28.6%	$31.4	44.3%

From 2010 to 2019, health clubs in the U.S. and Europe—led by Germany and the United Kingdom—accounted for more than two thirds of total global revenues every year. Europe contributed the largest share each year over the first half of the decade, but by 2015 the United States became the largest global market. Americans spent $35.0 billion in 2019, 36.2% of total global spending, while Europeans spent $31.5 billion, a 32.5% share. Europe's diminishing market share reflects the U.S. health and fitness club market's steady growth over the period. From 2010 to 2019, U.S. revenues grew at 5.6% per year, increasing from $20.3 billion to $35.03 billion (3).

Figure 9.7 shows how much U.S. health and fitness clubs depend on membership fees (3). Revenues from joining clubs (initiation fees) and maintaining memberships (monthly or annual fees) account for nearly 70% of U.S. clubs' total annual operational revenues.

FIGURE 9.7
Health & Fitness Club Revenue Source Contribution

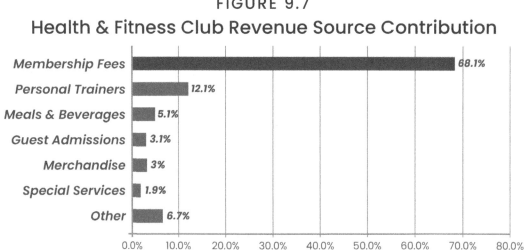

The clubs' membership-dependent operating model makes them vulnerable to changing economic conditions. Household and per capita disposable income levels and consumers' willingness to spend on gym and studio fitness memberships are critical for attracting and sustaining members.

Even in stable economies, health and fitness club operators historically have faced membership retention challenges. Research indicates many who join clubs cannot sustain commitment to a fitness regimen. Membership retention studies have found that a high percentage of those joining clubs lose interest early. A U.K. study found the fitness industry loses about 3.9 million members per year, with almost half quitting after the first 12 months (7). A large U.S. survey showed that 22% of health and fitness club members stopped going to the gym or studio six months into their membership (8).

Evidence indicates clubs can take several measures to enhance membership retention. Studies across several European countries found that members signing at least 12-month contracts were less likely to quit. The study concluded that "the restrictive nature of 12-month contracts by not allowing [members] to leave earlier" allowed gyms to achieve a 70% retention rate after one year (7). In the study, members signing 12-month agreements stayed with their gyms at a greater rate than those joining on a month-to-month basis but used the gym less frequently.

IHRSA, a global health and fitness association, reports a traditional health club retention rate of 71.4% (9). The Association of Fitness Studios reports a membership retention rate among small fitness studios of 75.9% (9). Because fitness and sports clubs must replace one quarter to one third of their members each year to maintain steady usage, overall fitness club memberships grew modestly at 2.5% per year during the several years prior to 2019.

The COVID-19 pandemic was particularly devastating to health and fitness clubs. Stay-at-home restrictions forced clubs to close in many countries and across the United States for most of 2020. The financial losses were significant, with clubs losing many members and reducing employment numbers.

Exercise Studios

Compared to full-service health clubs, exercise studios are smaller and less expensive. They offer classes typically focused on one or two specialty fitness areas, most prominently yoga and Pilates. Yoga's global popularity continues to grow. In India, yoga has been practiced for 6,000 years, and nearly one in four adults is now a practitioner. Consumer reports estimate anywhere from 300 million to 2 billion people around the world participate in yoga (10).

While the Best-Howard model cannot verify the participation figures, yoga's growing worldwide popularity is certain. The ancient Eastern discipline, which emphasizes flexibility and stress relief, has taken hold throughout Western nations. In the United States, yoga's participation numbers grew steadily from 2012 to 2019. Pilates's growth has not been as robust, but its overall numbers have increased modestly over the same period. *Figure 9.8* provides an annual breakdown of total and core participants in the activities (11).

Over 7 million more Americans participated in yoga in 2019 than in 2012. In 2019, total participants exceeded 30 million. Of the total, 11.5 million (38%) were committed yoga practitioners, having participated more than 50 times. Women over 50-years-old have largely driven the surge. Unlike strenuous fitness activities, yoga has no age limit, and seniors have increasingly gravitated to the activity. By 2019, the 50-plus age segment had grown to 38% of all Americans participating in yoga.

FIGURE 9.8
U.S. Exercise Studio Participation (thousands of participants)

Activity	Participant Type	2012	2013	2014	2015	2016	2017	2018	2019	1-Year Change	3-Year CAGR	5-Year CAGR
Pilates	Total (1+)	8,519	8,069	8,504	8,594	8,893	9,047	9,084	9,243	1.8%	1.3%	1.7%
	Core (50+)	3,307	3,287	3,373	3,394	3,367	3,346	3,325	3,168	-2.2%	-2.0%	-1.2%
Yoga	Total (1+)	23,253	24,130	25,262	25,289	26,268	27,354	28,745	30,456	6.0%	5.1%	3.8%
	Core (50+)	9,940	10,182	10,400	10,341	10,782	10,900	11,193	11,503	2.8%	2.2%	1.9%

As shown in *Figure 9.8*, Pilates participation rates increased at a 1.7% annual rate from 2010 to 2019, with core participants declining slightly over the last three years of the decade. Studios have struggled with increased external competition as many large health and fitness clubs have begun offering Pilates classes. And the discipline lost more than 225,000 of its most highly committed practitioners between 2015 and 2019. Still, the intimate studio setting remains attractive to many enthusiasts. The Sports and Fitness Industry Association reports 9.2 million Americans participated in Pilates in 2019.

Figure 9.9 shows exercise studios' financial performance in the United States and globally. In 2019, total yoga and Pilates revenues reached $53.2 billion worldwide and $12.7 billion in the United States (12). The revenues' annual growth rates were 6.5% globally and 6.3% in the United States from 2010 to 2019.

FIGURE 9.9
U.S. & Global Pilates/Yoga Revenues (billions)

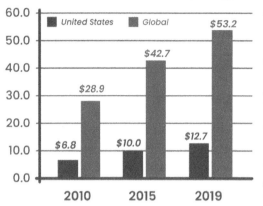

IBISWorld (12) breaks down the relative contribution of revenue sources to the total income U.S. exercise studios generated in 2019 (*Figure 9.10*). Yoga studios, with 30.5 million participants, claimed a dominant 75% of total spending. Americans spent $8.6 billion taking classes and buying yoga merchandise. Yoga instructors spent close to one billion dollars on specialty certification and continuing education programs.

FIGURE 9.10
2019 U.S. Yoga & Pilates Studio Revenue Sources (billions)

Source	Yoga (% of total)	Pilates (% of total)	Total
Class Registration	$6.67 (52.5%)	$2.21 (17.4%)	$8.87
Merchandise	$1.89 (75%)	$0.64 (25%)	$2.54
Accreditation / Certification	$0.96 (75%)	$0.32 (25%)	$1.28
TOTAL	**$9.54**	**$3.17**	**$12.7**

Pilates studios in the U.S. generated an estimated $3.2 billion in total revenues in 2019. Class registrations provided the largest share, $2.2 billion. Pilates merchandise and instructional training and certification courses totaled nearly $1 billion, about 30% of total spending.

COVID-19 deeply affected exercise studio revenues, but yoga, with its strong tradition and many committed practitioners, has shown evidence of a strong 2021 recovery. Yoga is likely to continue attracting elderly participants, ensuring the exercise studio segment's overall growth prospects.

Coaches & Trainers

Increased sports and fitness participation has resulted in continued demand for personal trainers, who provide services like customized workout regimens, injury rehabilitation, and nutrition and weight loss programs. By 2020, more than 300,000 personal fitness trainers were certified in 143 countries. Consumers spent more than $53 billion on personal trainer services around the globe in 2019 (*Figure 9.11*). U.S. clients and service providers (e.g., fitness clubs and rehab centers) spent the largest amount, $19.1 billion (14).

FIGURE 9.11
Coach & Personal trainer Revenues (billions)

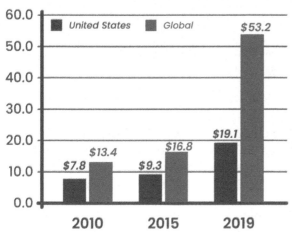

The largest revenue share, 40.9%, resulted from personal and small group training sessions at health and fitness clubs (14). In response to increasing customized training demand, major fitness chains have hired certified personal trainers to provide individual sessions. 24-Hour Fitness USA provides new members free trainer evaluation sessions and the option to purchase ongoing training. IBISWorld estimates 24-Hour Fitness generated $90.1 million from personal training programs in 2020.

Most personal trainers operate as independent instructors in their own homes, at private fitness studios (36.4%), or at clients' homes or offices (18.2%). The trainers charge on average $40 to $70 for one-hour sessions and $60 to $100 for 90-minute sessions (15).

Personal trainers' primary target market is adults between 35 and 54, who account for 54.2% of industry revenues (14). The group offers stable economic status and can afford high-priced training sessions. Personal trainers have also customized fitness programs for the Baby Boomers generation. With more than 70 million U.S. adults aged 57 to 75, the generation is the nation's wealthiest, accounting for more than half of its discretionary income (16). Aging demographics are a favorable trend for fitness coaches and trainers, as the large and affluent market spends more on health than any other population segment (14).

In 2020, COVID-19-induced gym closures drove many out-of-work trainers to adapt. Some were able to transition to offering classes outdoors or virtually, while many struggled and were part of the nearly 500,000 fitness industry jobs lost due to the pandemic (17).

Specialty Gyms

The specialty gyms segment of the Best-Howard Model's Fitness & Exercise core area incudes privately-operated small businesses offering unique services in activities like combat sports, rock climbing and high-intensity intervals. The segment is highly fragmented, and the Best-Howard Model finds limited credible participation and financial data, particularly on a global scale.

FIGURE 9.12
U.S. Specialty Gym Participation (thousands of participants)

Fitness Activity	Definition	2012	2013	2014	2015	2016	2017	2018	2019	1-year change	3-year CAGR	5-year CAGR
Boxing for Fitness	Total 1+	4,831	5,251	5,113	5,419	5,175	5,157	5,166	5,198	0.6%	0.2%	0.4%
	Core 13+	2,756	2,713	2,675	2,633	2,496	2,419	2,452	2,460	0.3%	-0.5%	-1.6%
Cross Training	Total 1+			11,265	11,710	12,914	13,622	13,338	13,542	1.5%	1.6%	3.8%
	Core 13+			5,579	5,672	6,483	6,744	6,732	6,442	-4.5%	-0.2%	3.1%
Martial Arts	Total 1+	5,075	5,314	5,364	5,507	5,745	5,838	5,821	6,068	4.2%	1.9%	2.6%
	Core 13+	3,869	3,781	3,765	3,714	3,780	3,816	3,830	3,890	1.6%	1.0%	0.7%
MMA for Fitness	Total 1+	1,977	2,251	2,455	2,612	2,446	2,376	2,365	2,405	1.7%	-0.5%	-0.3%
	Core 13+	1,161	1,052	1,190	1,173	1,116	1,091	1,096	1,097	-1.6%	-1.1%	-1.9%
Indoor Climbing Gyms	Total 1+	4,436	4,752	4,453	4,689	4,910	5,045	5,112	5,309	3.9%	2.8%	3.6%

The model relies on U.S. market data almost exclusively. Despite the limitations, the sector includes some of the fastest growing U.S. fitness activities—mixed martial arts (MMA), indoor climbing and high-intensity interval training, represented by CrossFit gyms. *Figure 9.12* presents participation data for the most prominent U.S. specialty gym categories (11).

Figure 9.13 presents revenue data for each specialized gym subsegment. The U.S. data is taken from IBISWorld and Statista, both reputable data aggregation firms; the Best-Howard Model extrapolates the global data. The model will add worldwide data as the specialty areas grow and information becomes available.

FIGURE 9.13
U.S. & Global Specialty Gym Revenues (billions)

SEGMENTS	U.S. 2010	Global 2010	% U.S.	U.S. 2015	Global 2015	% U.S.	U.S. 2019	Global 2019	% U.S.	U.S. CAGR	Global CAGR
Boxing	$1.0	$1.9	52.6%	$1.2	$2.5	48.0%	$1.4	$2.9	48.3%	3.42%	4.32%
CrossFit[1]	N.A.	N.A.	N.A.	$4.0	$6.0	66.7%	$5.0	$8.5	58.9%	4.56%	7.21%
Indoor Climbing	$0.4	$1.1	38.1%	$0.6	$1.6	37.5%	$0.7	$1.7	41.2%	5.76%	4.45%
Martial Arts	$3.8	$9.8	38.7%	$7.3	$18.8	38.8%	$9.9	$26.1	37.9%	10.1%	10.3%
TOTAL	$5.2	$12.8	40.6%	$13.1	$28.9	43.6%	$17.0	$39.2	43.4%	5.41%	6.29%

Sources: See (1) in this chapter's references section. [1] Based on 2015 to 2019 measurement

BOXING: Boxing gyms have been an American institution for more than 100 years. In 2019, more than 4,000 gyms around the country were dedicated to boxing. Many more boxing gyms operated around the world. Their growth from 2015 to 2019 was modest at 3.4%, with revenues reaching $1.36 billion in 2019 (18). The growing popularity of alternative combat sports, particularly MMA, has slowed boxing's growth. While young males 18- to 34-years-old traditionally have dominated boxing, young women increasingly participate in the sport for both its fitness and self-defense benefits. Many boxing clubs now offer classes exclusively for women. No-contact fitness programs targeting women, like iLoveKickboxing, have proven popular. Most analysts project a stable but flat growth trajectory for boxing gyms.

CROSSFIT: CrossFit has created a new fitness category, blending high-intensity weight training, cardiovscular exercise and gymnastics. Despite its enormous popularity, no major trade association or publication representing mainstream health and fitness clubs represents the activity. Club Industry's 2019 Top 100 Health Clubs ranking did not identify CrossFit, while LA Fitness and 24-Hour Fitness were ranked first and third.

The first CrossFit gym opened in 2000. Only 13 CrossFit franchises emerged in the next five years. But by 2019, more than 15,000 CrossFit gyms operated around the world. The United States now has about 6,700 affiliate CrossFit gyms, almost tripling LA Fitness's 2,391 establishments. The 2019 Outdoor Participation Report found that in 2018, 13.4 million Americans engaged in cross-training style workouts (19). CrossFit members pay $75 to $225 per month to "receive professional coaching, make a bunch of new friends in group workouts and get freakishly fit" (20).

CrossFit's low-cost affiliate business model has stimulated its tremendous growth. Prospective gym owners must complete a certification course for $1,000 and pay CrossFit, Inc. $3,000 per year to operate a branded affiliate. Unlike most franchise models, affiliate operators have almost complete decsion-making autonomy over hiring, programming, equipment, training methodology and hygiene (21). Depending on local real estate pricing, start-up costs can be under $100,000 for many CrossFit gyms, commonly called "boxes," as they are not lavishly outfitted. Boxes lack the amenities offered in traditional health and fitness clubs, such as pools, saunas, treadmills and steam rooms. Most boxes lack even mirrored walls (*Figure 9.14*).

Forbes estimates CrossFit gyms generated $4 billion in 2015 (22). No updated figure is available, though the brand's revenues are likely to have grown. In 2018, 2,500 new CrossFit affiliates opened—820 in the U.S (32.6%) and 1,680 internationally. By the end of 2018, international CrossFit gyms surpassed the number in the United States for the first time. Estimating a conservative annual growth rate of 5.8% would yield 2019 revenues of more than $5 billion. A more optimistic growth rate of 8.5% would raise CrossFit's total annual income to $5.5 billion in 2019.

FIGURE 9.14
CrossFit Gyms Explode in Popularity

CONTROVERSY SLOWS GROWTH: While analysts have labeled CrossFit a "unicorn," (i.e., a privately held startup valued at more than $1 billion), they have struggled to account for its enormous popularity. Whether it is the perpetually changing high-intensity exercises or camaraderie, CrossFit attracted many enthusiastic participants from 2015 to 2019. Still, 2020 proved a difficult year. The COVID-19 pandemic ignited a conflict between members supporting adherence to social distancing and masking and those strongly opposing the restrictions. The company made no policy requirements for COVID-19 compliance. CrossFit founder and former CEO Greg Glassman posted the following on the company website: "locking down the world … may be totally irrational." He later belitttled the pandemic in a social media post (20).

In March 2020, Glassman made racist remarks related to the police shooting of George Floyd in Minneapolis during a Zoom call with gym owners. In response, more than 1,000 owners disaffilated with CrossFit and "major sponsors fled" (21). The backlash led Glassman to resign and sell the company in late June 2020. The sale price was estimated at $200 million (20). The new CEO, former U.S. Navy SEAL and longtime CrossFit senior executive Dave Castro, pledged to make the company more diverse and inclusive. Under Castro's leadership, CrossFit has initated programs targeting underserved groups, such as trainer certification sholarships for teens in at-risk communites, and created a $7 milllon endowment, which includes free or low cost CrossFit memberships, for public health programs in low income communities (20).

By late 2020, Castro's efforts to change CrossFit's culture and image appeared to gain traction. The company restored its signature event, The CrossFit Games, in October 2020 after a two-year hiatus to help heal the fractured community. CBS, which had stopped broadcasting the event due to declining viewership, agreed to televise the 2020 Reebok CrossFit Games. An estimated 400,000 tuned in to the live broadcast, and more than 11 million more watched the games streaming on Facebook, YouTube and Pluto TV (23). Several major sponsors, including Reebok, the U.S. Army, Goruck and Whoop, renewed their partnerships with CrossFit. In early 2021, the company's new owner said, "In 10 years, my goal is to have 100 million people doing CrossFit" (20). Competitors in the high-intensity interval training market like Orangetheory may keep CrossFit from reaching the optimistic goal, but the company remains on an upward trajectory.

INDOOR CLIMBING: Outdoor rock climbing and mountaineering's increased popularity has created demand for indoor, artificial climbing walls and bouldering structures. The subsegment grew significantly from 2015 to 2019, with most new climbing gyms being built outside the United States. According to the Association of British Climbing Walls, enthusiasts made one million visits to indoor walls in 2017, and the numbers have grown annually by 15% to 20% since. The United Kingdom had more than 500 indoor climbing walls by 2019. The United States similarly reached 516 climbing gyms in 2019. The Chinese Mountaineering Association has also reported robust indoor climbing gym growth, with the country's total commercial rock climbing/mountaineering facilities increasing from 49 in 2012 to 338 by 2018. Statista forecasts China will have 899 indoor climbing walls by 2025 (24).

FIGURE 9.15
U.S. Indoor Climbing Participation (thousands of participants)

Fitness Activity	Definition	2012	2013	2014	2015	2016	2017	2018	2019	1-year change	3-year CAGR	5-year CAGR
Indoor Climbing Gyms	Total 1+	4,436	4,752	4,453	4,689	4,910	5,045	5,112	5,309	3.9%	2.8%	3.6%

U.S. participation in indoor climbing grew steadily after 2012 and hit an all-time high of 5.3 million people in 2019 (*Figure 9.15*) (11). Bouldering is the sport's fastest growing form. Bouldering participants mount 10- to 15-foot climbing walls without wearing harnesses or ropes (*Figure 9.16*). Of the 43 U.S. climbing facilities opened in 2017, 20 were bouldering-only, the most ever launched in a single year. Analysts believe bouldering-only facilities will continue to flourish in the United States and Canada.

FIGURE 9.16
A North American Bouldering Gym

A Technavio market report estimated the total global indoor climbing gym's market value was $1.72 billion in 2019 and forecast its CAGR at more than 7.3% (25). According to IBISWorld, the U.S. climbing wall industry has grown at an annualized rate of 6.7% since 2010 (26). In 2010, the U.S. market's value was estimated at $381 million. By 2019, total revenues from U.S. climbing facilities were $731 million.

FIGURE 9.17
Climbing Gym Revenue Source Contributions

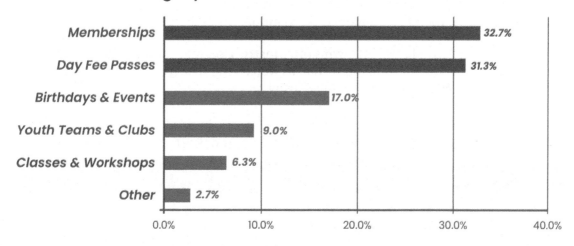

Figure 9.17 breaks down U.S. indoor climbing gyms' revenue sources (25). Memberships account for about one third of total revenues. While many gyms offer three to five-year options, most provide annual renewable memberships. Gyms differentiate their annual memberships by target audience and price, frequently offering single adult, student/military, youth and family

options. The operators often offer additional benefits to members willing to make pre-paid commitments. The perks often include private climbing lessons, six to 12 guest passes per year and 10% to 20% discounts on merchandise purchases. Other gyms offer day passes and "punch cards" granting a set number of visits. In 2019, day passes accounted for 31% of indoor rock climbing and bouldering revenues. No data exists indicating how many daily users become long-term members. The gyms generate their remaining revenues from targeted programs (e.g., youth teams and clubs), special-occasion events (e.g., birthday parties), classes and workshops.

Figure 9.18 offers a representative sample of indoor climbing gym participation costs in the United States. The annual and monthly costs are competitive with other popular specialty gyms, including Orangetheory at $159 per month for unlimited classes and CrossFit at $75 to $225 per month.

FIGURE 9.18
2019 U.S. Indoor Climbing Gym User Fee Ranges

Fee	Adult	Student/Youth	Senior/Vet	Family (3 people)
Annual Memberships	$450-$925	$450-$825	$450-$680	$1,699-$1,800
Monthly Memberships	$60-$99	$55-$75	$45-$85	$150-$200
Daily Pass Fee	$15-$25	$12-$19	$10-$20	–
10-Visit Punch Cards	$130-$180	$110-$152	$90-$180	–
Shoe Rental, Chalk	$2-$6	$2-$6	$2-$6	–

Climbing gyms across the United States struggled in 2020. The COVID-19 pandemic closed rock climbing and bouldering facilities for months, and their decade-long participation and revenue growth plunged. The gyms' total operating revenues fell 28% from $731 million in 2019 to $530 million in 2020. Despite the pandemic, 44 new climbing gyms opened in the United States in 2020—half were bouldering-only—and 61 more were slated to open in 2021 (27). U.S. consumers enthusiastically responded to climbing facilities' gradual reopening in 2021. IBISWorld projects industry revenues will grow 3.8% annually to $640 million by 2025 (26).

MARTIAL ARTS GYMS: Martial arts gyms offer instruction in traditional forms, such as karate, taekwondo, judo, jiu jitsu and muay thai, as well as the relatively new phenomenon, MMA. MMA combines techniques from many martial arts.

FIGURE 9.19
U.S. Martial Arts & MMA Participation (thousands of participants)

Activity	Participant Type	2012	2013	2014	2015	2016	2017	2018	2019	1-year change	3-year CAGR	5-year CAGR
Martial Arts	Total 1+	5,075	5,314	5,364	5,507	5,745	5,838	5,821	6,068	4.2%	1.9%	2.6%
	Core 13+	3,869	3,781	3,765	3,714	3,780	3,816	3,830	3,890	1.6%	1.0%	0.7%
Fitness & Competition MMA	Total 1+	2,726	3,232	3,690	3,902	3,578	3,423	3,382	3,383	0.03%	-1.8%	-1.7%
	Core 13+	1,343	1,246	1,447	1,446	1,425	1,371	1,382	1,336	-3.3%	-2.1%	-1.6%

U.S. martial arts participation grew steadily at an annualized rate of 2.5% from 2015 to 2019 (*Figure 9.19*) (11). In 2019, more than 6 million Americans took part in martial arts. Almost two thirds, or 3.9 million, were core participants engaging in martial arts at least 13 times annually.

Between 2010 and 2019, 23,580 new martial arts studios opened. By the end of the decade, 78,320 studios operated in the United States (28). Statista reports 13,600 studios were registered in South Korea in 2019 (29).

MMA gym participation grew rapidly from 2012 to 2015, peaking at 3.9 million. Increasing exposure for Ultimate Fighting Championship (UFC) MMA bouts on mainstream television propelled the growth. In 2011, UFC signed a seven-year deal with Fox Sports, which aired several fights on its flagship network. Many of the free telecasts drew millions of viewers. To capture the sport's sizeable, young audience, ESPN purchased the entire UFC broadcast package in 2018. ESPN committed $1.5 billion over five years to broadcast 30 UFC Fight Nights per year on television and stream another 20 events on its ESPN+ online platform (30).

FIGURE 9.20
UFC Training & Fitness Gyms Grow in Popularity

Despite the expanded television coverage, U.S. MMA participation gradually declined from 2015 to 2019. However, the continued loyalty of the sport's most committed patrons offset the losses. Core MMA participants increased from 37% of the total in 2015 to 40% in 2019. Analysts suggest maintaining an engaged core is critical for MMA gyms, which rely heavily on stable annual memberships. IBISWorld reports that MMA accounted for 34.9% of all U.S. martial arts gym revenues in 2019, or $3.45 billion of $9.9 billion (31).

UFC-branded gyms (*Figure 9.20*) generate a significant share of MMA revenues. Between 2009 and 2019, UFC's parent company Zuffa opened 150 branded gyms in the U.S. and five worldwide regions. In July 2016, Zuffa sold its majority stake in UFC to sports and entertainment company WME-IMG for $4.2 billion. The new ownership group has continued expanding globally. In 2018, UFC partnered with Lifestyle PLC of London to open more than 100 gyms throughout the United Kingdom and Ireland by 2028.

Despite its downturn in 2020 due to the COVID-19 pandemic, martial arts gyms stand to grow substantially in the coming years, driven largely by MMA gyms and UFC-branded facilities.

COVID-19's Impact on Fitness & Exercise

While 2021 may be looking up for the industry, 2020 was a nightmare for gyms and physical fitness.

Jackie Davalos, Bloomberg

Data suggest the Best Howard Model's Fitness & Exercise core area should rebound quickly from COVID-19 (32), but 2020 was difficult for every area segment. The heat maps in *Figures 9.21* and *9.22* highlight the pandemic's devastating impact both globally and in the United States. In 2020, health clubs and exercise studios worldwide lost a collective $77.6 billion across all four industry segments (*Figure 9.21*).

More than one third (37%) of the area's all-time high of $208 billion in 2019 revenues vanished as thousands of clubs closed. Many will not reopen. IHRSA reports that 30% to 50% of China's health clubs permanently closed. In Italy and Portugal, 40% to 50% of all gyms face permanent closure (33).

FIGURE 9.21
Global Fitness & Exercise Heat Map (U.S. billions)

Global Fitness & Exercise Segment	2019 (billions)	Growth Rate	2020 Forecast	-50% … 0% … 50%	2020 (billions)	2020 % Change
Health Clubs	$96.7	3.7%	$100.3	-47.1%	$51.1	-47.1%
Exercise Studios	$53.2	8.1%	$57.5	-27.6%	$38.5	-27.5%
Coaches & Trainers	$19.1	1.0%	$19.3	-32.5%	$12.9	-32.5%
Specialty Gyms	$39.2	0.5%	$39.4	-28.3%	$28.1	-28.3%
TOTAL	$208.2	3.7%	$216.5	-37.4%	$130.6	-37.4%

FIGURE 9.22
U.S. Fitness & Exercise Heat Map (U.S. billions)

U.S. Fitness & Exercise Segment	2019 (billions)	Growth Rate	2020 Forecast	-50% … 0% … 50%	2020 (billions)	2020 % Change
Health Clubs	$35.0	5.7%	$37.0	-58.2%	$14.6	-58.2%
Exercise Studios	$12.7	6.3%	$13.5	-33.1%	$8.5	-33.1%
Coaches & Trainers	$10.3	0.1%	$10.4	-34.0%	$6.8	-34.0%
Specialty Gyms	$17.0	7.6%	$18.3	-29.4%	$12.0	-29.4%
TOTAL	$75.0	5.6%	$79.2		$41.9	-44.1%

U.S. exercise and fitness gyms and studios suffered even greater declines in 2020. Revenues plunged 44%, with accumulated losses totaling $33 billion across all segments (*Figure 9.22*). IHRSA estimates that full-service U.S. health and fitness clubs lost $20.4 billion in 2020, a 58% decline from the record $35 billion they generated in 2019 (2). Extended club closures resulted in eight major fitness operators (e.g., Golds Gym and 24-Hour Fitness) filing for bankruptcy, an estimated 17% to 22% of all clubs closing permanently and more than 1.5 million industry employees losing their jobs.

The features making health club memberships attractive—personal instruction and a sense of community—provided ideal conditions for COVID-19 to flourish. Public health officials believed that crowded, high-exertion activity spaces were transmissive environments, and governments around the world mandated closures. In the United States, mandated closures began in mid-March 2020. Within a month, 48 states had shut down all gyms and studios.

Despite a continued infection rate increase in late spring 2020, many states began reopening businesses. Most imposed social distancing and/or capacity restrictions (25% to 50%). Some gyms and studios reopened, but 68% of members said they were reluctant to return because of COVID-19 (34). Many club operators began offering online classes and in-home programs, from apps with nutrition plans to customized video workout regimens. To preserve a connection with its members, Orangetheory launched digital classes across a "slew of platforms, including its own app, YouTube and Instagram" (35).

By July 2020, 52% of Americans were exercising at home (36). Survey respondents said they had invested on average $96 on home fitness in the previous three months, with 74% using at least one fitness app. Analytics firm App Annie reported that 71,000 new fitness apps launched in 2020 (37). In addition to gyms offering digital fitness services to members, many online-only fitness workout platforms emerged. Obé Fitness membership increased by a factor of 10 during the pandemic's first several months (38). The startup company offers members unlimited access to 14 live classes per day and more than 4,000 on-demand classes for $27 per month or $199 per year.

FIGURE 9.23
Pelotons Offers a Connected Workout Program

Fitness equipment manufacturers Peloton and MIRROR also reported "virus-fueled growth" (39). Both more than doubled sales of their interactive, in-home fitness systems, which connect hardware (e.g., stationary bikes, treadmills and full-length mirrors) with livestreaming workout programs (*Figure 9.23*). In addition to live spinning bike classes, Peloton allows members to race one another. MIRROR delivers thousands of live and on-demand at-home fitness programs through a full-length, interactive, reflective screen. The company provides personal training sessions for an additional fee. Peloton bikes sell for $2,245, and riders must pay $37 per month to access classes (40). MIRROR screens cost $1,495, with classes priced at $39 per month.

Evidence indicates that many consumers have adapted to in-home exercise apps and interactive fitness systems. A survey conducted at the COVID-19 pandemic's height found seven of 10 home exercisers felt "so confident staying fit at home they planned to cancel their gym membership altogether" (36).

Will members return to gyms and studios? Much depends on COVID-19 vaccinations. By August 2021, only nine worldwide nations had vaccinated more than 50% of their population (41). Vaccine distribution in low income nations has been slow. Nigeria, Sudan and Egypt were among 10 countries with fewer than 2% of their populations vaccinated by summer 2021. With only 15% of the world's population fully vaccinated, health experts believe it may be years before the global population reaches an appropriate immunity level.

In the United States, consumers seemed to begin returning to gyms by summer 2021. President Biden declared on July 4 that a "heroic" vaccination campaign had achieved U.S. "independence from the coronavirus. . . that no longer controlled our lives" (42). Research released in June 2021 revealed that fitness center traffic had reached 83% of January 2020 levels (43). A McKinsey & Company study found that half of former gymgoers were not as happy with their in-home workouts. The pre-pandemic club members said they struggled to stay motivated and wanted to return to the gym (44). The consumers further suggested they wanted to reestablish the personal connections made possible by live classes. As one fitness specialist said, "Everybody, right now, is just craving that sense of community" (45). Members of boutique clubs, yoga studios and climbing gyms frequently cite their close-knit fitness communities as critical to their motivation (46).

Still, many consumers will likely continue exercising wholly or in part online. Almost half those participating in online fitness classes said in a survey they would continue making virtual classes a regular part of their exercise regimen (47). Many grew accustomed to virtual fitness or heavily invested in at-home systems like Peloton. McKinsey & Company research supports the growing belief that the post-COVID fitness industry will move to a "hybrid service model" (44). The study found that 60% of Americans who exercise regularly would likely adopt both gym and at-home workouts. To recover and sustain viable membership, health club, boutique studio and specialty gym operators will need to adapt to the new behaviors and provide both brick-and-mortar and virtual services.

The emergence of rapidly spreading COVID-19 variants (to date, Delta and Omicron) around the world in 2021 perpetuate the challenges facing all segments of the fitness industry. Given the viruses' unpredictability, there is no assurance when and if the Fitness & Exercise core area will return to any semblance of pre-COVID normality. The industry's quick pivot to virtual and hybrid programming allowed many operators to survive the pandemic's initial blow. It's future recovery will depend on it's continued adaptability. It's highly likely that the "hybrid" programming in various forms will be a prominent service model into the foreseeable future.

References

We have added links to many references for direct and easy access. While we have tested each link, there are a few instances where the websites are no longer accessible. We will continue to monitor the accessibility of citation references and remove any links no longer active. In many instances the referenced data was purchased, this is noted.

1. Christina Gough, "Market size of global health club industry from 2009 to 2019," January 5, 2021, Statista (www.statista.com); Christina Gough, "Size of health and fitness club market worldwide in 2020 and 2024," June 17, 2021, Statista (www.statista.com); Christina Gough, "U.S. fitness center/health club industry revenue from 2000 to 2019," October 29, 2020, Statista (www.statista.com); Melisa Rodriquez, "U.S. fitness industry revenue dropped 58% in 2020," February 25, 2021, IHRSA (www.ihrsa.org); Cecilia Fernandez, "Pilates & Yoga Studios," March 2021, IBISWorld (my.ibisworld.com); Cecelia Fernandez, "Personal Trainers," April 2020, IBISWorld (my.ibisworld.com); Brigette Thomas, "Martial Arts Studios," January 2021, IBISWorld (my.ibisworld.com); Anna Miller, "Boxing Gyms & Clubs," May 2020, IBISWorld (my.ibisworld.com); Arnez Rodriquez, "Indoor Climbing Walls," May 2020, IBISWorld (my.ibisworld.com); and Mike Ozanian, "How CrossFit became a $4 billion brand," February 25, 2015, Forbes (forbes.com). (GSI Purchased Report)

2. Melisa Rodriquez, "U.S. fitness industry revenue dropped 58% in 2020," February 25, 2021. IHRSA (www.ihrsa.org).

3. Thi Le, "Gym, Health & Fitness Clubs in the US." April 2021. IBISWorld (my.ibisworld.com). (GSI Purchased Report)

4. "Fitness Industry in China (p. 8)," Statista. Deloitte (www2.deloitte.com).

5. "COVID-19: Gym & Fitness Impact Report," 2020, inMarket Insights (go.inmarket.com).

6. "The 2020 IHRSA Global Report," IHRSA (www.ihrsa.org).

7. "Member retention: A multi-country study on why members leave," Precor (www.precor.com).

8. Zachary Crockett, "Are gym memberships worth the money?" January 5, 2019. The Hustle (thehustle.co).

9. Chuck Leve, "Why your retention rate is the key to understanding fitness business success," Fitness Business Association (member.afsfitness.com).

10. Aleksandar Hrubenja, "Yoga statistics and facts: 2021 edition," January 21, 2021. Modern Gentlemen (moderngentlemen.net).

11. "2020 SFIA Topline Report," February 2020. Sports & Fitness Industry Association

12. Cecelia Fernandez, "Pilates & Yoga Studios," March 2021. IBISWorld (my.ibisworld.com). (GSI Purchased Report)

13. Baba Ramdev, "55 mm Americans could be doing asanas by 2020 as Yoga becomes big in the US, June 21, 2019. Business Standard (www.business-standard.com).

14. Cecilia Fernandez, "Personal Trainers," April 2020. IBISWorld (my.ibisworld.com). (GSI Purchased Report)

15. "How much does a personal trainer cost?," Lessons (lessons.com).

16. Alicia Adamczyk, "Millennials own less than 5% of all U.S. wealth," October 9, 2020. CNBC (www.cnbc.com).

17. Amir Vera, "COVID-19 took the personal out of personal training. Here's how trainers adapted," December 12, 2020. CNN (www.cnn.com).

18. Anna Miller, "Boxing Gyms & Clubs," May 2020. IBISWorld (my.ibisworld.com). (GSI Purchased Report)

19. Outdoor Foundation, "2019 Outdoor Participation Report," 2020. Outdoorfoundation.org *Outdoor Industry* (www.outdoorindustry.org).

20. Michael Easter, "Those two men are on a mission to save CrossFit," February 1, 2021. *Men's Health* (www.menshealth.com).

21. Spenser Mestel, CrossFit is feeling the weight of gym owners downplaying COVID-19, December 23, 2020. BuzzFeed *Spenser Mestel* (www.spensermestel.com).

22. Mike Ozanian, "How CrossFit became a $4 billion brand," February 25, 2015. *Forbes* (www.forbes.com).

23. Kay Wiese, (CrossFit Games' return to live TV. Brings 400,000 additional viewers, November 1, 2020. *Morning Chalk Up* (morningchalkup.com).

24. Lai Lin Thomala, "Number of total commercial indoor mountaineering gyms in China from 2012 to 2018, with forecasts until 2025," December 16, 2020, *Statista* (www.statista.com). (GSI Purchased Report)

25. "Climbing gym market by type and geography: Global forecast and analysis 2019-2023," September 2019. *Technavio* (www.technavio.com).

26. Arnez Rodriguez, "Indoor Climbing Walls," May 2020. *IBISWorld* (my.ibisworld.com). (GSI Purchased Report)

27. "Gyms and Trends 2020," February 7, 2021. *Climbing Business Journal* (www.climbingbusinessjournal.com).

28. Brigette Thomas, "Martial Arts Studios," January 2021. *IBISWorld* (my.ibisworld.com); and David Lang, "Martial Arts Studio Industry business count in the U.S. 2010-2020," February 16, 2021, *Statista* (www.statista.com). (GSI Purchased Report)

29. Jang Seob Yoon, "Number of martial arts studios registered in South Korea from 2010 to 2019," June 16, 2021. *Statista* (www.statista.com). (GSI Purchased Report)

30. "ESPN to broadcast 30 UFC events per year during 5-year deal," May 23, 2018. *ESPN* (www.espn.com).

31. "Martial Arts Studios," August 2019. *IBISWorld* (my.ibisworld.com). (GSI Purchased Report)

32. Jackie Davalos, "How Covid-19 has permanently changes the fitness industry," January 19, 2021. *Bloomberg* (www.bloomberg.com).

33. "IHRSA's TAKE 5: COVID's impact on industry becomes clearer," February 3, 2021. *IHRSA* (www.ihrsa.org).

34. "COVID-19: Gym & fitness impact report," 2021 *inMarket Insights* (go.inmarket.com).

35. Jessica Bursztynsky, "Boutique fitness studios are going digital during coronavirus pandemic, but are they making money yet," April 5, 2020. *CNBC* (www.cnbc.com).

36. SWNS, "Most Americans believe gyms will become a thing of the past after coronavirus," July 16, 2020. *NY Post* (nypost.com).

37. "The Omnichannel approach is here to stay," July 26, 2021. *Club Industry* (www.clubindustry.com).

38. Sarah Sluis, Obe Fitness grows memberships 10X as home fitness surges, May 14, 2020. *Ad Exchanger* (www.adexchanger.com).

39. Patti Waldmeir and Patrick McGee, "The online at-home fitness boom: Can it last? *Financial Times* (www.ft.com).

40. Aditi Shrikant, "Peloton sales are up 66% in the pandemic, but is a $2,200 bike worth it? Here's what users say," *Acorns* (acorns.com).

41. Statistics and Research, "Coronavirus pandemic." *Our World in Data* (ourworldindata.org).

42. Jennifer Jacobs and Sophia Cai, "Biden declares success in beating pandemic in July 4 speech," July 4, 2021, *Bloomberg* (www.bloomberg.com).

43. "Fitness Data Tracker Vol. 1: Ongoing recovery = Elongated season," April 30, 2021. <u>Jefferies Research Services</u> (www.integritysq.com).

44. Eric Faldardeau, John Glynn and Olga Ostromecka, "Sweating for the fitness consumer," June 21, 2021. <u>McKinsey</u> (www.mckinsey.com).

45. Kat Eschner, "COVID-19 has changed how people exercise, but that doesn't mean gyms are going away," June 11, 2020. Fortune

46. Joni Sweet, "7 big changes coming to yoga studios when they reopen," May 28, 2020. <u>Forbes</u> (www.forbes.com).

47. Jess Cording, "How COVID-19 is transforming the fitness industry," July 13, 2020. <u>Forbes</u> (www.forbes.com)

OUTDOOR RECREATION
CHAPTER 10

The Great Outdoors

How much do participants spend engaging in outdoor recreation activities? The costs associated with direct participation vary by activity but share a common core, including user fees (e.g., admission or entry, membership, rental, licensing, permits), operational costs (e.g., fuel, maintenance and repairs, boarding/storage) and travel (e.g., airfare, lodging, meals).

FIGURE 10.1
The Best-Howard Model's Outdoor Recreation Core Area

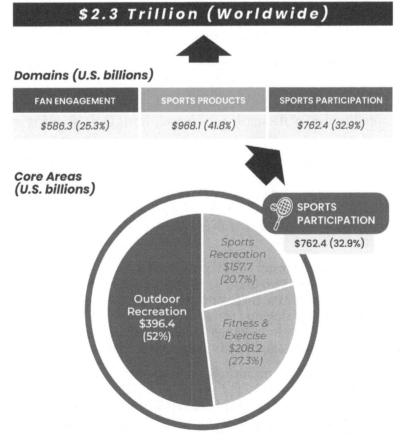

$2.3 Trillion (Worldwide)

Domains (U.S. billions)

FAN ENGAGEMENT	SPORTS PRODUCTS	SPORTS PARTICIPATION
$586.3 (25.3%)	$968.1 (41.8%)	$762.4 (32.9%)

Core Areas (U.S. billions)

SPORTS PARTICIPATION
$762.4 (32.9%)

Sports Recreation
$157.7 (20.7%)

Outdoor Recreation
$396.4 (52%)

Fitness & Exercise
$208.2 (27.3%)

Segments (U.S. billions)

Outdoor Recreation Segments	Revenues	Percent
Camping	$ 41.6	10.5 %
Hunting & Fishing	$ 87.2	22 %
Snow Sports	$ 25.3	6.4 %
Water Sports	$ 25.0	6.3 %
Equestrian	$ 217.3	54.8 %
TOTAL	**$ 396.4**	**100.0 %**

As shown in *Figure 10.1*, the Best-Howard model divides the Outdoor Recreation core area into five segments:

- **Camping:** Includes participants spending at least one night away from their primary residence in a tent, trailer, cabin, recreational vehicle (caravan) or motorhome at public or private campgrounds, RV parks, backcountry forests or wilderness areas.

- **Hunting & Fishing:** Combines all forms of recreational hunting and fishing. Hunting includes activities using rifles, shotguns or bows. Fishing includes both fresh and saltwater forms, as well as fly casting.

- **Snow Sports:** Includes participation and revenue data from the three most prominent winter sports activities, alpine and cross-country skiing and snowboarding.

- **Water Sports:** Recreational activities taking place in outdoor water settings, including canoeing, kayaking, pleasure boating, sailing, snorkeling, surfing and wakeboarding.

- **Equestrian:** Captures all expenses related to recreational horse ownership, including care, training, breeding and participating in competitions (e.g., showing, eventing, jumping, dressage).

Several sources provide relevant data on outdoor recreation participation and spending in the United States. Federal government agencies like the U.S. Forest Service, Fish & Wildlife Service and National Park Service collect and publish detailed annual data on participants and fees collected in a range of activities. Nonprofit and private organizations like the Outdoor Industry Association and Kampgrounds of America provide well-constructed, detailed reports on many outdoor recreation activities.

Few global data sources, with exceptions like the Global Camping and Caravanning Market Analysis, 2020 International Report on Snow & Mountain Tourism and The Equine Industry: A Global Perspective, offer credible participation and revenue figures for outdoor recreation activities, particularly hunting/fishing and water sports. Where the Best-Howard Model has limited confidence in available Outdoor Recreation data, it either uses conservative estimates based on the data's credibility or marks the annual record as not available (NA)).

Outdoor recreation activities are enormously popular around the globe. According to the 2020 Outdoor Participation Report, more than half the U.S. population participated in some outdoor recreation at least once in 2019 (1). And worldwide growth rates in several key areas have exceeded those in the United States. Led by Europe, the global camping and caravanning market is projected to grow at an annual rate of 7.6% from 2020 to 2030 (2). During the 2018/19 season, alpine skiing had its best worldwide year since 2000. Total skiers globally reached 135 million, due in large part to snow sports' continued development in Eastern Europe and Asia (3).

FIGURE 10.2
U.S. & Global Outdoor Recreation Participation Revenues (U.S. billions)

SEGMENT	U.S. 2010	Global 2010	% U.S.	U.S. 2015	Global 2015	% U.S.	U.S. 2019	Global 2019	% U.S.	U.S. Growth	Global Growth
Camping (RVs, recreational access, site fees)	$6.2	$23.7	23.6%	$7.5	$32.3	23.2%	$9.3	$41.6	22.4%	4.2%	5.8%
Hunting/Fishing (licenses, tags, permits, trips)	$46.0[1]	$115.0	40.0%	$38.4[1]	$95.9	40.0%	$34.9[2]	$87.2	40.0%	-2.7%	-2.7%
Snow Sports (lift tickets, lessons, equipment rental, meals, lodging)	$7.5	$21.3	35.2%	$8.3	$23.2	35.8%	$9.1	$25.3	36.0%	2.0%	1.7%
Water Sports (equipment operation, mooring, storage, license, admission)	$12.4	$20.8[3]	59.6%	$13.7	$22.9[3]	59.8%	$15.2	$25.0[3]	60.8%	2.1%	1.9%
Equestrian (boarding, feed, vets, lessons, trips)	N.A.	N.A.	N.A.	N.A.	N.A.	N.A.	$73.9[4]	$217.3[5]	34.0%	N.A.	N.A.
TOTAL	$-	$-	-%	$-	$-	-%	$142.4	$396.4	35.9%	-%	-%

[1] Figures drawn from 2011 and 2016 National Survey of Fishing, Hunting & Wildlife. [2] Estimate based on CAGR extension. [3] Estimate. [4] Extrapolation from 2018 Equine EIS report. [5] Extrapolation from global spending proportion.

The hundreds of millions participating in outdoor recreation around the world spent $396 billion on the activities in 2019 (*Figure 10.2*). U.S. spending, at $142 billion, accounted for nearly 36% of the world total.

Figure 10.2 provides 2010, 2015 and 2019 revenues for each of the major outdoor recreation industry segments. Four of the five areas demonstrated at least modest growth over the decade. Camping led the way, with annual revenue growth rates at 4.2% in the United States and 5.8% globally. Only hunting and fishing suffered declines over the period, with most of the loss in hunting. The equestrian segment is by the far the largest of any major outdoor activity category, with worldwide spending totaling $217 billion in 2019.

Camping

Camping is more popular than ever in the United States and around the world. A recent study found that 48.2 million U.S. households, about 39% of all American homes, camped at least once in 2020, an all-time high (4). In Canada, more than 5.7 million people spent $3.5 billion on camping in 2019, up 41% from 2015 (2). A 2020 global camping and caravanning market analysis reported that spending worldwide reached a new high of $41.6 billion in 2019 (*Figure 10.3*). While Europe and North America accounted for 68.3% of the total 2019 market (*Figure 10.4*), the most rapid growth from 2020 to 2030 is projected for East Asia, with forecast annual revenue increases of 13.1%.

FIGURE 10.3
U.S. and Global Camping Revenues (U.S. billions)

SEGMENT	U.S. 2010	Global 2010	% U.S.	U.S. 2015	Global 2015	% U.S.	U.S. 2019	Global 2019	% U.S.	U.S. Growth	Global Growth
Camping *(RVs, recreational access, site fees)*	$6.2	$23.7	23.6%	$7.5	$32.3	23.2%	$9.3	$41.6	22.4%	4.2%	5.8%

Source: "Camping and Caravanning Market," Global Market Insight, 2020-2030, Future Market Insights; IBISWorld (May 2020). RV & Camper Van Rental https://my.ibisworld.com/us/en/industry-specialized/od5841/key-statistics

FIGURE 10.4
Global Camping and Caravanning Revenues by Region

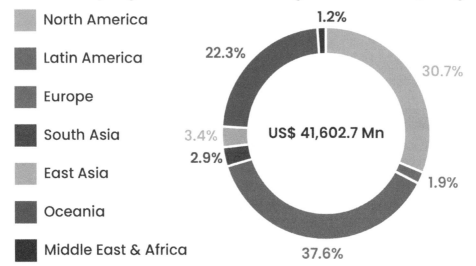

Source: "Camping and Caravanning Market," Global Market Insight, 2020-2030, Future Market Insights.

U.S. camping revenues grew to $9.3 billion in 2019, accounting for 22% of global spending. U.S. Census Bureau data reveal that a substantial share of camping-associated costs result from user, site and rental fees to access overnight campgrounds or RV parks. In 2018, the fees totaled an estimated $6.2 billion.

> *For every dollar spent on gear and vehicles, an estimated $4 is spent on trips and travel (food/drink, lodging, transportation, activities, souvenirs).*
>
> *Camping and Caravanning Market, 2020*

Emerging trends signal that camping participation and revenues will continue to grow, likely at an accelerated pace. Not only are more people camping across the globe, they are camping more frequently. The North American Camping Report found the percentage of survey respondents camping three or more times a year increased by 72% from 2014 to 2019 (5). Globally, 60% reported camping or caravanning more than three times in 2019, with 22% taking 12 or more trips (2).

Several key factors have driven camping's increased participation rates:

• Camping is increasingly popular with young adults. Millennials (age 23 to 38 years) make up the largest share of those new to camping in the United States, growing from 17% to 41% of new campers from 2017 to 2020. Camping and caravanning among the 18- to 24-year-old age group is also expected to grow significantly worldwide. And the young campers have altered the traditional experience. Large numbers of them stay in cabins, RVs or luxurious "glamping" accommodations instead of tents. Analysts have suggested that across the globe, "people are trading in sleeping in a tent on cold, rocky ground for a yurt and a comfortable bed" (6).

"More than 1.4 million households started camping last year: 56% are millennials, 51% identify as non-white."

Curbed.com

• According to the 2021 North American Camping Report, 50% of Millennials and Generation X (age 60 to 80) are interested in glamping, up from 25% in 2017. *Figure 10.5* shows an example of camping with enhanced services and amenities. Glamping, commonly referred to as "luxury camping" in Europe, is increasingly popular around the world.

FIGURE 10.5
Campers Enjoying the "Glamping" Experience

• While 2020 RV sales increased, declined, then increased again, most analysts project a coming surge (7). The coronavirus pandemic has driven demand. After months of restricted movement, many Americans found RV camping a safe way to return outdoors. The North American Camping Report revealed in 2021 that more than half of campers (52%) would consider buying an RV, with the highest interest among Generation X (41%) and Millennials (33%). After a slow spring, RV sales spiked in the early summer—orders "went from zero to 60," according to the RV Dealers Association president—and manufacturers began struggling to meet demand.

U.S. RV dealers saw a 170% sales increase through the first two quarters of 2021 compared to 2019 (8). A phenomenon known as the "van life" also became increasingly popular across the globe, most notably in Europe.

> *"I like to refer to RVs as the 'ultimate social distancing machine."*
> **Bob Rogers, Director of Marketing, Lance Campers**

• RV rentals skyrocketed along with sales. June 2020 bookings tripled compared to the previous year and jumped 1,600% from early April (9). With only 18% of U.S. travelers feeling safe in hotels or resorts during the pandemic, RV rentals became a desired alternative. Many families also can't afford to purchase RV vehicles at $60,000 and up. IBISWorld reported Americans spent $295 million renting recreational vehicles in 2019 (10). Given the participation increase over the second half of 2020, the Best-Howard Model forecasts U.S. RV rental revenues could exceed $500 million in 2021.

• Hispanic households represent 11% of campers, the largest non-white participant group. Hispanics were the largest group of new campers in 2018, at 22%, and the most willing to try all camping forms. Twenty-five percent of Hispanic campers use RVs, with a high number preferring towable vehicles. And Hispanics were found to be the most likely ethnic group to increase their level of camping participation (6).

Almost 48 million Americans aged 6 and over participated in camping in 2020, a 15% increase over 2019. Nearly 18 million RV campers accounted for 37% of the record number. More young people, particularly Millennials and Hispanics, are now camping with greater frequency. Tent camping remains the most common choice, but the increased preference for glamping indicates that participants will spend more in the years ahead. Still, while glamping costs are higher than for traditional tent camping, they are considerably cheaper than staying at resorts.

The Best-Howard Model expects RV sales and rentals to impact camping participation revenues profoundly in the short-term. More campers seeking safe, self-contained outdoor recreation experiences are likely to pay increased fees at campgrounds and for renting RVs.

Hunting & Fishing

Accurate global hunting and fishing participation estimates are not available. Estimates of recreational anglers, what the U.S. Fish & Wildlife Service and U.S. Census Bureau call fisherman, range from 220 million to a 700 million worldwide (11). The discrepancy results from methodological challenges. A European study of "recreational sea fishing," for example, acknowledged the "uncertainty" of participation rates obtained from several countries (12). A 2012 World Bank study offers the most recent credible global estimate, suggesting anglers spent approximately $190 billion annually at the time (13). Citing measurement challenges, the authors concluded that their findings should be taken with caution.

While the Best-Howard Model has located some relevant hunting data sources outside the United States, the model finds only one report providing hunting participation data on a regional scale. The German Hunting Association report measured the number of hunters per thousand for 26 countries in the European Union (14).

The German report revealed that France had the most hunters of any European country in 2020, 3 million, and Ireland had the largest number per 1,000 at 72.8. Applying the number to Ireland's population of 6.2 million yields 451,142 hunters. The partial data does not provide credible estimates of hunting or fishing participants globally. Consequently, the Best-Howard Model's analysis relies almost exclusively on pertinent U.S. data, where federal agencies collect information on the number of Americans hunting and fishing and how much they spend.

FIGURE 10.6
Annual U.S. Hunting & Fishing Participation (millions of participants)

Activity	2011	2016	2019*	Annual Growth (2011–2019)
HUNTING	13.67	11.45	9.95	-3.5%
Big Game (deer, elk)	11.6	9.2	7.68	-4.5%
Small Game (quail, rabbit)	4.5	3.5	2.91	-4.7%
Migratory Birds (duck, geese)	2.6	2.4	2.23	-1.8%
FISHING	33.12	35.75	38.15	1.6%
Freshwater	27.5	30.1	32.1	1.9%
Saltwater	8.9	8.3	8.0	-1.3%
Fly	5.7	6.5	8.1	4.4%

*Extrapolation using CAGR declines from 2011 to 2016.
Source: National Surveys of Fishing, Hunting and Wildlife-Associated Recreation

An estimated 40 million U.S. residents age 16 and over participated in fishing and/or hunting in 2019. *Figure 10.6* shows that the two pursuits' trajectories are moving in different directions (15). While the number of Americans fishing has grown modestly each year over the last decade, hunters have declined at an annual rate of nearly 3.5%, falling from 13.7 million in 2011 to under 10 million in 2019. The number of people fishing increased by 5 million during the same period, a 15% gain.

Considerable overlap exists among those who hunt and fish. Two thirds of hunters also fish, and 21% of anglers hunt (16). A 2018 U.S. Fish &Wildlife Service survey suggested that "about 5% of Americans (16 years and over) actually hunt … half of what it was 50 years ago" (16). The organization forecasts that the decline is likely to continue and may accelerate over the next decade.

> *"We're up against a demography wall…A wall of demographics when the number of hunters is really going to decline."*
>
> ### Keith Warnke, Hunting Coordinator, State of Wisconsin

Researchers suggest changing demographics, anti-hunting sentiment, restricted access to huntable areas, video games and even Netflix have contributed to hunting's declining popularity. Most evidence indicates that demographic changes are the root cause. Almost one third of hunters are Baby Boomers (aged 56 to 74). According to one analyst: "Sixty-five. That's when the average hunter stops buying licenses and picking up the rifle" (16). Big and small game hunting has experienced the greatest declines. The numbers participating in migratory bird hunting decreased only slightly from 2011 to 2019 at less than 2%.

The number of Americans aged 16 and over who fished in 2019 topped 38 million. A survey including U.S. residents aged 6 and older reported more than 49 million fished in 2019, making it the second most popular outdoor activity, behind only running, jogging and trail running at 57.8 million (15). From 2011 to 2019, freshwater fishing participation grew by 9%, while saltwater fishing declined by about 1%. Fly fishing grew over same period. The Outdoor Participation Report said 6.8 million Americans were fly fishing by 2019, up nearly 3 million from 2010 (15).

FIGURE 10.7
U.S. Hunting & Fishing Revenues (billions)

Segment	U.S. 2011	U.S. 2016	U.S. 2019*	Annual Growth (2011–2019)
Hunting (licenses, tags, permits, trips)	$19.7	$13.4	$9.9	-7.3%
Fishing (licenses, tags, trips, other)	$28.1	$25.0	$22.8	-2.3%
TOTAL	$47.8	$38.4	$32.7	-4.1%

*Estimate extrapolated from CAGR % declines between 2011 and 2106 from 2011 and 2016.
Source: National Surveys of Fishing, Hunting, and Wildlife-Associate Recreation

Recreational hunters and anglers spent an estimated $32.7 billion on the activities in 2019 (*Figure 10.7*). The estimates include travel, license, permit, federal and state tag and miscellaneous (e.g., boat fuel, guides, bait) expenses. Gear and equipment costs are omitted but accounted for in the Best-Howard Model's Sports Products core area. Overall revenues declined from 2011 to 2019, largely due to severe hunting participation losses. Hunting revenues plunged by nearly 50% from $19.7 billion in 2011 to $9.92 in 2019. Big game hunters, those who hunt animals like deer, elk and bear, comprise a majority of the activity's participants. Their numbers fell by more than 20% from 2011 to 2019. The number of days participants hunt big game is also down by 37%. Big game hunters spend on average $1,606 per hunting trip; migratory bird hunters spend on average $958 per trip. Hunting revenues represented less than half of the total spent on fishing in 2019.

A 2016 U.S. Fish & Wildlife Service national survey of hunting and fishing expenses (17) showed trip-related expenses—food, lodging and transportation—accounted for a dominant share of the total (*Figure 10.8*). Of the $25 billion spent on fishing, nearly 90%, or $21.7 billion, was allocated to food, lodging, transportation and miscellaneous trip-related expenses. Miscellaneous costs include land use fees, guide fees, equipment rental, boating expenses and bait. In 2019, the United States issued 41.4 million fishing licenses for $748 million.

FIGURE 10.8
Hunting & Fishing Participation Expenditures (billions)

Activity	Hunting	Fishing
TRIPS	$9.2 (69%)	$21.7 (87%)
Food & Lodging	$3.1	$7.8
Transportation	$3.2	$5.0
Miscellaneous	$2.9	$8.8
OTHER	$4.2 (31%)	$3.3 (13%)
Licensing Fees	$0.8	$0.6
Member Dues	$0.4	$0.2
Land (lease/own)	$2.9	$2.4
Magazines/Books/DVDs	$0.1	$0.1
TOTAL	$13.4	$25.0

Trip-related expenses also accounted for the largest share of hunting expenses in2019 at $9.2 billion, nearly 70% of total spending. U.S. state and federal agencies issued 35.91 million hunting licenses, stamps, tags and permits during the year, totaling $896 million. The number represented 1.1 million fewer licenses and tags than in 2018.

The aging hunting demographic suggests U.S. participation numbers will continue to decline. However, it appears the pandemic has had a positive impact. U.S. hunting license sales surged in 2020 (18), with the number of licenses, tags and permits issued increasing to 38.85 million from 35.91 million in 2019. South Carolina issued 306,000 more licenses in 2020 than in 2019, a jump of 39%, Idaho issued 250,100 (17%) more, Illinois issued 187,000 (13%) more and Missouri issued 149,000 (8.3%) more.

Fishing participation numbers were stable from 2011 to 2019. Freshwater fishing's numbers have grown steadily, accounting for more than 80% of the 5 million-person increase in anglers over the decade. The Best-Howard Model projects promising growth for fly fishing in the years to come.

Snow Sports

Sixty-eight countries had at least one outdoor ski area with lifts in 2019 (3). Almost half (47%) were located in Europe; the United States contained 21% of worldwide ski resorts. Global snow sports enthusiasts spent $25.3 billion on downhill and cross-country skiing and snowboarding in 2019 (*Figure 10.9*). The U.S. market share was around 36% at $9.1 billion. The segment's modest overall growth rate of 1% to 2% from 2010 to 2019 is largely the result of climate-driven fluctuations in the number of available skier days from one year to the next.

FIGURE 10.9
Snow Sports Revenues (billions)

SEGMENT	U.S. 2010	Global 2010	% U.S.	U.S. 2015	Global 2015	% U.S.	U.S. 2019	Global 2019	% U.S.	U.S. Growth	Global Growth
Snow Sports *(lift tickets, lessons, equipment rental, meals, lodging)*	$7.5	$21.3	35.2%	$8.3	$23.2	35.8%	$9.1	$25.3	36.0%	2.0%	1.7%

Sources: Laurent Vanat, "2020 International Report on Snow & Mountain Tourism - Overview of the key industry figures for ski resorts," April 2020, Vanat (vanat.ch); Ski & Snowboard Resorts in the US, December 2020, IBISWorld (my.ibisworld.com); Snowboard Resorts in the US – MyIBISWorld; Ski & Snowboard Rental in US, October 2020, IBISWorld (my.ibisworld.com); The Outdoor Recreation Economy, 2017, Outdoor Industry Association (www.scribd.com).

More than one third of ski areas, 80% of "major ski resorts," and nine of the 10 most visited resorts worldwide are in the European Alps (3). The highest ranked U.S. resort is Vail at number 14. Sixty-eight million people across Europe's 39 nations reported taking part in snow sports in 2018 (19). Germany had the highest number among the countries at 14 million, followed by France at 8.6 million and the United Kingdom at 6.3 million. In 2018, 12.1 million Americans participated in downhill and cross-country skiing.

China has recently emerged as a prominent snow sports nation. In 2019, 28 new ski areas opened in the country, bringing its total to 770. However, according to the 2020 International Report on Snow & Mountain Tourism, only 25 approach Western standards in terms of equipment and accommodations: "most are poorly equipped … with ski fields only for beginners." The prospect of hosting the 2022 Winter Olympics has generated enthusiasm for winter sports and accelerated development of four-season destination resorts and indoor "snow stadiums" across China.

FIGURE 10.10
Estimated U.S. Snow Sports Participants (millions of participants)

ACTIVITY	2011/12	2012/13	2013/14	2014/15	2015/16	2016/17	2017/18	2018/19	1-Year Change	7-Year CAGR
SKIING										
Downhill/Alpine[1,2]	6.2	7.1	7.1	6.5	6.2	6.8	7.0	8.0	14.3%	4.2%
Cross-Country[3]	4.3	4.5	4.3	4.1	4.6	5.1	5.1	4.9	-3.9%	3.6%
Sleeding/Tubing[3]	--	--	8.6	8.8	8.6	9.5	9.5	9.9	4.2%	2.4%
Snowboarding[3]	2.1	2.4	2.3	2.1	2.3	2.4	2.2	2.3	4.5%	1.8%
Snowshoeing[3]	4.1	4.0	3.6	3.9	3.6	3.7	3.5	3.4	-2.9%	-2.7%
TOTAL	**16.7**	**18.0**	**25.9**	**25.4**	**25.3**	**27.5**	**27.3**	**28.5**	**4.4%**	**2.3%**

1 Statista (November 26, 2020), Number of active skiers and snowboarders in the U.S. from 1996 to 2019. Statista (www.statista.com). 2 National Ski Areas Association, Industry Stats (nsaa.org). 3 2020 SFIA Topline Participation Report (sportsmarketanalytics.com).

The number of Americans participating in snow sports grew steadily from 2011 to 2019 (*Figure 10.10*). More than 28 million reported skiing, snowboarding, sledding, tubing or snowshoeing at least once in 2019. Except for snowshoeing, the activities showed growth over the decade's second half, with downhill skiing leading at an annual growth rate of 4.2%. The five-year average was influenced by a dramatic one-year jump of 14.3% in active skiers from 7 million in 2017/18 to 8 million in 2018/19. Snowboarding also experienced an increase in the 2018/19 season.

The ski industry uses "skier visits" or "skier days" interchangeably as its primary measure of annual attendance. The metric captures volume by measuring the number of times one person visits a ski area for any part of a day or night for skiing or snowboarding. *Figure 10.11* shows the annual skier days in the United States from 2010 to 2020 (20).

FIGURE 10.11
Total Skier Visits by Season (millions of visitors)

SEASON	2010/11	2011/12	2012/13	2013/14	2014/15	2015/16	2016/17	2017/18	2018/19	2019/20
Skier Visits	60.5	50.9	56.9	56.5	53.6	52.8	54.8	53.3	59.3	51.1
Seasonal Change	–	-15.9%	11.8%	-0.7%	-5.1%	-1.5%	3.2%	-2.7%	11.3%	-13.8%

Skier visits fluctuate dramatically from season to season. The most skier visits ever recorded was 60.5 million during the 2010/11 season. The following season, the number dropped almost 12% to 50.9 million. The 59.3 million visitors in 2018/19 was the fourth highest all-time total but followed by the second lowest total of the decade. The COVID-19 pandemic severely impacted the 2019/20 season, as ski areas across the United States shut down in early March 2020 (21). The National Ski Areas Association estimated the industry suffered a $2 billion loss during the shortened season.

Climate-driven weather patterns will continue to shape annual ski area visitation. Skier days are significantly influenced by weather conditions, as snowfall amounts and seasonal distribution impact the number of days ski areas can operate. The ski season's shortening length is also a concern. Since the early 1980s, annual snowfalls have decreased by 41% on average in the western United States (22).

Skiing's cost also poses a challenge to attracting and retaining participants. The 2020 World Report on Snow & Mountain Tourism reported that a daily lift ticket's average "window price" at a U.S. ski area increased from $59 in 2005/06 to $130 in 2018/19. Some destination resorts charge more than $200 for daily lift tickets. Recognizing the prices are a barrier for most American families, the industry and its resorts have begun offering affordable season passes. One analyst suggests the initiative has only attracted more money from fewer customers (3), and its appeal is to existing customers rather than new or beginning skiers.

According to the Family Skier newsletter, a day of downhill skiing or snowboarding can cost as little as $50 (23). But the cost is considerably more for most skiers. The newsletter provides three spending scenarios (*Figure 10.12*)

FIGURE 10.12
Skiing/Snowboarding Spending Scenarios

"Expensive"	"Moderate"	"Budget"
5 nights, slopeside lodging, $1,100 a night 4 lift tickets, $160 per day, 4 days 5 days of lunches on slope, dinners out Ski rentals, $40 per day per person	5 nights, near hill lodging, $475 a night 4 lift ticket packages, $400 per day, 4 days 5 days of lunches on slope, many meals in Ski rentals, $30 per day per person	5 nights, hotel room, $225 a night 4 lift tickets, $60 per day, 4 days Packed lunches, meals in or at inexpensive restaurants Bring own skis, gear
Full Cost: $9,985	**Full Cost: $4,800**	**Full Cost: $2,385**

Family Skier suggests it is impossible to provide blanket estimates for ski trip costs given travelers' many choices and spending decision constraints. Higher income families can afford amenity-rich ski resorts at more than $10,000 plus travel expenses. Airfare could double the cost of a four-person family's trip. A moderately priced option might still cost $5,000 plus travel, affording a family lodging at a condo near a resort like Big Sky or Park City. Families could choose a drivable, low-end ski area and pay thousands less. But even the low-price experience is relatively costly.

The United States is a mature skiing market. Not only have Americans engaged in the sport since the 1880s, but its existing participant base is also aging. Ski resorts have long depended on older, wealthier individuals who have the time and resources to ski often. A study examining total skier days by age finds that the highest average days skied were among those 72 and older, 63-71 and 53-62 every season from 1996/97 through 2016/17 (24).

> *"Skiing is not a growing sport. We have a problem—the baby boomers are aging out."*
>
> *Jim Powell, VP of Marketing, Park City Chamber*

While demographic trends present a challenge, climate change looms as the greatest threat to the ski industry. Skier visits are highly correlated with snow cover. While U.S. skier visits averaged 55.4 million between the 2010/11 and 2018/19 seasons, they were 5.7 million greater during the decade's four highest snow fall years than in the lowest snowfall years.

Climate forecasts predict increasingly short U.S. ski seasons (25). Critical to maintaining a sustainable snowpack are number of days at or below freezing. The Climate Impact Lab reports global greenhouse emissions will reduce the number of freezing days "by weeks or even a month" over the next 20 years (25). Not only do fewer freezing days mean less natural snow, they also restrict ski resorts from making artificial snow, which requires an ideal temperature of 28°F. The Climate Impact Lab study concludes that if global carbon dioxide emissions continue to increase at the same rate as they did from 2000 to 2010, ski resorts could experience half as many subfreezing days compared to their late 20th century historical averages.

Water Sports

The Best-Howard Model finds no credible data on worldwide outdoor water sports. Until improved global data becomes available, the model will include U.S. participation in 10 outdoor water activities: boardsailing/windsurfing, power boating, canoeing, kayaking, rafting, sailing, scuba diving, snorkeling, surfing and wakeboarding. Several highly reliable sources provide participation levels and trends for each of the sports.

In 2019, 48 million Americans participated in at least one of the 10 sports listed in *Figure 10.13*. Participation levels for surfing and kayaking remained stable, while all others modestly but consistently declined from 2012 to 2019. Only one of the activities, recreational kayaking, showed appreciable growth, with participation levels increasing every year over the period at an annual growth rate of 5.2%. Surfing participation showed modest annual growth of about 2%.

FIGURE 10.13
Annual U.S. Water Sports Participation
(thousands of participants aged 6+)

Activity	Definition	2012	2013	2014	2015	2016	2017	2018	2019	1-year change	5-year CAGR
Board / Windsurfing	Total (1+)	1,372	1,324	1,562	1,766	1,737	1,573	1,566	1,405	-9.7%	-1.8%
	Core (8+)	264	234	285	305	288	284	310	292	-5.8%	0.7%
Canoeing	Total (1+)	9,839	10,163	10,044	10,236	10,046	9,220	9,129	8,995	-1.5%	-2.1%
Kayaking (recreational)	Total (1+)	8,144	8,716	8,855	9,499	10,017	10,533	11,017	11,382	3.3%	5.2%
Rafting	Total (1+)	3,690	3,836	3,781	3,883	3,428	3,479	3,404	3,438	1.0%	-1.7%
Sailing	Total (1+)	3,841	3,915	3,924	4,099	4,095	3,974	3,754	3,618	-3.6%	-1.6%
	Core (8+)	1,276	1,233	1,225	1,281	1,262	1,254	1,159	1,141	-1.5%	-1.3%
Scuba Diving	Total (1+)	2,781	3,174	3,145	3,274	3,111	2,874	2,849	2,715	-4.4%	-2.8%
	Core (8+)	849	823	893	869	819	761	716	699	-5.1%	-4.8%
Snorkeling	Total (1+)	8,644	8,700	8,752	8,874	8,717	8,384	7,815	7,659	-2.0%	-2.6%
	Core (8+)	1,760	1,807	1,818	1,872	1,773	1,663	1,493	1,468	-1.7%	-4.1%
Surfing	Total (1+)	2,545	2,658	2,721	2,701	2,793	2,680	2,874	2,964	3.1%	1.8%
	Core (8+)	1,001	1,029	1,076	1,036	1,024	975	904	962	-1.9%	-2.1%
Wake-boarding	Total (1+)	3,368	3,316	3,125	3,226	2,912	3,005	2,796	2,729	-2.4%	-2.5%
	Core (8+)	1,132	1,010	926	918	895	903	896	890	-0.6%	-0.8%
Water Skiing	Total (1+)	4,434	4,202	4,007	3,948	3,700	3,572	3,382	3,203	-4.8%	-4.4%
	Core (8+)	1,312	1,133	1,095	1,112	1,033	997	863	847	-1.9%	-5.2%

Source: 2020 SFIA Topline Participation Report (www.sfia.org). 2020 Outdoor Participation Report (outdoorindustry.org).

The shared profile among other water sports reveals a gradual decline in both total and core participants. The sports' annual and overall participant losses, however, were moderate, ranging from less than 1% to just under 3% during the decade. The number of Americans who report sailing each year, for example, has remained around 4 million since 2012, with avid sailors at around 1.2 million. Sailboat sales mirror the activities' participation rates. During 2017's third quarter, 1,369 sail boats were sold in the United States at a price of $118 million. During the same quarter in 2018, 1,313 boats were sold for $114 million (26).

FIGURE 10.14
Estimated Annual Sailboat Ownership Costs

Registration/Taxes	$ 620
Insurance	$ 400
Moorage/Slip Fees	$ 2,500
Maintenance/Repair	$ 2,000
Dry Storage	$ 400
	$ 5,920

The high cost of recreational boating has curbed demand. As shown in *Figure 10.14*, routine sailboat ownership costs are nearly $6,000 per year (27). The estimate focuses on an older 30-foot fiberglass boat purchased for $7,500. The costs are variable depending on boat size; bigger boats draw higher state registration fees, which range from 4-10% of purchase price, and slip fees are based on boat length. Powerboat owners must pay all the expenses in *Figure 10.14* plus engine maintenance and fuel costs, adding up to several thousand more per year. With boat trailers, equipment and accessories (e.g., life jackets, water skis), annual operating expenses can exceed $10,000 to $15,000.

Not included in *Figure 10.14* are the membership costs associated with joining one of the more than 700 U.S. yachting and sailing clubs (28). The Yachting Club of America represents a membership of more than 300,000. Sail World's club database details 2,619 yacht clubs worldwide. In the United States, memberships with moorage privileges typically cost from $375 to $650 per month, depending on services. Most full-service yacht clubs charge initiation fees ranging from $1,000 to $2,000 (29). While no verifiable figure for annual U.S. yachting and sailing club revenues is available, a plausible estimate would fall between $300 million and $600 million per year.

U.S. recreational powerboat sales grew steadily from 2011 to 2019, reaching a near record level of 280,000 boats in 2019 (30). The sales include leisure boats, from inboard-motor cruisers and ski boats to small watercraft with attached motors. Small outboard boats used for recreational activities like fishing and crabbing accounted for nearly two thirds of all powerboats sold in 2019. Not only are Americans buying new recreational boats in increasing numbers, but previously owned boat sales are also surging. Nearly 1 million used powerboats have been sold every year since 2016.

Americans spent $15.2 billion participating in water sports in 2019, an annualized increase rate of 2.1% since 2010 (*Figure 10.15*). While water sports' overall participation numbers declined, the activities' costs increased, pushing revenues upward. The most significant cost increases related to sail and powerboat operation were in moorage/slip fees, dry storage and fuel costs (31). Marina operators had a record year in 2019, with revenues reaching $5.7 billion. More than three fourths of the revenues, $4.42 billion, were realized from docking and storage fees, fuel and merchandise sales, and repair and maintenance services (32).

FIGURE 10.15
U.S. Water Sports Participation Revenues (billions)

SEGMENT	U.S. 2010	Global 2010	% U.S.	U.S. 2015	Global 2015	% U.S.	U.S. 2019	Global 2019	% U.S.	U.S. Growth	Global Growth
Water Sports (maintenance/operation, mooring, storage, license, admin)	$12.4	$20.8[1]	59.6%	$13.7	$22.9[1]	59.8%	$15.2	$25.0[1]	60.8%	2.1%	1.9%

Sources: Industry at a Glance (March 2021), Marinas in the US. IBISWorld (my.ibisworld.com); Boat Dealership and Repair in the US (December 2020), Boat Dealerships and Repairs in the US. IBISWorld (my.ibisworld.com). 1 Estimate

Personal watercraft sales soared during the 2020 COVID-19 pandemic. While pleasure boat sales declined in the outbreak's early stages, they had increased 75% by May 2020. The National Marine Manufacturers Association forecast new powerboat sales would settle into an annualized growth rate of 6% to 10% through the mid-2020s (33). The Best-Howard Model expects increasing boat sales to drive increased spending across all boat operation and maintenance dimensions. Marina businesses will flourish as demand for moorage and storage space and repair services grows.

Equestrian

Europe has a vibrant horse industry, with a long-established tradition in racing, competitive jumping, eventing and dressage. A 2017 economic impact study, which measured personal wages, payments for goods and services and sales revenues, reported that European nations accounted for $140.5 billion (47%) of the global equine industry's $300 billion annual economic impact (34). The U.S. impact amounted to $102 billion, or 34% of the total. Canada ($16 billion) and Australia ($5 billion) also have growing equine sectors. China's horse industry is growing at an exponential rate, with equestrian center numbers increasing from 90 in 2010 to more than 500 in 2018 (35). The country has the world's second-highest number of horses owned at 3.6 million. In 2019, China's horse sector was valued at $1.5 billion (36).

The Best-Howard Model's analysis of the Outdoor Recreation core area's equestrian segment focuses on spending directly related to horse use and ownership. It includes spending on horses used for recreational activities like pleasure riding and trekking, as well as horses competing in shows and jumping and dressage competitions. The direct spending estimates are smaller than equestrian's broad economic impact figures but still amount to $217 billion globally, the single largest expenditure segment in the Best-Howard Model's Sports Participation domain.

An American Horse Council study found U.S. horse owners spent $54.76 billion in 2019 (37). Adding the $19.15 billion spent by non-horse owners on riding, lessons and traveling to events, the total spent directly on U.S. equestrian activity amounted to nearly $74 billion during the year.

The American Horse Council estimates the U.S. horse population at 7.2 million (37). The country's horse population, classified by use type, is as follows:

- Recreational/Pleasure—3,141,449.
- Showing—1,227,986.

- Racing—1,224,482.
- Working—537,261.

Owning a horse can cost from $3,500 to $14,000 per year (38). A significant percentage, about 40%, of those owning and boarding horses spend $1,000 to $2,000 per month. For competitive horse owners, breeding presents another cost. Owners campaigning their horses at the highest jumping and dressage levels pay annual training and transport costs into the hundreds of thousands of dollars per season (*Figure 10.16*). Competitors typically own two or more horses, each valued at $10,000 or more, and their total spending can extend into the billions. The American Horse Council estimates that competitive show participants (owners/riders) and spectators spend $27 billion annually (37).

FIGURE 10.16
U.S. Horse Ownership Costs

Category	Low	High	Median Estimate	Per Month
Boarding	$ 900	$ 9,600	$ 2,400	$ 200
Nutrition (Forage/Grain)	$ 240	$ 5,720	$ 1,200	$ 100
Hoof Care (Farrier)	$ 1,000	$ 2,000	$ 1,200	$ 100
Health Care (Vet)	$ 360	$ 2,000	$ 600	$ 50
Insurance	$ 1,000	$ 2,000	$ 1,200	$ 100
TOTAL	$ 3,500	$ 13,800	$ 6,600	$ 550

Total U.S. equestrian participation revenues reached nearly $74 billion in 2019 (*Figure 10.17*). The $217.3 billion spent globally that year is an estimate based on extrapolating the 34% U.S. share of the global market. Europe has the largest market share at 47%. The Best-Howard Model's global estimate assumes that the same bundled costs (e.g., boarding, feed, veterinary services) borne by U.S. horse owners apply to those in the rest of the world.

FIGURE 10.17
Equestrian Participation Revenues (billions)

SEGMENT	U.S. 2010	Global 2010	% U.S.	U.S. 2015	Global 2015	% U.S.	U.S. 2019	Global 2019	% U.S.
Equestrian (boarding, feeding, vet, lessons, trips)	N.A.	N.A.	N.A.	N.A.	N.A.	N.A.	$73.9[1]	$217.3[2]	34.0%

[1] The $73.9 billion spent by U.S. pleasure and competition owners/riders is the only credible participation spending estimate available. [2] Extrapolation based on U.S. proportion of global spending.

The global equestrian industry suffered in 2020 as the COVID-19 pandemic shut down teaching and training, competitive horse events and horse racetracks for months. Hundreds of horse shows were cancelled around the world, resulting in losses of billions in the United States alone. The reopening of many worldwide economies in late 2020 resulted in a significant boost to many horse industry sectors.

COVID-19 Impacts on Sports Participation

Figures 10.18 and *10.19* show COVID-19's differential impact on the five Outdoor Recreation segments. Demand for uncrowded, fresh air sports and leisure activities soared during the pandemic, producing substantial gains in 2020 for camping and water sports. Even the long declining hunting industry experienced a sharp uptick in participation. However, state and local government restrictions to curtail the virus adversely impacted both the recreational ski and equestrian segments.

FIGURE 10.18
Global Outdoor Recreation Revenues Heat Map (billions)

Global Outdoor Recreation	2019	Growth	2020	−50%		0%		50%	2020	2020
Segment	(billions)	Rate	Forecast						(billions)	% Change
Camping	$41.6	7.2%	$44.6				16.4%		$48.0	16.4%
Hunting & Fishing	$87.2	--	$--			4.6%			$91.2	4.6%
Snow Sports	$25.3	2.0%	$25.81		−21.0%				$20.0	−21.0%
Water Sports	$25.0	2.2%	$25.55			8.4%			$27.3	8.4%
Equestrian	$217.3	--	--			−5.3%			$205.8[1]	−5.3%
TOTAL	$396.4	--	--			−1.0%			$392.3	−1.0%

[1]Estimate

The global and U.S. heat maps depict modest overall losses of just 1%, as gains in traditional pursuits, particularly camping, moderated snow sports' steep declines.

FIGURE 10.19
U.S. Outdoor Recreation Revenues Heat Map (billions)

U.S. Outdoor Recreation	2019	Growth	2020	−50%		0%		50%	2020	2020
Segment	(billions)	Rate	Forecast						(billions)	% Change
Camping	$9.3	7.5%	$10.0				19.4%		$11.1	19.4%
Hunting & Fishing	$32.7	4.2%	$34.1				11.7%		$36.6	11.7%
Snow Sports	$9.1	2.2%	$9.3		−20.8%				$7.2	−20.8%
Water Sports	$15.2	2.6%	$15.6			9.2%			$16.6	9.2%
Equestrian	$73.9	--	--			−5.3%			$70.0[1]	−5.3%
TOTAL	$140.2	--	--			1.3%			$141.5	1.3%

[1]Estimate

Many outdoor recreation industry analysts said the coronavirus stimulated camping demand as families stuck in their homes sought to get outside in a safe and socially responsible way. RV camping soared in 2020. Summer RV sales in the United States increased 175% from the same period in 2019. RV camping provided a safe, self-contained bubble where people could avoid crowds while enjoying amenities like television, wireless internet and private bathrooms. Remote workers were able to take their offices on the road (39). Camping/caravanning both globally (15.4%) and in the United States (19.4%) showed the greatest gains of any outdoor activity in 2020, and forecasts indicate a bright future. The 2021 North American Camping Report survey found that 2020 campers intended to take more trips (64% more) and spend more nights camping (70% more) in 2021 (5).

While hunting's numbers have progressively dwindled since 2011, the COVID-19 pandemic revitalized the sport, at least temporarily. Nearly 3 million more hunting licenses were sold in the United States in 2020 than in 2019, an 8% increase (18). The increase coincided with a surge in hunter safety course enrollments. Many of the enrollees were young, female and first-time hunters (40). Industry insiders hope the infusion of young hunters will replace the many elderly white males leaving hunting and slow or reverse the sports' steady participation decline.

Recreational boat sales accelerated during the pandemic, reaching a 13-year high in 2020 (33). Pleasure boat sales declined at the start of the year but increased by 75% by May. The sale of wake boats, popular for wake surfing and water skiing, increased by 20%; freshwater fishing and pontoon boat sales were up 12% for the year. Personal watercraft (e.g., Jet Ski, Sea Doo, Wave Runner) sales increased by 8%. Yacht sales also boomed, buoyed by a "wave of first-time buyers" (41). The United States accounted for nearly half (47%) of worldwide yacht sales; Europe accounted for 41%. The sales spike was reflected in increased spending across all boat operation and maintenance dimensions. The global yacht market is now forecast to expand at an annual growth rate of 5.2% from 2021 to 2028 (41).

The global snow sports industry suffered serious losses as many countries shut down ski resorts mid-season during the pandemic. As COVID-19 spread across Europe in March 2020, Italy, France, Norway, Spain and Switzerland mandated ski resort closures. The economic impact was considerable, as the European Alps draw 43% of total skier visits worldwide (42). In the United States, an estimated 93% of ski areas ceased operations in March 2020. The timing coincided with spring break, "killing off the most profitable weeks of the season" (43). The shortened season resulted in estimated losses of $1.9 billion in the United States and $5 billion globally. The full financial impact was mitigated by the ski industry's recent efforts to sell advance season passes as a hedge against unpredictable weather conditions. While the discounted passes result in reduced revenues overall, they are resistant to area closures and poor ski conditions. Vail, which operates 37 ski areas, reported receiving 21% of its $486 million in revenues from season pass sales during the 2019/20 season.

North American ski resorts rebounded strongly in 2020/21. U.S. skier visits climbed to 59 million, the fifth highest all-time total (20). Pent-up demand from 2020 closures and aggressive promotional efforts, including deep season and day pass discounts and loyalty reward programs, were key factors in the recovery.

The European ski industry's immediate future remains uncertain. The 2020/21 season started slowly due to COVID-19's resurgence. A ski resort in Austria caused an outbreak the previous season, and many observers suggested resorts should shut down their 2020/21 season entirely (44). Germany called for the European Union to close ski resorts across the continent in November 2020. Europe's leading ski nations were divided on how to respond. By mid-December 2020, Germany, France and Italy closed ski areas, while locations in Switzerland, Spain and

Austria remained partially open under restrictions. The Swiss government limited visitors to domestic citizens only. Austria limited capacity on ski lifts and required people entering the country to quarantine. As the season progressed, Austria required negative COVID-19 tests for skiers and snowboarders, and several resorts closed due to the restrictions being too rigid. France and Italy briefly reopened ski areas but closed them in March due to rising infection rates. A turbulent 2021/22 European season appeared likely as the COVID Delta variant threatened openings.

While the pandemic impacted the entire horse industry, the competition sector was hardest hit. Operators around the world cancelled hundreds of shows, including premier global competitions like the Longines Global Champions Tour and U.S. shows like the Palm Beach Masters, Devon Horse Show (which attracts 126,000 spectators) and Hampton Classic (45). In mid-March 2020, the U.S. Equestrian Federation suspended all event activity, including shows, selection trials and training camps (46). The shutdown resulted in the cancellation of 130 major events across all disciplines, including 62 in eventing, 49 in hunting/jumping and five in dressage (47). The cancellations resulted in massive losses. While no credible source has provided an estimate of the financial losses, the volume of cancellations likely shaved billions from the nearly $19 billion spent on the segment in 2019. A conservative estimate of a 20% U.S. decline amounts to a loss of $3.75 billion in 2020. Assuming America accounted for 40% of global equine event spending, worldwide losses attributable to cancellations would be about $9.5 billion.

The U.S. Equestrian Federation lifted its event suspension on June 1, 2020, but implemented hundreds of rule modifications and safety protocols. Many events returned in 2021, including Devon and the AQHA World Championships. However, the coronavirus infection surge in summer 2021 led many state and local governments to reimpose social distancing restrictions and masking requirements at public events. Spectators, the lifeblood of the events, may not be able to attend horse shows in the near future. Eliminating or restricting spectators would present event organizers with serious financial challenges. Only unprecedented fundraising support led the world-class Kentucky Three Day event to reverse its announced cancellation in February 2021. Faced with a spectator ban, corporate sponsors like Land Rover and Rolex and $550,000 in grass roots donations rescued the event (48).

Similar to the ski industry, the equine industry's competitive event sector was hit hard by the COVID-19 pandemic. While participation demand for competitive equestrian events remain sufficient to ensure a solid post-pandemic recovery, until the crisis is controlled the prospects for a full recovery remain uncertain.

References

We have added links to many references for direct and easy access. While we have tested each link, there are a few instances where the websites are no longer accessible. We will continue to monitor the accessibility of citation references and remove any links no longer active. In many instances the referenced data was purchased, this is noted.

1. "2020 Outdoor Participation Report," December 31, 2020. Outdoor Industry Association (outdoorindustry.org).

2. "Camping and Caravanning Market 2020. Trend Analysis and Competition – Global Market Insight, 2020-2030," Future Market Insights.

3. Laurent Vanat, "2020 International Report on Snow & Mountain Tourism - Overview of the key industry figures for ski resorts," April 2020. Vanat (vanat.ch).

4. "2021 Outdoor Participation Trends Report," 2021. Outdoor Industry (outdoorindustry.org).

5. "The 2019 North American Camping Report – 5-Year Trends," sponsored by Kampgrounds of America, Inc. (koa.uberflip.com).

6. "The 2021 North American Camping Report," sponsored by Kampgrounds of America, Inc. Outdoor Recreation (outdoorrecreation.wi.gov).

7. "RV Manufacturing Trends," May 2020. Gordon Brothers (www.gordonbrothers.com).

8. Chris Woodyard, "More turning to RVs, motor homes to escape COVID-19 – and to get away from it all, June 11, 2020. USA Today (www.usatoday.com).

9. "RV owners poised to profit from surging rental demand in the U.S summer," June 10, 2020. RV share. PR Newswire (www.prnewswire.com).

10. Sean Eagen, "Recreational Vehicle dealers in the US," August 2020. IBISWorld (my.ibisworld.com). (GSI Purchased Report)

11. "The role of recreational fisheries in the sustainable management of marine resources," February, 2017. Food and Agriculture Organization of the United Nations (fao.org).

12. Hyder, et. al., "Recreational sea fishing in Europe in a global context – Participation rates, fishing effort, expenditure, and implications for monitoring and assessment," November 16, 2017. Fish and Fisheries. Wiley Online Library (onlinelibrary.wiley.com).

13. Kieran Kelleher and David Mills, "World Bank, 2012. The hidden harvest. The global contribution of capture fisheries," January 2012. World Bank, Food and Agricultural Organization. Research Gate (www.researchgate.net)

14. "Diese Webseite verwendet," October 2020. Deutscher Jagdverband e.V. (www.jagdverband.de).

15. "2020 Outdoor Participation Report" and "2011 National Survey of Fishing, Hunting, and Wildlife-Associated Recreation," Revised February 2014. U.S. Fish & Wildlife Service (census.gov); "2016 National Survey of Fishing, Hunting, and Wildlife-Associated Recreation," April 2018. U.S. Fish & Wildlife Service (fws.gov).

16. Nathan Rott, "Decline in hunters threatens how U.S. pays for conservation," March 20, 2018. National Public Radio (www.npr.org).

17. "2016 National Survey of Fishing, Hunting, and Wildlife-Associated Recreation," April 2018. U.S. Fish & Wildlife Service (fws.gov).

18. "Historical Hunting License Data," May 17, 2021. U.S Fish & Wildlife Service (fws.gov).

19. David Lange, "Global Breakdown of skiers 2020, by region of origin," September 10, 2020. Statista (www.statista.com). (GSI Purchased Report)

20. *National Ski Areas Association*, Industry Stats (Appendix B: Skier Visit Detail by Region) (nsaa.org).

21. "The economic impact of skiing and snowboarding," November 2020. *National Ski Areas Association* (nsaa.org); "Industry Stats," 2021. *National Ski Areas Association* (nsaa.org).

22. Diana Olick, "Climate change is taking a toll on the $20 billion winter sports industry – and swanky ski homes could lose value," March 21, 2019. *CNBC* (www.cnbc.com).

23. "How much does a ski trip cost?" *Family Skier* (www.familyskier.com).

24. Carolyn Webber, "As baby boomers leave ski slopes, millennials are failing to fill in the gaps," October 16, 2017, *The Aspen Times* (www.aspentimes.com).

25. Kelly McCusker and Hannah Hess, "America's Shrinking Ski Season," February 8, 2018. *Climate Impact Lab* (www.impactlab.org).

26. "Combined value of boats sold," November 2019. YachtWorld Market Index. *Boats Group* (www.boatsgroup.com).

27. Daniel Wade, "How much does sailboat upkeep cost?" March 9, 2021. *Life of Sailing* (www.lifeofsailing.com).

28. "Yachting Club of America," *Yachting Club of America* (www.ycaol.com)

29. Morten Storgaard, "How much do yacht club memberships cost? November 10, 2109. *Go Downsize* (godownsize.com).

30. "U.S. boat sales reached second highest volume in 12 years in 2019, expected to remain strong in 2020." January 7, 2020. *National Marine Manufacturers Association* (www.nmma.org).

31. Jack Daly, "Marinas in the U.S.," March 2021. *IBISWorld* (my.ibisworld.com). (GSI Purchased Report)

32. Brigette Thomas, "Boat Dealership and Repair in the US," December 2020. *IBISWorld* (my.ibisworld.com). (GSI Purchased Report)

33. "U.S. boating sales reached 13-year high in 2020, Recreational boating boom to continue through 2021," January 6, 2021. *National Marine Manufacturers Association* (www.nmma.org).

34. The Equine Industry: A Global Perspective (October 20, 2107). *Equine Business Association* (www.equinebusinessassociation.com).

35. "Equestrian Market in China: a fast & furious development," February 5, 2018. GMA. *Marketing to China* (www.marketingtochina.com).

36. "China to spur its horse industry," October 6, 2020. *CGTN* (news.cgtn.com).

37. "Economic Impact of the U.S. Horse Industry," 2018, American Horse Council Foundation; "US Horse Population – Statistics," *American Horse Council* (www.horsecouncil.org); and "The Horse Industry by the Numbers, Riding with the Quo," January 2017. *Ride with the Quo* (www.ridewithequo.com).

38. "What Are the costs of horse ownership," October 14, 2017. *Equine Chronicle* (www.equinechronicle.com); "Equestrian Market Research Report 2018: THE STATS," *Equivont* (www.equivont.com).

39. Heather Wilson, "The RV market is exploding thanks to COVID-19, June 6, 2020," *Kahn Media* (www.kahnmedia.com).

40. Alex Brown, "The pandemic created new hunters. States need to keep them," December 14, 2020, Stateline. *Pew* (www.pewtrusts.org)

41. Alexandra Kirkman, "The yachting industry is on track for a post-pandemic boom in 2021," May 31, 2021. *Forbes* (www.forbes.com).

42. Alice Hancock, "Europe's ski market crushed by COVID-19," December 20, 2020. Travel & Leisure Industry. *Financial Times* (ft.com).

43. Kyle Stock, "Sunday strategist: Months before snow, ski CEOs struggle to save the season," July 5, 2020.

Bloomberg (www.bloomberg.com).

44. "Ischgl: Austria sued over Tyrol ski resort's Covid-19 outbreak," September 23, 2020. *BBC* (www.bbc.com).

45. Richard Ilgenfritz, "2020 Devon Horse Show cancelled this year," May 2020. *Main Line Times* (www.mainlinemedianews.com).

46. Dani Schneider, "Can the equestrian industry afford to go on pause during the coronavirus," March 18, 2020. *The Plaid Horse* (www.theplaidhorse.com).

47. "Rolling Updates: Equestrian events cancelled/modified due to COVID-19 {Updated 8/22], March 12, 2020. *Jumper Nation* (www.jumpernation.com).

48. Staff writers, "Kentucky 5* Three-Day Event back on, but without spectators," February 2021. *The Horse of Delaware Valley* (www.thehorseofdelawarevalley.com).

PART V:
"Glocal" Vision

As businesses in the sports industry begin to reach their sales potential in their home countries, they often look for new opportunities internationally. The effort usually starts in adjacent countries, where potential customers are relatively close by and might understand the firms' culture and business infrastructure.

A global presence alone does not guarantee business success, local knowledge is also necessary (*Figure I*). A German sportswear company, for example, might first seek new customers in France. In the Asia-Pacific region, a Japanese baseball equipment firm might move into South Korea. In both cases, the company has a good chance of learning the local behaviors, lifestyles and preferences in the nearby countries and major cities that may be new markets for their products.

FIGURE I
Global Reach & Local Knowledge

As sports industry businesses expand their global reach, acquiring the needed local knowledge grows increasingly difficult. The German sportswear company must expend considerably more effort to gain the local knowledge necessary to enter an Asia-Pacific country like China than it does to enter European countries. The more distant a country, language, or culture from a business's own, the more challenging it is to achieve local success there. The further a business moves along the curve in Figure I the greater the challenge to expand into more distant international markets and more difficult the task of adapting to local cultures, lifestyles and economic conditions.

A "Glocal" vision combining the global and local perspectives is essential for international sports industry business success (1). It is a strategy global sports brands must employ to adapt to local needs. Glocal marketing aims to:

- Maintain global brand image and messaging.

- Adapt to the needs, languages and lifestyles of local cultures.

- Adapt to new marketing channels and trade regulations.

International brands must maintain brand consistency all around the world but adapt their products and message to local experiences. For example, McDonald's has 36,000 restaurants across 119 countries (2). The company preserves its brand message—offering simple and affordable fast food—but adapts its menu to suit the local people's dietary needs and the store layout familiar to consumers.

GLOBAL REACH—TOP 10 SPORTS COUNTRIES: The first step in building a Glocal strategy is achieving global reach. Where are a firm's best opportunities to grow outside its home country? It must begin in adjacent countries, then expand regionally and beyond. In the sports industry, many Chinese companies are still building share in their home market. However, Japanese brands like Asics and Mizuno are truly global, generating sales in all world regions.

Businesses must select new countries to enter based on opportunity (i.e., sales potential) and market knowledge. Chapter 11 of The Sports Industry considers sales potential at the country level. The countries are examined based on:

- **Fan Engagement**—Number of sports and pro teams.

- **Media Market**—Number of households.

- **Purchasing Power**—Consumer spending and spending per household.

Using a weighted index of the performance metrics, the Best-Howard Sports Industry Model presents its Sports Country Power Scores. The model reports the score, along with performance data, for the 35 largest countries in the world and ranks the top 10 sports countries.

The Best-Howard Model's analyses of the 35 largest countries in the world is intended to help industry analysts, students and businesses understand the world areas with the greatest sports potential.

LOCAL PRESENCE—TOP 50 SPORTS CITIES: The second step in building a Glocal strategy is serving local consumers. Companies looking to develop local authenticity must understand the critical cities within their target countries. Cities have their own culture, and the sports industry is built around professional sports teams that identify closely with their hometowns. In turn, the teams drive sports viewing, participation and product purchases.

Chapter 12 of The Sports Industry examines the top sports cities in the world. One might not expect the Metro area of Randstad, Netherlands, or Istanbul, Turkey, to be among the world's top 10 sports cities, but the Best-Howard Model finds that they are. Using the following metrics, the model offers Sports City Power Scores for 120 of the world's largest cities (50 in North America, 30 in Europe, 20 in the Asia-Pacific region, 10 in Latin America, and 10 in the Mid-East/Africa region):

- **Fan Engagement**—Number of professional sports teams.

- **Media Market**—Number of households.

- **Purchasing Power**—Consumer spending and spending per household.

The model employs a weighted average of the three sports city performance metrics to construct its Sports City Power Scores. All 120 cities are reported by region, along with their sports played and number of teams. The model then highlights the top 50 sports cities in the world based on their power scores. Sports industry analysts, students and businesses can use the lists to prioritize cities within countries.

Chapter 12 also explores city-centric sportswear and street sports. *Figure II* summarizes the number of men and women professional sports teams by region, top 3 countries and top 5 cities with a region.

FIGURE II
Global Professional Sports Teams

North America	Europe	Asia-Pacific	Latin America	Mid-East & Africa
203	*1945*	*470*	*524*	*517*

Top Countries	Top Countries	Top Countries	Top Countries	Top Countries
United States 179	Germany 184	China 139	Brazil 120	Turkey 104
Canada 24	England 106	Australia 164	Mexico 116	Israel 74
	Spain 98	Japan 98	Argentina 87	Egypt 64

Top Cities	Top Cities	Top Cities	Top Cities	Top Cities
New York 13	London 29	Tokyo 22	Sao Paulo 20	Cario 22
Los Angeles 11	Rhine-Rhur 26	Hong Kong 20	Buenos Aires 30	Johannesburg 33
Chicago 9	Randstad 40	Melbourne 38	Mexico City 9	Doha 18
Houston 6	Paris 13	Sydney 34	Lima 26	Lagos 12
Washington DC 8	Istanbul 38	Osaka 9	Rio de Janeiro 7	Tel Aviv 11

References

We have added links to many references for direct and easy access. While we have tested each link, there are a few instances where the websites are no longer accessible. We will continue to monitor the accessibility of citation references and remove any links no longer active. In many instances the referenced data was purchased, this is noted.

1. "Glocal Marketing Definition," Loomly (loomly.com).

2. "Number of McDonald's Restaurants Worldwide," Thought Co. (www.thoughtco.com).

TOP 10 SPORTS COUNTRIES
CHAPTER 11

Thinking Globally

The biggest challenge to companies thinking globally is seeing the world from outside their own country and region.

Consider women's professional cricket. In 2020, Australia defeated India in the Women's Cricket World Cup, played in Melbourne, Australia, in front of a crowd of 86,174 fans (1). Ten professional women's cricket teams represent 10 countries in the sport's international championship, launched in 1973. The 2020 event drew the second largest crowd to any women's sporting event in history. The FIFA Women's World Cup in soccer, which attracted 90,185 in 1999, holds the top spot. See *Figure 11.1* for a video highlighting the 2020 Women's Cricket World Cup.

FIGURE 11.1
The 2020 Women's Cricket World Cup

WT20WC: Ind v Aus final – Australia defend title

Scan to *Watch the Video*

Source: https://www.t20worldcup.com/video/1640569

Cricket currently boasts about 2.5 billion fans worldwide (2) Women's cricket recently has grown its fanbase, establishing new record event attendances, broadcast audiences and participation each year. The gear and equipment required for cricket is extensive, as are the number of fans willing to purchase team sportswear. North American audiences, however, are unfamiliar with the sport, and companies in the region fail to understand the opportunity to market sports products, fan gear, media broadcasts and wagering to cricket fans worldwide.

Sports-focused companies interested in expanding their international reach must understand the worldwide competitive landscape and country-level industry revenue potential before entering foreign markets. They must also recognize how different countries' passion for sports, population and buying power drives revenue potential.

Sports by Country

Three fundamental forces drive country-level sports industry revenues—fan passion, market size and buying power. A country's sports passion is tied to its popular sports, amplified by its professional teams . Professional teams compete in events drawing attendance and media broadcasts fans can watch on television or digital devices or listen to on the radio. Fans engage in both live and rebroadcast games and commentary. *Figure 11.2* provides a summary of the world's professional sports teams (3).

FIGURE 11.2
Worldwide Professional Sports Teams in 2019

SPORTS	North America	Europe	Asia Pacific	Latin America	Mid-East Africa	Multi Country	Total Worldwide	% Worldwide
Association Football	31	619	84	179	215	–	1128	30.3%
Basketball	50	365	110	81	142	–	748	20.1%
Volleyball	–	160	77	60	90	–	387	10.4%
Ice Hockey	32	164	20	–	–	24	240	6.4%
Handball	–	218	4	–	6	–	228	6.1%
Rugby	13	105	36	21	10	29	214	5.7%
American Football	32	63	20	47	8	–	170	4.6%
Baseball	30	43	34	44	–	–	151	4.1%
Futsal	–	38	–	92	–	–	130	3.5%
Field Hockey	–	68	14	–	18	–	100	2.7%
Cricket	–	44	22	–	26	–	92	2.5%
Gaelic Football	–	34	–	–	–	–	34	0.9%
Australian Football	–	–	32	–	–	–	32	0.9%
Badminton	–	–	17	–	–	–	17	0.5%
Bandy	–	14	–	–	–	–	14	0.4%
Kabaddi	–	–	–	–	12	–	12	0.3%
Netball	–	10	–	–	–	–	10	0.3%
Canadian Football	9	–	–	–	–	–	9	0.2%
Softball	6	–	–	–	–	–	6	0.2%
REGIONAL TOTAL	203	1945	470	524	527	53	3722	100.0%
% Worldwide	5.5%	52.3%	12.6%	14.1%	14.2%	1.4%	100.0%	
% Women's Teams	16.3%	24.5%	31.1%	15.1%	18.5%	0.0%	22.2%	

While there are many insights and surprises in the number of professional teams in these regions and worldwide, one that might catch the eye of many in North America is the number of professional leagues created to play American Football outside of United States. The NFL is massive with 32 pro teams. The other 138 teams are much smaller but still emerging in popularity. For example, Mexico has two pro leagues and a total of 16 pro teams that have become the second most watched sport in Mexico's (4). Perhaps even more surprising is the Egyptian Federation of American Football with 8 teams, two female shown below. (5)

American Pro Football in Egypt

Launched in 2014 the Egyptian Federation of American Football (EFAF) has 8 teams:

• **6 Men's Teams:** The Cairo Bears, GUC Eagles, Hellhounds, MSA Tigers, AUC Titans and Cairo Wolves.

• **2 Women's Teams:** The She-Wolves and Transforma Pink Warriors

https://www.youtube.com/watch?v=E6RwgbkNasM

Country-level sports industry revenues are a function of a nation's population and number of households. Countries with large populations and passion for sports offer companies better market opportunities than countries with the same passion but half the people.

Countries also must have buying power, as measured in consumer spending, to drive sports industry revenues. *Figure 11.3* shows the three forces shaping country-level sports industry revenues.

FIGURE 11.3
Country-Level Sports Industry Revenue Drivers

SPORTS PASSION	**MARKET SIZE**	**BUYING POWER**
Country Pro Sports Teams	Country Population & Households	Country Economy & Consumer Spending

The three forces can be defined as follows:

• **Sports Passion.** The extent to which people are emotionally attached to sports as fans and participants, which dramatically affects their likelihood of spending time and money on them.

• **Market Size.** A country's number of people and households creates a baseline for fan engagement, sports product purchases and sports participation spending.

• **Buying Power.** A country's consumer buying power is derived from the disposable income households can spend on sports participation, products and engagement.

Consider the sports markets in India, Brazil and Norway. As shown in *Figure 11.4*, each country has different passions based on the sports they play and professional teams they support. And each country has a unique sports culture revolving around its sports and professional teams.

FIGURE 11.4
Passion, People, Purchasing Power & Sportswear Revenues

INDIA	BRAZIL	NORWAY

INDIA

PASSION: Cricket, Soccer, Field Hockey, Badminton & Tennis.

- Number Pro Teams: 106
- % Women: 40%

PEOPLE: (millions)

- Population: 1368.1
- Households (HH): 306.8
- Household Size: 4.5
- Percent >65: 28%

BUYING POWER:

- GDP (U.S. billions): $2,800
- HH Income: $6,793
- HH Spending: $3,790

SPORTWEAR SALES:

- Country (U.S. billions): $9.0
- % Footwear: 44%
- % Apparel: 56%
- SW Sales/HH: $29
- % HH Spending: .77%

BRAZIL

PASSION: Soccer, Volleyball, Martial Arts, Basketball, Tennis.

- Number Pro Teams: 120
- % Women: 21%

PEOPLE: (millions)

- Population: 211.2
- Households (HH): 68.2
- Household Size: 3.1
- Percent >65: 30%

BUYING POWER:

- GDP (U.S. billions): $2,020
- HH Income: $19,408
- HH Spending: $4,405

SPORTWEAR SALES:

- Country (U.S. billions): $7.4
- % Footwear: 47%
- % Apparel: 53%
- SW Sales/HH: $108
- % HH Spending: 2.5%

NORWAY

PASSION: Cross-Country Skiing, Soccer, Ice Hockey & Ski Jumping.

- Number Pro Teams: 16
- % Women: 0%

PEOPLE: (millions)

- Population: 5.4
- Households (HH): 2.4
- Household Size: 2.3
- Percent >65: 17%

BUYING POWER:

- GDP (U.S. billions): $450
- HH Income: $73,708
- HH Spending: $69,083

SPORTWEAR SALES:

- Country (U.S. billions): $1.7
- % Footwear: 68%
- % Apparel: 32%
- SW Sales/HH: $696
- % HH Spending: 1.0%

Turning to market size, Norway's small population of 2.4 million households offers less sports industry revenue potential than Brazil with 68.2 million households, despite Norway's tremendous sports passion. Not all consumers can attend sporting events, but all those interested can follow teams via print and media broadcasts.

Considering buying power, India's average consumer spending is $3,790 per household. Despite the country's strong passion for soccer, cricket, field hockey and badminton and its second largest worldwide population of 1.37 billion people, its buying power is lower than Brazil's at $17,363 and far below Norway's at $67,984.

So, what are the three countries' sports industry sales potential? India has almost 1.4 billion people and 306.8 million households. Its average household income of $6,793 in 2019 limited its consumer spending to $3,790 per year and sportswear sales to $29 per household, or 0.77% of the total. India's 2019 sportswear sales were $9 billion, with 44% going to footwear and 56% going to apparel.

By contrast, Norway had only 5.4 million people and 2.4 million households in 2019. However, its average household income was $73,708 and consumer spending was $69,083. With greater buying power, Norwegian households spent an average of almost $700 per household on sportswear in 2019. The country's sportswear sales were $1.7 billion, with 68% on footwear and 32% on apparel. While sportswear sales were higher in India, it took 24 Indian households to buy as much product as one household in Norway.

Brazil's per household sportswear sales were $108 in 2019, and its total sportswear revenues were $7.4 billion. Forty-seven percent of the sales were in footwear; 53% were in apparel, similar to the numbers in India. The average Brazilian household allocated 2.5% of its consumer spending on sportswear. To achieve $1 million is sportswear sales, Brazil would therefore require 9,559 households.

The amount countries spend attending, watching, betting on and participating in sports varies greatly, given the enormous differences among populations, disposable income and sports event access worldwide. Every country has a unique sports industry revenue model.

The Best-Howard Sports Industry Model examines 35 countries' sports passion, market size and buying power and to generate its proprietary Country-Level Sports Power Scores (0 to 100).

Country-Level Sports Passion

The strong emotional connection fans form with their favorite teams is central to the popularity of professional sports around the world. For many, the connection is reinforced by what sociologists call "tribalism," a basic human urge to belong, particularly to a group identifying with the same thing. The shared sense of community among fans devoted to a team is one of several elements reinforcing sports team loyalty. Sports provide individuals with shared experiences, a sense of belonging and an emotional connection. Competition and the pride or pain at the end of a game or season heightens the shared feelings.

Every country has different sports passions. In the United States, passions are built around professional baseball, football, basketball, ice hockey and, more recently, soccer teams. In Europe and the Asia-Pacific region, baseball and football are not significant parts of the sports culture. Soccer, rugby, cricket, field hockey and volleyball instead dominate sports fans' interests.

Figure 11.5 shows the worldwide fanbases for several popular sports. Soccer has the largest number of fans, with 3.5 billion. Cricket has the second largest worldwide fanbase, despite not being played in North America or Latin America. Basketball, with 2.2 billion fans, is played in almost all world countries. Volleyball, with 900 million fans, is played mostly in Latin America and Europe. Baseball and football are popular in the United States but have fewer fans worldwide. The opposite is true for rugby, which has only begun to establish a U.S. presence.

FIGURE 11.5
Global Sports Fans (millions of people)

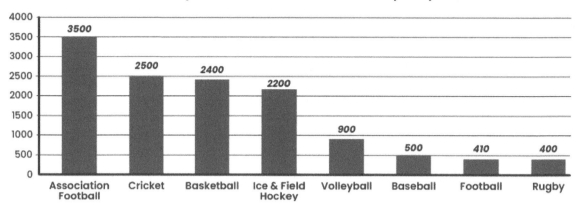

Every country in the world has a national soccer team and uniforms featuring specific colors. Through the uniforms, each country's pride and passion are on display in worldwide soccer events, as well during the Olympics. *Figure 11.6* shows the soccer team uniforms for multiple countries in the five world regions (6). Click on each region at the bottom of the figure to see the uniforms in detail.

FIGURE 11.6
National Soccer Team Uniform Colors

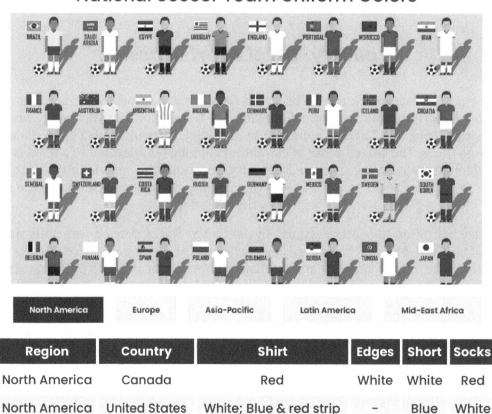

Region	Country	Shirt	Edges	Short	Socks
North America	Canada	Red	White	White	Red
North America	United States	White; Blue & red strip	–	Blue	White

View other graphs at the end of the chapter on page A11.1 Chapter 11 Appendix 1.

Due to many countries' enormous interest in soccer, national uniform colors are an important way for global brands to connect with local consumers. The colors have meaning and are easily recognized and associated with positive emotions. For example, the orange color worn by the Dutch soccer team (*Figure 11.7*) and its fans dates back almost 600 years to when the Netherlands sought independence from Spanish rule (7). During the 80-year war, Prince William III of England, known as William of Orange, helped liberate the Netherlands. After gaining independence, the Dutch adopted orange as a national color in honor of the prince, who was appointed governor in 1555. The Netherlands flag, on the other hand, is red, white and blue.

FIGURE 11.7
The Dutch National Soccer Team Wearing Orange

When sponsors use team colors for brand ads in stadium signage and digital advertising, consumers exhibit greater brand recall and purchase intention. For example, M&Ms uses the Brazilian soccer team's colors in digital advertisements (*Figure 11.8*) during important matches to achieve greater brand performance scores than its traditional brand colors provide (8). With companies increasingly focusing on digital advertising, the strategy represents a cost-effective way to build brand awareness and preference.

FIGURE 11.8
M&Ms Employs Brazil's National Soccer Team Colors

Country-Level Professional Sports Teams

While every country in the world has sports teams, many are not at the professional level. *Figure 11.9* identifies the top 35 worldwide countries based on their number of professional teams. The number of pro teams for these countries was determined by the pro leagues for each sport in a country and then the number of teams per sport (9). This database will also allow us to profile each country by sport and number of pro teams per sport. This data will be used extensively in the remainder of Chapter 11.

In the figure, professional team volumes range from 12 in Hungary to 184 in Germany. Countries not shown have fewer than 12 pro teams. The 35 countries average 84 teams and represent 78% of the world's 3,772 professional sports teams. The top 10 countries in the figure account for 1,459 teams, 51% of the top 35 and 39% of all teams around the globe. The top 10 countries range from 116 teams in Mexico to 184 in Germany. The United States has the second largest number at 179. By sport, soccer accounts for the most professional teams globally at 815, 27% of the 35 countries' teams and 22% of all teams worldwide.

FIGURE 11.9
Top 35 Sports Countries by 2019 Professional Team Volume

No.	Country	Pro Teams	% Top 35 Countries Teams	% Women Teams	Association Football	Assoc. Football % Pro Teams
1	Germany	184	6.2%	23.9%	30	16.3%
2	United States	179	6.1%	17.9%	32	17.9%
3	England	175	5.9%	39.3%	32	18.3%
4	Australia	164	5.6%	42.1%	20	12.2%
5	China	149	5.1%	31.5%	34	22.8%
6	France	144	4.9%	26.4%	32	22.2%
7	Spain	140	4.7%	31.4%	36	25.7%
8	Netherlands	133	4.5%	28.6%	27	20.3%
9	Brazil	120	4.1%	16.7%	20	16.7%
10	Mexico	116	3.9%	15.5%	36	31.0%
11	India	106	3.6%	22.6%	47	44.3%
12	Turkey	104	3.5%	35.6%	30	28.8%
13	Italy	101	3.4%	27.7%	32	31.7%
14	Sweden	99	3.4%	22.2%	28	28.3%
15	Japan	98	3.3%	24.5%	18	18.4%
16	Switzerland	90	3.1%	30.0%	28	31.1%
17	Belgium	88	3.0%	45.5%	22	25.0%
18	Greece	88	3.0%	45.5%	24	27.3%
19	Argentina	87	2.9%	12.6%	24	27.6%
20	Israel	74	2.5%	39.2%	22	29.7%
21	Egypt	64	2.2%	0.0%	18	28.1%
22	South Africa	61	2.1%	36.1%	28	45.9%
23	Russia	57	1.9%	31.6%	24	42.1%
24	Austria	56	1.9%	0.0%	12	21.4%
25	Canada	47	1.6%	2.1%	11	23.4%

26	Poland	46	1.6%	0.0%	16	34.8%
27	South Korea	45	1.5%	13.3%	12	26.7%
28	Finland	27	0.9%	0.0%	12	44.4%
29	Chile	18	0.6%	0.0%	18	100.0%
30	Portugal	18	0.6%	0.0%	18	100.0%
31	Norway	16	0.5%	0.0%	16	100.0%
32	Czech Republic	16	0.5%	0.0%	16	100.0%
33	Romania	14	0.5%	0.0%	14	100.0%
34	Denmark	14	0.5%	0.0%	14	100.0%
35	Hungary	12	0.4%	0.0%	12	100.0%
	TOTAL/AVERAGE	**2950**	**100%**	**18.9%**	**815**	**27.6%**
	% World	**78.2%**				
	Worldwide	**3772**			**1137**	**815**

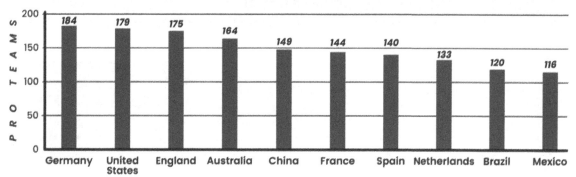

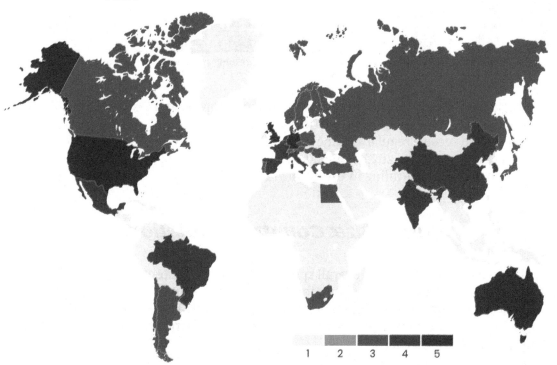

The top 10 countries based on professional team volume are of strategic importance for companies looking to grow beyond their borders. England, Germany, France, Spain and Italy would be critical targets for European firms, while Brazil and Mexico would be important in Latin America. China, Australia and Japan are the top opportunities in the Asia-Pacific region.

For major global companies, such as Nike, Adidas, Puma, Asics and Mizuno, the full 35-country list provides a way to prioritize targets. For example, a Europe-based sports products firm with an existing regional presence in the top 10 countries might also look to Italy, Turkey, Switzerland, Belgium, Greece, Russia, Austria, Sweden, Finland, Portugal, Norway and Denmark.

Because of the structure of professional sports leagues, the Best-Howard Model specifically looks at the percentage of women's teams among men's teams. *Figure 11.10* shows 40% of the world's soccer teams are composed of women (10). In professional basketball, 20% of teams are women's, making the two sports important strategic opportunities for companies selling women's footwear, apparel and equipment.

FIGURE 11.10
Women's Professional Team Percentages Worldwide in 2019

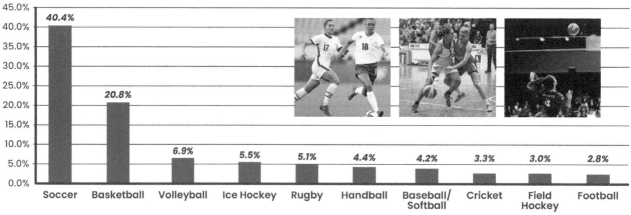

Women's sports participation and professional teams are growing at a faster rate than those for men, especially in countries outside the United States. The women's national cricket teams in India and England receive regular airtime on Sky Sports and Fox Sports. And with record attendance and viewing for the 2020 Women's Cricket World Cup, the Australian women's team won a $1 million prize for prevailing in the event. The men's national teams played for a similar prize in 2021.

Market Size: Country Population

Market size shapes every country's overall sports product sales potential. And market size is dependent on more than simply population. In addition to number of people, population age categories, households and household sizes have an effect. Two countries with the same number of people would behave differently if 40% of the population were over 64 in one and 40% were under 25 in the other.

Three critical market size metrics are (11):

- **Population**—number of people. The 2019 world population was 7.6 billion.

- **Households**—number of dwellings in which a group of people live together. The world contained 2.1 billion households in 2019.

- **Household Size**—number of people per household unit. The average worldwide household size was 3.5 in 2019.

The video in *Figure 11.11* discusses the way world population changes are expected to affect the global sports industry. According to the United Nations, the world's population will grow from 7.6 billion in 2019 to 9.7 billion by 2050. During the period, Japan and countries in Eastern Europe are expected to shrink in population. India is expected to surpass China as the world's most populous nation, and the African continent will become home to one third of global population. The world population will also age dramatically—half the people expected to be living in 2050 were already born by 2020. While it is impossible to know the shift's impact on the global sports market, the industry must continue to follow changing population dynamics.

FIGURE 11.11
Country & Regional Global Population Growth

Mapping global population and the future of the world | The Economist

Scan to *Watch the Video*

Source: https://www.youtube.com/watch?v=Ur77lDetl9Q

The Best-Howard Model uses Oxford Economics population data (11) to examine the 35 countries presented in *Figure 11.12*. The countries contain a large part of the world population:

- China is the largest country, with 1.43 billion people, followed by India with 1.37 billion. The two countries contain 59% of the people living in the largest 35 countries and 37% of the world population. India, with a higher average household size at 4.5 versus 3.0, is expected to overtake China as the world's largest population center.

- The top 10 countries account for 85% of the top 35 countries' population and 53% of the world's.

- Household size varies from a low of 2.1 in Denmark to 4.5 in India.

- The top 10 countries contain 56% of the world's households; the top 35 countries contain 70% of worldwide households.

Because they represent 56% of worldwide households and 34% of global professional teams, the top 10 countries provide sports products companies a strategic focus as they attempt to expand globally.

FIGURE 11.12
Country Populations & Professional Sports Teams in 2019

No.	Country	Pro Teams	% Top 35 Countries Teams	Population (millions)	Households (millions)	% Top 35 Households	Household Size
1	China	149	5.1%	1434.5	479.6	31.8%	3.0
2	India	106	3.6%	1368.1	306.8	20.4%	4.5
3	United States	179	6.1%	328.2	122.1	8.1%	2.7
4	Brazil	120	4.1%	211.2	68.2	4.5%	3.1
5	Russia	57	1.9%	145.9	56.7	3.8%	2.6
6	Mexico	116	3.9%	127.7	33.8	2.2%	3.8
7	Japan	98	3.3%	126.8	55.7	3.7%	2.3
8	Hungary	12	0.4%	104.1	38.0	2.5%	2.7
9	Egypt	64	2.2%	100.4	24.5	1.6%	4.1
10	Turkey	104	3.5%	83.5	24.1	1.6%	3.5
11	Germany	184	6.2%	83.1	41.5	2.8%	2.0
12	France	144	4.9%	67.1	30.0	2.0%	2.2
13	England	175	5.9%	66.8	28.0	1.9%	2.4
14	Italy	101	3.4%	60.3	26.1	1.7%	2.3
15	South Africa	61	2.1%	58.8	17.7	1.2%	3.3
16	South Korea	45	1.5%	51.2	19.8	1.3%	2.6
17	Spain	140	4.7%	47.1	18.9	1.3%	2.5
18	Argentina	87	2.9%	44.8	14.5	1.0%	3.1
19	Poland	46	1.6%	38.0	14.5	1.0%	2.6
20	Canada	47	1.6%	37.5	14.7	1.0%	2.5
21	Australia	164	5.6%	25.4	9.6	0.6%	2.6
22	Romania	14	0.5%	19.4	6.7	0.4%	2.9
23	Chile	18	0.6%	18.9	5.4	0.4%	3.5
24	Netherlands	133	4.5%	17.3	7.9	0.5%	2.2
25	Belgium	88	3.0%	11.5	5.0	0.3%	2.3
26	Czech Republic	16	0.5%	10.7	4.5	0.3%	2.4
27	Greece	88	3.0%	10.5	4.4	0.3%	2.4
28	Sweden	99	3.4%	10.3	4.7	0.3%	2.2
29	Portugal	18	0.6%	10.3	4.1	0.3%	2.5
30	Israel	74	2.5%	8.9	2.9	0.2%	3.1
31	Austria	56	1.9%	8.9	4.0	0.3%	2.2
32	Switzerland	90	3.1%	8.6	3.9	0.3%	2.2
33	Denmark	14	0.5%	5.8	2.7	0.2%	2.1
34	Finland	27	0.9%	5.5	2.7	0.2%	2.0
35	Norway	16	0.5%	5.4	2.4	0.2%	2.2
	TOTAL/AVERAGE	2950	100%	4762.7	1506.2	100.0%	3.2
	% World	78.2%		62.8%	69.9%		89.8%
	Worldwide	3772		7585.5	2153.3		3.5

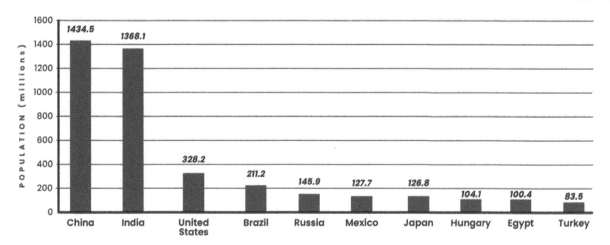

Buying Power: Country Economy

Passion, professional teams and a large population are necessary conditions for strong sports industry sales. But countries also need strong economies to drive revenues. Household income and consumer spending determine consumers' ability to purchase sports products. For example, 1.423 billion Chinese (19% of the world population) living in 474 million households spend about $3.37 per household per year on professional sports. The United States, with 4.4% of the world population and 120.7 million households, spends $260 per household.

With just 1.1% of the world's population, Germany accounts for 7.1% of total worldwide professional sports spending. German households average two residents but spend $135 per year, almost four times more than the $37.29 global average. The Best-Howard Model finds no statistically significant relationship between country-level professional sports revenues and raw population.

Gross domestic product (GDP) is the most used metric to determine a country's economic wellbeing and buying power. As shown in *Figure 11.13*, consumer spending drives 64.5% of GDP. GDP is determined as follows:

$$GDP = \begin{array}{c} Consumer \\ Spending\ (C) \end{array} + \begin{array}{c} Company \\ Investment\ (I) \end{array} + \begin{array}{c} Government \\ Spending\ (G) \end{array} + \begin{array}{c} Net\ Exports\ (NE) \\ (Exports - Imports) \end{array}$$

FIGURE 11.13
2019 Worldwide Gross Domestic Product

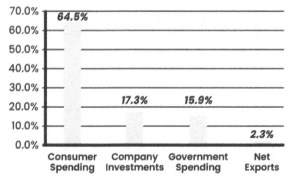

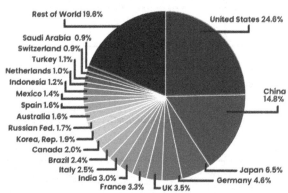

The video in *Figure 11.14* provides an overview of global and country-level GDP. The four components contributing to GDP are:

• **Consumer Spending (C).** Money individuals spend in a year on goods and services, from groceries to haircuts.

• **Company Investment (I).** Investments companies make in their businesses, such as on manufacturing facilities, equipment, and research and development.

• **Government Spending (G).** The amount a country's government puts into the economy via expenditures on infrastructure, government workers, equipment purchases, etc.

• **Net Exports (NE).** Annual sales value of a country's exports minus imports.

FIGURE 11.14
Country-Level Gross Domestic Product

Source: https://www.cnbc.com/video/2018/09/26/what-is-gdp.html

The world's top five countries' GDPs account for 50% of the worldwide total. Roughly 15 others account for another 30%. The remaining 180 countries make up 20% of worldwide GDP. Because consumer spending is the largest part of country-level GDP, the metric is critical for understanding sports entertainment, products and recreation spending.

FIGURE 11.15
Global GDP Growth

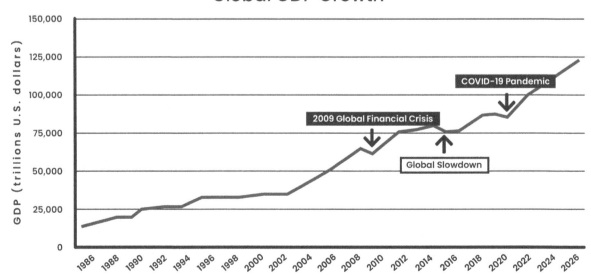

In 2019, global GDP was $87.4 trillion (*Figure 11.15*), representing total worldwide consumer spending, government spending, firm investments and net exports. The world economy contracted in 2009 following the 2008 financial crisis, leading to decreased consumer spending and global sports industry revenues. (12)

COVID-19 negatively impacted global GDP in 2020, causing it to drop to $84.5 trillion, and lowered consumer spending to about 70% of GDP. However, the economy rebounded to $93.7 billion in 2021 and was projected to grow at an increased rate to nearly $125 trillion in 2026. Sports companies interested in global growth can therefore be optimistic. The growing GDP will drive consumer spending, creating more opportunities for sports industry events, products and participation.

Figure 11.16 presents GDP for the top 35 countries in professional team revenues in 2019. The top 10 countries accounted for almost 75% of revenues and 68.4% of worldwide GDP. The United States represented 25.4% of global GDP and 42.8% of worldwide professional team revenues. While the United States therefore achieved greater revenues than would be expected based on GDP, China produced $1.9 billion in professional team revenues, well below expectations. Recognizing China's GDP of $13.6 trillion is 16.8% of the world's, the Best-Howard Model expects the country to spend more on professional sports as teams proliferate.

According to the Best-Howard Model, the more prosperous a country based on economic revenues, the more money its people will spend on professional team sports events. The high GDP countries would therefore also be expected to spend more on sports products and participation.

FIGURE 11.16
Top 35 Sports Country Economies in 2019

No.	Country	Pro Teams	% Top 35 Countries Teams	GDP (billions)	Disposable Income (billions)	Disposable Income per Household	Consumer Spending (billions)	Consumer Spending per Household
1	United States	179	6.1%	$21,433	$16,440.6	$134,597	$13,561	$111,022
2	China	149	5.1%	$14,280	$8,907.3	$18,573	$5,848	$12,194
3	Japan	98	3.3%	$4,955	$2,950.6	$52,971	$2,787	$50,033
4	Germany	184	6.2%	$3,861	$2,222.4	$53,489	$2,011	$48,402
5	England	175	5.9%	$2,831	$1,938.4	$69,249	$1,780	$63,589
6	Italy	101	3.4%	$2,005	$1,314.7	$50,441	$1,478	$56,707
7	France	144	4.9%	$2,716	$1,618.1	$53,964	$1,287	$42,922
8	Brazil	120	4.1%	$1,878	$1,324.6	$19,408	$1,185	$17,363
9	Canada	47	1.6%	$1,742	$993.0	$67,431	$1,000	$67,906
10	Spain	140	4.7%	$1,393	$858.9	$45,415	$857	$45,312
11	Russia	57	1.9%	$1,687	$954.5	$16,841	$809	$14,273
12	Mexico	116	3.9%	$1,269	$1,013.6	$29,981	$805	$23,811
13	Australia	164	5.6%	$1,397	$853.8	$88,794	$803	$83,512
14	South Korea	45	1.5%	$1,647	$852.6	$43,097	$790	$39,931
15	India	106	3.6%	$2,870	$2,083.8	$6,793	$559	$1,822
16	Turkey	104	3.5%	$761	$574.0	$23,853	$440	$18,284
17	Netherlands	133	4.5%	$907	$438.0	$55,098	$391	$49,189
18	Switzerland	90	3.1%	$731	$119.4	$30,603	$380	$97,556
19	Argentina	87	2.9%	$446	$137.5	$9,484	$323	$22,285
20	Belgium	88	3.0%	$533	$308.8	$62,080	$261	$52,476

21	Egypt	64	2.2%	$303	$3.7	$151	$250	$10,189
22	Sweden	99	3.4%	$531	$246.9	$52,831	$242	$51,783
23	Poland	46	1.6%	$596	$338.5	$23,428	$226	$15,640
24	South Africa	61	2.1%	$351	$210.0	$11,864	$218	$12,316
25	Israel	74	2.5%	$395	$171.0	$58,966	$214	$73,738
26	Austria	56	1.9%	$445	$246.4	$61,312	$179	$44,542
27	Chile	18	0.6%	$279	$253.0	$46,852	$177	$32,702
28	Norway	16	0.5%	$406	$176.9	$72,448	$166	$67,984
29	Portugal	18	0.6%	$240	$159.4	$38,496	$162	$39,129
30	Denmark	14	0.5%	$350	$175.0	$64,815	$161	$59,767
31	Romania	14	0.5%	$250	$8.4	$1,254	$157	$23,393
32	Greece	88	3.0%	$205	$148.0	$33,636	$142	$32,320
33	Finland	27	0.9%	$269	$37.0	$13,704	$141	$52,219
34	Czech Republic	16	0.5%	$251	$135.8	$30,178	$119	$26,362
35	Hungary	12	0.4%	$164	$85.5	$22,500	$80	$21,113
	TOTAL/AVERAGE	**2950**	**100%**	**$74,377**	**$48,300**	**$41,846**	**$39,989**	**$27,167**
	% World	**78.2%**		**85.1%**	**82.0%**	**87.8%**	**79.3%**	**116.1%**
	Worldwide	**3772**		**$87,400**	**$58,930**	**$47,650**	**$50,400**	**$23,406**

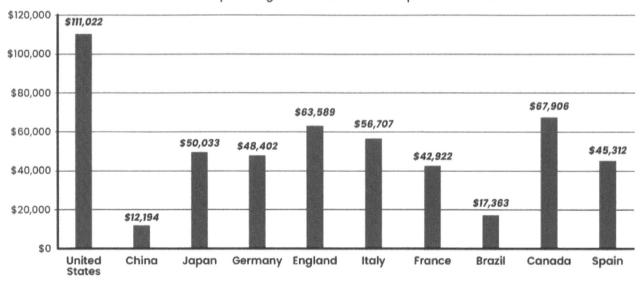

Consumer Spending Per Household - Top 10 Countries

While consumer spending is a key buying power metric, taking into account households provides the full picture. Among the top 10 countries in *Figure 11.16*, household buying power varies greatly, ranging from $12,194 in China and $17,363 in Brazil to $111,022 in the United States. The other seven top 10 countries range from roughly $42,000 to $67,000. As a result, some expensive sports products do not fit average household budgets. In India, where average per household consumer spending is $1,822, one pair of high-performance running shoes at $150 would be about 8% of the family's average annual budget. *Figure 11.17* links to a video describing Puma's strategy in India, where the company focused on low priced flip flops in its 365 company-owned stores.

FIGURE 11.17
Puma's Flip Flop Shoe in India

Source: https://www.youtube.com/watch?v=bTkMLr5Aobg

Puma's global chief executive Bjorn Gulden believes India's growing young population and increasing interest in fitness and sports will set the company up for success in the future. "It's great to see the brand record sustained growth in India," Gulden said. "It is a strategic market for Puma." According to Gulden, Puma's combination of global strength and local execution has accelerated its momentum in the country. The German sportswear maker said in 2020 that the Asia-Pacific region was its strongest market, with 26% sales growth the previous year at $1.8 billion. India and China drove the regional growth (13).

Country-Level Sports Power Scores

The Best-Howard Model uses professional team volume, market size and buying power data from the world's top 35 sports countries to generate its proprietary Country-Level Sports Power Scores.

The scores, which rank each country objectively, are composites based on the three country-level metrics and rely on the same methodology employed by the well-known buying power index (14). The Best-Howard Model begins by pegging each metric to a benchmark score:

- **Pro Teams Relative Index** = (Number Pro Teams / Benchmark Number Pro Teams) x 100

- **Households Relative Index** = (Number Households/ Benchmark Number Households) x 100

- **Consumer Spending Relative Index** = (Country Consumer Spending / Benchmark Consumer Spending) x 100

The benchmarks are taken from the maximum score for each metric among the 35 countries identified as top sports countries. In 2019, Germany had the highest number of professional teams, 184, making it the benchmark for the metric. The Pro Teams Relative Index ranged from 6.5 to 100, with an average of 45.8. For the households metric, China had the largest number at 479.6 million. The relative index ranged from 0.5 to 100, with an average of 8.8, across the 35 examined countries. The United States had the highest level of consumer spending at $13.6 trillion. The Consumer Spending Relative Index ranged from 0.6 to 100, with an average of 8.4, across the countries.

Analysts use the buying power index to estimate U.S. states' and cities' ability to purchase consumer goods. The index is estimated as:

Buying Power Index =

0.5 x Market's Buying Income Percentage

+ 0.3 x Market's Retail Sales Percentage

+ 0.2 x Market's Population Percentage

Similarly, the Best-Howard Model uses a regression analysis to determine the relative importance of its three country-level indices:

Country-Level Sports Power Score =

0.40 x Pro Teams Relative Index

+ 0.10 x Households Relative Index

+ 0.50 x Consumer Spending Relative Index

The analysis grants more weight to a country's professional team volume and consumer spending than it does to its number of households. Still, household number is a significant variable in explaining country-level sports revenue variance. As shown in the equation, the Best-Howard Model computes its final Country-Level Sports Power Scores using each country's relative index and their weighted averages. *Figure 11.18* shows the scores for all 35 countries. The figure also shows the relationship between Country-Level Sports Power Score and number of professional teams, which has a strong explained variance of 95% (R-squared equal to 0.9523).

FIGURE 11.18
Country-Level Sports Power Scores

No.	Country	Country Sports Power Score	Pro Teams (number)	Households (millions)	Consumer Spending (billions)	Consumer Spending per Household
1	United States	91	179	122.1	$13,561	$111,022
2	China	64	149	479.6	$5,848	$12,194
3	Germany	48	184	41.5	$2,011	$48,402
4	England	45	175	28.0	$1,780	$63,589
5	Australia	39	164	9.6	$803	$83,512
6	France	37	144	30.0	$1,287	$42,922
7	Spain	34	140	18.9	$857	$45,312
8	Japan	33	98	55.7	$2,787	$50,033
9	Brazil	32	120	68.2	$1,185	$17,363
10	India	32	106	306.8	$559	$1,822
11	Netherlands	31	133	7.9	$391	$49,189
12	Mexico	29	116	33.8	$805	$23,811
13	Italy	28	101	26.1	$1,478	$56,707
14	Turkey	25	104	24.1	$440	$18,284
15	Sweden	23	99	4.7	$242	$51,783
16	Switzerland	21	90	3.9	$380	$97,556

17	Argentina	20	87	14.5	$323	$22,285
18	Belgium	20	88	5.0	$261	$52,476
19	Greece	20	88	4.4	$142	$32,320
20	Israel	17	74	2.9	$214	$73,738
21	Russia	17	57	56.7	$809	$14,273
22	Egypt	15	64	24.5	$250	$10,189
23	South Africa	14	61	17.7	$218	$12,316
24	Canada	14	47	14.7	$1,000	$67,906
25	South Korea	13	45	19.8	$790	$39,931
26	Austria	13	56	4.0	$179	$44,542
27	Poland	11	46	14.5	$226	$15,640
28	Finland	6	27	2.7	$141	$52,219
29	Chile	5	18	5.4	$177	$32,702
30	Portugal	5	18	4.1	$162	$39,129
31	Norway	4	16	2.4	$166	$67,984
32	Czech Republic	4	16	4.5	$119	$26,362
33	Romania	4	14	6.7	$157	$23,393
34	Denmark	4	14	2.7	$161	$59,767
35	Hungary	3	12	3.8	$80	$21,113
	TOTAL/AVERAGE	23	2950	1472.0	$39,989	$42,337
	% World		78.2%	68.4%	83.9%	78.2%
	Worldwide		3772	2153.3	$47,650	$40,138

Number Pro Teams vs. Country Sports Power Score

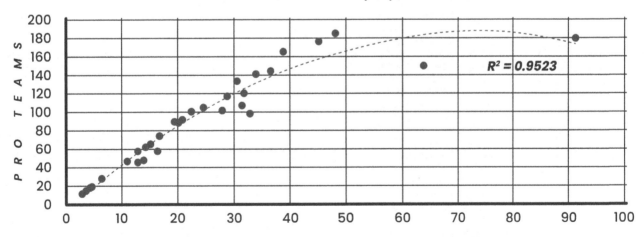

$R^2 = 0.9523$

The top 10 sports countries range from India and Brazil sharing power scores of 32 to the United States with a score of 91. China has the second strongest power score at 64. While China has fewer professional teams than Germany, its massive number of households and high consumer spending lifts it well above Germany, with a score of 48, and the third highest ranking country, England, at 45.

Australia, France, Spain and Japan post similar final scores but vary in performance metrics. Australia owes its slight lead over France to its large number of professional teams; Japan has many households and elevated consumer spending but fewer professional sports teams than the three countries just outranking it.

The top 10 countries account for 50% of the top 35 countries' professional teams and 39% of all teams worldwide, 79% of the top 35's households and 54% of households worldwide, and 77% of the top 35's consumer spending and 64% of worldwide spending.

Power Score Predictive Validity

The Best-Howard Model assesses the predictive validity of its proprietary Country-Level Sports Power Scores by comparing each country's score to its sportswear, camping equipment and gym/ health club revenues.

SPORTSWEAR REVENUES. Figure 11.19 shows the top 35 sports countries' sportswear revenues per household in 2019. The metric ranged from $14 per household in Egypt to $1,005 per household in the United States. The average for the 35 countries was $305.

FIGURE 11.19
Global Sportswear Revenues Per Household in 2019

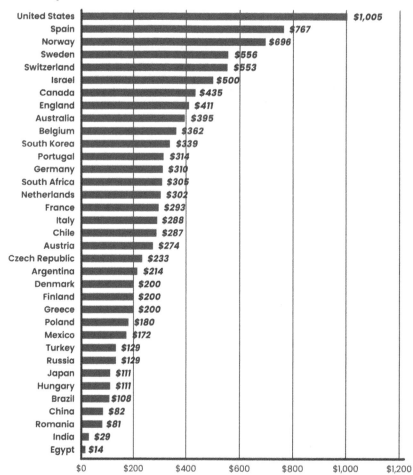

United States	$1,005
Spain	$767
Norway	$696
Sweden	$556
Switzerland	$553
Israel	$500
Canada	$435
England	$411
Australia	$395
Belgium	$362
South Korea	$339
Portugal	$314
Germany	$310
South Africa	$305
Netherlands	$302
France	$293
Italy	$288
Chile	$287
Austria	$274
Czech Republic	$233
Argentina	$214
Denmark	$200
Finland	$200
Greece	$200
Poland	$180
Mexico	$172
Turkey	$129
Russia	$129
Japan	$111
Hungary	$111
Brazil	$108
China	$82
Romania	$81
India	$29
Egypt	$14

　　　　　　　　　　　　　　　　　　　　　Copyright 2022 Global Sports Insights

Figure 11.20 presents the countries' sportswear revenues along with their Country-Level Power Scores and the metrics used to create them. The correlation between country-level sportswear revenues and power scores is 0.96. The relationship is non-linear, as sportswear revenues increase at a greater rate than Country-Level Sports Power Scores.

The correlations between sportswear revenues and all power score metrics are strong, ranging from 0.49 for households to 0.98 for consumer spending. Countries with high levels of any of the Best-Howard Model's sports industry metrics are therefore likely to have high sportswear revenues. The correlations suggest that as countries grow in households and consumer spending, they will increase sportswear purchases. Countries forecast to decline in households and consumer spending by 2030, such as Japan and some Eastern Europe nations, will likely decrease sportswear purchases.

FIGURE 11.20
Global Sportswear Revenue & Power Scores

No.	Country	Country Sports Power Score	Sportswear (billions)	Pro Teams	Households (millions)	Consumer Spending (billions)	Consumer Spending per Household	Sportswear % Consumer Spending
1	United States	91	$122.8	179	122.1	$13,561	$111,022	0.91%
2	China	64	$39.4	149	479.6	$5,848	$12,194	0.67%
3	Germany	48	$12.9	184	41.5	$2,011	$48,402	0.64%
4	England	45	$11.5	175	28.0	$1,780	$63,589	0.65%
5	Australia	39	$3.8	164	9.6	$803	$83,512	0.47%
6	France	37	$8.8	144	30.0	$1,287	$42,922	0.68%
7	Spain	34	$6.2	140	18.9	$857	$45,312	0.72%
8	Japan	33	$14.5	98	55.7	$2,787	$50,033	0.52%
9	Brazil	32	$7.4	120	68.2	$1,185	$17,363	0.62%
10	India	32	$9.0	106	306.8	$559	$1,822	1.61%
11	Netherlands	31	$2.4	133	7.9	$391	$49,189	0.61%
12	Mexico	29	$5.8	116	33.8	$805	$23,811	0.72%
13	Italy	28	$7.5	101	26.1	$1,478	$56,707	0.51%
14	Turkey	25	$3.1	104	24.1	$440	$18,284	0.70%
15	Sweden	23	$2.6	99	4.7	$242	$51,783	1.07%
16	Switzerland	21	$2.2	90	3.9	$380	$97,556	0.57%
17	Argentina	21	$3.1	87	14.5	$323	$22,285	0.96%
18	Belgium	20	$1.8	88	5.0	$261	$52,476	0.69%
19	Greece	20	$0.88	88	4.4	$142	$32,320	0.62%
20	Israel	17	$1.5	74	2.9	$214	$73,738	0.68%
21	Russia	17	$7.3	57	56.7	$809	$14,273	0.90%
22	Egypt	15	$0.35	64	24.5	$250	$10,189	0.14%
23	South Africa	15	$5.4	61	17.7	$218	$12,316	2.48%
24	Canada	14	$6.4	47	14.7	$1,000	$67,906	0.64%
25	South Korea	13	$6.7	45	19.8	$790	$39,931	0.85%
26	Austria	13	$1.1	56	4.0	$179	$44,542	0.61%
27	Poland	11	$2.6	46	14.5	$226	$15,640	1.15%
28	Finland	7	$0.54	27	2.7	$141	$52,219	0.38%
29	Chile	5	$1.6	18	5.4	$177	$32,702	0.88%
30	Portugal	5	$1.3	18	4.1	$162	$39,129	0.80%
31	Norway	4	$1.7	16	2.4	$166	$67,984	1.02%
32	Czech Republic	4	$1.05	16	4.5	$119	$26,362	0.89%

33	Romania	4	$0.54	14	6.7	$157	$23,393	0.34%
34	Denmark	4	$0.54	14	2.7	$161	$59,767	0.33%
35	Hungary	3	$0.42	12	3.8	$80	$21,113	0.52%
	TOTAL/AVERAGE	**23**	**$304.6**	**2950**	**1472.0**	**$39,989**	**$27,167**	**0.76%**
	% World		**86.3%**	**78.2%**	**68.4%**	**83.9%**	**116.1%**	**0.74%**
	Worldwide		**$353**	**3772**	**2153.3**	**$47,650**	**$23,406**	

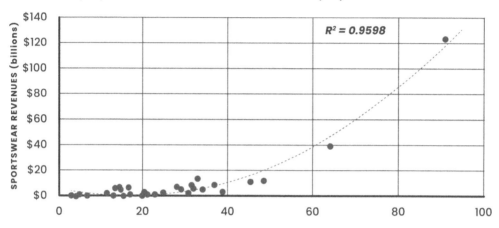

Country Sportswear Revenues vs. Country Sports Power Score

Figure 11.20 also shows the percentage of household consumer spending allocated to sportswear. The range is considerable, from Egypt at 0.14% to South Africa at 2.48%. The United States' 0.91% is above the average of 0.78%. Countries with a higher level of consumer spending per household have a higher percentage of household spending allocated to sportswear purchases.

CAMPING EQUIPMENT REVENUES. The Best-Howard Model next uses camping and caravanning revenues to assess its Country-Level Sports Power Scores' predictive validity (15). *Figure 11.21* highlights the purchases.

FIGURE 11.21

Country-Level Camping Equipment Revenues in 2019

Country	Country Sports Power Score	Camping Equipment (billions)	Camping CAGR	Households (millions)	Camping Equip. Revenue per Household	Consumer Spending (billions)	Consumer Spending per Households
United States	91	$9.30	5.5%	122.1	$76.14	$13,561	$111,022
China	64	$0.35	12.5%	479.6	$0.73	$5,848	$12,194
Germany	48	$4.25	3.8%	41.5	$102.29	$2,011	$48,402
England	45	$3.59	7.8%	28.0	$128.25	$1,780	$63,589
Australia	39	$5.74	7.4%	9.6	$596.96	$803	$83,512
France	37	$2.71	6.9%	30.0	$90.38	$1,287	$42,922
Spain	34	$1.03	6.6%	18.9	$54.46	$857	$45,312
Japan	33	$0.49	14.0%	55.7	$8.80	$2,787	$50,033
India	32	$0.15	12.5%	306.8	$0.49	$559	$1,822
Brazil	32	$0.20	8.8%	68.2	$2.93	$1,185	$17,363
Netherlands	31	$1.61	6.9%	7.9	$202.54	$391	$49,189
Mexico	29	$0.15	10.0%	33.8	$4.44	$805	$23,811

Canada	14	$2.5	8.8%	14.7	$169.77	$1,000	$67,906
South Korea	13	$0.26	7.7%	19.8	$13.14	$790	$39,931
TOTAL/AVERAGE	**39**	**$32.3**	**8.5%**	**1472.0**	**$103.7**	**$39,989**	**$46,929**
% World		**77.7%**	**129.0%**	**68.4%**	**118.6%**	**83.9%**	**113.9%**
Worldwide		**$41.6**	**6.60%**	**2153.3**	**87.4**	**$47,650**	**$41,203**

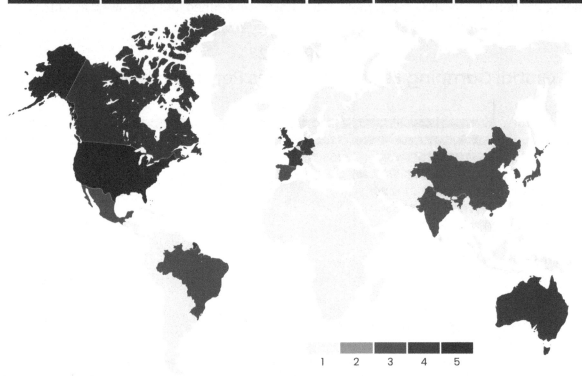

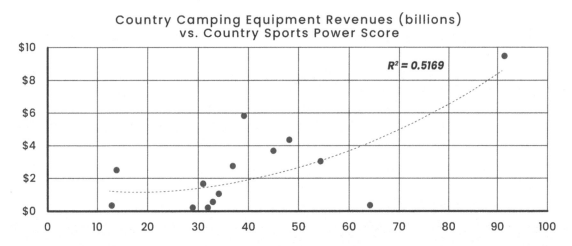

Country Camping Equipment Revenues (billions) vs. Country Sports Power Score

$R^2 = 0.5169$

The correlation between camping revenues and Country-Level Sports Power Scores is greater than 0.70, with an explained variance (r-squared) of 52%. As shown, camping revenues increase at a faster rate than Country-Level Sports Power Scores.

The United States generated the world's highest camping revenues in 2019 at $9.3 billion and has a Country-Level Power Score of 91. The second highest rated country on power score, China, generated few camping revenues. Australia, with a power score of 39, generated the second highest camping revenues in the world. China and Australia's variances weaken the correlation between camping revenues and Country-Level Power Score.

Figure 11.22 summarizes country-level camping revenue variance. Australia's average household spends about $597 per year on camping equipment, while Chinese households spend only $0.73. The United States falls near the middle at $76 per household. India has the lowest consumer spending per household, $1,822, among the 35 countries examined and the lowest camping revenues per household.

FIGURE 11.22
Global Camping Equipment Sales Per Household in 2019

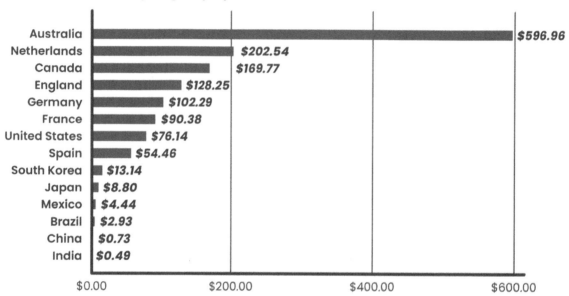

GYM & HEALTH CLUB REVENUES. The Best-Howard Model provides a third validity check for its Country-Level Power Scores via gym and health club revenues (16). *Figure 11.23* shows the revenues for the sports countries reporting them, as well as detail on country-level gym and health club revenues, members and locations. The United States has the world's highest power score and in 2019 featured the highest gym and health club revenues ($32.3 billion), largest number of members (64.2 million) and most locations (41,370). Brazil ranked second in locations (29,525) but lower in revenues than countries with similar power scores.

FIGURE 11.23
Global Gym & Health Club Revenues in 2019

No.	Country	Power Score Country Sports	Revenues (billions)	Members (millions)	Locations (number)	Households (millions)	Gym Revenue per Household	Spending (billions)	Spending per Household
1	United States	91	$32.3	64.2	41370	122.1	$264.44	$13,561	$111,022
2	China	64	$3.9	4.5	1767	479.6	$8.13	$5,848	$12,194
3	Germany	48	$6.7	11.7	9669	41.5	$161.26	$2,011	$48,402
4	England	45	$6.7	10.0	7239	28.0	$239.35	$1,780	$63,589
5	Spain	34	$2.6	5.5	4713	18.9	$137.47	$857	$45,312
6	Japan	34	$3.9	4.2	4950	55.7	$70.01	$2,787	$50,033

7	France	37	$2.9	6.2	4540	30.0	$96.72	$1,287	$42,922
8	Australia	39	$2.8	3.7	3715	9.6	$291.20	$803	$83,512
9	India	32	$0.8	2.0	2813	306.8	$2.61	$559	$1,822
10	Brazil	32	$2.2	10.3	29525	68.2	$32.24	$1,185	$17,363
11	Italy	28	$2.6	5.5	7760	26.1	$99.76	$1,478	$56,707
12	Mexico	29	$1.9	4.3	12871	33.8	$56.20	$805	$23,811
13	Netherlands	31	$1.6	3.0	2084	7.9	$201.28	$391	$49,189
14	Sweden	23	$0.9	2.3	1702	4.7	$192.58	$242	$51,783
15	Russia	17	$1.0	3.3	3900	56.7	$17.64	$809	$14,273
16	Argentina	21	$1.0	2.8	7910	14.5	$68.99	$323	$22,285
17	South Korea	13	$2.6	3.8	6590	19.8	$131.42	$790	$39,931
18	Canada	14	$3.0	6.2	6587	14.7	$203.72	$1,000	$67,906
19	Austria	13	$0.6	1.1	1299	4.0	$149.30	$179	$44,542
20	Poland	11	$1.1	3.1	2754	14.5	$76.12	$226	$15,640
21	Finland	7	$0.5	0.9	1824	2.7	$185.19	$141	$52,219
22	Norway	4	$0.6	1.2	1228	2.4	$245.72	$166	$67,984
	TOTAL/AVERAGE	30	$82.2	110.0	77963	785	$133.2	$28,934	$44,656.4
	% World					36.5%		60.7%	108.4%
	Worldwide					2153.3		$47,650	$41,203

Country Gym Revenues (billions) vs. Country Sports Power Score

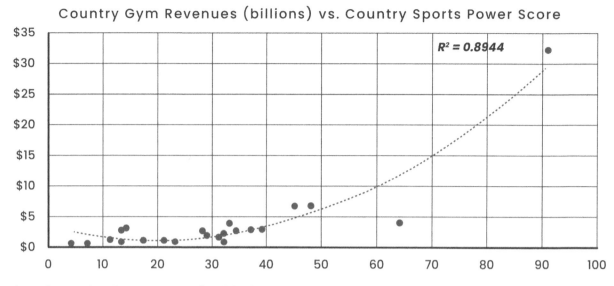

$R^2 = 0.8944$

The relationship between gym/health club revenues and Country Sports Power Score is strong, with a 0.94 correlation and explained variance (r-squared) of 89%. The relationship is curvilinear, with gym/health club revenues increasing at a faster rate than power scores. The United States largely drives the relationship.

Figure 11.24 considers per household gym/health club revenues. Australia leads the world at $291 per household per year. The United States is second at $264. Many European countries follow, with Russia ($17.64), China ($8.13) and India ($2.61) at the distribution's low end. The Best-Howard Model expects the countries to spend more as their household incomes increase and their populations build more awareness of exercise's health benefits.

FIGURE 11.24
Global Gym Revenue Per Household in 2019

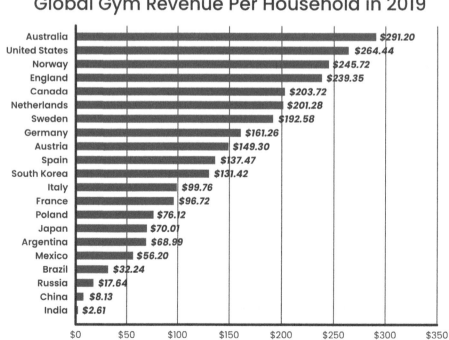

The Top 10 Sports Countries

The Best-Howard Model determines the world's top 10 sports countries based on professional team volume, household number and consumer buying power. *Figure 11.25* shows the countries' locations around the world. As shown, the United States is ranked the top sports country. China is second. While China had a lower number of professional teams in 2019, its market size and buying power elevate its position. Germany had the world's most professional teams and revenues in 2019, moving it to the third ranked spot despite its relatively small household number and consumer spending. England, Australia, France, Spain and Japan rank fourth to eighth; India and Brazil make up the bottom two countries in the top 10 sports countries.

FIGURE 11.25
The Best-Howard Model's Top 10 Sports Countries

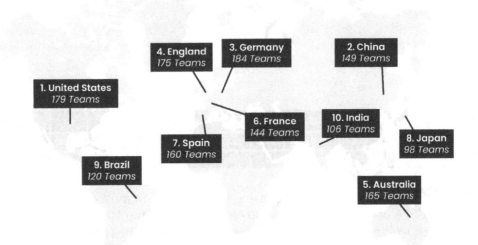

No.	Country	Country Sports Power Score	Pro Teams	Households (millions)	Consumer Spending (billions)	Consumer Spending per Household
1	United States	91	179	122.1	$13.561	$111,022
2	China	64	149	479.6	$5,848	$12,194
3	Germany	48	184	41.5	$2,011	$48,402
4	England	45	175	28.0	$1,780	$63,589
5	Australia	39	164	9.6	$803	$83,512
6	France	37	144	30.0	$1,287	$42,922
7	Spain	34	140	18.9	$857	$45,312
8	Japan	33	98	55.7	$2,787	$50,033
9	Brazil	32	120	68.2	$1,185	$17,363
10	India	32	106	306.8	$559	$1,822
	TOTAL/AVERAGE	45	1459	1160.5	$30,678	$47,617
	% World		38.7%	53.9%	64.4%	215.2%
	Worldwide		3772	2153.3	$47,650	$22,129

Figure 11.26 shows that soccer and basketball are the dominant professional team sports in the Best-Howard Model's top 10 sports countries. However, the countries differ in sports played and number of teams. For example, the United States has no professional handball, field hockey or cricket teams, but the sports are played extensively in other top 10 countries. Countries with all warm weather climates play no ice hockey. And while observers might expect football and baseball to be limited to the United States, the sports are growing in international appeal and may one day rival basketball on the global stage.

FIGURE 11.26
Top 10 Sports Countries' Sports & Pro Teams

No.	Top 10 Countries	Association Football	Basketball	Volleyball	Football	Ice Hockey	Handball	Rugby	Baseball	Field Hockey	Cricket	Others	Total	% Women Teams
1	United States	28	41	–	32	25	–	12	29	–	–	6	179	17.9%
2	China	34	53	28	20	–	–	–	4	–	–	10	149	31.5%
3	Germany	30	18	12	16	22	30	16	16	24	–	–	184	23.9%
4	England	32	23	–	12	10	8	42	–	20	18	10	175	36.6%
5	Australia	20	17	14	–	13	4	20	8	14	22	32	164	42.1%
6	France	32	32	14	–	12	28	14	–	–	–	12	144	26.4%
7	Spain	36	32	–	–	5	30	12	9	–	–	16	140	31.4%
8	Japan	18	30	22	–	–	–	16	12	–	–	–	98	24.5%
9	Brazil	20	22	24	31	–	–	–	–	–	–	23	120	16.7%
10	India	47	8	12	–	–	6	–	–	6	8	19	106	22.6%
	Top 10	**297**	**276**	**126**	**111**	**87**	**106**	**132**	**78**	**64**	**48**	**128**	**1459**	
	% Global	**26.3%**	**36.9%**	**32.6%**	**65.3%**	**36.3%**	**46.5%**	**61.7%**	**51.7%**	**64.0%**	**52.2%**	**48.5%**	**39.2%**	
	Global Total	**1128**	**748**	**387**	**170**	**240**	**228**	**214**	**151**	**100**	**92**	**264**	**3722**	**22.2%**

Women's professional team sports are growing in popularity in most countries; however, they comprise only 17.9% of U.S. teams, second lowest among the top 10 sports countries (*Figure 11.27*). In four countries, women's teams represent more than 30% of the total. Australia and England are the world leaders. The Best-Howard Model forecasts the percentages to increase around the world as women continue to become more involved in sports and their audiences grow.

FIGURE 11.27
Top 10 Countries' Women's Professional Team Percentage in 2019

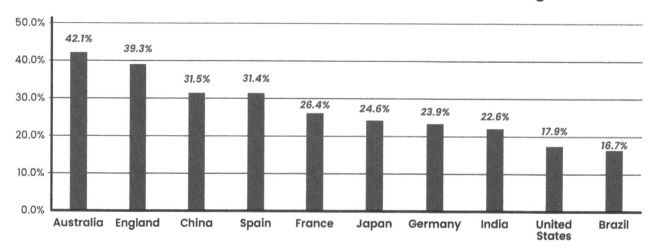

Top 10 Country Profiles

To better understand each of the top 10 sports countries and the pro team sports they support, the Best-Howard Model presents visual profiles of each nation, starting with the United States (*Figure11.28*). Select other top 10 sports countries by clicking on the names below.

FIGURE 11.28
Top 10 Sports Country Profiles

No.	Country	Country Sports Power Score	Number of Pro Teams	Households (millions)	Spending (millions)	Spending per Household
1	United States	85	179	122.1	$13,561	$111,022

FOOTBALL	BASEBALL	BASKETBALL	ICE HOCKEY	SOCCER
$13.66 billion	$9.4 billion	$7.46 billion	$4.56 billion	$0.82 billion
(32 teams)	(29 teams)	(41 teams)	(29 teams)	(32 teams)
0% Women	0% Women	29% Women	17% Women	28% Women

United States Sport	Football	Baseball	Basketball	Ice Hockey	Soccer	Rugby	Softball	Total
Pro Teams	32	29	41	29	32	10	6	**179**
Women's Teams	0	0	12	5	9	0	6	**32**
% Women's Teams	0.0%	0.0%	29.3%	17.2%	28.1%	0.0%	100.0	**17.9%**

United States	China	Germany	England	Australia
France	Spain	Japan	Brazil	India

View other graphs at the end of the chapter on page A11.8 Chapter 11 Appendix 2.

• **Country:** The United States' power score is more than double that of the second ranked country due to its many professional teams, considerable population and high consumer spending.

• **Pro Teams:** The United States ranks third in professional team volume at 179 teams, just below the benchmark set by Germany at 184.

• **Sports:** The United States is unique with football and baseball being its two leading sports. Neither is played in many world regions, but they are growing among top 10 sports countries.

COVID-19's Impact on World Sports

The Best-Howard Model does not have extensive data to examine COVID-19's impact on the top 10 sports countries. However, the pandemic's impact on sportswear revenues and major U.S. professional sports leagues provides insight.

Global sportswear revenues were $346.1 billion in 2019, roughly 15% of the global sports industry's $2.3 trillion in revenues. The heat map in *Figure 11.29* indicates 2020 global sports revenues decreased 15% worldwide to $292.5 billion (17).

Overall, the top 10 sports countries experienced a 14% decline in sportswear sales from $236.3 billion in 2019 to $213.2 billion in 2020. The countries accounted for 72% of 2019 worldwide sportswear sales. Because the top 10 were impacted by COVID-19 less than other countries, the number increased to 76% in 2020.

FIGURE 11.29
COVID-19's Impact on Top 10 Country Sportswear Revenues

No.	Top 10 Country	2019 (billions)	-50%	0%	50%	2020 (billions)	2020 % Change
1	United States	$122.8		-18%		$101.3	-18%
2	China	$51.2		-2%		$50.4	-2%
3	Germany	$12.9		-9%		$11.8	-9%
4	England	$11.5		-14%		$9.9	-14%
5	Australia	$3.8		-11%		$3.4	-11%
6	France	$8.8		-10%		$7.9	-10%
7	Spain	$6.2		-18%		$5.1	-18%
8	Japan	$14.5		-8%		$13.3	-8%
9	India	$9.0	-36%			$5.8	-36%
10	Brazil	$7.4	-42%			$4.3	-42%
	Total	$263.30		-19%		$213.20	-19%
	Worldwide	$346.10		-15%		$292.50	-15%

Four of the top 10 sports countries saw modest sportswear sales revenue declines of 2% to 10%. China experienced the smallest decline. The United States and three other countries saw sales declines ranging from 11% to 18%. India (36%) and Brazil (42%) were hardest hit for two reasons. First, they experienced more COVID-19 cases and were less able to address the problem through their health care systems. Second, they saw larger GDP decreases, which resulted in decreased consumer spending. India's average pre-pandemic, per household consumer spending was $1,822; Brazil's was $17,363.

In 2019, the United States produced $42.6 billion in major league sports revenues, almost half the world total (18). In 2020, U.S. major league revenues dropped 27% to $31.1 billion (*Figure 11.30*).

The decline represented an enormous erosion of sales and profits extending beyond professional teams. The sports media, which broadcasts the teams' games, saw similar losses. Likewise, the sports betting industry shut down for much of the year.

FIGURE 11.30

COVID-19's Impact on U.S. Professional Team Revenues

Top 10 League	2019 (billions)	-50%		0%		50%	2020 (billions)	2020 % Change
Football	$16.0		-25%				$12.0	-25%
Baseball	$10.7		-28%				$7.7	-28%
Basketball	$8.8		-23%				$6.8	-23%
Ice Hockey	$5.1		-29%				$3.6	-29%
Soccer	$2.0	-50%					$1.0	-50%
Top 10 Total	$42.6		-27%				$31.1	-27%

While the overall decrease in U.S. professional team revenues was 27%, baseball and soccer experienced the greatest relative declines among the five major sports. The Best-Howard Model does not have reliable post-COVID data on other top 10 sports countries, but evidence suggests they experienced similar declines.

The worldwide sportswear revenue decrease was far lower than the decline experienced by U.S. professional teams. The sportswear industry did not shut down, despite many of its in-person retail outlets suffering during the pandemic. Instead, the industry shifted to online sales. In 2020, sportswear purchases increased to 50% of total apparel in the United States. Many analysts believe the change in buying behavior will be permanent as more shoppers became more comfortable buying sports footwear and apparel online.

References

We have added links to many references for direct and easy access. While we have tested each link, there are a few instances where the websites are no longer accessible. We will continue to monitor the accessibility of citation references and remove any links no longer active. In many instances the referenced data was purchased, this is noted.

1. *"Women's T20 World Cup final: Australia beat India at MCG." BBC (www.bbc.com).*

2. *"Top 10 List of the World's Most Popular Sports" Topend Sports (www.topendsports.com).*

3. *Regional professional teams data are derived from our country-level database with 300+ links.*

4. *Mexico Liga de Fútbol Americano Profesional (7). Wikipedia (en.m.wikipedia.org) Mexico Fútbol Americano de Mexico (FAM) (9). Wikipedia (en.m.wikipedia.org).*

5. *"The Egyptian Federation of American Football | About EFAF". The Egyptian Federation of American Football*

6. *"National Team Soccer Uniform Colors" RSSSF (www.rsssf.com).*

7. *"Why Is The National Color Of The Netherlands Orange?" Netherlands Insiders (www. netherlandsinsiders.com).*

8. *Conor Henderson and Marc Mazodier, "The Color of Support: The Effect of Sponsor-Team Visual Congruence on Sponsorship Performance," Journal of Marketing, (March 2019).*

9. *Data used to create country pro teams by sport.*

10. *"How Women's Cricket Has Started To Soar In Popularity?", July 2, 2021. Female Cricket (femalecricket. com).*

11. *Oxford Economics, Global Population and Economic Data, 2020. (www.oxfordeconomics.com). (GSI Purchased Report)*

12. *"Global gross domestic product (GDP) at current prices from 1985 to 2026." Statista (www.statista. com). (GSI Purchased Report)*

13. *"India is driving Puma's global growth: CEO," The Economic Times (economictimes.indiatimes.com).*

14. *"Buying Power Index: Definition & Calculation," Study (study.com).*

15. *"Camping and Caravanning Market," Trend Analysis and Competition Tracking 2020-2030, Future Markets Insights.*

16. *Country Gym and Health Club Revenues, Memberships and Number Locations. Crossfit (map.crossfit. com), Exercise (www.exercise.com), Business Insider (www.businessinsider.com), Health & Fitness Journal (journals.lww.com) and Wellness Creatives (www.wellnesscreatives.com).*

17. *Apparel and Footwear: Euromonitor from trade sources/national statistics, 2021. (GSI Purchased Report)*

18. *"The NFL's Most Valuable Teams 2021: Average Team Value Soars To $3.5 Billion As League Shrugs Off Pandemic Year" Forbes (www.forbes.com); "NFL revenue by team" Statista (www.statista.com); "NHL Team Values 2020: Hockey's First Decline In Two Decades" Forbes (www.forbes.com); "NHL revenue by year" Statista (www.statista.com); "Total NBA revenue 2001-2018" Statista (www.statista.com); "NBA Team Values 2021: Knicks Keep Top Spot At $5 Billion, While Warriors Seize No. 2 From Lakers" Forbes (forbes.com); "MLB revenue by team US 2020" Statista (www.statista.com); "Baseball's Most Valuable Teams 2021: New York Yankees On Top At $5.25 Billion" Forbes (www.forbes.com); "Forbes Releases 24th Annual Valuations Of Major League Baseball's 30 Teams; Despite Lockdown, MLB Teams Gain Value In 2020" Forbes (www.forbes.com); and "Major League Soccer's Most Valuable Teams 2019: Atlanta Stays On Top As Expansion Fees, Sale Prices Surge" Forbes (www.forbes.com). (GSI Purchased Report)*

Chapter 11 Appendix

APPENDIX 1

FIGURE 11.6
National Soccer Team Uniform Colors - Europe

Region	Country	Shirt	Edges	Short	Socks
Europe	Albania	Red	Black	Black	Red
Europe	Andorra	Yellow	Red & Blue	Red	Blue
Europe	Armania	Red	Blue	Blue	Orange
Europe	Austria	White	Black	Black	White
Europe	Belarus	White	Green & Red	Green	White
Europe	Belgium	Red	Black & Yellow	Red	Red
Europe	Bosnia-Herzegovina	White	Blue	Blue	White
Europe	Bulgaria	White	Green & Red	Green	Red
Europe	Croatia	Red & White checks	–	White	Blue
Europe	Cyprus	Blue	White	White	Blue
Europe	Czech Republic	Red	White & Blue	White	Blue
Europe	Denmark	Red	White	White	Red
Europe	England	White	Red	Blue	White
Europe	Estonia	Blue	Black	Black	White
Europe	Faroe Islands	White	Blue & Red	Blue	White
Europe	Finland	White	Blue	Blue	White
Europe	France	Blue	White & Red	White	Red
Europe	Georgia	White	–	Black	White
Europe	Germany	White	Black	Black	White
Europe	Gibraltar	Red	White	Red	Red
Europe	Greece	Blue	White	Blue	Blue
Europe	Hungary	Red	White & Green	White	Green
Europe	Iceland	Blue	White	White	Blue

Europe	Ireland Republic	Green	White	White	Green
Europe	Italy	Blue	–	White	Blue
Europe	Kosovo	Blue	White	Blue	Blue
Europe	Latvia	Carmine Red	White	White	Carmine Red
Europe	Liechtenstain	Blue	White	Red	Blue
Europe	Lithuania	Yellow	Green	Green	Red
Europe	Luxembourg	Red	White	White	Blue
Europe	Macedonia FYR	Red	Yellow	Red	Red
Europe	Malta	Red	White	White	Red
Europe	Moldova	Yellow	Red & Blue	Blue	Red
Europe	Montenegro	Red	Yellow	Red	Red
Europe	Netherlands	Orange	White	White	Orange
Europe	Northern Ireland	Green	White	White	Green
Europe	Norway	Red	Blue	White	Blue
Europe	Poland	White	Red	Red	White
Europe	Portugal	Red	Green	Green	Red
Europe	Romannia	Yellow	Red & Blue	Yellow	Yellow
Europe	Russia	White	Blue	Blue	Red
Europe	San Marino	Sky Blue	White	White	Sky Blue
Europe	Scotland	Marine Blue	White	White	Marine Blue
Europe	Serbia	Red	White	Blue	White
Europe	Slovakia	Blue	White	Blue	Blue
Europe	Slovenia	White	Green	Green	White
Europe	Spain	Red	Yellow	Blue	Black
Europe	Sweden	Yellow	Blue	Blue	Yellow
Europe	Switzerland	Red	White	White	Red
Europe	Ukraine	Yellow	Blue	Blue	Yellow
Europe	Wales	Red	White	White	Red

FIGURE 11.6
National Soccer Team Uniform Colors - Asia-Pacific

Region	Country	Shirt	Edges	Short	Socks
Asia-Pacific	American Samoa	Blue	White	Black	White
Asia-Pacific	Australia	Green	Yellow	Red	Green
Asia-Pacific	Bangladesh	Orange	Dark Green	Dark Green	Orange
Asia-Pacific	Bhutan	Yellow	Red	Black	Red
Asia-Pacific	Brunei Darssulam	Yellow	Black	Green	Yellow
Asia-Pacific	Cambodia	Blue	White & Red	Red	Blue
Asia-Pacific	China	White	Red	Blue	White
Asia-Pacific	Chinese Taipei	Blue	White & Red	Green	Red
Asia-Pacific	Cook Islands	Green	White	White	Green
Asia-Pacific	East Timor	Red	White	White	Red
Asia-Pacific	Fiji	White	Black	White	White
Asia-Pacific	Guam	Blue	White	White	Blue
Asia-Pacific	Hong Kong	Red	White & Black	Blue	Red
Asia-Pacific	India	Sky Blue	White & Blue	Black	Blue
Asia-Pacific	Indonesia	Red	White	Blue	Red
Asia-Pacific	Japan	Blue	White	Blue	Blue
Asia-Pacific	Kazakhstan	Blue	Yellow	White	Yellow
Asia-Pacific	Korea DPR	Red	White	Black	Red
Asia-Pacific	Korea Republic	Red	White	Black	Red
Asia-Pacific	Laos	Red	White	Red	Red
Asia-Pacific	Macao	Green	White	Blue	Green
Asia-Pacific	Malaysia	Yellow	Black	White	Yellow
Asia-Pacific	Maldives	Green	White	White	Green
Asia-Pacific	Mongolia	Red	White & Blue	White	White
Asia-Pacific	Myanmar	Red	White & Blue	White	Blue
Asia-Pacific	Nepal	Red	White & Blue	Blue	Red

Asia-Pacific	New Caledonia	Grey	Red & White	White	Grey
Asia-Pacific	New Zealand	White	Black	Red	White
Asia-Pacific	Papua New Guinea	Red	Yellow & Black	Green	Yellow
Asia-Pacific	Philippines	Blue	White & Red	White	Red
Asia-Pacific	Samoa	Blue	White & Red	Red	Red
Asia-Pacific	Singapore	Red; White sleeves	–	White	Red
Asia-Pacific	Solomon Islands	Yellow	Blue & Green	Blue	White
Asia-Pacific	Sri Lanka	White	Brown & Yellow	Red	White
Asia-Pacific	Tahiti	Red & white stripes	–	White	White
Asia-Pacific	Thailand	Red	White & Blue	White	Red
Asia-Pacific	Tonga	Red	White	White	Red
Asia-Pacific	Vanuatu	Yellow	Black	Red	Yellow
Asia-Pacific	Vietnam	Red	Yellow	Green	Red

FIGURE 11.6
National Soccer Team Uniform Colors - Latin America

Region	Country	Shirt	Edges	Short	Socks
Latin America	Anguilla	Sky Blue	Orange	Sky Blue	Orange
Latin America	Antigua & Barbuda	Red	White, Black & Yellow	Black	Black
Latin America	Argentina	Sky Blue & White Stripes	–	Black	White
Latin America	Aruba	Yellow	Sky Blue	Sky Blue	Yellow
Latin America	Bahamas	Yellow	Black	Black	Yellow
Latin America	Barbados	Yellow	Blue	Blue	Yellow
Latin America	Belize	Dark Blue	White & Red	Red	Red
Latin America	Bermudas	Blue	White & Red	White	Blue
Latin America	Bolivia	Green	White	White	Green
Latin America	Brazil	Yellow	Green	Blue	White
Latin America	British Virgin Islands	Green	Yellow	Green	Green
Latin America	Cayman Islands	Red	White	Blue	Blue
Latin America	Chile	Red	White	Blue	White
Latin America	Colombia	Yellow	Blue	Blue	Red
Latin America	Costa Rica	Red	White & Blue	Blue	White
Latin America	Cuba	Red	White	Red	Red

Latin America	Curacao	Blue	White & Yellow	White	White
Latin America	Dominica	Green	Red	Black	Green
Latin America	Dominican Republic	Red; Red Sleeves	White	Blue	Red
Latin America	Ecuador	Yellow	Blue & Red	Blue	Red
Latin America	El Salvador	Blue	White	Blue	Blue
Latin America	Grenada	Yellow	Black	Black	Red
Latin America	Guatemala	Sky Blue	White	Sky Blue	Sky Blue
Latin America	Guyana	Green & Yellow Stripes	-	Green	Yellow
Latin America	Haiti	Blue & Red Stripes	-	Blue	Red
Latin America	Honduras	Blue & White Stripes	-	White	White
Latin America	Jamaica	Yellow	Green & Black	Black	Yellow
Latin America	Mexico	Green	Green & Red	White	Red
Latin America	Monserrat	Dark Green	White & Black	Black	White
Latin America	Nicaragua	Blue	White	White	Blue
Latin America	Panama	Red	White	Red	Red
Latin America	Paraguay	Red & White Stripes	Blue	Blue	White
Latin America	Peru	White; Red Sash	-	White	White
Latin America	Puerto Rico	Red	White	Blue	Red
Latin America	St. Kitts & Nevis	Red	Yellow, Green & Black	Green	Red
Latin America	St. Lucia	Sky Blue	Yellow & Black	Yellow	Blue
Latin America	St. Vincent & Grenadines	Yellow	Green & Blue	Green	Blue
Latin America	Surinam	White	Green & Red	Green	White
Latin America	Trinidad & Tobago	Red; Black & norrow white stripes	-	Black	Red
Latin America	Turks & Caicos Islands	Turquoise	White	White	White
Latin America	Uruguay	Sky Blue	Black	Black	Black
Latin America	US Virgin Islands	Blue & Yellow Stripes	-	Blue	Blue
Latin America	Venezuela	Claret	White	White	White

FIGURE 11.6
National Soccer Team Uniform Colors - Mid-East Africa

Region	Country	Shirt	Edges	Short	Socks
Mid-East Africa	Afghanistan	Red	White	White	Red
Mid-East Africa	Algeria	White	Green	White	White
Mid-East Africa	Angola	Red	Black & Yellow	Black	Red
Mid-East Africa	Azerbaijan	White; Blue, Red Green stripes	-	Blue	White
Mid-East Africa	Bahrain	Red	White	Red	Red

Region	Country				
Mid-East Africa	Benin	Green	Yellow	Yellow	Red
Mid-East Africa	Botswana	Sky Blue	White & Black	Black	White
Mid-East Africa	Burkina Faso	Red	Green	Green	Red
Mid-East Africa	Burundi	Red	White & Green	Green	Green
Mid-East Africa	Cameroon	Green	Yellow & Red	Red	Yellow
Mid-East Africa	Cape Verde Islands	Blue	White, Red & Yellow	Red	Blue
Mid-East Africa	Central African Republic	Blue & White hoops	Red	Green	White
Mid-East Africa	Chad	Blue	Yellow	Yellow	Red
Mid-East Africa	Comoros Island	Green	White	Green	Green
Mid-East Africa	Congo	Red	Yellow & Green	Red	Red
Mid-East Africa	Congo DR	Yellow	Blue	Blue	Yellow
Mid-East Africa	Djibouti	Blue & White stripes; Red Star	–	Blue	Blue
Mid-East Africa	Egypt	Red	White & Black	White	Black
Mid-East Africa	Equitarial Guinea	Red, White & Green stripes	Blue	Blue	Red
Mid-East Africa	Eritrea	Blue	White	White	White
Mid-East Africa	Ethiopia	Green	Yellow & Red	Yellow	Red
Mid-East Africa	Gabon	Green	Yellow	Yellow	Blue
Mid-East Africa	Gambia	Red	White	Blue	Green
Mid-East Africa	Ghana	White	Black	White	White
Mid-East Africa	Guinea	Red	Yellow & Green	Yellow	Green
Mid-East Africa	Guinea-Bissau	Red	Yellow & Green	Red	Green
Mid-East Africa	Iran	White	Red & Green	White	White
Mid-East Africa	Iraq	White	Black & Green	White	White
Mid-East Africa	Israel	Sky Blue	White	White	Sky Blue
Mid-East Africa	Ivory Coast	Orange	White	White	Green
Mid-East Africa	Jordan	Red; White loops	–	White	Red
Mid-East Africa	Kenya	Red	White, Green & Black	Black	Red
Mid-East Africa	Kuwait	Blue	White	White	Blue
Mid-East Africa	Kyrgystan	Red	White & Black	Red	Red
Mid-East Africa	Lebanon	Red	White	White	Red
Mid-East Africa	Lesotho	Blue & White stripes	–	Green	White
Mid-East Africa	Liberia	Red	White & Blue	Blue	White
Mid-East Africa	Libya	Green	White	Green	Green
Mid-East Africa	Madagascar	Green	White	Green	Green
Mid-East Africa	Malawi	Red	Black & Green	Red	Red
Mid-East Africa	Mali	Green	Yellow	Yellow	Red
Mid-East Africa	Mauritania	Green	Yellow	Green	Green

Mid-East Africa	Mauritius	Red	Blue, Yellow & Green	Red	Red
Mid-East Africa	Morocco	Red	Green & White	Red	Green
Mid-East Africa	Mozambique	Red	Black	Black	Red
Mid-East Africa	Namibia	Red	White, Blue, Green & Yellow	Red	Red
Mid-East Africa	Niger	Orange	White	White	Green
Mid-East Africa	Nigeria	Green	White	Green	Green
Mid-East Africa	Oman	Red	Green & White	Red	Red
Mid-East Africa	Pakistan	Dark Green; White sleeves	–	White	Dark Green
Mid-East Africa	Palestine	Green	Black, White & Red	Black	Red
Mid-East Africa	Qatar	Brown	White	White	Brown
Mid-East Africa	Rwanda	Yellow; Blue sleeves	–	Blue	Yellow
Mid-East Africa	Sao Tome e Principe	Green; Yellos Black & Red hoop	–	Yellow	Green
Mid-East Africa	Saudi Arabia	White	Green	Green	White
Mid-East Africa	Senegal	White	Green, Yellow & Red	White	White
Mid-East Africa	Seychelles	Blue; Yellow hoop	Red	Blue	Blue
Mid-East Africa	Sierra Leone	Green	White & Blue	White	Blue
Mid-East Africa	Somalia	Blue	White	Blue	Blue
Mid-East Africa	South Africa	Yellow	Green & White	Green	White
Mid-East Africa	South Sudan	White	Black, Red & Green	Black	White
Mid-East Africa	Sudan	Red	White	Red	Red
Mid-East Africa	Swaziland	Blue	Yellow & Red	Blue	Blue
Mid-East Africa	Syria	Red; Black sleeves	–	Black	Red
Mid-East Africa	Tajikistan	White	Green	White	White
Mid-East Africa	Tanzania	Green	Yellow & Blue	Black	Blue
Mid-East Africa	Togo	Red	Green & Yellow	Green	Yellow
Mid-East Africa	Tunisia	Red	White	White	Red
Mid-East Africa	Turkey	Red	White	Red	Red
Mid-East Africa	Turkmenistan	Green	White	White	Green
Mid-East Africa	Uganda	White	Black, Yellow & Red	Black	Yellow
Mid-East Africa	United Arab Emirates	White	Red	White	White
Mid-East Africa	Uzbekistan	White	Blue	White	White
Mid-East Africa	Yemen	Red	White	White	Black
Mid-East Africa	Zambia	Green	White & Orange	White	Green
Mid-East Africa	Zimbabwe	Green	Yellow, Black & Red	Yellow	Green

APPENDIX 2

FIGURE 11.28
Top 10 Sports Country Profiles - China

No.	Country	Country Sports Power Score	Number of Pro Teams	Households (millions)	Spending (millions)	Spending per Household
2	China	64	149	479.6	$5,848	$12,194

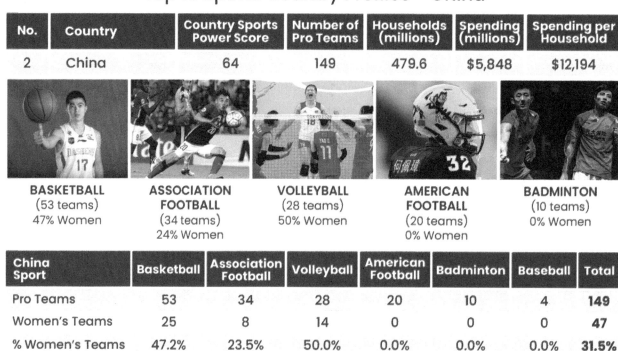

BASKETBALL (53 teams) 47% Women · **ASSOCIATION FOOTBALL** (34 teams) 24% Women · **VOLLEYBALL** (28 teams) 50% Women · **AMERICAN FOOTBALL** (20 teams) 0% Women · **BADMINTON** (10 teams) 0% Women

China Sport	Basketball	Association Football	Volleyball	American Football	Badminton	Baseball	Total
Pro Teams	53	34	28	20	10	4	149
Women's Teams	25	8	14	0	0	0	47
% Women's Teams	47.2%	23.5%	50.0%	0.0%	0.0%	0.0%	31.5%

FIGURE 11.28
Top 10 Sports Country Profiles - Germany

No.	Country	Country Sports Power Score	Number of Pro Teams	Households (millions)	Spending (millions)	Spending per Household
3	Germany	48	184	41.5	$2,011	$48,402

ASSOCIATION FOOTBALL (30 teams) 40% Women · **HANDBALL** (30 teams) 40% Women · **FIELD HOCKEY** (24 teams) 50% Women · **ICE HOCKEY** (22 teams) 36% Women · **BASKETBALL** (18 teams) 0% Women

Germany Sport	Association Football	Handball	Field Hockey	Ice Hockey	Basketball	Rugby	Baseball	American Football	Volleyball	Total
Pro Teams	30	30	24	22	18	16	16	16	12	184
Women's Teams	12	12	12	8	0	0	0	0	0	44
% Women's Teams	40.0%	40.0%	50.0%	36.4%	0.0%	0.0%	0.0%	0.0%	0.0%	23.9%

FIGURE 11.28
Top 10 Sports Country Profiles - England

No.	Country	Country Sports Power Score	Number of Pro Teams	Households (millions)	Spending (millions)	Spending per Household
4	England	45	175	28.0	$1,780	$63,589

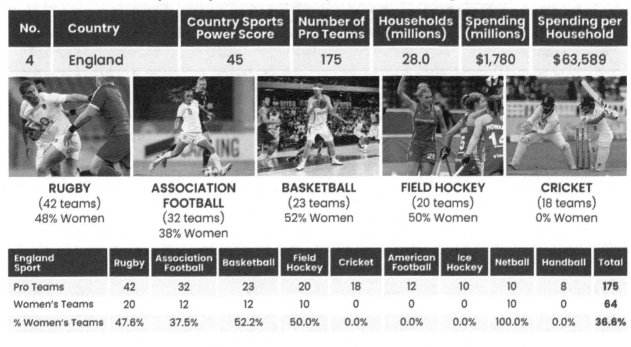

RUGBY (42 teams) 48% Women   **ASSOCIATION FOOTBALL** (32 teams) 38% Women   **BASKETBALL** (23 teams) 52% Women   **FIELD HOCKEY** (20 teams) 50% Women   **CRICKET** (18 teams) 0% Women

England Sport	Rugby	Association Football	Basketball	Field Hockey	Cricket	American Football	Ice Hockey	Netball	Handball	Total
Pro Teams	42	32	23	20	18	12	10	10	8	175
Women's Teams	20	12	12	10	0	0	0	10	0	64
% Women's Teams	47.6%	37.5%	52.2%	50.0%	0.0%	0.0%	0.0%	100.0%	0.0%	36.6%

FIGURE 11.28
Top 10 Sports Country Profiles - Australia

No.	Country	Country Sports Power Score	Number of Pro Teams	Households (millions)	Spending (millions)	Spending per Household
5	Australia	39	164	9.6	$803	$83,512

AUSTRALIAN FOOTBALL (32 teams) 44% Women   **CRICKET** (22 teams) 64% Women   **ASSOCIATION FOOTBALL** (20 teams) 45% Women   **RUGBY** (20 teams) 20% Women   **BASKETBALL** (17 teams) 47% Women

Australia Sport	Australian Football	Cricket	Association Football	Rugby	Basketball	Field Hockey	Volleyball	Ice Hockey	Baseball	Handball	Total
Pro Teams	32	22	20	20	17	14	14	13	8	4	164
Women's Teams	14	14	9	4	8	7	8	5	0	0	69
% Women's Teams	43.8%	63.6%	45.0%	20.0%	47.1%	50.0%	57.1%	38.5%	0.0%	0.0%	42.1%

FIGURE 11.28
Top 10 Sports Country Profiles – France

No.	Country	Country Sports Power Score	Number of Pro Teams	Households (millions)	Spending (millions)	Spending per Household
6	France	37	144	30.0	$1,287	$42,922

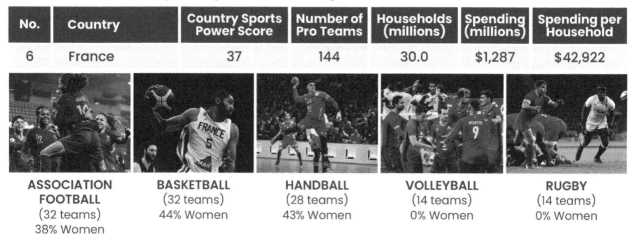

ASSOCIATION FOOTBALL (32 teams) 38% Women **BASKETBALL** (32 teams) 44% Women **HANDBALL** (28 teams) 43% Women **VOLLEYBALL** (14 teams) 0% Women **RUGBY** (14 teams) 0% Women

France Sport	Association Football	Basketball	Handball	Volleyball	Rugby	Futsal	Ice Hockey	Total
Pro Teams	32	32	28	14	14	12	12	**144**
Women's Teams	12	14	12	0	0	0	0	**38**
% Women's Teams	37.5%	43.8%	42.9%	0.0%	0.0%	0.0%	0.0%	**36.1%**

FIGURE 11.28
Top 10 Sports Country Profiles – Spain

No.	Country	Country Sports Power Score	Number of Pro Teams	Households (millions)	Spending (millions)	Spending per Household
7	Spain	34	140	18.9	$857	$45,312

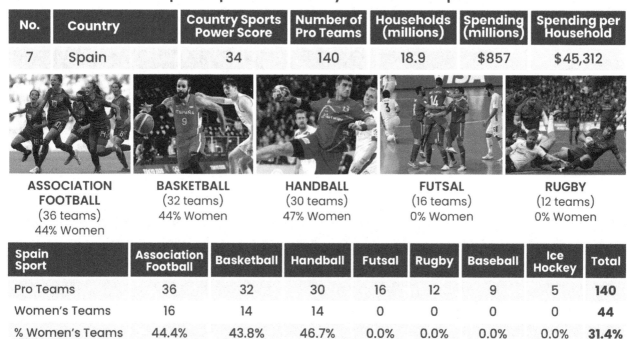

ASSOCIATION FOOTBALL (36 teams) 44% Women **BASKETBALL** (32 teams) 44% Women **HANDBALL** (30 teams) 47% Women **FUTSAL** (16 teams) 0% Women **RUGBY** (12 teams) 0% Women

Spain Sport	Association Football	Basketball	Handball	Futsal	Rugby	Baseball	Ice Hockey	Total
Pro Teams	36	32	30	16	12	9	5	**140**
Women's Teams	16	14	14	0	0	0	0	**44**
% Women's Teams	44.4%	43.8%	46.7%	0.0%	0.0%	0.0%	0.0%	**31.4%**

FIGURE 11.28
Top 10 Sports Country Profiles - Japan

No.	Country	Country Sports Power Score	Number of Pro Teams	Households (millions)	Spending (millions)	Spending per Household
8	Japan	33	98	55.7	$2,787	$50,033

BASKETBALL (30 teams) 40% Women | **VOLLEYBALL** (22 teams) 55% Women | **ASSOCIATION FOOTBALL** (18 teams) 0% Women | **RUGBY** (16 teams) 0% Women | **BASEBALL** (12 teams) 0% Women

Japan Sport	Basketball	Volleyball	Association Football	Rugby	Baseball	Total
Pro Teams	30	22	18	16	12	**98**
Women's Teams	12	12	0	0	0	**24**
% Women's Teams	40.0%	54.5%	0.0%	0.0%	0.0%	**24.5%**

FIGURE 11.28
Top 10 Sports Country Profiles - Brazil

No.	Country	Country Sports Power Score	Number of Pro Teams	Households (millions)	Spending (millions)	Spending per Household
9	Brazil	32	120	68.2	$1,185	$17,363

AMERICAN FOOTBALL (31 teams) 0% Women | **VOLLEYBALL** (24 teams) 50% Women | **FUTSAL** (23 teams) 0% Women | **BASKETBALL** (22 teams) 36% Women | **ASSOCIATION FOOTBALL** (20 teams) 0% Women

Brazil Sport	American Football	Volleyball	Futsal	Basketball	Association Football	Total
Pro Teams	31	24	23	22	20	**120**
Women's Teams	0	12	0	8	0	**20**
% Women's Teams	0.0%	50.0%	0.0%	36.4%	0.0%	**16.7%**

FIGURE 11.28
Top 10 Sports Country Profiles - India

No.	Country	Country Sports Power Score	Number of Pro Teams	Households (millions)	Spending (millions)	Spending per Household
10	India	32	106	306.8	$559	$1,822

ASSOCIATION FOOTBALL
(47 teams)
51% Women

KABADDI
(12 teams)
0% Women

VOLLEYBALL
(12 teams)
0% Women

CRICKET
(8 teams)
0% Women

BASKETBALL
(8 teams)
0% Women

India Sport	Association Football	Kabaddi	Volleyball	Cricket	Basketball	Badminton	Field Hockey	Handball	Total
Pro Teams	47	12	12	8	8	7	6	6	**106**
Women's Teams	24	0	0	0	0	0	0	0	**24**
% Women's Teams	51.1%	0.0%	0.0%	0.0%	0.0%	0.0%	0.0%	0.0%	**22.6%**

TOP 50 SPORTS CITIES
CHAPTER 12

Acting Locally

New York City is one of the top sports cities in the world. Why?

The city has 13 professional sport teams that generated more than $3 billion in sales in 2019, a large population of 20.5 million people, 7.4 million households and consumer spending greater than $1 trillion per year (*Figure 12.1*). Cities with fewer professional sport teams, fewer people, and less consumer spending cannot generate the same revenue from sporting events, sportswear sales, and sports participation. The three critical variables are:

- **Professional Teams.** A city's number of professional teams builds passion among its residents. The teams generate sports event revenues, as well as entertainment revenues via sports betting, fantasy sports and sports bars.

- **Population.** Cities with more people and more households have more sports fans. Large sports media markets create revenues via sports broadcasting, digital media subscriptions and advertising.

- **Purchasing Power.** Cities with large economies, measured in gross domestic product (GDP), have great purchasing power, allowing residents to buy event tickets, sportswear, sports equipment, fitness club and gym memberships.

FIGURE 12.1
New York City's Sports

The Best-Howard Sports Industry Model uses the three metrics (*Figure 12.2*)—focusing on professional team volume, raw population, household number, consumer spending and consumer spending per household—to develop proprietary City-Level Sports Power Scores. Using a similar methodology to the one employed at the country level, the model examines the top sports cities in North America, Europe, the Asia-Pacific region, Latin America, and the Middle East and Africa region. The model then determines the top 50 sports cities from its initial inventory.

FIGURE 12.2
Building the Sports City Model

PRO TEAMS:

Local teams offer sports events, media and entertainment.

POPULATION:

Larger concentrations of people create elevated demand for sports tickets, products and participation.

PURCHASING POWER:

Wealthy consumers have the capability to buy tickets, sports products, and fitness club and specialty gym memberships.

What Makes a Sports City Unique?

Beyond the metrics used to identify the City-Level Sports Power Scores, each sports city the Best-Howard Model examines has a unique culture. While two cities may have similarly high power scores, they might also be radically different based on the sports they value. *Figure 12.3* shows how the sports shaping city-level sports cultures vary by world region.

In North America, football and baseball, along with basketball, ice hockey and a growing interest in soccer, shape sports culture. The European culture is different, with 625 professional soccer, 300 basketball, 108 handball, 89 volleyball, 64 rugby and 44 cricket teams. In the Asia-Pacific region, soccer and basketball represent about half the sports played, but rugby (36 teams), cricket (22 teams) and baseball (34 teams) are also popular. Soccer drives the Latin American and Middle East and Africa regions. The number of pro teams for these countries was determined by the pro leagues for each sport in a country and then the number of teams per sport (1). This database will also allow us to profile each country by sport and number of pro teams per sport. This data will be used extensively in the remainder of Chapter 11.

Sports are often a leading source of city pride. Whether the teams are perennial winners or losers, they have legacy fans built over generations (2). Some cities with multiple professional teams, large populations and great buying power generate more sports industry revenues than entire countries.

FIGURE 12.3
Regional Sports & Professional Teams

SPORTS	North America	Europe	Asia Pacific	Latin America	Mid-East Africa	Multi Country	Total Worldwide	% Worldwide
Association Football	31	619	84	179	215	–	1128	30.3%
Basketball	50	365	110	81	142	–	748	20.1%
Volleyball	–	160	77	60	90	–	387	10.4%
Ice Hockey	32	164	20	–	–	24	240	6.4%
Rugby	13	105	36	21	10	29	214	5.7%
Handball	–	215	4	–	6	–	228	6.1%
Baseball	30	43	34	44	–	–	151	4.1%
Cricket	–	44	22	–	26	–	92	2.5%
Field Hockey	–	68	14	–	18	–	100	2.7%
American Football	32	63	20	47	8	–	170	4.6%
Other Pro Teams	15	96	49	92	12	–	264	7.1%
REGIONAL TOTAL	203	1945	470	524	527	53	3722	100.0%
% Worldwide	5.5%	52.3%	12.6%	14.1%	14.2%	1.4%	100.0%	

Local professional teams drive fan engagement, sports product purchasing and sports participation. Local sports media and entertainment, such as wagering, team merchandise retail and sports bars, further support fan engagement (3). The teams contribute to city sports personality inspiring street sports and fashion (*Figure 12.4*), and top sports cities are likely to have many health and fitness clubs, exercise studios and specialty gyms.

FIGURE 12.4
City Sports Personality

PRO TEAMS   **STREETWEAR**   **STREET SPORTS**

Fan Engagement

Sports Products

Sports Participation

Each city's professional sports teams fuel a unique streetwear aesthetic. Los Angeles sports streetwear is different from that in New York City, Tokyo or London. Likewise, cities have unique street sports. Basketball and skateboarding might be found in most major sports cities, but London features a street soccer scene unlike anything in U.S. cities. Where and when athletes engage in street sports also varies. In Tokyo, skateboarders take to the streets after midnight, while Los Angeles has multiple skate parks and other dedicated venues.

Sports-obsessed cities can have a major impact on industry-wide revenues. With 20.2 million people and 7.2 million households, New York City has considerable potential based on its size alone. It also has buying power—in 2019, the average New York household spent $143,750 on consumer goods, 28% higher than the U.S. average of $112,344 (4). The global average consumer spending per household was $22,025, less than one fifth that of New York. While major sports cities significantly impact sportswear and health revenues, they affect equipment more moderately, as their populations are less likely to spend on outdoor activities and recreational vehicles.

To understand how a city's professional teams, population and purchasing power work together, consider five major sports cities (5): Tokyo, New York City, London, Los Angeles and Shanghai (*Figure 12.5*). Each city is an important sports epicenter but has different professional teams, population and purchasing power.

As shown in the figure, Tokyo has 22 professional teams, with baseball and soccer representing 13 of them. New York has fewer teams, 13, but generates more sports industry revenue than Tokyo. London has the most pro teams at 29, with soccer (nine) and field hockey (eight) accounting for 17 of them. All five cities have two or three basketball teams. Los Angeles and New York have football teams, while Tokyo and London each have five professional rugby teams. The two Asian cities lack ice hockey teams.

FIGURE 12.5
Five Major Sports Cities' Professional Teams

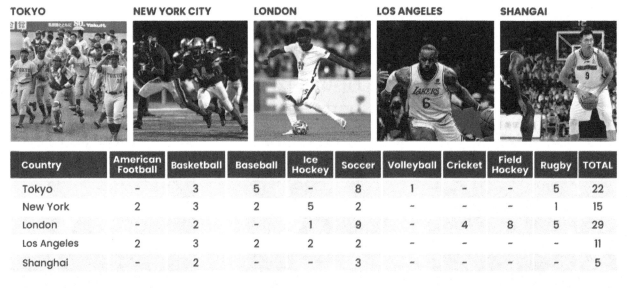

Country	American Football	Basketball	Baseball	Ice Hockey	Soccer	Volleyball	Cricket	Field Hockey	Rugby	TOTAL
Tokyo	-	3	5	-	8	1	-	-	5	22
New York	2	3	2	5	2	-	-	-	1	15
London	-	2	-	1	9	-	4	8	5	29
Los Angeles	2	3	2	2	2	-	-	-	-	11
Shanghai	-	2	-	-	3	-	-	-	-	5

Figure 12.6 breaks down New York City sports revenues in detail. The full impact of New York sports includes revenues produced by sports product sales, fees and memberships related to sports participation, team events, sports media and wagering.

FIGURE 12.6
Professional Sports Teams' Impact in New York City

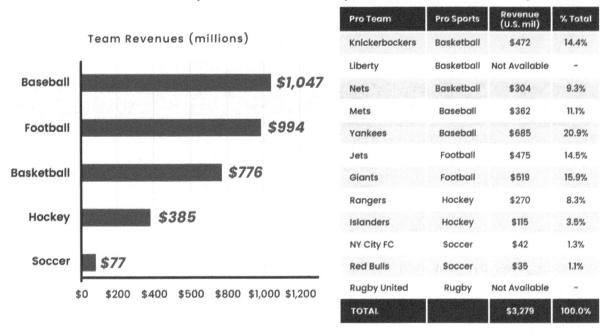

Team Revenues (millions)

Baseball	$1,047
Football	$994
Basketball	$776
Hockey	$385
Soccer	$77

$0 $200 $400 $500 $800 $1,000 $1,200

Pro Team	Pro Sports	Revenue (U.S. mil)	% Total
Knickerbockers	Basketball	$472	14.4%
Liberty	Basketball	Not Available	–
Nets	Basketball	$304	9.3%
Mets	Baseball	$362	11.1%
Yankees	Baseball	$685	20.9%
Jets	Football	$475	14.5%
Giants	Football	$519	15.9%
Rangers	Hockey	$270	8.3%
Islanders	Hockey	$115	3.5%
NY City FC	Soccer	$42	1.3%
Red Bulls	Soccer	$35	1.1%
Rugby United	Rugby	Not Available	–
TOTAL		**$3,279**	**100.0%**

New York's professional teams produced $3.3 billion in 2019 revenues (6), 7.5% of all U.S. revenues and 3.4% of global sports revenues. The value is greater than the revenues produced by any country in the world except the United States itself, Germany and the United Kingdom. The revenues are three times those of Russia. In addition to the 13 professional sports teams New York offers its 20.2 million people, the city is home to the New York Marathon, tennis's U.S. Open and seven racetracks. The additional revenue streams likely add another $1 billion.

Population & Purchasing Power

Leading up to 2019, the world was experiencing a major population shift from rural areas to cities. The global urban population at the time was growing by 65 million people annually, equivalent to adding seven new Chicago-size cities per year. For the first time in history, more than half of the world's population was living in towns and cities at the end of 2019.

The population of top sports cities is therefore changing. Following are city population growth projections for the top 600 cities worldwide from 2015 to 2025 (7):

- 136 of the top 600 cities in 2015 will be replaced by new cities in 2025.

- The new cities in 2025's top 600 will come from China (100 cities), India (13 cities) and Latin America (8 cities).

- The cities leaving the top 600 will be from North America and Europe. The cities will still be large based on population but no longer among the 600 largest worldwide.

A city's population profile includes its number of people and households, household size and age distribution (8). Cities with professional sports teams typically have large populations, but not all large cities have professional teams.

The five cities in *Figure 12.7* have populations ranging from 13.4 million to 37 million and households varying from 4.3 million to 17 million. Their populations consume local sports events, media broadcasts and wagering opportunities. Even those who cannot afford event tickets can follow their teams with live and recorded broadcasts and buy sports merchandise.

FIGURE 12.7
Major Sports Cities' Populations

City	Population (millions)			Age Categories			Households (millions)	Households Size
	2019	CAGR	2025	<15	15 to 59	>59		
Tokyo	37.0	0.00%	37.0	12%	57%	31%	17	2.2
New York	20.2	0.39%	21.0	18%	62%	20%	7.2	2.8
London	14.0	1.34%	16.0	19%	62%	19%	6.4	2.2
Los Angeles	13.4	0.72%	14.4	19%	64%	17%	4.3	3.1
Shanghai	26.0	3.10%	32.0	8%	72%	20%	9.0	2.9

Purchasing power gives city residents the ability to engage with their teams, buy sports products and participate in fee-based activities. The stronger a city's buying power, the more sports industry revenue it creates. The five major cities shown in Figure 12.8 have larger populations than many countries and significant purchasing power (9). Tokyo's GDP of $1.7 trillion is larger than 90% of the country-level GDPs in the world. Los Angeles's GDP of $0.9 trillion is larger than that of Sweden, Belgium, Norway, Demark, Finland, Poland, Switzerland, Netherlands and Turkey. As consumer spending is typically 70% of GDP, the cities have tremendous buying power.

FIGURE 12.8
Sports City Purchasing Power

City	GDP (U.S. trillions)	Household Income (thousands)				Spending (U.S. millions)	Consumer Spending per Household
		<$7.5	$20	$70	>$70		
Tokyo	$1.71	1%	5%	63%	31%	$1,300	$76,471
New York	$1.46	2%	4%	28%	60%	$1,035	$143,750
London	$1.01	2%	5%	44%	49%	$670	$111,667
Los Angeles	$0.90	2%	4%	34%	60%	$625	$145,349
Shanghai	$0.49	7%	29%	53%	11%	$337	$37,444

Annual consumer spending per household further explains a city's purchasing power. New York City has 7.2 million households that each spend greater than $143,750 per year. While Tokyo has 16.8 million more households, they contain only 2.2 people on average and spend half that of New York's households. In New York and Los Angeles, 60% of households have incomes greater than $70,000, compared to 11% in Shanghai and 31% in Tokyo.

Figure 12.9 shows the top 25 global cities based on 2015 consumer spending and projections for 2025. The cities shaded in gray will leave the top 25 by 2025; those in yellow will move into the top 25. The figure also displays the top 75 world cities based on consumer spending by region (10).

North America and Europe will each lose five cities from the top 75 by 2025 based on consumer spending, while the Asia-Pacific region will gain 10.

FIGURE 12.9
Top Consumer Spending Cities

NORTH AMERICA

CITIES	2015	2025	Change
New York	$1,034	$1,261	22%
Los Angeles	$625	$780	25%
Chicago	$410	$490	20%
Houston	$341	$500	47%
Washinton DC	$315	$411	30%
Dallas	$300	$425	42%
Philadelphia	$256	$308	20%
San Francisco	$250	$330	32%
Atlanta	$211	$300	42%
Seatle	$200	$260	30%
Miami	$200	$274	37%
Boston	$200	$265	33%
Top 25 Cities	**$4,342**	**$5,604**	**29%**

EUROPE

CITIES	2015	2025	Change
London	$670	$871	30%
Paris	$311	$367	18%
Rhine-Ruhr	$356	$409	15%
Milan	$191	$202	6%
Randstand	$184	$215	17%
Istanbul	$157	$249	59%
Top 25 City	**$1,869**	**$2,313**	**24%**

ASIA-PACIFIC

CITIES	2015	2025	Change
Tokyo	40	625	100
Osaka	41	300	110
Nagoya	–	89	35
Hong Kong	29	92	20
Seoul	10	64	36
Shanghai	–	108	4
Beijing	29	18	34
Tianjin	–	44	22
Top 25 City	**$2,080**	**$2,977**	**43%**

LATIN AMERICA

CITIES	2015	2025	Change
Sao Paulo	$260	$340	31%
Mexico City	$230	$346	50%
Buenos Aires	$192	$226	15%
Top 25 City	**$846**	**$1,095**	**29%**

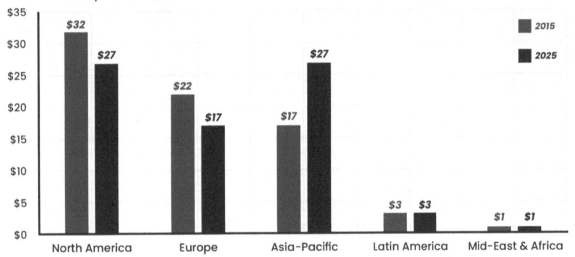

Top 75 Global Cities Based on Consumer Spending (billions)

Sports City Streetwear & Sports

Streetwear has been a defining part of city sports cultures for more than 40 years. Over the period, streetwear has evolved from a basic expression to high fashion. Today, streetwear is evident among individuals wearing tracksuit bottoms as they once wear jeans and celebrities seeking designer brands like Vetements and Off-White (11).

The designer Dapper Dan played a pivotal role in elevating streetwear to a luxury product in the 1980s in Harlem, N.Y., developing styles for hip-hop artists shunned by traditional high-end brands (12). Pioneer streetwear producers include the skate brand Supreme and the surf-focused firm Stüssy (13).

The term streetwear was initially used to describe comfortable clothing predominately worn by those engaged in skateboarding and surf culture in Los Angeles. Surfboard manufacturer Stüssy began making t-shirts with its iconic logo. Streetwear soon evolved to refer to casual street fashion encompassing many styles, from hip hop to punk rock, and is often found in independent surf/skate shops and thrift stores or from internet-based start-ups (14).

Figure 12.10 highlights five streetwear brands founded in major sports cities. Supreme started in New York and has expanded globally. A Bathing Ape (also BAPE) originated in Tokyo (15) and has become a dominant brand throughout the Asia-Pacific region. Palace started as a skateboard company in London (16) and now sells a growing line of streetwear products worldwide. In Shanghai, DOE is a leading streetwear brand (17) with locations across Asia.

FIGURE 12.10
City Streetwear Brands

A streetwear brand's exclusivity as a status symbol has long been integral to its popularity. However, comfort and community identity also play a role, as shown in *Figure 12.11*. (18), along with product quality, design and celebrity endorsements. One additional factor is authenticity, which relates directly to streetwear's role in major cities' sports culture.

FIGURE 12.11
Consumers' Most Preferred Streetwear Attributes

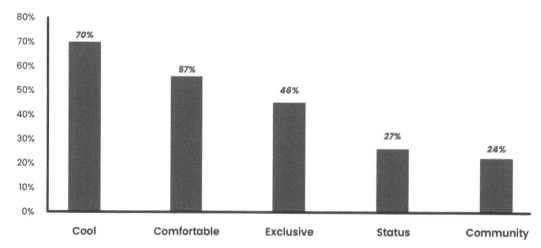

The Tokyo streetwear video presented in *Figure 12.12* provides an overview of streetwear brands sold in the city, as well as how the clothing and culture evolved in Tokyo and now includes brands from New York, London and Los Angeles.

FIGURE 12.12
Exploring Tokyo Streetwear

Source: https://www.youtube.com/watch?v=nvRoF88S4Lw

Street sports, another critical aspect of a city's sports culture, are those adapted to play in urban areas. The origins of street sports are traceable to the earliest evidence of sports themselves in Greek and Roman civilization (19). Street sports are self-organized, informal and often played with local rules created by the participants. Most, such as street basketball, soccer, cricket and football, originate from traditional sports and are adapted to the urban space and local culture (20). Some sports, like skateboarding, scootering and breakdancing, originate directly from the street.

Street sports vary by city and according to the dominant local professional teams. New Yorkers played the stickball adaptation of baseball for years, with its popularity peaking in the 1950s and 1960s (21). The game is played with a broomstick serving as a bat and a rubber ball. In some versions, players bounce the ball, hit it, and run to a created base; in others, opposing players pitch to the batter as in baseball. *Figure 12.13* shows Willie Mays playing stickball on the streets of Harlem in 1950. By the 1980s, stickball largely gave way to new cultural patterns and recreational interests, but it can still be found in some New York City neighborhoods.

FIGURE 12.13
Willie Mays Playing Stickball in New York

Stickball is just one unique aspect of New York City street sports. "The Cage" at West 4th Street in Greenwich Village is an iconic street basketball venue. Street football, soccer, baseball, skateboarding and break-dancing are also commonplace. While breaking has been around since the 1970s, it is scheduled to be included in the 2024 Summer Olympics and will likely grow in popularity (22). The dance form originated in Black and Latino communities in the Bronx and quickly spread. Cultures outside the United States have created their own version of breaking, which serves as a unique intersection among a city's music, streetwear and sport.

The video in *Figure 12.14* highlights a street soccer tournament in London. According to tournament host COPA90, the adapted sport keeps many London youths from engaging in illegal activities. Street sports are often played by lower income youth with no access to gyms and fitness clubs. Some researchers have suggested introducing sports in inner cities could affect crime and teen pregnancy levels. According to the COPA90 video, street soccer also improves personal wellbeing and builds community.

FIGURE 12.14
Street Soccer in London

Source: https://www.youtube.com/watch?v=jEJQ5ZgXSho

City-Level Sports Power Scores

The Best-Howard Sports Model's proprietary City-Level Sports Power Scores are composites based on municipalities' professional sports teams, households and consumer spending, each of which have been shown to correlate with city sports revenues in North America. The number of pro sport teams by city was determined by using the pro leagues in a country and then examining each pro league by city. This database can be accessed to further examine these city sport teams (23)

The Best-Howard Model indexes the three metrics using benchmark scores, similar to the model's country-level methodology and the strategy used to create the well-known buying power index (24):

- Pro Teams Relative Index = (City's Pro Team Number / Benchmark City's Pro Team Number) x 100

- Households Relative Index = (City's Household Number / Benchmark City's Household Number) x 100

- Consumer Spending Relative Index = (City's Consumer Spending / Benchmark City's Consumer Spending) x 100

Tokyo, with 22 professional sports teams, 17.8 million households and $1.3 trillion in consumer spending, serves as the benchmark city for all three metrics. The Best-Howard Model creates an index for each metric based on each city's performance divided by the benchmark. The overall score is a weighted average of the three metrics.

Analysts use the buying power index to estimate U.S. states' and cities' ability to purchase consumer goods. The index is estimated as:

$$\textit{Buying Power Index} = \textit{0.5 (Market's Buying Income Percentage)}$$
$$+ \textit{0.3 (Market's Retail Sales Percentage)}$$
$$+ \textit{0.2 (Market's Population Percentage)}$$

Similarly, the Best-Howard Model uses a regression analysis to determine the relative importance of its three indices for explaining variance in city sports sales and finds the following relationships:

> *City-Level Sports Power Score* = *0.2 (Pro Teams Relative Index)*
>
> *+ 0.2 (Households Relative Index)*
>
> *+ 0.6 (Consumer Spending Relative Index)*

To better understand the process, consider New York City, which has 13 professional sports teams, 7.4 million households and $1,120 billion in consumer spending:

> *Pro Team Relative Index* = *(13 teams / 22 teams) x 100 = 59*
>
> *Households Relative Index* = *(7.4 million / 17.8 million) x 100 = 42*
>
> *Spending Relative Index* = *($1,120 billion / $1,300 billion) x 100 = 86*

The weighted average of New York's three city-level indices is 72, as shown in *Figure 12.15*. Relative to Tokyo with a score of 100, New York has almost half as many professional teams and 10.4 million fewer households but close to the same level of consumer spending.

FIGURE 12.15
New York City's Power Score

NEW YORK – CITY-LEVEL SPORTS POWER SCORE (72)

PRO TEAMS (number)	HOUSEHOLDS (millions)	CONSUMER SPENDING (billions)
• Benchmark: 22 • New York: 13 • City Index: 59	• Benchmark: 17.8 • New York: 7.4 • City Index: 42	• Benchmark: $1,300 • New York: $1,120 • City Index: 86

Sport	Football	Basketball	Baseball	Ice Hockey	Soccer	Rugby	Other	TOTAL
Pro Teams	2	3	2	2	2	1	1	13

Each index used to create the Best-Howard Model's proprietary City-Level Sports Power Score is capped at 100. Some cities report data as metropolitan areas and include surrounding cities and small revenue sports like field hockey, handball and volleyball. For example, the Randstad metro area in Netherlands includes at least 10 adjacent cities with 40 professional teams. The average team revenues for the sports are less than $10 million. The average Tokyo-based professional team's revenue is greater than $30 million. Randstad earns a score of only 100 on its Pro Team Relative Index, still receiving considerable weight for its team volume without minimizing the revenue potential of major sports teams like the 22 located in Tokyo.

The Best-Howard Model applies its City-Level Sports Power Scores to at least 150 cities and breaks them down via five regions: North America, Europe, Asia-Pacific, Latin America, and Middle East and Africa.

North America

Forbes magazine produces an annual report on all North America's professional teams and their revenues (25). The Best-Howard Model therefore tests the validity of its North American City-Level Sports Power Scores against revenues. The model computes power scores for the top 50 North American sports cities; details on the top 10 are shown in *Figure 12.16*.

The results are shown in five tiers, each with 10 sports cities. New York City has the region's highest power score at 62. New York and the other Tier I, top 10 cities encompass almost 40% of North America's professional teams, 24% of its population and 23% of its consumer spending.

FIGURE 12.16
North America's Top 10 Sports Cities

TIER I	TIER II	TIER III	TIER IV	TIER V
76 Teams	52 Teams	24 Teams	19 Teams	11 Teams

No.	Tier I City	Score	Pro Teams
1	New York	72	13
2	Los Angeles	46	11
3	Chicago	32	9
4	Houston	26	6
5	Washington DC	26	8
6	Dallas	24	6
7	Boston	21	6
8	San Francisco	20	6
9	Philadelphia	20	5
10	Atlanta	19	6
	TOTAL/AVERAGE	31	76

No.	Tier I City	City-Level Sports Power Score	Pro Teams	Population (millions)	Households (millions)	Spending (billions)	Spending per Household
1	New York	72	13	20.5	7.4	$1,120	$151,493
2	Los Angeles	46	11	13.8	4.3	$682	$158,573
3	Chicago	32	9	9.8	3.6	$438	$121,544
4	Houston	26	6	7.1	2.3	$398	$172,940
5	Washington DC	26	8	6.4	2.3	$351	$152,414
6	Dallas	24	6	7.7	2.6	$345	$132,764
7	Boston	21	6	4.9	1.8	$293	$162,638
8	San Francisco	20	6	4.9	1.7	$280	$164,706
9	Philadelphia	20	5	6.1	2.3	$276	$119,803
10	Atlanta	19	6	6.2	2.1	$243	$115,680
	TOTAL/AVERAGE	31	76	87.4	30.4	$4,425	$145,255

No.	Tier I City	Football	Soccer	Baseball	Basketball	Canadian Football	Ice Hockey	Rugby	Softball	TOTAL
1	New York	2	2	2	3	0	3	1	0	13
2	Los Angeles	2	2	2	3	0	2	0	0	11
3	Chicago	1	2	2	2	0	1	0	1	9
4	Houston	1	2	1	1	0	0	1	0	6
5	Washington DC	1	2	1	2	0	1	1	0	8
6	Dallas	1	1	1	2	0	1	0	0	6
7	Boston	1	1	1	1	0	2	0	0	6
8	San Francisco	1	1	2	1	0	1	0	0	6
9	Philadelphia	1	1	1	1	0	1	0	0	5
10	Atlanta	1	1	1	2	0	0	1	0	6
	TOTAL/AVERAGE	12	15	14	18	0	12	4	1	76
	Percentage	16%	20%	18%	24%	0%	16%	5%	1%	100%
	Women's Teams	0	3	0	6	0	3	0	1	13
	% Women's Teams	0%	4%	0%	8%	0%	4%	3%	1%	17%

View other graphs on page A12.1 Chapter 12 Appendix 1

Strategically, each of the Tier I cities offer companies looking to market products in North America large populations with enormous purchasing power. The top 10 North American cities offer fewer opportunities for companies targeting female consumers than other regions, as only four of their 76 professional teams are women's teams. In Tier I sports cities in other regions, 13% to 34% of professional teams are comprised of women. The United States does have a strong collegiate program for women.

North America's Tier II cities have 52 professional teams. Click on Tier II, III, IV and V in *Figure 12.16* to see the various cities and their details. Each tier offers different insights related to the metrics used to compute power scores.

Figure 12.17 graphs North America's top City-Level Sports Power Scores against the cities' 2019 sports revenues (26). New York City, for example, receives a score of 72 and has 2019 revenues of $3.3 billion.

FIGURE 12.17
North America - City Sports Revenues (millions) Vs. Sports City Power Score

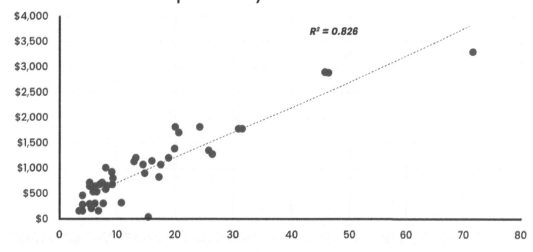

The Best-Howard Model finds the relationship between power score and revenue to be strong and meaningful, with a correlation of 0.91 and r-squared of 83%. In other words, City-Level Sports Power Scores are a good indicator of professional sports revenues. *Figure 12.18* shows the relationship between professional sports teams in the 50 top cities and sports team revenues. The correlation (.93) and r-squared (86%) both are high.

FIGURE 12.18
North America - City Sports Revenues (millions) Vs. Number Pro Teams

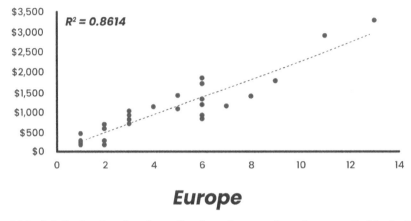

$R^2 = 0.8614$

Europe

The Best-Howard Model finds city-level professional team data less available in Europe than in North America. The model therefore turns to the professional European leagues, which lists teams by city. No single reference offers the data, and the resources do not provide team revenues. Major European soccer teams do, however, provide revenue data (27). Team revenues for other sports are not reported, making a complete estimate of city-level professional sports revenues impossible.

England, France, Germany, Spain and Italy have five major soccer leagues and many smaller organizations in cities across the continent, as summarized in *Figure 12.19* (28).

FIGURE 12.19
Europe's Big 5 Soccer Leagues

Premier League City	UK Teams	Premier League City	UK Teams	Ligue 1 City	France Teams	Serie A City	Italy Teams	Bundesliga City	Germany Teams	La Liga City	Spain Teams
Barnsley	1	London	9	Anfers	1	Bergamo	1	Augsburg	1	Vitoria-Gasteix	1
Birmingham	2	Manchester	2	Bordeaux	2	Benevento	1	Berlin	2	Bilbao	1
Blackburn	1	Middlesbrough	1	Brest	1	Bologna	1	Beilefeld	1	Madrid	2
Blackpool	1	Newcastle	1	Dijon	1	Cagliari	1	Bremen	1	Barcelona	1
Bolton	1	Norwich City	1	Lens	1	Florence	1	Cologne	1	Cadiz	1
Bournermouth	1	Oldham	1	Lille	1	Genoa	2	Dortmund	1	Vigo	1
Bradford	1	Portsmouth	1	Lorient	1	Verona	1	Frankfurt	1	Getafe	1
Brighton	1	Reading	1	Lyon	1	Milan	2	Freiburg	1	Huesca	1
Burnley	1	Sheffield	2	Marseille	1	Turin	2	Gelsenkirchen	1	Valencia	2
Carfidd	1	Southampton	1	Metz	1	Rome	2	Leipzig	1	Palmones	1
Coventry	1	Stoke City	1	Monaco	1	Naples	1	Leverkusen	1	San Sebastian	1
Derby	1	Sunderland	1	Montpellier	1	Parma	1	Mainz	1	Valladolid	1
Huddersfield	1	Swansea	1	Nantes	1	Sassuoto	1	Monchegladbach	1	Villarreal	1
Ipswich	1	Swindon	1	Nice	1	La Spezia	1	Munich	1		
Kingston	1	Watford	1	Nimes	1	Udine	1	Sinsheim	1		
Leeds	1	West Bridgford	1	Paris	1			Stuttgart	1		
Leicester	1	West Bromwich	1	Reims	1			Wolfburg	1		
Liverpool	2	Wigan	1	Rennes	1						
		Wolverhampton	1	St. Etienne	1						
				Strasbourg	1						
	Total		**48**	**Total**	**21**	**Total**	**19**	**Total**	**18**	**Total**	**15**

Figure 12.20 shows 2019 professional soccer revenues for the top 10 European sports cities (29). London produced $1.86 billion in revenues from four teams, 20% of the top cities' revenues and 11% of all Europe's "Big 5" leagues. Manchester produced $1.47 billion and Liverpool $867 million, both with just two teams. The 10 cities produced $9.13 billion, 54% of all Big 5 team revenues.

FIGURE 12.20
Top European Cities' 2019 Soccer Team Revenues

Ligue 1 City	Country	Team	League	Revenue (millions)	Percent Top 10	Percent Euro Big 5
London				$1,864	20.4%	11.0%
London	England	Chelsea	Premier	$597	6.5%	
London	England	Arsenal	Premier	$520	5.7%	
London	England	Tottenham Hotspur	Premier	$511	5.6%	
London	England	West Ham United	Premier	$236	2.6%	
Manchester				$1,474	16.1%	8.7%
Manchester	England	Manchester City	Premier	$795	8.7%	
Manchester	England	Manchester City	Premier	$679	7.4%	
Madrid				$1,259	13.8%	7.4%
Madrid	Spain	Real Madrid	La Liga	$896	9.8%	
Madrid	Spain	Athletico de Madrid	La Liga	$363	4.0%	
Liverpool				$867	9.5%	5.1%
Liverpool	England	Liverpool	Premier	$613	6.7%	
Liverpool	England	Everton	Premier	$254	2.8%	
Barcelona	Spain	Barcelona	La Liga	$824	9.0%	4.9%
Munich	Germany	Bayern Munich	Bundesliga	$751	8.2%	4.4%
Paris	France	Paris Saint-Germain	Ligue 1	$646	7.1%	3.8%
Milan				$583	6.4%	3.4%
Milan	Italy	Inter Milan	Serie A	$335	3.7%	
Milan	Italy	AC Milan	Serie A	$248	2.7%	
Turin	Italy	Juventus	Serie A	$480	5.3%	2.8%
Dortmund	Germany	Borussia Dortmund	Bundesliga	$379	4.2%	2.2%
Total				$9,127	100.0%	53.8%

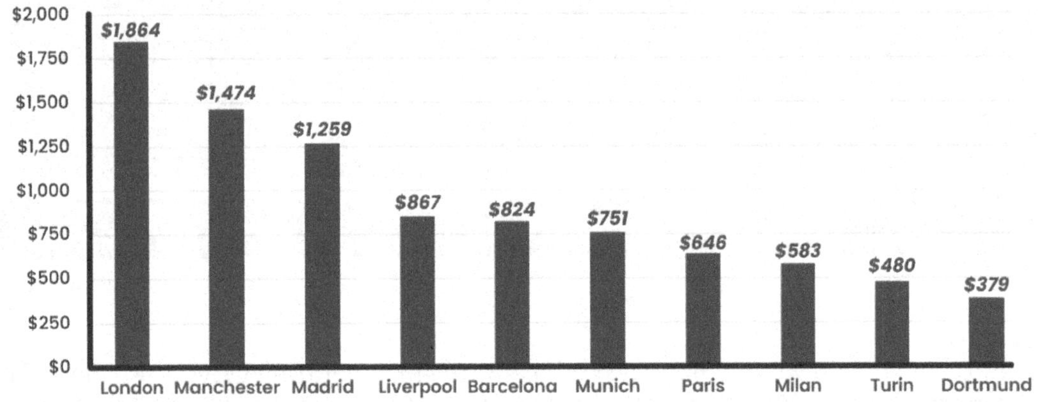

Using its City-Level Sports Power Score methodology, the Best-Howard Model presents Europe's top 30 sports cities. The data is obtained using information from leagues, teams and cities (30). *Figure 12.21* presents the scores for the top 10 cities. All are large metropolitan areas covering significant geographical space and many neighborhoods and boroughs. Cities with many professional teams tend to have high power scores; however, consumer spending carries more weight and shifts the rankings. For example, Randstad has the most professional teams in Europe but does not match other cities' households or consumer spending.

FIGURE 12.21
Europe's Top 10 Sports Cities

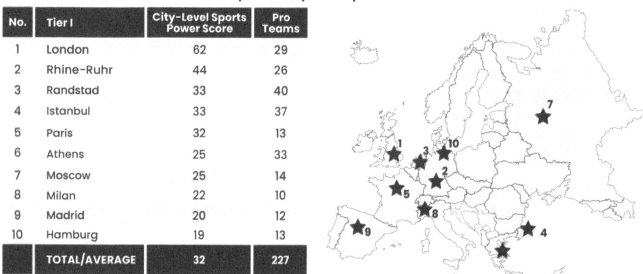

No.	Tier I	City-Level Sports Power Score	Pro Teams
1	London	62	29
2	Rhine-Ruhr	44	26
3	Randstad	33	40
4	Istanbul	33	37
5	Paris	32	13
6	Athens	25	33
7	Moscow	25	14
8	Milan	22	10
9	Madrid	20	12
10	Hamburg	19	13
	TOTAL/AVERAGE	32	227

London is the leading sports city in Europe based on City-Level Sports Power Score (*Figure 12.22*). The city is home to 29 professional teams and four of the top revenue producing teams across Europe's Big 5 soccer leagues. The city has a population of almost 9 million and 4 million households.

FIGURE 12.22
London's Power Score

LONDON – CITY-LEVEL SPORTS POWER SCORE (62)		
PRO TEAMS (number)	**HOUSEHOLDS** (millions)	**CONSUMER SPENDING** (billions)
• Benchmark: 22 • London: 18 • City Index: 82	• Benchmark: 17.8 • London: 6.4 • City Index: 37	• Benchmark: $1,300 • New York: $744 • City Index: 57

Sport	Association Football	Basketball	Volleyball	Rugby	Field Hockey	Cricket	Hand Ball	Ice Hockey	TOTAL
Pro Teams	9	2	0	6	0	1	0	0	18

While professional team volume plays a significant role in generating City-Level Sports Power Scores, leagues are structured differently around the world. For example, Istanbul has eight professional basketball teams in a country with 16 total teams. In the United States, cities with two teams are above average. So while marketers can't ignore a North American city like Chicago, easily-overlooked Istanbul might be equally attractive for its sports revenues across fan engagement, sports products and sports participation.

Europe has 1,418 professional sports teams. The top 30 sports cities have 18% of them and almost 20% of the region's households. They account for 54% of Europe's consumer spending. As a result, sportswear brands can realize their greatest sales potential by focusing on the region's top 30 cities.

The Best-Howard Model reports the top 30 European sports cities in three tiers of 10 cities each. *Figure 12.23* presents the tiers.

FIGURE 12.23
Europe's Top 30 Sports Cities

	TIER I 227 Teams	TIER II 81 Teams	TIER III 34 Teams

No.	Tier I Cities	City-Level Sports Power Score	Pro Teams	Population (millions)	Households (millions)	Spending (billions)	Spending per Household
1	London	62	29	12.3	6.4	$744	$116,606
2	Rhine-Ruhr	44	26	11.6	6.2	$376	$60,744
3	Randstad	33	40	8.2	3.6	$196	$55,089
4	Istanbul	33	37	15.6	3.7	$189	$50,949
5	Paris	32	13	12.1	4.6	$333	$72,478
6	Athens	25	33	3.2	1.7	$72	$41,365
7	Moscow	25	14	12.7	4.9	$135	$27,655
8	Milan	22	10	5.1	3.4	$195	$58,032
9	Madrid	20	12	6.8	2.5	$132	$52,800
10	Hamburg	19	13	1.8	1.7	$117	$69,467
	TOTAL/AVERAGE	32	227	89.5	38.6	$2,489	$60,518

No.	Tier I City	Association Football	Basketball	Rugby	Volleyball	Field Hockey	Handball	Ice Hockey	Football	Baseball	Cricket	Other	TOTAL
1	London	10	2	6	0	0	2	0	4	0	3	2	29
2	Rhine-Ruhr	8	1	0	0	6	4	3	1	3	0	0	26
3	Randstad	11	7	3	0	9	4	1	0	5	0	0	40
4	Istanbul	10	10	4	8	0	0	1	4	0	0	0	37
5	Paris	3	2	1	1	0	5	0	0	0	0	1	13
6	Athens	7	12	0	7	0	7	0	0	0	0	0	33
7	Moscow	7	4	3	0	0	0	0	0	0	0	0	14
8	Milan	4	1	0	2	0	0	1	2	0	0	0	10
9	Madrid	8	3	0	0	0	1	0	0	0	0	0	12
10	Hamburg	0	1	1	1	5	1	1	1	1	0	1	13
	TOTAL/AVERAGE	68	43	18	19	20	24	7	12	9	3	4	227
	Percentage	30.0%	18.9%	7.9%	8.4%	8.8%	10.6%	3.1%	5.3%	4.0%	1.3%	1.8%	100%
	Women's Teams	29	17	4	9	7	8	1	0	0	0	3	78
	% Women's Teams	43%	40%	22%	47%	35%	33%	14%	0%	0%	0%	75%	34.4%

View other graphs on page A12.5 Chapter 12 Appendix 2.

Tier I include 227 professional sports teams, almost 14% of Europe's total. The cities represent about 10% of Europe's households and 29% of its consumer spending, with average spending of $62,022 per household. The number is 267% higher than Europe's average household.

Europe's top 10 sports cities have far more professional teams, 277, than North America at 76. North America has few or no professional rugby, field hockey, handball, volleyball or cricket teams. However, the sports produce less revenue than soccer and basketball. Europe's Tier I cities have 78 women's teams, 35.4% of the total. North America's Tier I sports cities have only four professional women's teams.

Europe's Tier II cities have 94 professional teams; Tier III has 34. Click on the icons in *Figure 12.23* to see the cities in each tier, along with their team numbers, populations, households, consumer spending and average spending per household. The top 10 cities provide global brands their greatest sales opportunity, but Tier II cities offer some potential, likely with lower marketing costs.

Each major European sports city has its own streetwear brands, with several shown in *Figure 12.24*. Pigalle is an underground French firm focusing on young streetwear consumers. The company has expanded its line by collaborating with Nike on basketball-inspired sportswear. Palace is a well-known London streetwear brand that evolved from skateboarding, while Kappa is a fashion brand found in Milan and other large cities across Italy. DTF is a Dutch brand that seeks authenticity via culturally relevant messages. Les Benjamin is a luxury streetwear brand initially launched in Istanbul with printed t-shirts; it has since attracted interest across Europe and in major U.S. retailers, such as Saks Fifth Avenue and Harvey Nichols.

FIGURE 12.24
European Streetwear Brands

London – Palace   **Paris – Pigalle**   **Italy – Kappa**   **Netherlands – DTF**   **Istanbul: Les Benjamin**

Asia-Pacific

The Asia-Pacific region is perhaps the most diverse in the five examined by the Best-Howard model in culture, language and sports (*Figure 12.25*). The region spans Japan, China, Korea and India in the north to Australia and New Zealand in the south.

FIGURE 12.25
The Diverse Asia-Pacific Region

Soccer is among the most popular sports in the region's major cities, but Japan is also known for baseball, China for basketball, India for cricket and Australia for Australian Rules Football (as well as cricket).

Tokyo is the Asia-Pacific region's top sports city with a City-Level Sports Power Score of 100, as shown in *Figure 12.26*.

FIGURE 12.26
Tokyo's Power Score

TOKYO – CITY-LEVEL SPORTS POWER SCORE (100)		
PRO TEAMS (number)	**HOUSEHOLDS** (millions)	**CONSUMER SPENDING** (billions)
• Benchmark: 22 • Tokyo: 22 • City Index: 100	• Benchmark: 17.8 • Tokyo: 17.8 • City Index: 100	• Benchmark: $1,300 • Tokyo: $1,300 • City Index: 100

For the Asia-Pacific region, the Best-Howard Model presents the top 20 sports cities based on their professional team volume, household number and consumer spending. The model determines professional team numbers based on league reports (31). Populations, households and consumer spending are obtained using the McKinsey Urban World database.

The Tier I, top 10 Asia-Pacific sports cities are shown in *Figure 12.27*. The cities contain 162 professional teams and 63.4 million households with average consumer spending of $56,347.

Soccer and basketball are the top sports, but the cities exhibit clear differences. Chinese athletes do not play volleyball at the professional level, while only Australia and India play cricket. Baseball is played extensively.

The 10 cities have a high number of women's professional teams. Of the 162, 35 are women's teams (22%). The number is more than eight times larger than that of North America's Tier I sports cities.

FIGURE 12.27
Top 20 Asia-Pacific Sports Cities

TIER I	TIER II
162 Teams	39 Teams

No.	Tier I Cities	City-Level Sports Power Score	Pro Teams	Population (millions)	Households (millions)	Spending (billions)	Spending per Household
1	Tokyo	100	22	37.3	17.8	$1,300	$73,034
2	Osaka	44	9	19.7	8.8	$569	$64,659
3	Hong Kong	31	20	7.5	2.6	$210	$80,769
4	Sydney	29	34	5.0	1.8	$153	$85,000
5	Melbourne	27	38	4.7	1.7	$121	$71,176
6	Nagoya	26	8	9.3	3.8	$315	$82,895
7	Beijing	22	7	24.3	8.5	$130	$15,294
8	Shanghai	22	5	28.0	9.0	$152	$16,889
9	Mumbai	20	11	20.8	5.4	$94	$17,407
10	Seoul	19	8	9.8	4.0	$166	$41,500
	TOTAL/AVERAGE	34	162	166.5	63.4	$3,210	$56,347

No.	Tier I City	Association Football	Basketball	Volleyball	Rugby	Australian Football	Baseball	Cricket	Other	TOTAL
1	Tokyo	8	3	1	5	–	5	–	–	22
2	Osaka	2	1	4	–	–	2	–	–	9
3	Hong Kong	9	8	–	–	–	–	–	3	20
4	Sydney	4	2	2	11	3	1	5	6	34
5	Melbourne	4	3	2	1	16	1	5	6	38
6	Nagoya	1	3	2	1	–	1	–	–	8
7	Beijing	2	3	–	–	–	1	–	1	7
8	Shanghai	3	2	–	–	–	–	–	–	5
9	Mumbai	2	1	2	–	–	–	2	4	11
10	Seoul	1	2	2	–	–	3	–	–	8
	TOTAL/AVERAGE	36	28	15	18	19	14	12	20	162
	% Team Sports	20.8%	16.2%	8.7%	10.4%	11.0%	8.1%	6.9%	11.6%	93.8%
	Women's Teams	6	7	6	2	8	0	6	0	35
	% Women's Teams	3.5%	4.1%	3.5%	1.2%	4.6%	0.0%	3.5%	0.0%	20.3%

View other graph on page A12.7 Chapter 12 Appendix 3

Click on Tier II to review the Asia-Pacific cities ranked 11 to 20. The second tier represents cities containing 39 professional sports teams, roughly 25% of those in the Tier I cities. Seven of the 10 Tier II cities are in China, two are in Japan and one is in India. The Tier II cities are growing rapidly and could move to Tier I over time.

Latin America

The Latin American people are passionate about sports. *Figure 12.28* identifies the region's top 10 sports cities using the Best-Howard Model's City-Level Sports Power Score. Professional team numbers are determined based on league reports (32). City populations, households and consumer spending are obtained using the McKinsey Urban World database.

The top 10 Latin American sports cities have 56 professional soccer teams, 41% of their 137 total teams. Volleyball, with 38 teams (28% of the total), is uniquely popular in the region. Like all regions, basketball is among the top three sports, with 30 professional teams among the top 10 Latin American sports cities.

Women are represented in 41, or 30%, of the region's 137 Tier I teams. Thirteen of the 56 Tier I soccer teams are women's teams. Volleyball has 24 women's teams, 63% of the total. Latin America has more women's teams in its Tier I cities than any other world region.

FIGURE 12.28
Top 10 Latin American Sports Cities

No.	City	City-Level Sports Power Score	Pro Teams	Population (millions)	Households (millions)	Spending (billions)	Spending per Household
1	São Paulo	38	20	21.8	7.2	$261	$36,250
2	Buenos Aires	33	30	14.4	4.4	$170	$38,636
3	Lima	26	26	9.8	2.5	$76	$30,400
4	Mexico City	26	9	21.8	6.1	$231	$37,869
5	Rio de Janeiro	17	7	12.5	4.4	$115	$26,136
6	Bogota	16	10	9.8	2.8	$73	$26,071
7	Santiago	14	9	6.7	2	$88	$44,000
8	Caracas	14	12	5.1	1	$37	$37,000
9	Monterrey	12	8	4.4	1.3	$78	$60,000
10	Belo Horizonte	10	6	6.1	1.9	$55	$28,947
	TOTAL/AVERAGE	21	137	112.4	33.6	$1,184	$36,531

No.	Tier I Latin America	Association Football	Basketball	Volleyball	Football	Baseball	Other	TOTAL
1	Buenos Aires	12	8	10	-	-	-	30
2	Lima	8	7	11	-	-	-	26
3	São Paulo	3	5	10	1	-	1	20
4	Caracas	8	1	1	-	1	1	12
5	Bogota	6	2	-	-	-	2	10
6	Mexico City	5	1	-	2	1	-	9
7	Santiago	6	1	2	-	-	-	9
8	Monterrey	4	1	-	1	1	1	8
9	Rio de Janeiro	2	3	2	-	-	-	7
10	Belo Horizonte	2	1	2	-	-	1	6
	TOTAL/AVERAGE	56	30	38	4	3	6	137
	% Team Sports	40.9%	21.9%	27.7%	2.9%	2.2%	4.4%	100.0%
	Women's Teams	13	4	24	0	0	0	41
	% Women's Teams	23.2%	13.3%	63.2%	0.0%	0.0%	0.0%	29.9%

São Paulo is Latin America's top sports city with a City-Level Sports Power Score of 38 (*Figure 12.29*). The city has 20 professional teams and 7.2 million households with average consumer spending of $36,250. São Paulo's power score compares to that of cities like Chicago, Paris and Hong Kong.

FIGURE 12.29
São Paulo's Power Score

SÃO PAULO – CITY-LEVEL SPORTS POWER SCORE (38)

PRO TEAMS (number)	HOUSEHOLDS (millions)	CONSUMER SPENDING (billions)
• Benchmark: 22 • São Paulo: 20 • City Index: 91	• Benchmark: 17.8 • São Paulo: 7.2 • City Index: 40	• Benchmark: $1,300 • São Paulo: $261 • City Index: 20

Soccer is a way of life in much of Latin America. São Paulo is the sport's epicenter and home to the region's most important soccer clubs, such as Corinthias, São Paulo FC, Santos, Palmeiras, Juventude, Nacional and Portuguesa. Latin American teams compete annually for the Copa Libertadores de America, and each of São Paulo's major clubs have won the tournament at least once. São Paulo is home to several historic stadiums, including the Palestra Italia, Parque Sao Jorge, Rua Javari and the Morumbi. Morumbi, home of São Paulo FC, is one of the biggest sports stadiums in the world.

Buenos Aires achieves a City-Level Sports Power Score of 33. The score would be among the top five cities in North America, Europe and the Asia-Pacific region. With 30 professional teams, Buenos Aires has the most of any Latin American city. The city has 12 soccer, 10 volleyball and five basketball teams, making it an attractive market for aspiring global sports products companies.

Latin America is also notable for the extensive streetwear brands populating its top sports cities. *Figure 12.30* shows a limited sample. Many of the brands are the work of musicians, artists and designers focused on local culture and street fashion. Their goal is to reflect what is happening on Latin America's streets (33).

FIGURE 12.30
Latin American Streetwear Brands

Mexico City – Moonrise **Mexico City – Lv Ciudvd** **Santiago – Whats Up Wear** **Panama – Papaupa**

Middle East & Africa

The Middle East and Africa region includes more than 59 countries and 1.56 billion people (*Figure 12.31*). It contained 20% of the global population in 2019 and was projected to grow to 33% by 2050. About 60% of Africa's population is under 25, making it the world's youngest continent. The region's average household is larger, at more than four people per dwelling, and its consumer spending per household is lower than that of other world regions.

FIGURE 12.31
The Massive Middle East & Africa Region

The region has roughly 600 million internet users, with 525 million in Africa and 174 million in the Middle East. The number is greater than that of Latin America, at 447 million and North America, at 184 million (34). The widespread internet access makes sports broadcasts and replays accessible across the region and has created a large group of e-sports followers.

The Middle Eastern and African people are passionate about sports and the region's 192 professional teams (35). One hundred forty-two of the teams are in the region's top 10 cities (*Figure 12.32*). The Best-Howard Model examines the top 20 Middle Eastern/African sports cities based on professional team numbers, households and consumer spending. Teams are determined using league reports (36). City population and spending data is obtained using the McKinsey Urban World database.

FIGURE 12.32
Top 10 Middle East & Africa Sports Cities

No.	City	City-Level Sports Power Score	Pro Teams	Population (millions)	Households (millions)	Spending (billions)	Spending per Household
1	Cairo	38	23	21.2	4.7	$280	$59,038
2	Johannesburg	28	22	9.8	3.7	$74	$20,000
3	Doha	22	18	2.4	0.4	$113	$282,500
4	Lagos	19	12	14.1	4.1	$68	$16,513
5	Tehran	18	14	8.4	2.2	$56	$25,455
6	Tel Aviv	17	11	3.6	2.2	$97	$44,091
7	Ankara	17	13	4.40	1.5	$69	$46,000
8	Luanda	16	15	5.9	1.2	$32	$26,667
9	Riyadh	11	7	6.1	1.1	$68	$61,818
10	Alexandria	6	7	5.4	1.3	$67	$50,870
	TOTAL/AVERAGE	**19**	**142**	**81.3**	**22.5**	**$924**	**$63,295**

No.	Tier I Mid-East Africa	Association Football	Basketball	Volleyball	Field Hockey	Rugby	Other	TOTAL
1	Cairo	9	6	2	-	-	6	23
2	Johannesburg	6	3	-	12	-	1	22
3	Doha	8	5	5	-	-	-	18
4	Luanda	4	11	-	-	-	-	15
5	Tehran	3	8	3	-	-	-	14
6	Ankara	1	5	7	-	-	-	13
7	Lagos	1	4	-	-	7	-	12
8	Tel Aviv	5	3	2	-	-	1	11
9	Riyadh	3	2	2	-	-	-	7
10	Alexandria	2	5	-	-	-	-	7
	TOTAL/AVERAGE	**42**	**52**	**21**	**12**	**7**	**8**	**142**
	% Team Sports	**29.6%**	**36.6%**	**14.8%**	**8.5%**	**4.9%**	**5.6%**	**100.0%**
	Women's Teams	**9**	**14**	**7**	**6**	**3**	**0**	**39**
	% Women's Teams	**21.4%**	**26.9%**	**33.3%**	**50.0%**	**42.9%**	**0.0%**	**27.5%**

Soccer, with 42 professional teams, and basketball, with 52, account for 67% of the region's top 10 cities' total teams. Volleyball (14.8%) and field hockey (8.5%) are more popular in the region than others, particularly when compared to North America.

Cairo is the region's top sports city, with a City-Level Sports Power Score of 38 (*Figure 12.33*). Cairo has 23 professional teams, 4.7 million households and consumer spending of $280 billion.

FIGURE 12.33
Cairo's Power Score

CAIRO – CITY-LEVEL SPORTS POWER SCORE (38)		
PRO TEAMS (number)	**HOUSEHOLDS** (millions)	**CONSUMER SPENDING** (billions)
• Benchmark: 22 • Cairo: 23 • City Index: 100	• Benchmark: 17.8 • Cairo: 4.7 • City Index: 27	• Benchmark: $1,300 • Cairo: $280 • City Index: 22

In addition to Cairo, Johannesburg is an important Middle East and Africa region sports city, with a power score of 28. Johannesburg's power score and 22 professional sports teams make it similar in profile to cities like Sydney, Moscow, Milan and Washington, D.C. Uniquely, Johannesburg has 12 professional field hockey teams. It is the only city among the region's top 10 with field hockey teams. The teams are likely a result of Dutch colonial influence. By comparison, Netherlands' Randstad region has nine field hockey teams.

Middle Eastern women face many obstacles in professional sports. For example, men will not play against women in the same stadiums. Faiza Haidar recently broke one of the region's barriers, becoming Egypt's first female coach to train a male soccer team (37). Haidar has been made coach of Ideal Goldi, a fourth division club in the Egyptian Premier League. Female swimmers in the region must wear full body suits (*Figure 12.31*). Historically, the region's culture and religion prohibited women's participation in sports (38). The video in *Figure 12.34* shows how conditions are changing for women playing soccer in Turkey.

FIGURE 12.34
Women Playing Soccer in Turkey

Female soccer players shoot down Turkish Taboos

Scan to Watch Video

Source: https://sites.duke.edu/wcwp/research-projects/middle-east/muslim-women-in-sport/the-state-of-womens-football-in-muslim-countries/

Top 50 Sports Cities

Tier I sports cities, with the highest City-Level Sports Power Scores, are well represented in the world's top 50 sports cities. *Figure 12.35* shows the total professional teams in each region's top 10 sports cities. As shown in the figure:

- North America has the fewest professional teams in its top 10 sports cities.

- Europe has the most professional teams among its top cities.

- North America has the lowest number of women's professional teams (5.3% of the total).

- Latin America has the highest number of women's teams at 41 (41% of the total).

- The Middle East and Africa region has 142 professional teams, of which 21.5% are women's.

FIGURE 12.35
The Top 10 Sports Cities' Professional Teams by Region

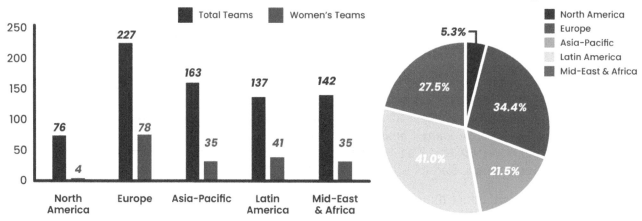

North America offers more sports revenues than any other regional market given its number of households and tremendous buying power. However, sports cities outside North America are growing in population and consumer spending.

Figure 12.36 shows the Best-Howard Model's top 50 sports cities based on City-Level Sports Power Score.

FIGURE 12.36
The Best-Howard Model's Top 50 Sports Cities

No.	Tier I Cities	No.	Tier II Cities	No.	Tier III Cities	No.	Tier IV Cities	No.	Tier V Cities
1	Tokyo	11	Istanbul	21	Washington DC	31	Mumbai	41	Tehran
2	New York	12	Paris	22	Mexico City	32	San Francisco	42	Rhein-Main
3	London	13	Chicago	23	Athens	33	Madrid	43	Miami
4	Los Angeles	14	Hong Kong	24	Moscow	34	Philadelphia	44	Tianjin
5	Rhine-Ruhr	15	Sydney	25	Dallas	35	Seoul	45	Stockholm
6	Osaka	16	Johannesburg	26	Doha	36	Hamburg	46	Vienna
7	Sao Paulo	17	Melbourne	27	Milan	37	Atlanta	47	Helsinki
8	Cairo	18	Houston	28	Beijing	38	Lagos	48	Tel Aviv
9	Randstad	19	Lima	29	Shanghai	39	Toronto	49	Ankara
10	Buenos Aires	20	Nagoya	30	Boston	40	Seattle	50	Rio de Janeiro

The Best-Howard Model again divides its top 50 sports cities into five new tiers. Tier I (*Figure 12.37*) contains the top 10 sports cities in the world. Tokyo, New York, London, Los Angeles and Rhine-Ruhr/Osaka make up the top five. The Tier I cities contain 224 professional sport teams, 37% of top 50's total. The Tier I cities represent 34% of the top 50's households and 35% of its spending.

FIGURE 12.37
Exploring the Top 50 Cities by Tier

TIER I 224 Teams		TIER II 122 Teams	TIER III 77 Teams	TIER IV 83 Teams	TIER V 41 Teams

No.	Tier I City	City-Level Sports Power Score	Pro Teams	Households (millions)	Spending (billions)	Spending per Household
1	Tokyo	100	22	17.8	$1,300	$73,034
2	New York	72	13	7.4	$1,120	$151,493
3	London	62	18	6.4	$744	$116,606
4	Los Angeles	46	11	4.3	$682	$158,573
5	Rhein-Ruhr	44	9	8.8	$569	$64,659
6	Osaka	44	26	6.2	$376	$60,744
7	São Paulo	38	18	7.2	$261	$36,250
8	Cairo	38	23	4.7	$280	$59,038
9	Randstad	33	37	3.7	$189	$50,949
10	Buenos Aires	33	30	4.4	$170	$38,636
	TOTAL		224	69.7	$5,607	$80,603
	% TOP 50		36.7%	34.2%	35.2%	

View other graphs on page A12.8 Chapter 12 Appendix 4.

Click on Tier II to see the details for the 10 cities ranked 11 to 20, which contain 122 professional sports teams. Tier III has 95 teams, Tier IV has 69 teams and Tier V has 37 teams.

The top 10 sports cities include two from North America, three from Europe, two from the Asia-Pacific region, two from Latin America and one from the Middle East and Africa region. North America has 26% of the top 50 sports cities, Europe has 28% and the Asia-Pacific region has 22%. Latin America and the Middle East and Africa region combine to make up 24% of the top 50 sports cities. *Figure 12.38* shows each region's number of top 50 sports cities.

FIGURE 12.38
Top 50 Sports Cities by Region

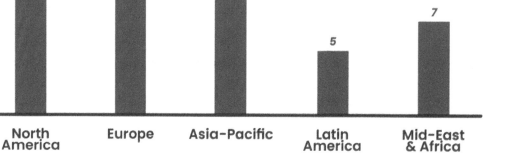

City-Based Brand Strategies

Sports—and particularly women's sports—are growing in popularity, and the Best-Howard Model's top 50 sports cities are likely to change in the coming years. Those most likely to break into the top 50 are large cities adopting women's sports teams as part of their culture and entertainment.

Leading sports industry brands are acutely aware of changing demographics and growing urbanization and are recalibrating their marketing approaches (39). City-based brand strategies recognize what makes certain areas unique, special and relevant. The strategies develop consistent, coherent and long-term messaging through ongoing actions, activities and policies aligned with target cities' sports culture, consumer lifestyle and social media preferences (40).

For example, adidas built a marketing strategy across six global cities where the company wants to grow its market share: London, Los Angeles, New York, Shanghai, Tokyo and Paris (41). The six cities represent 1.6% of the world's population and households (*Figure 12.39*) and, more importantly, 11.1% of worldwide consumer spending and 8.6% of retail sales. On average, the cities represent about 11% of their country's retail sales, making them attractive to sports product companies. The top sports cities' large populations have considerable disposable income and professional sports revenues greater than those of many countries.

FIGURE 12.39
Adidas's Top Sports City Strategy

City	Pro Teams	Population (millions)	AGE CATEGORIES			Households (millions)	Spending (billions)	Spending per Household
			<15	15 to 59	>59			
Tokyo	22	37.0	12%	57%	31%	17.0	$1,300	$76,471
New York City	13	20.2	18%	62%	20%	7.2	$1,035	$143,750
London	29	14.0	19%	62%	19%	6.0	$670	$111,667
Los Angeles	11	13.4	19%	64%	17%	4.3	$625	$145,349
Shanghai	5	26	8%	72%	20%	7.7	$337	$43,766
Paris	8	8.0	21%	60%	19%	10.3	$333	$32,330
TOTAL/AVERAGE	88	118.6	16%	63%	21%	52.5	$4,300	$81,905
% of World	3.5%	1.6%	-	-	-	2.5%	9.0%	364%
World	2549	7575.5	26%	51%	23%	2118.8	$47,650	$22,489

Adidas's brand strategy allowed it to grow net sales in the key cities by 33% and market by 1.7 percentage points. *Figure 12.40* summarizes the company's marketing strategies, each customized to the target cities and their sports cultures and buying behaviors. The strategy focused on retail stores and social media marketing to deliver adidas's brand message and reach consumers where they were (42).

FIGURE 12.40
Adidas City Brand Strategy Touchpoints

Nike targeted 12 areas for its own city-based strategy: New York City, London, Shanghai, Beijing, Los Angeles, Tokyo, Paris, Berlin, Mexico City, Barcelona, Seoul and Milan (43). The company observed that consumer trends travel primarily from city to city, not country to country. The 12 cities, which represent almost 10% of global GDP, were targeted not only because of their size, but also because their streetwear cultures influenced other cities (*Figure 12.41*).

Nike expected the targeted locations to represent 80% of its future growth, and brand research showed the cities' young consumers highly valued brand relevance. Nike therefore designed its city-based strategy to deepen one-on-one connections with consumers and create sportswear products meeting their needs. The company knew it was critical to communicate with the consumers digitally but in an authentic style and language.

Because of social media, trends flow more rapidly and haphazardly than ever before, as major cities are linked in real time. The world follows what happens in its cultural capitals, and social media connects once isolated communities. To build relevance and drive sales, companies must therefore focus their resources on influencing culture in major metropolitan areas.

FIGURE 12.41
Nike's Global City-Based Strategy (billions)

Key Cities	GDP	Key Cities	GDP	Key Cities	GDP	Key Cities	GDP
Tokyo	$1,706	Los Angeles	$902	Beijing	$416	Seoul	$321
New York	$1,463	Paris	$558	Milan	$369	Berlin	$190
London	$1,012	Shanghai	$487	Mexico City	$324	Barcelona	$145

At home in North America, Nike attempts to influence culture in many ways. One way it builds local authenticity in New York is through sponsoring the West 4th Street basketball court in Greenwich Village known as "The Cage". The Cage is an icon in New York Street basketball, and the video in *Figure 12.42* offers a glimpse of its role.

FIGURE 12.42
New York Street Basketball in The Cage

The legendary West Fourth basketball courts, aka "The Cage"

Scan to Watch Video

Source: https://www.youtube.com/watch?v=HmxDjhVMoLI&

References

We have added links to many references for direct and easy access. While we have tested each link, there are a few instances where the websites are no longer accessible. We will continue to monitor the accessibility of citation references and remove any links no longer active. In many instances the referenced data was purchased, this is noted.

1. Country Pro Sports Database: Data used to create country pro teams by sport can be accessed HERE. This link lists all the leagues and pro teams by country.

2. "5 Reasons Why Sports Matter in American Cities," Dec. 17, 2017. *Huffpost* (www.huffpost.com).

3. "The importance of Sports in City Marketing," Dec. 12, 2017. *Fox Sports Stories* (foxsportsstories.com).

4. Oxford Economics. (GSI Purchased Report)

5. "Most Exciting Sports Cities in the World" *Contiki* (www.contiki.com).

6. "New York City Pro Team Sports Revenues – MLB, NFL, NBA, NHL, MLS," Statista.com, The Statistics Portal for Market Data, Market Research and Market Studies. (GSI Purchased Report)

7. "Urban world: Mapping the economic power of cities" *McKinsey* (www.mckinsey.com).

8. McKinsey Urban World, "Urban world: What's next?" Oct. 21, 2016. *McKinsey* (www.mckinsey.com).

9. The data provided in Figure 12.8 was obtained from the McKinsey Urban World database.

10. "Urban world: Mapping the economic power of cities" *McKinsey* (www.mckinsey.com).

11. The History of Streetwear: From Stüssy to Vetements. *Who What Wear* (whowhatwear.com).

12. *Business Of Fashion* (businessoffashion.com).

13. Supreme, "Charting the Rise of Supreme, From Cult Skate Shop to Fashion Superpower" *Vogue* (www.vogue.com).

14. Decoding Men's Streetwear and Street Style, John Jones, December 3, 2018. *The Manual* (www.themanual.com).

15. *Medium* (medium.com).

16. *HypeBeast* (hypebeast.com).

17. *HypeBeast* (hypebeast.com).

18. The 10 Best Streetwear Brands to Buy in 2021", Ty Gaskins, November 18, 2020. *The Manual* (www.themanual.com).

19. "What is Street Sport? Why Is it important for our Youth?" *Malta Street Sports Association* (mssa.mt).

20. "STREET SPORTS & CULTURE" *Game* (game.ngo).

21. "Remembering… STICKBALL!," April 16, 2020. *Tenement Museum* (www.tenement.org).

22. "Break Dancing Will Be An Olympic Sport In 2024," December 20, 2020. *NPR* (www.npr.org).

23. "What is the Buying Power Index?", July 27, 2021. *The Business Professor* (thebusinessprofessor.com).

24. City Pro Sports Database: used to create city pro teams by sport can be accessed HERE.

25. "The World's Most Valuable Sports Teams 2020" *Forbes* (www.forbes.com).

26. "World's Most Valuable Sports Teams."

27. "The World's Most Valuable Soccer Teams 2019: Real Madrid Is Back On Top, At $4.24 Billion," *Forbes* (www.forbes.com).

28. "The European Leagues comprises of 37 Member Leagues, Associate Members and Development Members," *European Leagues* (europeanleagues.com).

29. *"Annual Review of Football Finance 2021," The Deloitte Annual Review of Football Finance (www2. deloitte.com).*

30. *European cities and sports teams are compiled by listing all pro teams in a country and selecting the sports with teams in top cities based on population and consumer spending.*

31. *Asia-Pacific cities and sports teams are compiled by listing all pro teams in a country and selecting the sports with teams in top cities based on population and consumer spending.*

32. *Latin America cities and sports teams are compiled by listing all pro teams in a country and selecting the sports with teams in top cities based on population and consumer spending.*

33. *"7 Latin American Streetwear Brands You Need to Know," Remezcla (remezcla.com).*

34. *Esports and its vast potential for the African continent, June 25, 2021. Benjamin Dada (benjamindada. com).*

35. *"Sports and the Middle East," MEI (www.mei.edu).*

36. *Middle East and Africa cities and sports teams are compiled by listing all pro teams in a country and selecting the sports with teams in top cities based on population and consumer spending.*

37. *"Meet Egypt's first female coach of a men's soccer team," Nov. 13, 2020. Al Monitor (www.al-monitor. com).*

38. *"The Current State of Women's Football in Muslim Countries" Duke (sites.duke.edu).*

39. *Douglas, S.P., Craig, C.S. & Nijssen, E.J. 2001, "Integrating Branding Strategy Across Markets: Building International Brand Architecture," Journal of International Marketing, 9(2): 97-114.*

40. *Talay, M. B., Townsend, J. D., & Yeniyurt, S. 2015, "Global Brand Architecture Position and Market-Based Performance: The Moderating Role of Culture," Journal of International Marketing, 23(2): 55-72.*

41. *"The Basics of a Successful Country or City Brand Strategy," Bloom Consulting Journal (www.bloom-consulting.com).*

42. *"Adidas Best Practice Brand Distribution Strategy" June 2018. Brand Experts (www.brand-experts.com).*

43. *"Nike's 12-city strategy", Sep. 06, 2018. Seeking Alpha (seekingalpha.com).*

Chapter 12 Appendix

APPENDIX 1

FIGURE 12.16
North America's Top 10 Sports Cities – Tier II (2019)

No.	Tier II City	Score	Pro Teams
11	Toronto	19	10
12	Miami	18	5
13	Seattle	18	7
14	Minneapolis	16	7
15	Phoenix	16	6
16	Denver	13	6
17	Detroit	13	4
18	San Diego	11	2
19	Portland	10	2
20	Tampa	9	3
	TOTAL/AVERAGE	142	52

No.	Tier II City	City-Level Sports Power Score	Pro Teams	Population (millions)	Households (millions)	Spending (billions)	Spending per Household
11	Toronto	19	10	6.3	2.1	$153	$72,517
12	Miami	18	5	6.5	2.3	$226	$98,330
13	Seattle	18	7	3.9	1.5	$221	$147,648
14	Minneapolis	16	7	3.7	1.4	$174	$124,051
15	Phoenix	16	6	5.1	1.7	$179	$105,106
16	Denver	13	6	3.0	1.1	$140	$126,983
17	Detroit	13	4	4.2	1.7	$163	$95,962
18	San Diego	11	2	3.5	1.1	$165	$150,391
19	Portland	10	2	2.6	1.0	$143.2	$138,357
20	Tampa	9	3	3.2	1.2	$114	$95,066
	TOTAL/AVERAGE	142	52	41.8	15.1	$1,679	$1,154,412

No.	Tier II City	Football	Soccer	Baseball	Basketball	Canadian Football	Ice Hockey	Rugby	Softball	TOTAL
11	Toronto	0	3	1	1	2	2	1	0	10
12	Miami	1	1	1	1	0	1	0	0	5
13	Seattle	1	2	1	1	0	1	1	0	7
14	Minneapolis	1	1	1	2	0	2	0	0	7
15	Phoenix	1	0	1	2	0	2	0	0	6
16	Denver	1	1	1	1	0	1	1	0	6
17	Detroit	1	0	1	1	0	1	0	0	4
18	San Diego	0	0	1	0	0	0	1	0	2
19	Portland	0	2	0	1	0	0	0	0	3
20	Tampa	1	0	1	0	0	1	0	0	3
	TOTAL/AVERAGE	7	10	9	10	2	11	4	0	53
	Percentage	13%	19%	17%	19%	4%	21%	8%	0%	100%
	Women's Teams	0	2	0	3	0	3	0	0	8
	% Women's Teams	0%	4%	0%	6%	0%	6%	0%	0%	15%

FIGURE 12.16
North America's Top 10 Sports Cities – Tier III (2019)

No.	Tier III City	Score	Pro Teams
21	Baltimore	9	2
22	Pittsburgh	9	3
23	St. Louis	8	2
24	Cleveland	8	3
25	Charlotte	8	2
26	Cincinnati	8	3
27	Orlando	8	2
28	Montreal	8	2
29	Kansas City	7	3
30	Indianapolis	7	2
	TOTAL/AVERAGE	80	24

No.	Tier III City	City-Level Sports Power Score	Pro Teams	Population (millions)	Households (millions)	Spending (billions)	Spending per Household
21	Baltimore	9	2	2.8	1.0	$136	$136,232
22	Pittsburgh	9	3	2.4	1.0	$114	$114,364
23	St. Louis	8	2	2.8	1.1	$113	$102,441
24	Cleveland	8	3	2.0	0.9	$92	$102,007
25	Charlotte	8	2	2.7	1.0	$107	$106,551
26	Cincinnati	8	3	2.2	0.8	$89	$111,851
27	Orlando	8	2	2.7	0.9	$105	$116,257
28	Montreal	8	2	4.2	1.7	$85	$50,709
29	Kansas City	7	3	2.1	0.8	$84	$104,907
30	Indianapolis	7	2	2.1	0.8	$92	$114,437
	TOTAL/AVERAGE	80	24	26.0	10.0	$1,016	$1,059,757

No.	Tier III City	Football	Soccer	Baseball	Basketball	Canadian Football	Ice Hockey	Rugby	Softball	TOTAL
21	Baltimore	1	0	1	0	0	0	0	0	2
22	Pittsburgh	1	0	1	0	0	1	0	0	3
23	St. Louis	0	0	1	0	0	1	0	0	2
24	Cleveland	1	0	1	1	0	0	0	1	4
25	Charlotte	1	0	0	1	0	0	0	0	2
26	Cincinnati	1	1	1	0	0	0	0	0	3
27	Orlando	0	2	0	1	0	0	0	0	3
28	Montreal	0	1	0	0	0	1	0	0	2
29	Kansas City	1	1	1	0	0	0	0	0	3
30	Indianapolis	1	0	0	2	0	1	0	0	4
	TOTAL/AVERAGE	7	5	6	5	0	4	0	1	28
	Percentage	25%	18%	21%	18%	0%	14%	0%	4%	100%
	Women's Teams	0	1	0	1	0	0	0	1	3
	% Women's Teams	0%	4%	0%	4%	0%	0%	0%	4%	11%

FIGURE 12.16
North America's Top 10 Sports Cities - Tier IV (2019)

No.	Tier IV City	Score	Pro Teams
31	Nashville	7	3
32	Columbus	7	2
33	Austin	7	2
34	Sacramento	6	1
35	San Antonio	6	1
36	Buffalo	6	3
37	Milwaukee	6	2
38	Vancouver	6	2
39	New Orleans	5	2
40	Las Vegas	5	1
	TOTAL/AVERAGE	61	19

No.	Tier IV City	City-Level Sports Power Score	Pro Teams	Population (millions)	Households (millions)	Spending (billions)	Spending per Household
31	Nashville	7	3	1.9	0.7	$78	$110,782
32	Columbus	7	2	2.1	0.8	$89	$111,491
33	Austin	7	2	2.2	0.88	$90.5	$102,841
34	Sacramento	6	1	2.4	0.9	$97	$110,896
35	San Antonio	6	1	2.6	1.0	$90.8	$92,602
36	Buffalo	6	3	1.1	0.46	$58	$125,000
37	Milwaukee	6	2	1.6	0.6	$68	$112,584
38	Vancouver	6	2	2.6	0.9	$59	$65,552
39	New Orleans	5	2	1.3	0.5	$63	$125,859
40	Las Vegas	5	1	2.3	0.8	$79	$98,780
	TOTAL/AVERAGE	31	19	20.2	7.5	$771	$1,056,388

No.	Tier IV City	Football	Soccer	Baseball	Basketball	Canadian Football	Ice Hockey	Rugby	Softball	TOTAL
31	Nashville	1	1	0	0	0	1	0	0	3
32	Columbus	0	1	0	0	0	1	0	0	2
33	Austin	0	1	0	1	0	0	0	0	2
34	Sacramento	0	0	0	1	0	0	0	0	1
35	San Antonio	0	0	0	1	0	0	0	0	1
36	Buffalo	1	0	0	0	0	2	0	0	3
37	Milwaukee	0	0	1	1	0	0	0	0	2
38	Vancouver	0	1	0	0	0	1	0	0	2
39	New Orleans	1	0	0	1	0	0	0	0	2
40	Las Vegas	0	0	0	1	0	1	0	0	2
	TOTAL/AVERAGE	3	4	1	6	0	6	0	0	20
	Percentage	15.8%	21.1%	5.3%	26.3%	0%	31.6%	0%	0%	100%
	Women's Teams	0	0	0	1	0	0	0	0	1
	% Women's Teams	0%	0%	0%	5%	0%	0%	0%	0%	5%

FIGURE 12.16
North America's Top 10 Sports Cities - Tier V (2019)

No.	Tier V City	Score	Pro Teams
41	Salt Lake City	5	2
42	Raleigh	4	1
43	Jacksonville	4	1
44	Oklahoma City	4	1
45	Calgary	4	1
46	Memphis	4	1
47	Edmonton	3	1
48	Ottawa	3	1
49	Winnipeg	2	1
50	Green Bay	2	1
	TOTAL/AVERAGE	36	11

No.	Tier V City	City-Level Sports Power Score	Pro Teams	Population (millions)	Households (millions)	Spending (billions)	Spending per Household
41	Salt Lake City	5	2	1.2	0.4	$59	$134,905
42	Raleigh	4	1	1.5	0.5	$57	$113,053
43	Jacksonville	4	1	1.5	0.6	$54	$89,181
44	Oklahoma City	4	1	1.2	0.5	$56	$111,065
45	Calgary	4	1	1.5	0.5	$52	$95,863
46	Memphis	4	1	1.4	0.5	$51	$102,292
47	Edmonton	3	1	1.2	0.5	$44	$87,887
48	Ottawa	3	1	1.4	0.5	$36.9	$67,706
49	Winnipeg	2	1	0.8	0.3	$18.5	$58,571
50	Green Bay	2	1	0.32	0.14	$15	$111,111
	TOTAL/AVERAGE	36	11	12.1	30.4	$442	$971,635

No.	Tier V City	Football	Soccer	Baseball	Basketball	Canadian Football	Ice Hockey	Rugby	Softball	TOTAL
41	Salt Lake City	0	1	0	0	0	1	0	0	2
42	Raleigh	1	1	0	0	0	0	0	0	2
43	Jacksonville	0	0	0	1	0	0	0	0	1
44	Oklahoma City	0	0	0	0	0	1	0	0	1
45	Calgary	0	0	0	1	0	0	0	0	1
46	Memphis	0	0	0	0	0	1	0	0	1
47	Edmonton	0	0	0	0	0	1	0	0	1
48	Ottawa	0	0	0	0	0	1	0	0	1
49	Winnipeg	1	0	0	0	0	0	0	0	1
50	Green Bay	0	1	0	0	0	0	0	0	1
	TOTAL/AVERAGE	2	3	0	2	0	5	0	0	12
	Percentage	17%	25%	0%	17%	0%	42%	0%	0%	100%
	Women's Teams	0	2	0	0	0	0	0	0	2
	% Women's Teams	0%	17%	0%	0%	0%	0%	0%	0%	17%

APPENDIX 2

FIGURE 12.23
Europe's Top 30 Sports Cities – Tier II

No.	Tier II Cities	City-Level Sports Power Score	Pro Teams	Population (millions)	Households (millions)	Spending (billions)	Spending per Household
11	Rhein-Main	18	8	5.8	2.28	$167	$73,480
12	Stockholm	14	10	2.4	1.31	$83	$63,599
13	Vienna	17	11	1.9	1.81	$108	$59,395
14	Helsinki	17	15	1.3	0.77	$53	$68,887
15	Manchester	16	12	2.7	1.24	$84	$68,158
16	Barcelona	16	11	4.9	1.74	$88	$50,835
17	Berlin	16	8	5.3	2.52	$118	$46,855
18	Zurich	14	9	1.4	0.94	$104	$110,665
19	Belgian Metro	14	4	2.1	2.45	$162	$65,992
20	Munich	13	3	2.9	2.11	$162	$76,592
	TOTAL/AVERAGE	15	81	30.7	17.2	$1,130	$68,446

No.	Tier II City	Association Football	Basketball	Rugby	Volleyball	Field Hockey	Handball	Ice Hockey	Football	Baseball	Cricket	Other	TOTAL
11	Rhein-Main	2	2	0	0	0	3	1	0	0	0	0	8
12	Stockholm	3	1	2	0	0	1	2	1	0	0	0	10
13	Vienna	2	1	2	1	0	1	1	2	0	0	1	11
14	Helsinki	3	2	0	0	0	0	2	3	0	0	5	15
15	Manchester	4	2	3	0	0	0	0	1	0	1	1	12
16	Barcelona	3	1	1	1	0	1	1	1	1	0	1	11
17	Berlin	0	1	0	0	3	1	1	1	1	0	0	8
18	Zurich	3	0	0	1	0	2	2	1	0	0	0	9
19	Belgian Metro	2	1	0	1	0	0	0	0	0	0	0	4
20	Munich	1	1	0	0	0	0	1	0	0	0	0	3
	TOTAL/AVERAGE	23	12	8	4	3	9	11	10	2	1	8	81
	Percentage	25.3%	13.2%	8.8%	4.4%	3.3%	9.9%	12.1%	11.0%	2.2%	1.1%	8.8%	100%
	Women's Teams	7	2	0	1	0	1	2	0	0	0	0	13
	% Women's Teams	30.4%	16.7%	0%	25.0%	0%	11.1%	18.2%	0%	0%	0%	0.0%	14.3%

FIGURE 12.23
Europe's Top 30 Sports Cities – Tier III

No.	Tier III Cities	City-Level Sports Power Score	Pro Teams	Population (millions)	Households (millions)	Spending (billions)	Spending per Household
21	Rome	11	4	4.4	1.88	$102	$54,313
22	Rhein-Neckar	10	4	2.4	1.54	$98	$63,666
23	Stuttgart	10	3	0.6	1.54	$111	$72,436
24	Birmingham	10	3	2.6	1.64	$109	$66,449
25	Warsaw	9	4	7.9	1.24	$75	$60,801
26	Lyon	8	4	1.7	1.00	$63	$62,813
27	Naples	7	4	1.1	1.54	$43	$27,905
28	Liverpool	7	3	0.9	1.00	$70	$69,917
29	Lille	6	2	0.2	1.44	$64	$44,268
30	Turin	6	3	1.8	1.00	$44	$44,000
	TOTAL/AVERAGE	8	34	23.6	13.8	$779	$56,657

No.	Tier III City	Association Football	Basketball	Rugby	Volleyball	Field Hockey	Handball	Ice Hockey	Football	Baseball	Cricket	Other	TOTAL
21	Rome	4	0	0	0	0	0	0	0	0	0	0	4
22	Rhein-Neckar	1	0	0	0	0	1	1	1	0	0	0	4
23	Stuttgart	0	1	0	0	0	2	0	0	0	0	0	3
24	Birmingham	3	0	0	0	0	0	0	0	0	0	0	3
25	Warsaw	1	1	0	1	0	0	0	1	0	0	0	4
26	Lyon	2	1	1	0	0	0	0	0	0	0	0	4
27	Naples	2	1	0	0	0	0	0	1	0	0	0	4
28	Liverpool	3	0	0	0	0	0	0	0	0	0	0	3
29	Lille	1	0	0	1	0	0	0	0	0	0	0	2
30	Turin	3	0	0	0	0	0	0	0	0	0	0	3
	TOTAL/AVERAGE	20	4	1	2	0	3	1	3	0	0	0	34
	Percentage	58.8%	11.8%	2.9%	5.9%	0%	8.8%	2.9%	8.8%	0%	0%	0%	100%
	Women's Teams	9	0	0	0	0	0	0	0	0	0	0	9
	% Women's Teams	26.5%	0%	0%	0%	0%	0%	0%	0%	0%	0%	0%	26.5%

APPENDIX 3

FIGURE 12.27
Top 20 Asia-Pacific Sports Cities - Tier II

No.	Tier II Cities	City-Level Sports Power Score	Pro Teams	Population (millions)	Households (millions)	Spending (billions)	Spending per Household
11	Tianjin	18	6	13.7	5.4	$130	$24,074
12	Guangzhou	14	5	13.4	4.8	$94	$19,521
13	Shenzhen	14	4	12.6	4.5	$122	$27,067
14	Fukuoka	13	4	5.5	2.5	$150	$60,000
15	Delhi	13	5	18.5	4.4	$67	$15,227
16	Wuhan	11	3	11.5	3.9	$81	$20,769
17	Nanjing	10	3	8.6	3.5	$67	$19,143
18	Hangzhou	9	3	7.7	3.1	$67	$21,613
19	Shenyang	9	3	7.4	2.9	$63	$21,724
20	Sapparo	7	3	2.6	1.4	$67	$47,857
	TOTAL/AVERAGE	–	39	101.5	36.4	$908	$276,995

No.	Tier II City	Association Football	Basketball	Volleyball	Rugby	Australian Football	Baseball	Cricket	Other	TOTAL
11	Tianjin	1	1	2	0	0	1	0	1	6
12	Guangzhou	2	1	0	0	0	0	0	2	5
13	Shenzhen	1	1	2	0	0	0	0	0	4
14	Fukuoka	1	0	0	2	0	1	0	0	4
15	Delhi	1	1	0	0	0	0	1	2	5
16	Wuhan	2	0	0	0	0	0	0	1	3
17	Nanjing	1	1	0	0	0	0	0	0	2
18	Hangzhou	1	0	0	0	0	0	0	2	3
19	Shenyang	0	1	2	0	0	0	0	0	3
20	Sapparo	1	1	0	0	0	1	0	0	3
	TOTAL/AVERAGE	11	7	6	2	0	3	1	8	38
	% Team Sports	28.9%	18.4%	15.8%	5.3%	0.0%	7.9%	2.6%	21.1%	100.0%
	Women's Teams	3	0	3	0	0	0	0	0	6
	% Women's Teams	27.3%	0.0%	50.0%	0.0%	0%	0.0%	0.0%	0.0%	15.8%

APPENDIX 4

FIGURE 12.37
Exploring the Top 50 Cities by Tier - Tier II

No.	Tier II City	City-Level Sports Power Score	Pro Teams	Households (millions)	Spending (billions)	Spending per Household
11	Istanbul	33	13	4.59	$333	$72,478
12	Paris	32	9	2.8	$438	$156,270
13	Chicago	32	32	1.8	$153	$85,000
14	Hong Kong	31	17	2.6	$210	$80,769
15	Sydney	29	6	2.3	$398	$172,940
16	Johannesburg	28	22	3.7	$74	$20,000
17	Melbourne	27	38	1.7	$121	$71,176
18	Houston	26	9	6.1	$231	$37,869
19	Lima	26	26	2.5	$76	$30,400
20	Nagoya	26	6	2.6	$345	$132,764
	TOTAL		122	33.8	$2,908	$100,105
	% TOP 50		20.0%	16.5%	18.3%	

FIGURE 12.37
Exploring the Top 50 Cities by Tier - Tier III

No.	Tier III City	City-Level Sports Power Score	Pro Teams	Households (millions)	Spending (billions)	Spending per Household
21	Washington DC	26	10	3.37	$195	$58,032
22	Mexico City	26	5	9	$152	$16,889
23	Athens	25	33	1.75	$72	$41,365
24	Moscow	25	6	1.8	$293	$162,638
25	Dallas	24	6	1.7	$280	$164,706
26	Doha	22	18	0.4	$113	$283,500
27	Milan	22	12	2.5	$132	$52,800
28	Beijing	22	8	4	$166	$41,500
29	Shanghai	21	13	1.68	$117	$69,467
30	Boston	21	6	2.1	$243	$115,680
	TOTAL		77	36.9	$1,983	$81,681
	% TOP 50		12.6%	18.1%	12.5%	

FIGURE 12.37
Exploring the Top 50 Cities by Tier - Tier IV

No.	Tier IV City	City-Level Sports Power Score	Pro Teams	Households (millions)	Spending (billions)	Spending per Household
31	Mumbai	20	11	5.4	$94	$17,047
32	San Francisco	20	5	2.3	$226	$98,330
33	Madrid	20	8	2.28	$167	$73,480
34	Philadelphia	20	6	1.5	$221	$147,648
35	Seoul	19	13	1.31	$83	$63,599
36	Hamburg	19	11	1.81	$108	$59,395
37	Atlanta	19	7	1.4	$174	$124,051
38	Lagos	19	12	4.1	$68	$16,513
39	Toronto	19	5	1.7	$179	$105,106
40	Seattle	18	9	0.94	$104	$110,665
	TOTAL		**83**	**17.1**	**$1,504**	**$90,563**
	% TOP 50		**13.6%**	**8.4%**	**9.5%**	

FIGURE 12.37
Exploring the Top 50 Cities by Tier - Tier V

No.	Tier V City	City-Level Sports Power Score	Pro Teams	Households (millions)	Spending (billions)	Spending per Household
41	Tehran	18	4	2.45	$162	$65,992
42	Rhein-Main	18	7	1.7	$121	$71,176
43	Miami	18	4	2.5	$150	$60,000
44	Tianjin	18	6	1.1	$140	$126,983
45	Stockholm	17	4	1.7	$163	$95,962
46	Vienna	17	13	1.31	$83	$63,599
47	Helsinki	17	15	0.77	$53	$68,887
48	Tel Aviv	17	11	2.2	$97	$44.09
49	Ankara	17	13	1.5	$69	$46,000
50	Rio de Janeiro	17	3	1.54	$111	$72,436
	TOTAL		**41**	**18.3**	**$1,390**	**$83,005**
	% TOP 50		**6.7%**	**9.0%**	**8.7%**	

Made in the USA
Las Vegas, NV
18 August 2022

53534660R10210